BORDER WORK

D1596517

CULTURE AND SOCIETY AFTER SOCIALISM
edited by Bruce Grant and Nancy Ries

A list of titles in this series is available at
www.cornellpress.cornell.edu.

BORDER WORK

Spatial Lives of the State in Rural Central Asia

MADELEINE REEVES

Cornell University Press
Ithaca and London

First published 2014 by Cornell University Press
First printing, Cornell Paperbacks, 2014

Printed in the United States of America

Library of Congress Cataloging-in-Publication Data

Reeves, Madeleine, author.
  Border work: spatial lives of the state in rural Central Asia / Madeleine Reeves.
    pages cm
  Includes bibliographical references and index.
  ISBN 978-0-8014-4997-0 (cloth : alk. paper)
  ISBN 978-0-8014-7706-5 (pbk. : alk. paper)
  1. Borderlands—Fergana Valley. 2. Ethnology—Fergana Valley.
3. Fergana Valley—Politics and government. 4. Fergana Valley—
Ethnic relations. I. Title.
  DK855.4.R44 2014
  958.7—dc23   2013036994

Cornell University Press strives to use environmentally responsible suppliers and materials to the fullest extent possible in the publishing of its books. Such materials include vegetable-based, low-VOC inks and acid-free papers that are recycled, totally chlorine-free, or partly composed of nonwood fibers. For further information, visit our website at www.cornellpress.cornell.edu.

Cloth printing   10 9 8 7 6 5 4 3 2 1
Paperback printing   10 9 8 7 6 5 4 3 2 1

Photos are by the author unless otherwise indicated.

Dedicated to Christopher Reeves, 1939–2012

CONTENTS

ACKNOWLEDGMENTS

As work on the manuscript comes to an end it is a pleasure to acknowledge the many friends, colleagues, and interlocutors without whom this book would not have been possible. The initial idea for this book emerged over a decade ago when I was working at the American University-Central Asia in Bishkek, Kyrgyzstan. This was a young, self-consciously experimental, and uniquely stimulating environment in which to teach and research. Several one-time colleagues and students have become close scholarly collaborators and friends. For illuminating conversations at various stages of research I am grateful to Zulfia Abdullaeva, Abdujalil Abdurasulov, Mehrigul Ablezova, Medina Aitieva, Gulnara Aitpaeva, Aida Alymbaeva, Michael Andersen, Nina Bagdasarova, Norma-Jo Baker, Aisalkyn Botoeva, Gulzat Botoeva, the late Aron Brudny, Aminat Chokobaeva, Bill Hansen, Gulnara Ibraeva, Dasha Isachenko, Emil Joroev, Shairbek Juraev, Anara Karagulova, Mirgul Karimova, Anna Kirey, Russell Kleinbach, Martha Merrill, Valia Papoutsaki, Vanessa Ruget, Balihar Sangherra, Colin Spurway, Muzaffar Suleymanov, Chad Thompson, Bermet Tursunkulova, Burul Usmanalieva, Tom Wood, Amanda Wooden, and Tanya Yarkova. Vika Lavrova—student, colleague, and friend—left us too early and is dearly missed.

The book took initial shape at the University of Cambridge, where Nikolai Ssorin-Chaikov inspired and challenged me with his uncanny ability to make connections between material and across literatures. Piers Vitebsky and the Magic Circle Seminar fostered a supportive and creative environment in which to try out ideas. I am grateful to colleagues with whom I shared writing seminars, and in particular to the incisive feedback offered by Barbara Bodenhorn, Tod Hartman, Steven Hugh-Jones, Caroline Humphrey, Elena

Khlinovskaya-Rockhill, Jon Mair, Polly McMichael, Yael Navaro-Yashin, Eleanor Peers, David Sneath, Maja Petrović-Šteger, Marilyn Strathern, Katie Swancutt, and Olga Ulturgasheva.

As the manuscript developed, I have benefited from the insight and expertise of many scholars of Central Asia who have pointed me to new sources, read drafts of chapters, or shared conversation about the themes that emerge in this book. I am grateful to Sergei Abashin, Laura Adams, Sarah Amsler, Gazi Babayarova, Judith Beyer, Sally Cummings, Eva-Marie Dubuisson, Adrienne Edgar, Jeanne Féaux de la Croix, Olivier Ferrando, Dave Gullette, John Heathershaw, Aksana Ismailbekova, Deniz Kandiyoti, Botakoz Kassymbekova, Sarah Kendzior, Adeeb Khalid, Mateusz Laszczkowski, Morgan Liu, Nick Megoran, David Montgomery, Alexander Morrison, Till Mostowlansky, Kirill Nourzhanov, Stephanie Ortmann, Serguei Oushakine, Mathijs Pelkmans, Johan Rasanayavam, Sophie Roche, Jeff Sahadeo, Elmira Satybaldieva, John Schoeberlein, Regine Spector, Julien Thorez, Stina Torjesen, and Rano Turaeva. Christine Bichsel was a friend and inspiration during my period of research in Batken, and our conversations about borders, irrigation, and the work of conflict prevention have profoundly shaped this book. Gerry Fagan proved a wonderful writing partner as we both sought to bring books to fruition (she got there first by several months). Claire Malone-Lee, Andrew Barry, and Juliana Ochs generously read a draft of the entire manuscript, giving detailed and insightful feedback on matters of substance and style. The series editors, Bruce Grant and Nancy Ries, provided pages of astute and generous feedback on the manuscript, and the helpful comments of an anonymous reader helped me to clarify parts of my argument. At Cornell University Press I am indebted to John Ackerman for his enthusiasm, responsiveness, and patience, and to Susan Specter and Irina Burns for their careful edits to the manuscript. Bill Nelson drew the maps. Any errors, of course, remain my own.

At the University of Manchester and the ESRC Centre for Research on Socio-Cultural Change (CRESC), this research has grown in several ways as I have been immersed in new conversations about borders, politics, and the materiality of state projects. Penny Harvey and Sarah Green have inspired me by their intellectual curiosity and ability to weave together theory and ethnography. Jackie Stacey has pointed me to new questions and ways of conceiving of the political, and Nina Glick-Schiller always encouraged me to look beyond the nation-state. Mike Savage has provided a model for productive interdisciplinary collaboration and created a generous working environment in Waterloo Place. Jeanette Edwards and Gillian Evans have shown by example why anthropology matters. I hope that each of these scholars will see traces of their inspiration here, personal and professional. For their stimulating support, conversation, and in some cases detailed reading, I am grateful to colleagues Michelle Bastian, Felica Chan, Jan Grill, Hannah Knox, Adi Kuntsman, Stef Jansen, Gemma John, Petra Kalshoven, Heather Latimer, Keir Martin, John Law, Niamh Moore, Adriana Nilsson, Michelle Obeid, Ewa Ochman, Damian O'Doherty, Annabel Pinker, Evelyn Ruppert, Atreyee Sen, Tony Simpson, Katie Smith, Ebru Soytomel, Nick Thoburn, Galin Tihanov, and Angela Torresan.

A number of institutions and organizations have provided the material and practical support to make this book possible. I would like to acknowledge the generous support offered by the UK's Economic and Social Research Council; the Cambridge Committee on Central and Inner Asia, and Trinity College Cambridge, which funded the main period of field research for this book. The East-West Center at the American University-Central Asia provided research affiliation and working space in Bishkek, as well as a ready group of colleagues with whom to share ideas and beers. A postdoctoral Research Fellowship from the Research Councils UK enabled me to develop the manuscript at the University of Manchester, and a short-term Visiting Fellowship at the Centre for Arab and Islamic Studies at the Australian National University afforded me two wonderful months to focus exclusively on revisions at a time when I was becoming submerged in other projects. I am deeply grateful to Amin Saikal and Kirill Nourzhanov for making this happen, and to a remarkable group of graduate students at CAIS for welcoming me. Research visits to Kyrgyzstan in 2009–2010 were supported by the Nuffield Foundation and a Travelling Fellowship from Newnham College, Cambridge.

A portion of chapter 4 was previously published in "Unstable Objects: Corpses, Checkpoints, and 'Chessboard Borders' in the Ferghana Valley," *Anthropology of East Europe Review* 25 (1): 72–84. Parts of chapter 6 were previously published in "Fixing the Border: On the Affective Life of the State in Southern Kyrgyzstan," *Environment and Planning D: Society and Space* 29:905–923, by permission of Pion Ltd., London, www.pion.co.uk, and in "The Time of the Border: Contingency, Conflict, and Popular Statism at the Kyrgyzstan-Uzbekistan Boundary," in *Ethnographies of the State in Central Asia: Performing Politics*, edited by Madeleine Reeves, Johan Rasanayagam, and Judith Beyer, 198–220, by permission of Indiana University Press.

My thanks to friends and acquaintances in Kyrgyzstan, Uzbekistan, and Tajikistan are greater than I can express in words. Over the past decade several families have welcomed me as a guest, friend, and adoptive daughter during research visits, and taught me about their lives and hopes. Dozens more have patiently responded to my questions. I am indebted to the four generations of the Malabaev family, and particularly to Ovalbek-Aka, Salima-Eje, Aitkul, and Sultanali for their generosity over many years; to Dastan Nadyrov and his extended family, who provided a particularly acute insight into life at the border; to Medet-Baike and Gulnara-Eje in Ak-Örgö for patiently allowing me to practice my Kyrgyz; to Guljan-Eje and Janybek Botoev for welcoming to me into their home on countless evenings in Bishkek; to the family identified here as Parviz and Sharofat, who taught me much about life in a post-Soviet enclave. Rakilya Jusupova, Tynarkul Ryskulova, Elnura Osmonalieva, Nodirbek Abduhalatov, Dilshod Sharipov, Almaz Kalet, and Matliuba Azamatova have inspired me by their courage, and provided friendship and practical support at various stages of researching this book. Kishimjan Osmonova, Dariha Erketaeva, Jyldyz Beishenalieva, Tilek Bolotov, Yulia Lysenko, and Behzod Sharipov helped me at various times to translate or interpret material; Dilya Dorgabekova, Sunatullo Jonboboev, Tohir Kalandarov, and Mohira Suyarkulova provided some insightful translations of Tajik phrases by e-mail; and Batma-Ejeke, Zainiddin-Agai, Sadyr-Agai, Ominakhon-Opa, Sapargul, Mavliuda-Opa, and members of the Mehr collective helped me to conduct the household survey in the Sokh and Isfara valleys. Daniil Kislov, Igor Rotar´, David Trilling, and Altynai Koichumanova responded generously to my requests to reproduce photographic material. Above all I am grateful to the dozens of people in Batken, Sokh, and the Isfara Valley who generously shared their experiences and reflections with me. I hope that I have done justice to their experiences in this book.

Finally, I would like to thank my family and close friends. My sister, Margaret, has brought a medic's eye to early drafts of these chapters and known just when to ask how the book is going. Brian Goddard has taught me to observe beauty in detail. My niece, Aisulu-Rose, has been a constant reminder of what is most important in life. Above all, I thank my parents, Christopher and Claire, for their love, encouragement, and enthusiasm. They always encouraged me to pursue my passions, without losing sight of what scholarship is for. Dad left us too soon to see this book in print, but without his support, his interest, and his care for words, it would probably never been written. It is to him that I dedicate this book.

A NOTE ON NAMING AND TRANSLITERATION

This book explores the politics of place in Central Asia, a region where four languages are regularly used: Kyrgyz, Tajik, Uzbek, and Russian. Place names and surnames, forms of address and regional dialects attest to the fact that this is a region of intense linguistic borrowing, just as it is of cultural contact. Many villages that I refer to in this book are regularly called by two, or even three, quite different names. Often these names are used interchangeably, with speakers switching names (and sometimes languages) within the course of a single conversation. Other are emphatically "marked," with my informants preferring to use an older Tajik or Kyrgyz version of a place name that is now rendered differently in official geographies. I have used the current standard name for any given settlement in my own narrative description, but have been faithful to the names used by the people I was speaking with when I reproduce their words. Where there is a standard English usage for particular place names, I have used the regular English variant rather than the transliterated official version (thus Andijan rather than Andijon or Anjian; Ferghana rather than Farg'ona or Fergana; Kokand rather than Qoqon or Kokon, and Alay rather than Alai). In the case of all other place names, I have transliterated the name according to its standard spelling in the country where it lies. The one significant exception is the Uzbekistani enclave Sokh. I use this spelling, rather than the official Uzbek So'x since the former scans more easily to an English-speaking reader. I have changed the names of my informants, except in those instances where I quote someone who was speaking in an official capacity or where they explicitly requested that I do not change their name. Further, to protect my informants' confidentiality, I have changed the name of the Sokh *mahallas* referred to in the text.

Most of my research was conducted in Kyrgyz and Russian, languages that I had studied and used for everyday communication before beginning fieldwork. I occasionally refer to comments made in Uzbek and Tajik. In Uzbekistan, the Uzbek language has increasingly been rendered in the Latin script since 1995 (in Kyrgyzstan, the Uzbek language is still taught and written in Cyrillic script). This introduces some complexities in transliteration, particularly given the considerable degree of Uzbek borrowing in southern-dialect Kyrgyz. My approach has been a pragmatic one, seeking to combine ease of reading for an Anglophone audience with ease of reference for those seeking to trace particular sources. I have used nonstandard spellings for comments in dialect quoted verbatim.

I have retained forms of address that I used in the field: *Eje* (pronounced "eh-jay") and *Opa* for an older woman; *Ejeke* for a female teacher; *Aka* or *Baike* for an older man; *Agai* for a male teacher; *Hojai* (in Sokh) for an older man who has completed the Hajj. In the choice of anonymized names I have sought to remain faithful to the preponderance of Persianate and Arabic names found in and around Batken; in the case of Kuba/Kolia who is introduced in chapter 5, I have sought to capture the degree of aural proximity between the Kyrgyz and Russian versions of his name.

The system of transliteration that I use in the text is as follows: for Russian words, I use the Library of Congress system of transliteration, except for some proper nouns that are conventionally spelled differently in English (e.g., Yeltsin, Bayaman). For Uzbek, except for those place names mentioned above, I use the official Latin script that was approved in 1995. For Kyrgyz quotes in the text, I use the same system of transliteration as that used for Russian, with the following exceptions. ж = j; ө = ö; ү = ü; ң = ng. For bibliographic references I have been guided by the language of the source in transliterating the author's surname. For this reason some authors referenced in the bibliography appear with more than one spelling (e.g., Dzhakhonov, Jahonov).

BORDER WORK

INTRODUCTION

On Border Work

On a blistering summer day in 2005 at the southern fringes of Central Asia's Ferghana Valley, a group of children bathe in the meter-wide irrigation canal that runs along the edge of their village. Some of the older boys wrestle under the surface and splash each other with water. Others jump from a small concrete ledge at the side of the canal, shouting and laughing. One of the girls, recognizing me and spotting my camera, calls out for me to take a picture of the group. The concrete ledge is briefly transformed into a platform on which to squeeze and wave and pose for a photo.

The canal in which these children are playing, the Machoi or Ak-Tatyr canal as it is variously called, winds its way along and between garden plots for 400 meters, providing irrigation for homes on either side. The canal is one of several in this part of rural Central Asia built during the 1970s to channel water from glacial rivers at the mountainous rim of the Ferghana Valley into the parched hilly hinterland below, turning arid foothills (*adyr*) into permanent, irrigated villages.[1] This particular canal winds through, and thus connects, the villages of Khojai-A′lo, Üch-Döbö, and Ak-Tatyr. In so doing it also connects—and sometimes divides—two neighboring post-Soviet states: Kyrgyzstan and Tajikistan. Yet although the children are technically playing at, or perhaps even in, an international boundary, there is little of the paraphernalia here that we might associate with such spaces. There are no flags,

---

[1] The Ferghana Valley is a large intermontane basin approximately 300 kilometers long and 70 kilometers wide at its widest point. The Syr Darya River runs through the middle of the basin, while several tributary valleys, including Sokh and Isfara, enter the basin to the north and south. On the role of irrigation as a vehicle of social and spatial transformation in late Soviet Central Asia, see Thurman (1999, 223–247), Lam (2009, 196–242), and Bichsel (2012).

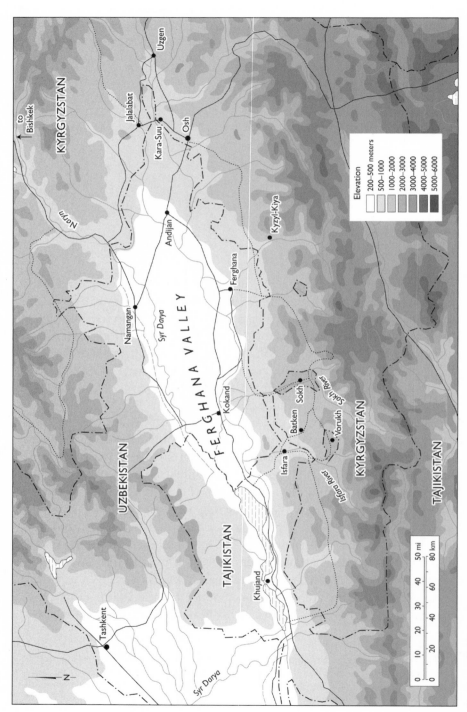

Ferghana Valley

Playing at the border: The Ak-Tatyr/Machoi canal, July 2005.

no signs announcing exit from one state or entry into another, no border posts, no barbed wire, and on quiet days like today no soldiers manning this stretch of border. Indeed, the only state insignia visible here belongs to a different era. In faded red capitals on the concrete ledge where the children pose for their photo are the Cyrillic letters КПСС (CPSU): a reminder that this canal was a gift from the Communist Party of the Soviet Union and a feat of socialist engineering.

There is a further complication to this scene. Not only do the canal and border transect one another here—the concrete channel built at a time when infrastructure was seen as properly knitting constituent republics together into a single Soviet state. At several points on either side, the official, juridical boundary between today's Kyrgyzstan and Tajikistan has never been conclusively determined. Areas of land that were unirrigated and uninhabited until this canal was built have since been appropriated, built on, legalized, sold, and resold, creating what is locally called a "chessboard" (*shakhmat*) formation of alternating and contested jurisdiction. In official discourse the border here is referred to as "contested" (*spornaia*) or simply "unwritten" or "undescribed" (*neopisannaia*)—a term that often appears in English translation as "indescribable," gesturing poetically to our difficulty of conceiving of a state border that is not always-already a line (Ingold 2008).

When this "indescribable" border is described, as it has been with increasing frequency in print and online media in recent years, the tone is often one of alarm at the dangers of territorial indeterminacy, or incredulity at the inability of states to sort out where the border "really" lies. Writing of this region in 2009, Kyrgyz journalist Aidar Kenenbaev noted sardonically that "any European country that has signed the Schengen agreement could be forgiven for envying Tajikistan and Kyrgyzstan. For these two countries have virtually no clear territorial divisions between them." In contrast to the determinate-but-crossable borders that mark out Europe's Schengen zone the lack of state regulation in the Ferghana Valley was rather cast as a mark of failure. Borders are indeterminate here, Kenenbaev (2009) argued, "not because [Kyrgyzstan and Tajikistan] are brothers in misfortune and therefore understand one another well, for that is not the case. The reason is rather different: for they themselves don't know, indeed, they can't even guess [*ne dogadyvaiutsia*] where their state borders lie."

During one of my early visits to his home in the summer of 2004, Pirmat-Ata, a Kyrgyz elder from Üch-Döbö whose house lies in part of this ambiguous administrative space, told me about the arrangement that led to him paying for his electricity to Kyrgyzstan and collecting his water from a standpipe in Tajikistan. Sitting on the terrace (*aivan*) in front of his house, surrounded by crates of apricots that he had recently picked from his orchard on the other side of the canal, Pirmat-Ata traced with a finger the spatial configuration of homes and orchards:

PIRMAT-ATA: Around here it's half Tajik, half Kyrgyz. Mixed up [*aral-ash*]. You've got one Kyrgyz [home], then one Tajik, then another Kyrgyz. A long time ago one Tajik came and after that, they all started gathering around. So there's no way you could divide all that up!

MADELEINE: But how is it decided for instance to which state people should pay taxes?

PIRMAT-ATA: The Kyrgyz pay to Kyrgyzstan, the Tajiks pay to Tajikistan. It's the same with the passports. The Tajiks have Tajik passports [i.e. they are citizens of Tajikistan], the Kyrgyz have Kyrgyz passports. It's just their houses are mixed up. They are all neighbors.

As our conversation moved to the need for more land for newly married couples, and the acute shortages of irrigation water faced by families in and around Üch-Döbö, I asked Pirmat-Ata what he thought would happen if a commission were to come and try to determine the border decisively.

PIRMAT-ATA: It's a difficult situation, that's why people don't like it. Here you've got a Tajik, and the wall of his home is like that [showing with his

"Here you've got a Tajik, and the wall of his home is like this, and the Kyrgyz house is just there, sharing a wall." Apricot orchard at the "chessboard" border, July 2005.

hands] and the Kyrgyz house is just here, sharing a wall. And here you've got a Tajik home, and so on. So how are you going to divide all of that? There is no way you can divide them [*ich bölüshkö tuura kelbei jatat*]! Otherwise you're going to have serious quarrels [*chatak*] appearing.

Pirmat-Ata's remarks about homes, neighborliness, and the difficulties of separation at the canal border between Üch-Döbö and Khojai-A″lo point to concerns that are at the heart of this book—the making and working of new borders in rural Central Asia after the collapse of the Soviet Union. What is at stake in fixing the bounds of the state, transforming space into territory? And how do new borders work—and get worked—in practice, when the edges of the states in question are nonlinear, full of gaps, their precise geographical coordinates disputed or unknown? These are questions I explore through an ethnographic study of two regions of post-Soviet borderland at the southern rim of the Ferghana Valley, where Kyrgyzstan and Uzbekistan, and Kyrgyzstan and Tajikistan meet. My focus is on the sites of ordering and bordering through which new international boundaries in former Soviet Central Asia come to take on material form in daily life: in practices of narration, of classification, of mapping; in the building or dismantling of infrastructure; in mundane and exceptional enactments of exclusion and belonging. I am equally interested in how new international borders with few material traces on the landscape—such as the one that winds between the villages of Khojai-A″lo and Üch-Döbö—are encountered, talked about, and worked. Under what circumstances might an irrigation canal morph from a summer pool for children into a source of cross-border tension or even open conflict—its flow deliberately blocked or diverted by those living on one or other side, as has periodically occurred at these villages? When is danger seen to reside in too much separation, as Pirmat-Ata seems to suggest in his comment about the consequences of demarcating an interstate boundary here—and when from an excess of connection?

My story, in short, concerns border work: the messy, contested, and often intensely social business of making territory "integral." This leads me to engage in a broader, comparative conversation about the transformation of borders globally at a time when the cross-border circulation of things, people, currencies, and ideas seems at once more pervasive and more embattled than before. There is an empirical concern motivating this exploration: to contribute to pluralizing the global study of borders and bordering by exploring ethnographically lives that are lived around, across, through, and from the sporadically securitized land borders of rural Central Asia.[2] The range of ethnographic studies of international borders has increased dramatically since the 1990s, as scholars have sought to grasp the changed configuration of borders brought about by the fall of the iron curtain, the enlargement of the European Union (EU), the (re)emergence of ethno-nationalisms, the securitization of migration, and the proliferation of new technologies and

---

[2]In doing so I build on path-building contributions to the regional literature. In geography, Megoran (2004, 2005) has examined the relationship between domestic political concerns and the intensification of border controls on the Kyrgyz-Uzbek border and Lam (2009) has explored the role of habitus and social networks in sustaining cross-border cooperation. In political science Raballand (2005) has investigated the economic costs of mounting border controls; and Gavrilis provides a trenchant critique of internationally sponsored border assistance programs in the region, which have "increased [governments'] self-assurance, and encouraged their expectations of unconditional patronage" (2012, 7).

techniques for policing trans-border movement.[3] However, it is still the case that we know a great deal more about the boundaries between heavily securitized great powers and their neighbors or about emergent sites of highly technologized surveillance, than we do about the everyday workings of power at the edge of new, or newly poor, states.[4]

Moreover, although the complex spatiality of borders has been an increasing focus of exploration in anthropology and human geography (Mountz 2010, 2011; Parker and Vaughan-Williams 2009), their temporality has tended to garner less attention: their ability to appear or disappear, to materialize at certain times or for certain groups of people with sudden intensity; to morph, or acquire the quality of permanent fixtures (Green 2010; Mountz 2011; Radu 2010; Reeves 2014; Zartman 2010). I explore how and when new borders become socially salient and how authority is negotiated in a setting where the technology for border surveillance at many rural crossing points often consists, if it exists at all, of a pair of conscript soldiers with Kalashnikov rifles, a paper ledger, and a stamp.

My ethnography starts out from the small town of Batken in southwestern Kyrgyzstan and the two river valleys, Isfara and Sokh, which lie to its east and west. Habitual geographies in this region have been reconfigured by the transformation of administrative boundaries between Kyrgyz, Tajik, and Uzbek Soviet Socialist Republics (SSRs) into new international borders and, since the late 1990s, by varied and sometimes expressly performative attempts to nationalize state space through prohibitions on cross-border movement and trade.[5] By attending to local discussion around the everyday

---

[3]See, for instance, Berdahl (1999) on the ambivalent reception of German reunification in an East German border town; Pelkmans (2006) on the policing of new divides between Islam and Christianity on the Georgian-Turkish border; Green (2005) on the reproduction of marginality; and Jansen (2009) on new experiences of entrapment at the EU's "immediate outside." Recent scholarship has also explored how domestic and international political dynamics are reshaping borders globally, including the relationship between new borders and waning sovereignty (Brown 2010); the securitization of immigration (Bigo 2002; Bigo and Guild 2005); the proliferation of border-like surveillance and use of biometrics (Amoore 2006; Pallitto and Heyman 2008).

[4]The everyday working of borders between countries of the global south have been the focus of rich ethnographic studies. See, for example, Roitman (2005), Flynn (1997); Lentz (2003); Chalfin (2010); and Horstmann and Wadley (2006). Within the field of border studies, the United States-Mexico "hyperborder" (Romero 2008) retains paradigmatic status and has been singularly important in generating theory about what borders are and how they work (see also Wilson and Donnan 2012, 7). The range of empirical studies of borders has increased dramatically in the past two decades, but undemarcated borders have received comparatively little ethnographic attention, despite their importance for exploring the everyday dynamics of state spatialization (see also van Schendel 2001).

[5]On the relationship between state building and the regulation of international boundaries in Central Asia, see Gavrilis (2008).

entailments of sovereignty and territorial integrity in this region, I seek to foreground the subjective experience of state spatiality at borders, or what Sarah Green, drawing on geographer Doreen Massey, has called the sense of border as the location of "stories so far" (2012a, 575). This is a perspective alert to the reality both that borders themselves shift through time, and that understandings of what "border" should index or "territorial integrity" should entail are historically contingent. Throughout this book I track a shift from what Achille Mbembe (2000, 263) has described in an African context as "itinerant territoriality," constituted by the imbrication of spaces that are "constantly joined, disjoined, and recombined through wars, conquests and the mobility of goods and persons," toward an understanding of territory as properly having finite geometrical coordinates—and of border as therefore properly contiguous and linear. This logic of border underlies many contemporary initiatives to stabilize space and preempt cross-border conflict in the margins of the Ferghana Valley through programs of border management and so-called preventive development (see chapter 2). Such an approach to border does not erase other modes of apprehending or producing space premised on seasonal mobility, the obligations of kinship, and the interdependence of pastoral and agricultural modes of life. Moreover, translating a particular spatial imaginary into concrete arrangements on the ground is complex, laborious, and as Pirmat-Ata pointed out to me, liable to generate its own new sources of contention.

While my aim in this book is in part to explore the impact of new international borders on those who find themselves living at the new state edge, it is also to make bordering itself the object of ethnographic attention, and through this to explore the complex, messy, and often contested work of spatializing the post-Soviet state. Studied ethnographically, borders are less a simple reflection or manifestation of territorial sovereignty that is already fully formed than a site from which "to reflect on the *project* of territorial sovereignty" (Chalfin 2010, 58); a project that here is contested among multiple state and quasi-state figures (see also Galemba 2012a).

The period that I explore roughly corresponds with the Central Asian states' second decade of independence (2001–2011). This is a period marked by the progressive intensification of state presence at and near these new international boundaries through the building of new national infrastructures and in the form of multiple new "faces of the state" (Navaro-Yashin 2002), including customs officers, road police, ecological inspectors, members of the security services, parliamentary deputies, governors, and border guards. It is also a decade characterized by progressive state attempts to "fix" new borders, discursively and materially, in a region where administrative boundaries have been moved and debated, asserted and ignored since the 1920s. As I explore ethnographically, however, this process of spatializing the state is neither smooth nor uncontested. The dynamics of interaction in the border zones of the Ferghana Valley reveal that state power here functions less through a smooth spreading out of disciplinary techniques than through sporadic assertions of sovereignty—the claims of strongmen (*kattalar*, literally "big men") to embody the state's authority; the power to determine whose rules rule. It follows that we can better grasp the dynamics of border work by exploring state territoriality as process: to shift from asking about what the state (as a singular locus of sovereign power) "does" at borders to inquiring about how, where, and in which situated practices the state is done and undone, invoked and ignored (see also Rasanayagam 2002a; Beyer 2009; Rasanayagam, Beyer, and Reeves 2014). Fixing the state at its edge and making such edges connect with centers of state power is never a smooth process of inscription. "Manning the border," for the customs officers and border guards who work in and around Batken, entails a series of situated judgments concerning who is local, which car should go through unstopped, which truck to check for contraband, how to balance respect for elders with the entailments of law.

The dynamics of border work in the Ferghana Valley are inseparable from the particular history of the Soviet Union's ethno-territorial formation and its subsequent socio-spatial transformation since the 1920s (I explore this history in detail in chapters 1 and 2). The socio-spatial transformations in and around Batken are generative for thinking comparatively about the remaking of international borders at a moment when the Westphalian logic of border-as-line is being simultaneously transformed (by new sites, materials and techniques of inclusion and exclusion often distant from the state's geographical boundary) *and* often violently reasserted through kilometers of barbed wire fencing and the laying of landmines to prevent unsanctioned entry.[6] Sites like the "chessboard" border between Üch-Döbö and Khojai-A″lo provide fertile ground from which to reflect on the paradoxical detachment of sovereignty from the nation-state and

---

[6]For a succinct statement of the need to recast border studies to take account of the transforming relationship between territory and borders, see Parker and Vaughan-Williams (2009). Recent work in political geography has stressed the need to think the sites of bordering that occur throughout the state, as well as the proliferation of agents of bordering (Amoore 2006; Amoore and Hall 2009, 2010; Mountz 2010; and Vaughan-Williams 2010). Stuart Elden (2006) has explored the significance of these changes for recasting our understanding of sovereignty. Although I have found this recent turn to the "deterritorialization" of border provocative, my ethnography also points to the way in which the image of border as *line* continues to have a powerful hold on political imaginaries, among state officials as well as those living near the border. These dynamics are not unrelated; indeed "rather than resurgent expressions of nation-state sovereignty, the new walls [being built around many states] are icons of its erosion" (Brown 2010, 24).

the simultaneous frenzy of border building with which this moment has been accompanied in diverse global settings (Brown 2010, 24). They reveal how those charged with enacting state authority at its limits are embedded in relations of mutual dependence and friendship. They bring into focus the "invisible spatial narratives" (Turnbull 2005, 757) that underpin accounts of contemporary statehood. And they highlight the ways in which the coercive powers of the state may thrive on the continued specification of threat and the putative violation of its sovereignty at its territorial limits.[7] As such, the contested and often decidedly nonlinear borders that characterize this part of rural Central Asia should be deemed neither exceptional, nor marginal, but *diagnostic*. They are sites that expose with particular clarity the contestation over the limits of the state—spatial, institutional and personal—in a context of stark new inequalities after socialism.

"Strong Weak States" and Other Beasts: Implications for the Study of Central Asia

Approaching the state through its geographical margins and attending to the work of making it cohere as a singularity opens up a space for critically exploring the way the state has come to be written and studied in the growing scholarly literature on Central Asian statehood (see chapters 4 and 5). Political scientists working in the region have often noted that the states of Central Asia present a particular conceptual challenge to theories of the state, since the history of these republics' incorporation into, and unanticipated emergence from, the Soviet Union means that they appear simultaneously strong and weak, overbearing and fragmented. They are *strong* in the sense that the state is often experienced as intrusively authoritarian, penetrating into domains of social life that in Western-type liberal democratic states would be considered private; for example, by requiring that public sector employees provide free labor to the state through cotton-picking or participation in choreographed public performances for national holidays (Adams 2010; Kandiyoti 2003). Conversely, Central Asian states are to varying degrees *weak* in their capacity to provide for their populations—and, in the case of Kyrgyzstan and Tajikistan, in the degree to which the formal institutions of state governance can be deemed sovereign over the entire territory of the country.

Frederick Starr, in the introduction to an edited volume on the Ferghana Valley, puts the dilemma in terms of a problem of over- and under-governance.

---

[7]See also Bayart (2009); Lombard (2012); Mbembe (2001, 72–77); Roitman (2005).

"In all three countries that meet in the Ferghana Valley it is customary to speak of authoritarian rule," Starr notes. "But the habit of governments imposing decisions from the top down does not necessarily mean that the affected region is over-governed. On the contrary, performances of authoritarian rule may coexist with a situation in which decisions are implemented poorly at the community level, or not at all" (2011, xviii). Scott Radnitz, writing of Kyrgyzstan, characterizes state weakness as the source of what he calls "subversive clientalism," in which elites form asymmetrical dependencies with communities, providing welfare and symbolic support in exchange for votes and political loyalty, thereby "usurp[ing] the functional role and legitimacy of the state" (2010, 28). Pauline Jones Luong, in a theoretical discussion of Central Asia's contribution to theories of the state, identifies such practices as illustrative of the state "acting against itself." "In contrast to other developing countries," Jones Luong argues, "local 'strongmen' in Central Asia developed within, not outside, the state apparatus" (2004, 277). Consequently, state actors "who are ostensibly engaged in the same enterprise—namely, achieving state predominance over society" are nonetheless acting in ways that "compete with the state and challenge its authority" (ibid., 275). The dilemma is resolved in this institutionalist account through paradox: the "strong-weak state"; the state "acting against itself."

My ethnography supports the empirical findings of this literature: the borderlands of the Ferghana Valley are indeed characterized by weak state governance, and relationships of patronage are important, and often decisive, for accessing basic goods and services. In several Kyrgyz villages around Batken, for instance, newly constructed bridges bear the name of the wrestler-turned-businessman-turned-politician, Bayaman Erkinbaev, who provided this critical piece of infrastructure in return for loyalty at election time. The administration building for the village district (*aiyl ökmötü*) in which Üch-Döbö is situated is adorned by a large sign with the logos of multiple donor agencies that have invested in the development of the community with budgets that far exceed financial transfers from the central government. The state is indeed often empirically weak and experienced as fragmented. However, my ethnography questions the premise of much scholarly and policy analysis that proceeds from an a priori analytical separation between state and society. Much analysis (and much international intervention aimed at bolstering "civil society" in Central Asia) is premised on an assumption that the initial Soviet setting from which to measure the changes of transition was one "wherein the state once appeared to be omnipotent" (Jones Luong 2004, 280). The indication of a successful transition is then understood to be the extent to which society is able to "regain" its autonomy from the state (ibid.). This is the model that explicitly informs several of the initiatives of conflict prevention operating in the region, which I explore in later chapters.[8]

Viewed ethnographically such a characterization is striking in at least two senses. First, historical ethnographies of seemingly strong, Soviet-type states have shown how, studied close-up, the "omnipotent" state was often chronically weak in its capacity to get things done (Grant 1995; Humphrey 1998; Northrop 2004; Poliakov 1992; Verdery 1991). Moreover, these apparent failures in state capacity were central to the very operation of Soviet-type power—for it is precisely in the identification of failure and fragmentation that power is entrenched. As Ssorin-Chaikov argues in his historical ethnography of deferral in the Siberian Subarctic region, "Soviet-type governmentality thrived on the formal weaknesses of the Soviet system" (2003, 202): the condition of failure enables an expansion of governmental projects and the reproduction of the very "traditionalism" that has to be overcome. This is instructive for thinking about contemporary manifestations of the "strong weak state." For example, to understand the ubiquity and entrenchment of contemporary Uzbek authoritarianism, it might be less useful to look for smooth lines of power flowing from an omnipotent center than to explore the micro-sites of fragmentation, the sites of "failure" that allow the invocation of state rule for personal gain, and the gaps between life and law on which coercive technologies thrive (see also Asad 1992, 336–337). Borders are good places to explore these dynamics in practice, not because they are simple geographical "edges" (the place where one state begins and another one ends), but because they highlight the blurring of the legal and the extra-legal that "runs right within the offices and institutions that embody the state" (Das and Poole 2004, 14).

Second, the "strong weak state" characterizations arise from an initial assumption that the state "ought" to be a singular rather than a multiple entity, analytically distinct from society in both a normative and descriptive sense. In Radnitz's model of elite mobilization in rural Kyrgyzstan, for example, the state is represented as an entity distinct from and conceptually above society. In the visual representation of this model the state hovers over a dense network of elite networks, clientalist ties, and communities to be mobilized, visually detached from these "because it is detached from both communities … and autonomous elites" (2010, 31). My ethnography points me to a rather

---

[8] See, for instance, the Mercy Corps Civil Society Strengthening Framework, premised on a three-partner approach between government, business, and civic organizations (Young 2003, 37). For programmatic statements on the importance of civil society to conflict prevention in the Ferghana Valley, see Lubin and Rubin (1999, 23–26) and Maasen et al. (2005).

different position: the problem is not an a priori disjuncture between "state" and "society," but rather that the work entailed in producing the former as a separate, autonomous, disembedded, finitely territorial domain is effortful, contested, and often undermined in reality by structural inequalities and the practical demands of mundane getting along. Viewed in this way we see the perplexing "strong weak state" as a problem of detachment: emerging in a situation in which there are "too many actors competing to perform as state" (Aretxaga 2005b, 258).

To explore these issues ethnographically I take my lead from accounts that have sought to understand the production of the state beyond the realms of finite institutional settings, focusing on the "creative energy" of ordinary subjects in "maintaining the illusion of states' concreteness" (Greenhouse 2002, 1). Rather than asking how the state "sees" (Scott 1998), this literature examines how embedded subjects themselves see (but also imagine and fantasize about, invoke and undermine, mock and reify) the "state."[9] The state in this reading is understood to be the often irrational outcome of dispersed imaginings: a "privileged setting for the staging of political fantasy in the modern world" (Aretxaga 2005c, 106), rather than the outcome of the successive rationalization of society. In exploring public life in Turkey, Navaro-Yashin (2002) has emphasized how the Turkish state persists despite its cynical deconstruction in daily life. To understand why, she argues, we must look to the myriad minor activities, many of them "more statist than the state" (2002, 121) through which we act on the world "as if" it survived. Specifically, the state survives because ordinary people normalize the idea of the state, because "people with power" (e.g., statesmen, generals, mafia, journalists) are "successfully able to produce truth about the existence of the state through their bureaucratic practices," and because the material forces produced around the signifier, state, remain intact (2002, 178–179).

In Navaro-Yashin's ethnography, it is the first of these (the circulation of state-as-fantasy in everyday life) that receives primary ethnographic attention. During the course of my fieldwork, I was increasingly intrigued by the second: how and when do low-level state officials come to be seen as embodying state authority? What are the material practices through which they are successfully able to "produce truth" about the existence of the state, and what happens when such attempts fail? To put the question in ethnographically

---

[9]See Aretxaga (2000) on fantasies about state violence in Spain; Nelson (1999) on the state fetishism of Mayan activists in Guatemala; John and Jean Comaroff (2006) on "criminal obsessions" in South Africa; and Friedman (2011) on the paternalistic imaginings of magistrates in Namibia.

relevant categories, when is an eighteen-year old in an army uniform manning the border to be viewed as a border guard vested with state authority, and when is he a mere "goat in uniform"—as Batken slang would have it—to be ignored or mocked? In many everyday settings, such questions may seem merely indulgent musings on the origin of law. But at the state's limits, they have real urgency. What a border region reveals, perhaps more starkly than other state sites, is the fluidity and contingency of such claims. When the border guards of two neighboring states have a fistfight to determine which of them properly should control a lucrative site of cross-border trade—both claiming that they "represent" the state—the violence at the heart of law loses its abstraction and becomes ethnographically accessible (see also Das and Poole 2004).

Chapter 5 explores this question in theoretical terms: How it is that the state comes to be *impersonated*—to take on material consistency and human form? The term "impersonation" is definitionally ambiguous between the idea of identity (in the Oxford English Dictionary rendering: "to manifest or embody in one's own person"; "to invest with actual personality, to embody") and pretense ("to invest with supposed personality; to represent in personal or bodily form"). "Impersonating the state" thus wavers between a sense of embodying the state's authority and mimicking its effects; between enactment and pretense. As Sheila Fitzpatrick notes in her study of identity and imposture in Soviet Russia, impersonation "is always trembling on the brink of imposture" (2005, 19).

It is this "trembling on the brink" that makes it conceptually generative. In talking of impersonation, my point is not that coming to be seen to represent the state is a mere act of pretense or imposture, analogous to that of the stand-up comedian whose successful imitation of the official is premised on a general recognition of "real" versus "fake" authority. Nor is it to suggest that anyone can simply claim to represent the state successfully, and that the loudest (or the most powerful, or the better armed) necessarily wins. It rather seeks to draw attention to the fact that being seen to embody state authority also requires a certain external recognition: recognition that is empirically variable and spatially contingent. In order for a border guard successfully to regulate cross-border movement he must come to be seen as something other than a "goat in uniform."

In the context of Central Asia, focusing on the embodied performance and contingent recognition of state authority allows us to move beyond conceptual debates concerning the relationship between "local institutions," civil society, and the state (how do we insert "clans" into our political models? Is the *mahalla* [neighborhood] part of the state? Can Kyrgyzstan be really considered a "state" or merely a "globalized protectorate"?) to focus instead on the processes through which the state is produced as a separate domain.[10] It also enables us to separate out and thereby more rigorously analyze situations in which state agents are involved in illegal practices. A formal theory of the state tends to view illegal or semilegal activities undertaken by state agents as a corruption of a normative functioning system. If, by contrast, we start from a perspective where the state is conceived as a work-in-progress, and therefore recognize the "positional character of legality and illegality" (Heyman and Smart 1999, 14), we can better grasp when and why certain law-breaking activities come to be seen as corruptions of systems that ought to function differently, and when and why other law-breaking activities are locally accorded moral legitimacy.[11] It allows us to recognize the contestation over where the licit and illicit lie, and to see how violent practices, such as economic appropriation through seizure, "can also be produced as a legitimate mode of the exercise of power" (Roitman 2004, 193; see also Engvall 2011, 15; Galemba 2012b; van Schendel and Abraham 2005, 8).

To assert this is not to sink into ethical relativism or legal nihilism. It is rather to recognize the variable character of law as a regulatory force and to pose as an empirical question the extent to which particular institutional formations, languages of legitimation, economic imbalances, and regional geographies constrain the efficacy of law and its enforcement in different settings. In the case of Central Asia, where collusion in illegal activities by state officials is often naturalized by reference to "black box" explanations ("mentality" and "the Soviet legacy" being perhaps the most insidious), an emphasis on how and when certain authoritative claims are efficacious provide a much sharper analytical tool. What initially appear as violations of a preexisting boundary between "state" and "society," "legal" and "illegal," can be understood as constitutive acts. It is precisely through the struggle to define certain activities as falling within the domain of "state law" or particular encounters as being subject to the norms of "official" interaction (rather than those of friendship and kinship) that the state is made at its limits, coming to figure in daily life and political imaginaries as an autonomous structure.

---

[10]For contributions to these discussions, see Schatz (2004) on "clans"; Noori (2006) on the *mahalla*; and Pétric (2005) on Kyrgyzstan as a "globalized protectorate."

[11]This is a point well made by Michele Rivkin-Fish in another post-Soviet context where informal payments proliferate. In her study of Russian users of maternity care, she shows how in a setting where official channels of payment are themselves "viewed as ethically problematic or unjust," actors often view unofficial payments "as constituting important, *moral* forms of exchange" (2005, 49)—less the flouting of a transparent, legible law than the constitution of normative action in a setting where law is itself inscrutable.

Researching Border Work

Foregrounding the processual dynamics of fixing state space raises both methodological and conceptual challenges. Researching *across* a border, rather than on just one side of it, entails multiple practical and administrative obstacles, not least the need for multiple visas and affiliations (Donnan and Wilson 1999, 59). Research outside the bounds of the nation-state is a privilege, not always a possibility. There are also conceptual challenges in trying to bring bordering into ethnographic focus. How to explore the materialization of state space without taking the state's own narrative of itself (as encompassing, coherently bounded, and "above" society) as the framework of analysis? How, further, to attend to the institutional unboundedness and multiplicity of the state without denying its experiential reality as a singular, determinate, and powerfully consequential entity (Ferguson and Gupta 2002)? Bourdieu's observation concerning the difficulties of thinking the state "which still thinks itself through those who attempt to think it" (1999, 55) is salutary here. The dynamics of border work are hard to write because our narrative and methodological strategies so readily take the boundedness of state, the "difference" a border makes, or the coherence of power structures through which state personnel operate, as given a priori (see also Abraham and Van Schendel 2005; Harvey 2005; Scott 1998; Wimmer and Glick Schiller 2002).

To begin to gain empirical grasp on these dynamics I came to delimit my "field" for this project according to the riverways that mark the approximate boundaries of the Batken zone (*Batken zonasy* or *Batken aimagy*): the Isfara Valley in the west, where the villages of Khojai-A''lo and Üch-Döbö can both be found; and the Sokh Valley in the East.[12] Along their course, the Sokh and Isfara rivers sustain livelihoods for villages that are habitually identified in terms of each of the three major ethnic communities in the region: Tajik, Kyrgyz, and Uzbek. These two rivers tack back and forth across more than one state, connecting multiple administrative entities and passing through two of the world's largest sovereign enclaves (or exclaves, depending on your perspective)—stretches of land belonging to one state that are entirely enclosed within the territory of another.[13] To the west, glacial tributary valleys

---

[12]The Batken zone corresponds roughly to the official administrative boundaries of Kyrgyzstan's Batken district but the term is used locally to index social and geographical connection rather than to describe an administrative entity. Batken oblast (*oblus* in Kyrgyz) consists of three districts (Kadamjai, Leilek, and Batken), thus Batken is the center of both the smaller district and the larger province.

[13]An exclave refers to a portion of territory of one state completely surrounded by territory of another state or states, as viewed by the home territory. An enclave refers to the same territorial phenomenon viewed from the perspective of the state by which it is surrounded. The

Batken zone. The location of borders and settlements is approximate and should not be taken as authoritative.

of the Isfara River begin in the Alay Mountains in Kyrgyzstan, before entering the Vorukh enclave (administratively part of Tajikistan), reentering Kyrgyzstan, then passing through Tajikistan again before flowing downstream into Uzbekistan, watering the western end of the Ferghana Valley. This is the river that provides irrigation for the villages of Khojai-A″lo, Üch-Döbö, and Ak-Tatyr, sustaining one of the most densely populated agricultural zones of Central Asia. To the east, the Sokh Valley begins as a series of tributary streams in the high Alay peaks in Kyrgyzstan, watering summer pastures, then providing a dense zone of irrigation in the Sokh district (a geographical exclave of

Ferghana Valley contains multiple juridical enclaves/exclaves, some of them only a few hectares in size, the largest, Sokh and Vorukh, with sizeable populations and extending over a substantial area (54,000 and 23,000 inhabitants; and 238 square kilometers and 97 square kilometers, respectively). Vorukh, administratively part of Tajikistan's Isfara district, is a territorial exclave of Tajikistan and an enclave of Kyrgyzstan. Sokh is an exclave of Uzbekistan and an enclave of Kyrgyzstan. The absolute number of enclaves and exclaves in the Ferghana Valley is disputed because the question of whether a particular village or new settlement is actually connected to

Sokh Valley, with the Alay Mountains in the south, August 2005.

Uzbekistan), reentering Kyrgyzstan before fanning out into an intricate network of canals and irrigation channels inside Uzbekistan's Ferghana oblast.

By researching and writing across international borders that are often spoken of as ruptures to a past order of things; in spaces where the sovereignty of the state is often contested; and where people frequently laugh at the idea that friends, kin, or workmates from nearby villages might just have become citizens of different states, I foreground the complex and contested relationship between the state and sovereignty in the interstices of everyday life. How and when do certain ideas about the relationship between citizenship, territory, and proper cross-border movement take hold? When does border-crossing fuel and cooking oil become "contraband," both de jure and in popular understanding? When does a canal winding through border villages come to be imagined in national terms? And when does once-communal grazing land come to be understood, even fought over, as sovereign state territory or as private property?

---

its "home" state depends on where the borders are understood juridically to lie. Eight enclaves/exclaves are generally recognized in the Ferghana Valley, three of which are administratively subordinate to Tajikistan (Vorukh, Sarvak, and Kairagach); four to Uzbekistan (Halmion, Qalacha/Chong-Kara, Shahimardan, and Sokh); and one to Kyrgyzstan (Barak) (Alamanov 2005, 89). For a detailed discussion, see Thorez (2005, 489–504).

There is also a pragmatic reason for seeking to "follow the water" in my ethnography. Christine Bichsel notes in a detailed exploration of water conflicts in the Ferghana Valley that water is at once crucial to sustaining livelihoods and "a mobile, fluid and fugitive natural resource with an inherent uncertainty about its quantity and location" (2009, 49). Rivers, canals and reservoirs structure and constrain social relations here just as international borders do.[14] Within and between villages, the relation of places to water often acts as the geographical point of orientation. Homes are typically spoken of simply as "higher" (*jogorku; tepada* in Batken dialect) or "lower" (*pasta*); directions are given in relation to this spatial gradient or according to whether they lie on the village's sunny or shady side. Reference points to identify neighbors or relatives often distinguish whether a given household is "above the canal" (*kanaldyn üstündö*) or "before the canal" (*kanaldyn aldyda*). Such designations have social correlates. Homes "above" (that is, higher than) the canal typically have to pay for their irrigation water—or, at least for the electricity that pumps the water upstream. Homes near the source or "head" of the water, *suu bashyda,* tend to be better irrigated and their garden plots concomitantly more abundant. Stopping or "cutting" the water to a neighboring village by blocking a shared water source with stones and gravel, as has periodically occurred at times of heightened tension along the Machoi/Ak-Tatyr canal, can be a powerful vehicle for forcing demands and bringing concerns to the attention of authorities.[15] Appropriating water to a private garden plot through illicit outfalls from an uncared-for public canal can be interpreted as a source of domestic survival, an index of disregard for the commons, and a provocation to downstream communities. The Isfara and Sokh valleys afford a means of exploring the intersections of ecology, lived geography, and political formations without taking the contemporary state boundaries between the three states they transect as the delimiting contours of the ethnography.

Such sites also afford a way of understanding how past spatial orders inflect the present. For the other side of this uneven access to water is an

---

[14]On the importance of flowing water to Kyrgyz understandings of place and landscape, see Féaux de la Croix (2011).

[15]In the Isfara Valley, where Khojai-A″lo, Üch-Döbö, and Ak-Tatyr lie, there have been several well-documented instances of water-related conflict. Between April and July 1989, following attempts by the authorities of the Kyrgyz SSR to prevent expansion onto free but undemarcated lands by villagers from Khojai-A″lo, the upstream residents of this Tajik-majority village blocked the flow of water into the lower-lying Kyrgyz villages with stones and gravel, apparently ruining their apricot harvest. This conflict, locally well-remembered by Pirmat-Ata as the "war of the spades" (*voina ketmenei*) resulted in two dozen injuries, several deaths, and the introduction of Soviet troops to calm the disturbances (Foundation for Tolerance International n.d.a and n.d.b; Niksdorf 1989; Popov 1989; Shozimov, Beshimov, and Yusunova 2011, 193–194).

Disputed canal infrastructure, Isfara Valley. Image courtesy of David Trilling/Eurasianet.org.

intense historical interdependence between agricultural and mobile pastoral livelihoods, with social relations embedded in, and constrained by, systems of shared irrigation, as well as common grazing lands, trade routes, and sacred sites.[16] This region of southern Ferghana thus represents a distinct cultural zone in which social distinctions between Kyrgyz, Tajiks, and Uzbeks—although locally noted and culturally elaborated—are often less salient at the level of habitual practice than those practices that distinguish the Kyrgyz of Batken from their coethnics in northern Kyrgyzstan, or the Tajiks of Sokh from those of Bukhara (in Uzbekistan) or Dushanbe (in Tajikistan). In stressing these cultural and kin connections I do not mean to imply that differences between the new states into which the Ferghana Valley is carved are immaterial or insignificant. Indeed, in the chapters that follow I show how cartographic boundaries can come to shape social life in sometimes powerfully disciplining ways, and explore how these processes have been intensified by divergent political projects in capital cities distant from the Ferghana

---

[16]For an early Soviet statement concerning this interdependence, see Bartol'd ([1925] 1991); on irrigation interdependence in the Ferghana Valley under the Kokand Khanate, see Batrakov (1955). As these issues relate specifically to the Sokh and Isfara valleys, see Kisliakov (1953) and Dzhakhonov (1989). On interdependence as it related to use of grazing pastures and irrigated lands, see Batrakov (1947).

Valley. The work of bordering highlights the *improvisatory* work of everyday state formation, and affords an insight into a mode of governance in which power thrives less on rendering populations and places legible than on working the gap between life and law.

Ethnographic Locations

I conducted my field research for this book from February 2004 to August 2005, a period of considerable political upheaval in Kyrgyzstan and increasing tensions over the stakes and political corollaries of Islamic piety in Uzbekistan (Hilgers 2006 and 2011; Khalid 2007; Liu 2012; Rasanayagam 2006 and 2010). I also draw on research visits in 2008 and 2009–2010 when I returned to the Isfara Valley to explore some of the changes occurring in these border villages as a result of extensive outmigration to Russia in search of work (Reeves 2009 and 2012).

My interest in the impact of new borders in Central Asia extends several years earlier, however, when, in 1999 on my first extended visit to the region I spent a summer working with the Ferghana Valley Development Program (FVDP) in Osh city, at the eastern end of the Ferghana Valley, 200 kilometers from Batken. The FVDP was an ambitious UN-funded initiative that sought to reduce the potential for cross-border and interstate conflict between Uzbekistan, Kyrgyzstan, and Tajikistan through trilateral cooperation on issues of trade, income generation, education, and border security. As one of the program's early enthusiasts noted, the FVDP "seemed to embody virtually every item in the catechism of conflict prevention," grounded in transparent and equal collaboration between states, international organizations and local nongovernmental organizations (Rubin 2002, 113). By the summer of 1999, just a year after the FVDP had officially been launched, the program's promise of regional integration through cross-border cooperation seemed increasingly remote. Uzbekistan refused to be involved in a program that it felt undermined state sovereignty, and in September of that year the Uzbek foreign minister, Abdulaziz Kamilov, criticized the FVDP in a speech to the United Nations for interfering with the security of the region (ibid., 115).

My brief encounter with the politics of conflict prevention in the Ferghana Valley made me keen to understand better how and why initiatives aimed at cross-border cooperation could be perceived as threatening to state sovereignty. It also left me curious to explore how habitual geographies were being transformed by the progressive materialization of new international borders, in ways that often fell below the radar of newspaper headlines and policy reports. As I visited the Kyrgyz and Uzbek parts of the Ferghana Valley between 2000 and 2003, I was struck by the considerable variation in the degree to which new borders were visible on the landscape. I was also interested in the degree to which lived geographies and senses of place had or had not been altered by the progressive securitization of borderland space. In the border town of Kara-Suu, at the eastern end of the Ferghana Valley, I recorded angry accounts of the way that the dismantling of a bridge between Kyrgyzstan and Uzbekistan had disrupted local cross-border trade (Reeves 2003). I collected news reports of farmers in the Sokh valley who had lost livestock to landmines planted by Uzbekistan to prevent overland incursion by Islamic militants (e.g., *Vechernii Bishkek* 2003). And I read of villages that now found themselves with barbed wire running through their streets to mark the new international boundary (Frantz 2000a; Megoran 2002, 190–195). In Batken I also heard stories of how it was the business of getting to Russia to earn a living as migrant workers, rather than getting across the borders locally, that was crucial now to securing a viable, economically secure future.

It was this simultaneous salience and multiplicity of the borders around Batken that made me keen to return to the town for a more sustained period of research, something that I eventually did in 2004. My primary hosts and first gate-openers at that time were the family that I call the Sadyrbaevs. Their generosity, piety, and easy domestic harmony taught me far more than I ever learned from formal interviews or household surveys about place and belonging in and around Batken. Four generations of the Sadyrbaevs lived in the family's spacious house close to the town's stadium. Their youngest daughter, twenty-two-year-old Bübüsara, became a close friend and companion during fieldwork. We shared living space, housework, and a great deal of evening conversation about our backgrounds, aspirations, religious beliefs, and hopes concerning family, work, and marriage. Bübüsara taught Arabic and hadith to women who attended Batken's small women's madrassa. Several of her friends and acquaintances had begun extending their knowledge and practice of Islam in preceding years, and many visited Bübüsara at home, to hear her advice on wearing the hijab (*joluk*), to borrow Islamic tapes and DVDs, and to share their experiences of public and domestic responses to their decision to veil. As in other parts of Central Asia, the mid-2000s represented a moment of increasing religious exploration among young people in Batken, and several neighbors sent their children to Bübüsara to study the Arabic alphabet and to learn how to perform the five-time daily Muslim prayer, *namaz.*[17]

---

[17]McBrien (2008) provides a subtle account of social and religious exploration among Kyrgyzstan's "newly pious" in Jalalabat oblast; on the role of female fellowships as a site of social and spiritual knowledge transmission, see Borbieva (2012).

Exploring new expressions of Muslim piety, Batken, May 2004.

Like many of their neighbors, the Sadyrbaevs had moved to Batken in the mid-1970s. In 1971 the building of a large reservoir drawing water from the Isfara River allowed 9,000 hectares of otherwise uncultivated "stony land" (*tashtyk jer*) to be irrigated and brought under collective agriculture, transforming Batken from the small settlement that had initially been founded in 1934 into a large, planned "village of urban type" (*poselok gorodskogo tipa*) and district (*raion*) center. These Brezhnev-era transformations shaped the identity of the community and are often remembered as marking a high point in Batken's development. In 2004 the town's main street was still named after the Soviet cosmonaut, Yuri Gagarin; the town's boarding school was referred to simply as "Lenin," and some of the buses leaving for rural villages still listed destinations according to their long-disused sovkhoz names, One hundred years of Lenin and the First of May.

For seventy-five-year-old Ene, the oldest member of the Sadyrbaev family, the move by a Kamaz truck from the high mountains where she was raised to Batken—her first encounter with motorized transport and high socialist interventionism—was a decisive moment of transformation. Growing up in the tiny encampment of Döngmön, a thousand meters above Batken in a steep tributary of the Sokh River, she had been married at fourteen and spent all of her adult life in the mountains (*toodo*). Ene had not gotten used to working for the state farm in the dry, dusty hinterland (*boz adyr*)—though she did now appreciate the modest pension she received for her work on the collective. Her youngest son, Abdumital, who inherited Ene's home and who cared for her in old age, had, by contrast thrived on the Soviet state farm, working as a driver throughout the Soviet Union, transporting livestock and fuel between collective farms. After independence, Abdumital's extensive knowledge of the surrounding geography, along with the links his family retained with the Döngmön pastures, enabled the Sadyrbaevs to survive the sharpest upheavals of post-Soviet economic transition and the privatization of former collectively owned land. The family had a sizeable flock of sheep and cattle that they pastured there in the summer; they had apricot orchards in the mountains; and they had acquired a gasoline tanker which, until the cross-border trade became too risky, the family's eldest son, Kadyr, would use to transport gasoline from Uzbekistan for resale in Batken.

The Sadyrbaev family retained an intense spiritual connection with Döngmön. They described it now as their *jailoo*, their summer pasture, a place of rest and celebration where they would go to mark major lifecycle events.[18] Arapat-Eje, Bübüsara's mother, would regularly play her Döngmön videos with their green vistas and waterfalls, their scenes of racing games and raucous sliding down high glaciers, to friends and visitors, the images rolling silently in the background as guests sat on the floor and shared tea. Like the family photos carefully preserved in albums and the posters of Mecca that were pinned to the eastern walls of the Sadyrbaevs' house, such videos formed a constant visual connection to *this other place*, high above dusty Batken: a place in which it was truly possible to feel clean (*taza*), free (*erkin*), and magnanimous (*keng*). Arapat-Eje once described Batken to me as a "crossroads," the place to which families had been resettled, but where people's orientation often remained outward: to villages from which people had been relocated only a generation earlier; to kin who remained in the mountains; to summer pastures that provided both material security and spiritual solace.

The "Batken Events" and Their Aftermath

Despite its largely rural mode of life during my period of research, Batken had recently changed status from a "village of urban type" to a town and provincial capital of the newly formed Batken oblast. This sudden shift had been prompted by itinerant fighters' incursions across the region's southern mountain borders in the summers of 1999 and 2000, which heightened official anxiety over what appeared to be dangerously porous borders with its war-ravaged neighbor, Tajikistan. According to official versions of what came

---

[18]On the importance of the *jailoo* as a site of spiritual enrichment, spatial expansiveness, and material abundance, see Féaux de la Croix (2010, 62–66).

to be known as the "Batken events" (*Batken okuialary*), the incursions across Kyrgyzstan's southern borders were undertaken by extremist militants (*boevikter*) of the Islamic Movement of Uzbekistan who sought to enter Uzbekistan from Tajikistan through the high mountains above the Sokh enclave with the aim of overturning the government of Uzbekistan. In the village of Zardaly, close to the Döngmön pastures used by the Sadyrbaev family, the militants seized hostages, among them a Kyrgyz general and four Japanese geologists who had been excavating in the area. Kyrgyz mountain encampments were evacuated, with families who were pasturing their flocks during the summer taken in by relatives lower down the valley. In August 1999, apparently on Kyrgyzstan's request, Uzbek military planes dropped several bombs on and around Zardaly hoping to destroy this "terrorist threat," and more refugees arrived, turning Batken's small town stadium into a temporary sea of tents. Although the threat of incursion did not disappear, this unilateral military action did have the effect of bringing the region to national and international headlines, exposing its isolation and the poverty that had allegedly led many Zardaly villagers to offer the militants accommodation in exchange for cash.[19]

For the Uzbek authorities threatened by perceived terrorist activity, the events demonstrated the degree to which Islamic extremism posed a threat to the very continuity of the state, legitimating a discourse of extreme vigilance and an aggressive crackdown on those practicing Muslims whose piety or practices lead them to be deemed "Wahhabi."[20] For Kyrgyz leaders, meanwhile, the 1999 incursions were decisive in crystallizing a discourse of danger around the province's undefended and largely unmarked borders in Batken. The 1990s had been characterized by relatively open borders between the Central Asian states, in part because of the sheer costs and logistical difficulties of securing new international boundaries that had previously been internal Soviet borders, and in part because of an early (and short lived) aspiration toward interstate cooperation on the part of Kyrgyzstan's leadership. At a 2007 public lecture the head of Kyrgyzstan's committee for border delimitation and demarcation, Salamat Alamanov, commented nostalgically of the early discussions surrounding border delimitation and the atmosphere in which they had been conducted. When negotiations over border delimitation started with China soon after Kyrgyzstan's independence, Alamanov noted,

---

[19]A detailed chronology of the Batken events as they unfolded in 1999 can be found in Kurbskii (2000); Omuraliev and Elebaeva (2000); and Suslova (2000). On the hostage crisis and subsequent convergence of refugees in Batken, see Pannier (1999a and b).

[20]On the politicization of the category of "Wahhabi" as a means of delegitimizing religious piety in Uzbekistan, see Rasanayagam (2006); Khalid (2007, 46–47).

We never thought that we would have to undertake the same kind of work with our neighbors—with Kazakhstan, Tajikistan and Uzbekistan. The experts who conducted the work of determining the line of our border with China said, "well, we can get this work finished and then we can get on to other business.". . . The same was true for heads of state. If you leaf through the documents from those early meetings of the heads of state [1992–1993], it is written there that we wouldn't have any borders [*u nas ne budet granits*], we won't bother with any of that business [of changing borders], that we would keep the same community [*obshchnost'*] that we had in the Soviet Union. As a result, when we formulated our international relations with our neighbors, it was written there that we would recognize the existing administrative-territorial boundaries. We thought that would be enough to be able to live in our community [*v nashem soob-shchestve*] without any kind of border problems. (Alamanov 2008, 39)

Such openness rapidly came to figure in political discourse as a mark less of collegiality with former Soviet neighbors than of political naïveté. As one analytical report noted in the wake of the 1999 Batken events, the "transparency of borders between [the] republics of Central Asia" had created "happy circumstances for the movement of Islamic emissaries and extremists around the territory of these countries" (Tursunov and Pikulina, 1999). Concerns such as these came to inflect national policy-making in Tashkent, Dushanbe, and Bishkek. Even as fighting continued in the mountains high above Batken, border posts were hastily set up in mountain villages deemed at risk of incursion; border guards took up temporary residence in homes and tea-houses; Uzbekistan began to mount barbed wire along those stretches of its border with Tajikistan and Kyrgyzstan that had been delimited—sometimes right through the middle of villages—and swathes of pastureland deemed vulnerable to attack were mined by the Uzbek army (see Megoran 2002, 183).[21]

This is the context in which Batken oblast was hastily formed as a separate administrative unit—from the larger Osh oblast—in October 1999. By shifting in status from village to town and provincial capital, Kyrgyz president

---

[21]According to the International Landmine and Cluster Munition Monitor, Uzbekistan began mining its border with Afghanistan in 1998, with Kyrgyzstan in 1999, and with Tajikistan in 2000 (www.the-monitor.org/custom/index.php/region_profiles/print_profile/401). The mines around Sokh were reportedly cleared in 2004 and 2005, following requests from the Kyrgyz government, though it is unclear whether the mines laid along the Uzbek-Tajik border have been entirely removed (Integrated Regional Information Networks News 2005). In the early 2000s several incidents led to allegations that Uzbekistan had laid mines along territory, the status of which was formally contested (Kim and Gruzdov 2003a).

Askar Akayev argued, previously marginal Batken would become better securitized militarily, better resourced financially, and under more direct control of central government. Batken's discursive identification as a region peculiarly vulnerable to threat and to dangerous seepage from outside was thus rhetorically overdetermined from the start of the new province's existence. By 2004, official celebrations in Batken regularly featured the conscript soldiers posted to the region's borders as both guardians and symbolic guests of honor. Visits from dignitaries would typically include meetings with border units and appeals to public support for their work. The outer wall of Batken's military training ground, visible to passersby, was painted with slogans reminding Batken people (in Russian) to "strengthen and defend Kyrgyz statehood." Seven years later, legislation aimed at preventing the illegal sale of land and property among Batken's border villages to citizens of neighboring states had included measures to "strengthen the military-patriotic preparation" of those living in border villages and to create material incentives for Kyrgyz from outside Batken to move to the province to help strengthen popular border defenses (Proekt 2011).[22]

For Batken's residents, it was the material repercussions of these administrative changes that were more generally remarked on than the threat of incursion from militants. The shift in administrative status from village to town and oblast capital meant that within a few years Batken acquired a renovated administration building, a two-room television station, several newly asphalted roads, and a large new military barracks along the border with Tajikistan. As the Sadyrbaevs' youngest son, Üsön, would point out to me as we walked around the town together, these were signs that Batken was finally regaining its forward trajectory toward modernity—a trajectory that had been stalled for a decade during the 1990s and which was now, with this shift in administrative status, finally able to be regained. In 2004, to mark the fifth anniversary of the creation of the new province, a monument to freedom (*erkindik*) was unveiled in the center of the town, mirroring one that had been erected months earlier in Bishkek. The House of Culture began to be renovated and the provincial administration building or White House (*Ak Üi*) was given a facelift. Plans were announced for new roads that would consolidate the region's "transport independence." And in late 2004 the small Batken airport, which had been closed for the previous fifteen years, began scheduled flights to Kyrgyzstan's capital, Bishkek.

---

[22]Collectively, as the preamble to the draft law suggests, such measures are intended to "strengthen the border territories of the Kyrgyz Republic; to guarantee her national security and to protect her territorial integrity and the inviolability of the national border" (Proekt zakona Kyrgyzskoi Respubliki, preamble). I have discussed this proposed law in more detail in Reeves (2011b).

Soldiers on guard at the spring New Year (*Nooruz*) celebration in Batken, March 2004.

For Üsön it mattered little that few Batken people were able to afford the flights, or that most of the passengers were not even citizens of Kyrgyzstan. In 2004–2005 the majority of the Batken airport's traffic consisted of visiting development workers, high-ranking military officials, and traders from Khujand city in Tajikistan who purchased goods in Bishkek's vast wholesale market for resale across northern Tajikistan. The two-room airport, its interior unchanged since its Soviet incarnation, and typically operating in an atmosphere of friendly informality, materialized connection, mobility, and incorporation into a forward-moving world. As Üsön remarked on one occasion, "from here you can connect to anywhere. You could be in New York in a day."

Legacies of Enclavement: Sokh

Batken remained the home to which I returned throughout fieldwork, as well as the town in which I would catch up on news, make phone calls from the central telegraph office, and purchase provisions for the families in whose homes I stayed. As my social network grew, I traveled regularly to the villages of the Isfara and Sokh valleys. The Sadyrbaev family had many relatives in Kyrgyz villages to whom they introduced me. A university student, Jengish, who became both a key informant and a close friend, introduced me to his relatives in the villages of Ak-Tatyr, Üch-Döbö, and Ak-Sai, on the Kyrgyz side of the border along the Isfara River. Other social networks brought me to the Tajik-majority villages in the fertile river floor of the Sokh and Isfara valleys.

I spent four months between November 2004 and March 2005 living in the *mahalla* that I call Dehkonobod in the Sokh enclave, administratively part of Uzbekistan's Ferghana oblast, thirty kilometers east of Batken.[23] Sokh is at once anomalous within the Uzbek nation-state and paradigmatic of the complex legacies bequeathed to the Ferghana Valley by the national-territorial delimitation of 1924–1927 and the transformation of the landscape through artificial irrigation. The district (*tuman* in Uzbek, administratively equivalent to the Russian *raion*), with a population of 54,000 living in twenty-three *mahallas*, forms a fertile ribbon along the Sokh River on which wheat, corn, and rice are sown, alongside apricot and apple orchards. When Soviet republic boundaries were first drawn up here in the 1920s, Sokh was geographically contiguous with the Soviet Uzbek Republic (the UzSSR).[24] This is visible in the 1928 Soviet atlas of the USSR, which shows Sokh (and Vorukh in the Isfara Valley) connected to the UzSSR via narrow fingers of territory (*Atlas* 1928 reproduced here on page 30; Koichiev 2001).

As the area under cultivation grew in the 1930s, land was leased between the Kyrgyz and Uzbek SSRs, initially as an informal mechanism to rationalize the payment of land tax for what were then uncultivated pasturelands.[25] The story of Sokh's transformation into a geographical exclave of Uzbekistan is tied to the history of postwar industrialization and resettlement campaigns. It was in this period that the building of a new canal, Bürgündü, made an area of otherwise arid foothills at the northern end of Sokh habitable, leading to the resettlement

---

[23]Dehkonobod and other smaller villages in Sokh are identified using pseudonyms. In Uzbekistan, the *mahalla*, generally with a population of 1,000–2,000 is used to indicate a residential group (often related by ties of kinship and organized around a single mosque and associated burial ground), and to refer to the smallest official administrative unit of the state. *Mahalla* is subordinate to the administrative district (*tuman*), which is in turn subordinate to oblast (*viloyat*). On the significance of legislation in Uzbekistan aimed at reviving the *mahalla* as an institution at once secular, grassroots, and statist, see Noori (2006, 1–39).

[24]There was, however, considerable discussion in the 1920s as to whether Sokh should be administratively transferred to become part of the Kyrgyz Autonomous Soviet Socialist Republic (since it was economically connected to this region), or whether it should be joined to the newly formed Tajik SSR in 1929 (Bergne 2007, 52–53, 101, 147n22; Jahonov 1995, 34).

[25]It is often erroneously asserted that the Ferghana Valley's complex republican borders and multiple enclaves were deliberately created by Soviet authorities to foster cartographic confusion and dependence on Moscow (see, e.g., Lewington 2010, 224; Lewis 2008, 6; Shishkin 2013, 238). In fact the geographical enclavement of these regions follows from later policies. Both Vorukh and Sokh became territorially separated from the mainland of the Tajik and Uzbek SSRs as a

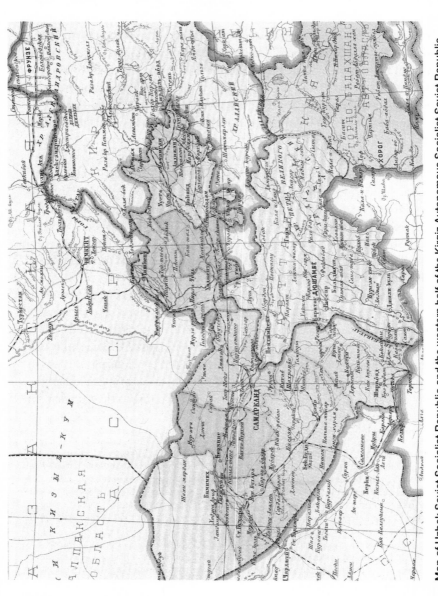

Map of Uzbek Soviet Socialist Republic and the western half of the Kirgiz Autonomous Socialist Soviet Republic from the 1928 atlas of the Soviet Union. The map shows today's Sokh and Vorukh exclaves as deep protrusions into the Kirgiz ASSR, but territorially contiguous with the UzSSR mainland.

there of Kyrgyz farmers from higher villages in the 1970s and the formation of two new state farms.[26] When the Soviet Union collapsed in 1991 and constituent republics became juridically independent, such informal arrangements took on dramatically new political significance. Sokh was transformed into an administrative exclave of Uzbekistan, a geographical "island" entirely enclosed within the territory of Kyrgyzstan. Meanwhile much of the region of northern Sokh— including a significant area of natural gas extraction—that had been the site of land leases in the previous decades acquired ambiguous administrative status. The object of occasional high-level political discussion, it also became the focus of sometimes polemical exchanges on Central Asian Internet sites about which state rightfully has jurisdiction over a given stretch of land.[27]

This administrative complexity is compounded by the fact that the majority population of the Sokh enclave, although citizens of Uzbekistan, are Tajik-speaking and Tajik-identifying, creating, as one of my acquaintances there put it, a "double box" (*dvoinaia korobka*) of separation from their broader ethno-linguistic group.[28] The sense of cultural isolation is particularly acute for those middle-age Sokh men who left Sokh to study in the Tajik SSR while the Soviet Union was still in existence and who now constitute the district's intelligentsia. Although the Sokh district was part of the *Uzbek* SSR, the district's brightest and best had been sent to receive a Tajik-language higher education in Khujand

---

result of lands leased "for long-term use" (*na dolgosrochnoe pol'zovanie*) in the 1930s to collective farms belonging to the Kyrgyz SSR (Alamanov 2005, 81; Gorshenina 2012, 296–297). In the case of Sokh, a 1955 parity commission sought to establish the borders of the Kyrgyz and Uzbek republics conclusively, and indicated that 70,000 hectares of uncultivated pasturelands should pass from Uzbekistan to Kyrgyzstan. However, the agreement, ratified by the Council of Ministers and Presidium of the Kyrgyz republic, was not ratified by the Presidium of the Supreme Council of the Uzbek SSR, or the Presidium of the USSR. The transfer of lands to the Kyrgyz SSR is regarded as a juridical fact in Kyrgyzstan, but not in Uzbekistan (Arslonzoda and Olimov 2004). With independence the de facto boundaries of Kyrgyz and Uzbek collective farms in this densely cultivated region north of Sokh became the de jure boundaries between the new states. Many of these areas remain disputed.

[26]According to Salamat Alamanov, the head of Kyrgyz commission on delimitation and demarcation, the exchanges of land at this time ended up with the drawing of "fussy, illogical borders, which made no sense to people living in this region" (2005, 89). Nonetheless, resettlement into this area has continued long after independence, with the Kyrgyz government promising in 2011 that 15,000 families from Batken province would be allocated land plots of up to 40 sotok (4 hectares) in this region instead of the usual 5–6 (Aimak News 2011).

[27]See, for instance, *Vechernii Bishkek* (2001), Arslonzoda and Olimov (2004), Samadov (2008), Asanov (2012), Mikhailov (2012), and Zokirov (2012).

[28]There are several Kyrgyz-identifying families in some of the outlying *mahallas*, where Kyrgyz-Tajik intermarriage has historically been common, but most "Kyrgyz" families currently living within the Sokh district speak Tajik and give their children Persian names. This is in marked contrast to the villages higher up the Sokh Valley, administratively part of Kyrgyzstan, where Kyrgyz-identifying and Kyrgyz-speaking villagers scorned the idea of Kyrgyz-Tajik intermarriage and emphasized the cultural, linguistic, and economic differences between the two ethnic groups.

or Dushanbe: cities that today, administratively in Tajikistan, can be reached only with difficulty, and from where university diplomas are no longer recognized (Nadzhibulla 2010). Many more Sokh people have kin who are citizens of Tajikistan, with whom practical and affective contacts in the form of telephone conversations, letters, and visits have been rendered perilous by the vagaries of bilateral visa regimes, interstate tensions, international calling charges, and the rising cost of travel (Reeves, 2007a, 2009b; Yusupov 2004).

Roles and Relations in the Field

Everywhere I conducted fieldwork I lived with families, my role shifting with time along a continuum between lodger, family guest, and adopted daughter. As my involvement within domestic networks grew, my sense of familial incorporation and obligation also shifted, and with the Sadyrbaev family in Batken, I came gradually to identify and be identified more as an adopted family member. Although my movement between these roles was gradual and occasionally reversed if I returned after a long absence, I became generally more observant of the subtle codifications of gender and generational hierarchy, aware that my dress, demeanor, and research routines indexed not just my own honor (*namys*), but that of the family with whom I was living.

This had implications for the kind of fieldwork that it was possible for me to pursue at different times. During my early months of research, when my outsider status gave me considerable freedom of movement, spending time with those charged with manning and working the borders around Batken was easy enough. I was invited to share beer with customs officers, play cards with border guards, and "ride the border" with the Sadyrbaevs' oldest son. As I came to fill more of the social roles associated with female "incomers" (*kelinder*) to the family, and as I spent more time sharing conversation with women of my age, I became increasingly aware of gendered dimensions of mobility and immobility.[29] The kinds of hanging out that I had earlier enjoyed in Batken's cafes with other incomers to the town felt increasingly disjointed from home life with an observant Muslim family. Although I started to spend proportionately less time talking with those responsible for guarding the integrity of state borders

---

[29]*Kelin* refers to a bride or daughter-in-law, but can be used generically to refer to young women who are "in" but not "of" a given household. The term derives from the root *kel-, kelmeq*, which means "to come," and my positioning as an outsider who had come "into" the household meant that I was often inserted into this category. Although I was not married at the time of research, being in my late twenties put me firmly in the category of those who "ought" to be married, and because my female friendships were mostly with those who were already daughters-in-law, it was natural that I would be associate with this group.

around Batken, I came to learn an increasing amount about domestic experiences of movement and its limits. Conversations with women whose husbands had left for seasonal work in Russia taught me that feelings of freedom and enclosure (or entrapment), of connection and separation, were mediated by far more than the presence or absence of an international boundary: in the highly coded relations of domestic deference, female subordination was often articulated in spatial terms.[30]

As I became attuned to domestic practices over their daily and yearly cycles, I became increasingly aware that the border had to be studied in the context of broader flows, ruptures, and productions of distance. Long-distance migration, to the respective capital cities and beyond to Russia, is inscribed in personal and familial biographies and patterns of consumption. Conversations with married women about sons and crops making it, or not making it, to their destinations increasingly focused my attention on roads, canals, train tracks, as well as the ways in which daughters, livestock, gifts, news, and accusations circulated across multiple boundaries. In my final months of research, between January and July 2005, I conducted a household survey in four Kyrgyz-majority villages in the Isfara Valley and in six Tajik-majority *mahallas* in Sokh to gain a better understanding of these dynamics of domestic and international mobility. The survey, which included a total of 586 households (encompassing a total population of about 3,800) gives an insight into the degree to which family livelihoods are progressively oriented toward migrant remittances as an important—indeed often primary—source of domestic livelihoods, in part because of increasing obstacles to local cross-border mobility (for more on this, see chapter 3).

Although my research occurred over various sites, it was not strictly "multi-sited" in Marcus's (1998) sense of the term. Indeed, it was precisely because of complex, asymmetrical flows of knowledge *between* Batken and Sokh that I came to be invited to the latter. Parviz, a former teacher and later an NGO-employed conflict analyst with whose extended family I lived in Dehkonobod, traveled regularly to Batken, collaborating in cross-border conflict prevention projects with colleagues from Batken-based organizations. I had become acquainted with several of Parviz's Kyrgyz partners through my research and as an English teacher. It was in this capacity that Parviz initially sought me out and presented me to the local district governor (*hokim*) in Sokh raion. For four months, at the *hokim*'s invitation, I conducted research and taught English at one of the district's newly renovated technical colleges.

---

[30]I have explored this theme in greater depth in Reeves (2011c); see also Liu (2012, 135–142) for a subtle account of the gendered dynamics of spatial presence in an Osh Uzbek *mahalla*.

As well as affording me a role and a routine, the college collective (*kollektiv*) provided a point of entry to social networks in two of Sokh's *mahallas,* and I would often spend afternoons during the winter months with the family of one of my colleagues, visiting, cleaning rice, cooking, chatting, and helping children with their English homework.[31] Late fall and winter mark the wedding season in Sokh, and my involvement in the preparations for two large family celebrations alerted me in new ways to the processes through which social reputation was premised on overcoming and circumventing restrictions on movement: How to get relatives from Tajikistan into Sokh without visas? How to import cases of commercially produced (*firmennaia*) Kyrgyz vodka for the wedding feast in a way that avoided customs duties? How to get hold of musical recordings in Tajik to accompany the wedding feast, and how to obtain the Tajik currency that would enable one to buy these recordings across the border in Isfara?

If the range of activities in which I was involved gave a surface similarity to my research on either side of the Kyrgyz-Uzbek border, the contexts of research in either case were nonetheless significantly different. My ability to communicate freely in Kyrgyz (a Turkic language), but not in Tajik (a Persianate language mutually incomprehensible with Kyrgyz and Uzbek), meant that conversation tended to be more spontaneous and subtle in Kyrgyz-speaking villages; but mediated through a second language (Kyrgyz, Uzbek, or Russian) in Tajik-speaking Sokh.[32] Moreover, my growing familiarity with Kyrgyz cultural codes over several years meant that Batken, while a remote field site in terms of the urban worlds in which I had previously worked, was one nevertheless imbued with familiar cultural, linguistic, and spatial referents to a far greater degree. A more significant difference had to do with the everyday presence of the state on the two sides of the Kyrgyz-Uzbek border. In rural Kyrgyzstan the state was often talked about as frustratingly remote (see also Beyer 2007, 2009). However, in Sokh—subject to Uzbekistan's capillary mechanisms of societal surveillance through the structures of the residential district or *mahalla*—everyday conversation was inflected with an awareness of the state's expansive presence in village life (Noori 2006). We might attribute this difference to the fact of Uzbekistan's greater authoritarianism: a fact for which the comparative indices of "freedom" of numerous monitoring organizations provide ample evidence.[33] Uzbekistan is an intrusive, illiberal state in a way that Kyrgyzstan is not, or at least was not in the mid-2000s.

---

[31]*Kollektiv* is a Russian term, but widely used in Kyrgyz and Uzbek, to refer to the social group with whom one works.

[32]Uzbek is the state language in Sokh and understood and spoken in the district by most men, women, and children (though many elderly women only speak Tajik). Russian is primarily spoken by middle-age men and by the mid-2000s was rarely understood and spoken by young people.

[33]See the Freedom House's assessment of Uzbekistan, which gives it the lowest possible score on five of the seven criteria by which it measures regime freedom (Pannier 2012).

From an ethnographic perspective, however, such distinctions raise important questions of how such difference is produced and encountered in the everyday. Which distinctions make a difference? How to capture, ethnographically, the experience of crossing from a state that is "unfree" to one that my informants often spoke of as excessively free and lacking in order (*tartib*)? How to capture the quality of stateness in a state that is deemed illiberal by outside observers: the sense of being subject to a state that is simultaneously intimate and intimidating in a way that neither belittles nor romanticizes that experience (see also Navaro-Yashin 2003)? Some of my interlocutors in Sokh spoke of fear and intimidation—particularly those who were more pious in their expression of Islam, or more explicit in their celebration of their Tajik ethno-linguistic heritage. Yet others seemed to have found a modus vivendi within the Uzbek polity and spoke of the importance of strong-armed leadership when so many threats lay across Uzbekistan's borders (see also Trevisani 2014). One Sokh neighbor, eager to send his son to Tashkent so that he might eventually join the state security services, asked that he be photographed along with his passport "so that people who read your book know that I belong to a great state." Other acquaintances, by contrast, reeled out jokes that spoke of popular complicity in their own oppression, subtly mocking the president of Uzbekistan, Islam Karimov, or questioning the anodyne displays of well-being that characterized Uzbekistan's highly censored news broadcasts.[34]

My first day of teaching in the district, on November 1, 2004, coincided with one of the largest and most vocal public demonstrations of recent years in the nearby city of Kokand against draconian new trading regulations.[35] Throughout the winter and spring of 2005, friends in Sokh followed with a mixture of alarm and awe news of increasing political mobilization across the border in Kyrgyzstan, which culminated in the ousting of the country's president in March 2005. Television news reports condemning "anarchy" across the border signaled a degree of official nervousness that the political turmoil that was gripping Kyrgyzstan, characterized by road closures and the violent

---

[34]Commentary on the nature of the state and its insertions into daily life often seemed to be the subject of conversation in Sokh. On one occasion, as the husband of one of my colleagues at the technical college was telling me about the debts he had to enter into in order to meet the costs of his son's wedding, the single light bulb in the room where we were sitting went out. Although this was not an unusual occurrence, the man's reaction linked our conversation to a commentary on the limits of permissible speech: "You see? Karimov doesn't want me to tell you about this!" On another occasion, a lively meal that was interrupted by the start of the evening news on Uzbek state television prompted a joke from my host: "Why are self-cleaning televisions so popular in Uzbekistan? Because our TVs get showered in spit every time the news comes on!"

[35]See Azamatova (2004); Whitlock (2004).

seizure of administrative offices by an assortment of opposition groups, would destabilize Uzbekistan. The traders, water engineers, and conflict analysts like Parviz who engaged in "nongovernmental" activities of various kinds became subject to increasingly restrictive laws on trade, export activities, and the use of commercial bank accounts throughout 2004. Condemnation of "alien ideologies" was a staple of official Uzbekistani broadcasting during the winter that I lived in Sokh.

In May 2005, Uzbekistan's willingness to employ violent force against a crowd of bystanders following a prison break in the valley's most populous city grabbed international headlines and sent shock waves throughout the Ferghana Valley.[36] Dozens, perhaps hundreds, of innocent bystanders were killed on Andijan's Bobur Square on May 13, 2005—an incident that profoundly reoriented attitudes toward Uzbekistan's "slow but steady" post-Soviet reforms both among Uzbek citizens and Uzbek-identifying citizens of Kyrgyzstan.[37] "Ordinary" fieldwork following what almost immediately came to be known as the Andijan events (*Andijon voqeasi*) suddenly felt far from ordinary; the bounds of legitimate violence and the integrity of the state themes now woven into everyday conversation. When I returned to Sokh in the summer of 2005, the tape-recorder and notebook that had often felt to be intrusive tools of research the previous winter were now appropriated by friends and acquaintances in new ways, recording grievances and grief that

---

[36]The prison break followed a highly politicized trial against thirteen pious and economically successful businessmen in Andijan, whose model of popular provisioning, grounded in an Islamic ethic, was intensely threatening to local authorities. The network of businesses they had established in Andijan over the previous few years provided for many Andijan families a form of alternative protection and authority from that of the state. The men's religious conservatism, together with their substantial popular support made for an extended show trial grounded in accusations of religious extremism and anticonstitutionalism. The lack of independent investigation of the Andijan events means that contemporary accounts of the events are polarized in their assessments and often sketchy in their analysis of the complex precipitating factors. The diversity of assessments of the Andijan events can be gained from comparing the conclusions drawn by Human Rights Watch (2005); International Crisis Group (2005c); Akiner (2006); Polat (2007). Khalid (2007, 192–198) situates the uprising and the state's response in historical context, noting that the crackdown on perceived militants was a "logical continuation" of earlier attempts to regulate spiritual and civic life in Uzbekistan (2007, 198).

[37]With regard to Osh's Uzbek population, Liu writes: "It was the Andijan events of 2005 that sealed the conviction for most Osh Uzbeks that they could look neither to Uzbekistan as an exemplary post-Soviet state nor to [Uzbekistan's president] Karimov as Khan. Most realized that Karimov had fired upon unarmed citizens in Andijan's central square, where people had gathered for peaceful protest, and killed possibly hundreds." After Andijan, "the Soviet-style control of the economy and dissent, the decisive ruthlessness against the nation's evil enemies, the condition of "state rich, people poor," the paternalism of "khan knows best what is good for the country," the policy of "short-term hardship for long-term benefit," the perpetual deferment of the "future great state" all came crashing at the gates of Osh" (2012, 194–195; 2014).

transformed the meaning of my fieldwork and left me struggling to define the bounds of "participant" observation. Neither the fieldwork, then, nor the resultant ethnography, should be read as a symmetrical cross-border comparison.

The story that I trace throughout this book emerges from this specifically ethnographic engagement. It is through the ethnography of a place and the people that live there that I seek to explore "territorial integrity" in anthropological terms: how space is made into territory when the geographical contours of the state and the entailments of independence are themselves contested. My ethnographic field was full of gaps and bumps; the "border" whose social life I explore was a plural, not a singular object. By moving from the border as it materializes in maps, in conversations, in administrative regulations, in encounters with border guards, in water pipes, and in bridges, I seek to destabilize the taken-for-grantedness of territorial "integrity" and through this to inquire about the way in which effects of state singularity are produced (Harvey 2005; Mitchell 1999).

This is not a historical ethnography of a particular state institution; an approach that has generated a rich strand of ethnographic work in Central Asia as elsewhere in the former Soviet space (Abramson 1998; Zanca 1999). Nor it is an attempt to grasp the life of the Kyrgyz or Uzbek state as an object of political imagination (Gullette 2010; Rasanayagam 2002a; see also Friedman 2011). By leaving unqualified the "state" in the title of my book, I want to draw attention to the practical work of limiting and delimiting "it" as a singularity, and to problematize the production of difference across a border. As such I also seek to contribute to a growing interdisciplinary debate on contemporary Central Asian statehood. For it is often in the epistemic gaps, the places where ideas do not quite translate, where perspectives do not quite coincide, where things "relate but don't add up . . . share a space but cannot be mapped in terms of a single set of three-dimensional coordinates" (Mol and Law 2002, 1) that some generative insights can emerge. Or so I hope to argue in the chapters that follow.

1. LOCATIONS

Place and Displacement in Southern Ferghana

It is the last day of August 2004 in Batken town in Kyrgyzstan's far southwest: a dry, windless day typical of late summer when life congregates on the shady side of the street. I join the crowd that has gathered in the rectangular shadow of the town's post office to await the daily bus bound for Ak-Sai, a border village thirty kilometers to our west lying in the valley of the Isfara River. There is always a throng of people here long before the bus's scheduled departure at 5 pm. The bus often leaves early, and those who arrive first have the best chance of a seat for the two-and-a-half-hour ride. On this occasion the crowd is larger than usual. August 31, 2004 marks the thirteenth anniversary of Kyrgyzstan's independence, and the town's usually empty stadium has today been bustling with activity. Officials in suits and ties, school girls in Kyrgyz national costume and conscript soldiers from the nearby barracks have joined the dozens of families who have come to take part in this annual celebration.

Independence Day is a state holiday in Kyrgyzstan, and the back wall of the stadium bears a large banner reminding onlookers that 2004 is, by presidential decree, the year of "conscientious leadership and social mobilization."[1] In the center of the stadium's soccer field, parched from the summer sun, a yurt-shaped podium has been installed with a sound system to broadcast speeches from the regional governor and members of his administration. Much the busiest part of the stadium, however, is far from these proceedings, where a series of tables has been set up in the shade, selling *plov*—the meat and rice dish that is a staple at celebratory occasions in Batken, as well as ice cream and succulent kebobs.

---

[1]Kyrgyz: *Akyikat bashkaruu jana sotsialdyk mobilizatsialoo jyly.*

Most of the people visiting the festivities, adults and children alike, seem largely oblivious to the content of the speeches ringing out from the center of the stadium. "Independence Day" is the opportunity for a celebration: a day off from work; the chance to dress up children in their best clothes; the excuse to share news with kin from other villages; and, for many rural families, the opportunity for some last minute shopping in the district's central market before the start of the new school year. Down the road from the stadium, as the cluster of passengers awaiting the Ak-Sai bus swells with families returning from the festivities, conversation moves from the celebrations here in the district center to the growing cost of school uniforms and the state of this year's apricot crop.

By 2004, the yellow Soviet-era Pazik bus, which I took on multiple occasions during the course of my research in and around Batken, had been making this journey once daily in each direction for the previous thirty years. Names and years scratched in a child's handwriting into the peeling paint date the bus to the early 1970s, the period when several of the villages that we will travel through on our way to Ak-Sai had been established and many of today's elders were forcibly relocated from smaller pastoral settlements in the mountains to the town's south. Bales of sweet-smelling fleece wool stuffed under the back row seats remind of the continued seasonal migration that links these newer, gridded villages in the valley basin with the summer pastures (*jailoo*) in the mountains above. The bus's demographic mix as we clamber aboard speaks of newer kinds of movement on which the region has come to depend for its livelihood. Most of the adult passengers boarding in Batken are women. Many—perhaps even a majority of the young mothers on board—have husbands and sons working on construction sites in urban Russia for months or years at a stretch. By 2004 Kyrgyzstan had become one of the most remittance-dependent countries in the world, and of its seven provinces, Batken has some of the country's highest rates of out-migration for work.[2] Little wonder, then, that elders here would often compare the seasonal departure of young men to construction sites in urban Russia to the wartime departure "to the front" of their parents' generation.

As new passengers join and standing room is filled to the limit, infants are passed to seated strangers to be cared for during the journey. Older men and women who board later in the journey will be provided with sitting space, entailing a careful rearrangement of people and goods at each new stop. Kyrgyz

---

[2] On the impacts and changing dynamics of international labor migration from Batken region see Bichsel, Hostetler and Strasser (2005); Röhner (2007); Reeves (2009b, 2012); Lukashova and Makenbaeva (2009).

and Tajik elders, known as *aksakals* in Kyrgyz, *mūisafed* in Tajik (in both languages meaning "white beards"), for whom seats have been found at the front of the bus, greet each other with a "peace be with you" (*assalomu aleikum*), followed by a rapid exchange of questions in a dialect of Kyrgyz heavily inflected with Tajik and Uzbek vocabulary. How is your health? Are you sitting peacefully? How are your children? Are they peaceful? Is everything in order (*duruspu*)? Followed by an "ah, good, ah good" (*tüzük tüzük*) before settling back into silence.[3]

The Batken Zone

Our journey from Batken, Kyrgyzstan's newest oblast capital with a population of roughly 13,000 people, takes us through one-half of the Batken zone (*Batken zonasy* or *Batken aimagy*), the irrigation-dependent plateau that extends for sixty kilometers from the Sokh River in the east to the Isfara River in the west. Located today at the cusp of three new states, this region of southern Ferghana has historically been a site of considerable social, ecological, and linguistic contact. Place names and demography reflect the historical interdependence between settled and pastoral modes of life and the dynamic interaction between speakers of Turkic and Persianate languages. Many places along our route are commonly called by two (and sometimes three) names—including Tajik, Kyrgyz, and more recent Russian variants.[4]

---

[3]This form of exchange is linguistically revealing. In their standard literary forms, Tajik and Kyrgyz are mutually incomprehensible: the former belongs to the Persian language family, whereas Kyrgyz is a Turkic language. In this exchange, however, we find a kind of linguistic hybrid—not only in the use of the religious greeting, *assalomu aleikum* (from Arabic), which occurs in both languages; but also in the use of the question, *duruspu*, which takes a typical northern Tajik greeting (*shumo durust mī?* ["is everything in order?"]) and renders it in Kyrgyz form, dropping the double consonant and adding the question particle, -*pu*. This regional greeting, a combination of Turkic and Persian forms, is at once locally inclusive (marking its speakers and hearers as part of a shared speech community) and regionally distinct (it would rarely be used by people from outside this region).

[4]Examples of villages in this region for which more than one name is regularly used include Kyrgyz Orto-Boz, which older generations tend to refer to using its previous, etymologically "Tajik," name as Govsuvor or Govsuar; Tajik Khojai-A″lo, known in Kyrgyz as Matchai and in Russian as Oktiabr′; Kyrgyz Kapchygai, which is often referred to by its former Tajik name, Tangi; and the new Tajik settlement of Tojikon, which Kyrgyz speakers nearby tend to refer to simply as Poselka, using a calque of the Russian word for village, *poselok*. Although these names are often used interchangeably, the identification of historical primacy through toponyms has become integral to the project of nation-building in Central Asia as a means of demonstrating autochthonous residence in the Ferghana Valley. For a detailed exploration of the ethnic history of the valley through an analysis of the region's toponyms, see Gubaeva (1983).

The very name Batken, which means "confluence of winds," can be traced etymologically to both Kyrgyz and Tajik. "You can expound on the meaning of the word in any language you like," one local poet writes at the start of her study of the region, before telling her reader, matter-of-factly, that she would rather describe the region with a song (Joosh kyzy 1997, 4).

Concrete waterways crisscross this landscape, running alongside roads and fanning through a complex network of mud channels that serve as irrigation ditches (*aryks*) under walls and into gardens. As the Ak-Sai bus traces a route west out of town the gray, parched hills where the water doesn't reach remind just how vital that irrigation is to sustaining homes and livelihoods. To our north lies the large fertile basin of the Ferghana Valley: densely populated and intensely cultivated with the cotton that sustains Uzbekistan's exports. To the south lie the high slopes of the Alay Mountains, the farthest of them still snow-capped on this late August day. In between lies the hilly hinterland of sharp grays and reds—the *boz adyr* (gray hills)—of the Batken zone.

This is a region decisively transformed by the ambitious arc of soviet modernization. The rock and asphalt road through this landscape was established in the heyday of "developed socialism" in the 1960s and 1970s when the region was undergoing a period of profound social and economic transformation.[5] The development of artificial irrigation on an industrial scale in the post-war period had opened barren landscapes to collectivized agriculture, transforming the de facto boundaries of collective farms and administrative districts. In the same period, high mountain villages and summer encampments, some of them well over 2,000 meters above sea level and only a few households in size, were consolidated and their populations moved to more "economically productive" areas in the lower-altitude *adyr* zone.[6] Ak-Sai, at

---

[5]Valentin Bushkov notes that it was in these decades that Batken came to be fully incorporated into Soviet industrial agriculture. Batken district (*raion*) was established in 1964, and this marked a major shift toward settled agriculture, large-scale stockbreeding and the "radical restructuring of the district's basic infrastructure" (1990, 6). It was also during this period that the first major resettlement of ethnic Kyrgyz began in Batken, with mountain Kyrgyz from the Teiit and Noigut descent groups resettled in low-lying Chong-Kara and Kara-Bak villages in 1959 and 1961, respectively. In general the wartime experience and postwar transformation of Central Asia remain significantly understudied in the historical literature on the region, although several scholars have hinted at the importance of this period for understanding both the relative stability of the postwar years and the sources of post-Soviet conflicts over territory and autochthony (Bichsel 2011, 2012; Dudoignon 1998; Liu 2012, 209n18; Northrop 2004, 349).

[6]The resettlement policy saw the voluntary, and later forcible resettlement of mountainous populations to the Ferghana Valley to contribute to lowland agriculture and cotton production. A detailed analysis of the policy as it pertained to the Tajik SSR and an insightful exploration of the consequences of this policy for subsequent articulations of identity politics in the valley are discussed in Ferrando (2011a, 2011b). Internal resettlement in Tajikistan is also discussed by

Soviet-era irrigation infrastructure in the Isfara Valley. Locally the road and canal are taken to mark the border: to the left is Tajikistan, to the right is Kyrgyzstan.

the far end of the Batken bus route, built in the early 1970s to resettle Kyrgyz pastoralists from higher mountain settlements at the source of the Isfara river was one such village. Batken was another, with gridded structure, municipal buildings, and landmarks reflecting its consolidation as a Soviet Kyrgyz "village of urban type" (*poselok gorodskogo tipa*).

In this late-Soviet period of socio-spatial transformation, the Batken–Ak-Sai bus would have tacked back and forth between the Kyrgyz and Tajik Soviet Socialist Republics, connecting several collective farms with each other and with their district centers, and integrating two distinct linguistic communities into a shared socialist space. By the mid-2000s, several decades of sedentarizing, collectivizing, settling and resettling of populations, irrigating and swapping of land had transformed this barren "stony place" (*tashtyk jer*) into a series of densely populated zones of tightly grouped courtyards,

Abulkhaev (1983), Bushkov (1995), Schoeberlein (2000), Loy (2006), and Kassymbekova (2011). The resettlement program as it was conducted in the 1960s and 1970s from mountainous to low-lying Batken region in the Kyrgyz SSR has not received comparable scholarly treatment.

cultivated fields and apricot orchards; splashes of green and white in an otherwise arid landscape of gray-red rock and scree. It had also created a border between now-independent states that is complex, contested and, in many areas, still awaiting conclusive delimitation: indeed, two decades after independence, nearly half of the 970-kilometer border between Tajikistan and Kyrgyzstan remains to be conclusively delimited.[7]

To trace the route of the Batken–Ak-Sai bus on a map of the region would reveal that we crossed back and forth over this new international border no fewer than six times in the course of the fifty-kilometer journey, with some of these stretches of alternating jurisdiction just a few dozen meters in length. We passed from Kyrgyzstan into Tajikistan at Surh, then back into Kyrgyzstan at Samarkandek, then into Tajikistan again for 200 meters as we crossed over the Isfara River, then Kyrgyzstan again for the village of Kök-Tash, then back into Tajikistan as we followed the river upstream through Khojai-A″lo and into Kyrgyzstan again at Ak-Sai, before the bus pulled up meters away from the border with Tajikistan at the enclave village of Vorukh.

From a cartographic perspective the bus was winding its way through an enormously complex area of borderland: a "chessboard border" on which a variety of political games could be played at moments of political tension. This patchwork of state territoriality created enormous administrative obstacles and fostered considerable local anxiety over rightful access to land, water, and pastures.[8] Yet in August 2004 the thick orange boundary lines that make

---

[7]According to Kyrgyz officials, 467.5 kilometers of the Kyrgyzstan–Tajikistan border await demarcation and delimitation, much of this in densely populated regions on the boundaries between Kyrgyzstan's Batken oblast and Tajikistan's Sogd oblast (Centrasia.ru 2011). Progress on delimitation remains slow because of disagreement over which Soviet era normative acts (and corresponding maps) are to serve as the basis for discussion. Tajikistan refers to maps from 1929, claiming that later agreements between the respective Soviet republics were not ratified by the Tajik Supreme Soviet and therefore do not have juridical force. Kyrgyzstan refers to maps from 1952 as the basis for negotiation. Neither of these, however, bears much correspondence to the actual territorial distribution of "Kyrgyz" and "Tajik" villages as it existed at the time of independence in 1991, still less as it appears today (Alamanov 2005, 84; 2010).

[8]For the normative foundations regulating the demarcation, control and movement across the Ferghana Valley borders see Polat (2002), Musabekova (2003), and Imanaliev et al. (2006a and 2006b). The history of recent delimitations between Kyrgyzstan and its neighbors is outlined in Alamanov (2005) and International Crisis Group (2002). The agreements (*soglasheniia*) between Kyrgyzstan and Uzbekistan, and between Uzbekistan and Tajikistan regulating cross-border movement in the Ferghana Valley at the time of my research in the mid-2000s are reproduced in *Dolina Mira* (2004, 28–47). For details of the administrative structures regulating border control in each of the Ferghana Valley states, see Appei and Skorsch (2002); on the relationship between state building and border control, see Gavrilis (2008, 93–129).

"Welcome to Vorukh." The Kyrgyz-Tajik border in the Isfara Valley, 2004. Land shortage in Vorukh has led to extensive residential construction on the southern (Tajikistan) side of this boundary since 2004.

the map of this area so complex still bore few material traces in the landscape. Citizens of Kyrgyzstan and Tajikistan both took this bus and passed freely, for the most part, from one state to another. In contrast to other parts of the Ferghana Valley, where barbed wire and plate-glass customs posts had taken shape on the landscape and borderland pastures had been laid with landmines, there were few formal markers here to indicate in which of the two states one happened to be. Indeed, only the hand-painted sign welcoming visitors to Vorukh (in Tajik rather than Kyrgyz) indicated that this stop also marked the territorial limit of Kyrgyzstan.

Contested Trajectories

To note this complexity is not to suggest that landscapes here were and are not read locally in terms of "rightful" Tajik and Kyrgyz ownership. Nor is it to deny that discussion about such ownership often animated the journey between Batken and Ak-Sai, morphing into sometimes heated debate over the primacy of claims upon, and fair access to water, land, or pastures. Local disputes over access to land and water between upstream and downstream users along the Isfara River have been a source of tension since the 1930s and have intensified considerably since the 1970s, when population growth and resettlement programs placed an acute strain on shared sources of irrigation.[9] The borders between Soviet republics in this part of the Ferghana Valley were negotiated and redefined until the very last years of the USSR's existence, as new lands were rendered habitable and new villages created in the previously unirrigated *adyr* zone. Tensions over rights to water and land periodically erupted into open conflict long before the reforms of perestroika enabled the more contentious consequences of Soviet modernization to be openly debated.[10]

The narrative recountings of such moments of transformation are striking for their discursive consistency and emotional force. Batken is a storied place (Stewart 1996)—and the stories often speak of comparisons with other places through which territorial disputes and historical grievances are rendered legible: with Palestine, with Kosovo, or with Nagorno-Karabakh. The stories of the region's transformation differ from place to place: they are often fragmentary and inconsistent, and the heroes and victims of such accounts differ according to who is narrating and who is the audience. But in their multiple iterations such narratives serve at once to describe and reenact feelings of loss and betrayal that mirror each other across the border (see also Green 2012b; Jackson 2002). This, for instance, is how one of Ak-Sai's first residents, sixty-two-year-old Ömürbek-Ata, recalled the process whereby Kyrgyz mountain settlements high in the Isfara Valley were consolidated into a single collective farm from the 1930s onwards:

ÖMÜRBEK-ATA: Kyrgyz people had been living up in the mountains. Bedek, you've seen Bedek, right, on the road going up to Keravshin and Kishemish pastures, above Tangi?[11] Where there's a border post now. There's a river there and a little village, Bedek. It's become a Tajik village

---

[9]For a chronology of such incidents, see *Regional'nyi dialog i razvitie* (2004) and Bichsel (2009, 106–112). For a frank contemporary account of the role of land exchanges in exacerbating conflict, see Popov 1989.

[10]In 1990, when sources of tension were publicly aired for the first time, Russian anthropologist Valentin Bushkov (1990, 1995) wrote ominously of the consequences of rapid population growth in the Isfara valley, which had grown elevenfold between 1870 and 1990 (from 13,500 to 162,200). "World experience shows that with such a speed of population growth, even the most modern economy cannot cope, without a radical transformation in the structure of society ... In the conditions of absolute and relative over-population that faces the Isfara district the Tajik population naturally sees in the Kyrgyz, who have settled on traditionally 'Tajik' lands and using 'Tajik' water, as the source of all of their problems" (Bushkov 1990, 4, 8). Meanwhile, policies of resettlement, sedentarization, and "consolidation" had meant that previous overwintering sites (*kyshtoo*) were transformed into permanent villages and grew rapidly. Bushkov estimates the Kyrgyz population dependent on the Isfara River to have grown fifty-seven times (from 83 to 4,715 households) between 1903 and 1989 (ibid., 7).

[11]This is the same village that is marked as Kapchygai on the map of the Batken zone, on page 17. Ömürbek is using the older "Tajik" name for the village, which refers to a steep gulley between mountains.

now, but it used to be Kyrgyz land [*kyrgyzdardyn jeri bolgon*]. There are still two Kyrgyz cemeteries [*mazar*] there, one is shaped like this, the other is like that. At present the Tajiks have been moving the fences little by little, squeezing the land around the cemetery. . . . This place used to be all Kyrgyzstan [*myna biakka polnost'iu Kyrgyzstan*]. But then after the October Revolution, after 1917, people were divided into collective farms. Ours was Kolkhoz Communism. I forget the name of the Tajik one. But we were all divided into collectives. All the Kyrgyz people were grouped into one place [*toptogon*] and made into a kolkhoz. The Party required it. People from Bedek were gathered up, brought and joined with Tangi. They brought people from other places too. . . . First they were made into one farm: Kolkhoz Communism. But then all those places where people had come from were all emptied out [*bul jer bosh kylat*], no Kyrgyz people should live there anymore; *no one* should live there.

MADELEINE: Do you mean that people moved down from the mountains above Vorukh?

ÖMÜRBEK-ATA: People were *brought* down [*köchü alyp kelgen*]. The Party demanded it [*Partiia zastavit kylyp*]. They gathered up the Kyrgyz people into one group.

MADELEINE: By force?

ÖMÜRBEK-ATA: By force [*majbur*]! People were obliged to resettle. This was during the time of collectivism [*kollektivizm ubagynda*]. Everyone should be one collective. And then after the Kyrgyz had moved, by the 1980s, by about 1982 the Tajiks started taking over this land. It started. Vorukh was getting too full: people would have to leave in order to take care of their children. And so they started settling down on what had been our land. But the Kyrgyz couldn't stop them. It was the Union at that time! The Union! Moscow didn't give its permission [to contest the land seizure]. Moscow issued a decree [*prikaz chygat*]. It said, "the land that is being lived on now by Tajiks belongs to the Tajik [SSR]; the land being lived on now by the Kyrgyz belongs to the Kyrgyz!" So that meant the Kyrgyz couldn't stop them [from claiming that land].

Comments such as these often came up during my journeys to, and walks through, Ak-Sai and its surroundings. Such stories would often weave together personal recollection, official history, and shared, almost mythic accounts of historical wrongdoing concerning illicit exchanges of land or the impossibility of redress in the face of decrees from Moscow.

The Batken zone is a region characterized, then, by acute constraints on shared resources, and by sometimes ardently voiced regrets that political leaders "gave away" land to the neighboring republic during the later years of the Soviet Union. And yet equally significant is that, in 2004 at least, the dominant discourse on the Ak-Sai bus was one of necessary cooperation in the face of growing attempts to regulate cross-border movement and entrench state presence. Mythicized accounts of Soviet leaders who forcibly moved populations or gave away land coexisted with an equally passionate and performative narrative of local cooperation in the face of external obstacles. Different idioms coexisted: plaintive recollections of historical wrongdoing often coupled with a quiet pragmatism about the need to get on with making a living in a harmonious (*yntymaktuu*) manner despite the increasing presence of conscript soldiers, or "boys in uniform" (*formadagy baldar*) patrolling the region. "Why do we need [border] posts here?" Akhmat-Agai, the director of the Ak-Sai school, asked me rhetorically one June afternoon as we sat in his office, less than 200 meters from the state border. "We use the same market, the same pastures, we drink from the same stream." Akhmat-Agai went on to tell me how an incident of violent escalation the previous winter, in which newly established Kyrgyz and Tajik customs posts were overturned by men from Vorukh and Ak-Sai unhappy at the inevitable document checks and customs fees they faced to visit their local markets, illustrated the degree of connection that existed between Kyrgyz and Tajik villages.

> [The government] started putting up all sorts of posts, customs posts and border posts, and all those stop people from living [*vse meshaiut liudiam zhit'*]. . . . It's mostly after the Batken events [1999] that they started putting up these posts; many of them. [They] started to check various of those, you know, documents, and these posts aren't good. People aren't happy with them because we have lived here almost a hundred years as neighbors! So, well, in the winter, people themselves, that is Kyrgyz and Tajiks, they came to an agreement you see, and they went there and turned over those posts. They went themselves, without any kind of state directive, they came to the opinion that if the state cannot solve the problem, let's sort it out ourselves. And since then there are no posts left.

Akhmat-Agai took considerable pride in narrating to me, an outsider, how people had taken the law into their own hands in the interests of maintaining cross-border peace. A year after this incident, there were still few indicators of where one state began and another one ended in the Isfara Valley. Most people would refer to the ethnicity of people living on a particular residential street to determine to which state it belonged. If this is where Tajiks lived, then it was Tajikistan; if Kyrgyz lived here, this was Kyrgyzstan. In 2004, the "border" in the Isfara Valley was only encountered as an administrative limit point at certain times, and in the form of particular people: a Tajik customs officer posted on the bridge that marked one part of the border on market day; a group of camouflage-clad conscript soldiers who would patrol disputed areas at moments of heightened tension; a series of boulders moved into the road to signal the appearance of an informal road block; or a policeman checking for the import of contraband at a rural crossroad.

By 2008, however, when I returned to Batken and Ak-Sai for a period of follow-up fieldwork, boundaries were appearing in other ways too. The dilapidated yellow bus, state-owned and increasingly costly to repair, had been replaced by private Mercedes minibuses, operating the same route at greater speed and transporting passengers in greater comfort. Stretches of previously uncultivated and administratively indeterminate land showed new signs of appropriation, with land plots marked with stones and the foundations of future homes laid in concrete. Blue painted signs along the route in Kyrgyz, English, and Russian announced that the European Commission had donated 6.5 million euros to build a detour route through Kyrgyzstan that would bypass Tajik villages, enabling Ak-Sai and neighboring Kyrgyz villages to be accessed from Batken without leaving Kyrgyz territory. The symbolic weight of this infrastructure in materializing state space was not lost on the regional governor. Visiting the construction site of the detour road in the summer of 2008, he lamented the territorial obstacles that had prevented Batken from experiencing "true" independence until now:

> On the territory of this oblast there are five enclaves, and all communication goes exactly through these enclaves. To tell you the truth, it is precisely for this reason that for already fifteen years now the local population has not yet experienced the taste of real freedom [vkus nastoiashchei svobody]. The taste of independence. Such problems can be resolved in one way only. We must build detour roads around these enclaves. (Anarkulov 2008)

In the mid-2000s, borders around Batken were beginning to materialize in new ways. New infrastructures were being built, often with outside funding; new stories about the need for territorial integrity were being told; and in national and regional capitals new arguments were being made about the

Sign announcing the building of a bypass road with European funding to circumvent the territory of Tajikistan at Surh and Chorkuh, March 2008.

importance of fixing Batken's borders conclusively, and the dangers of depriving border people of the "taste of independence." Such transformations were neither smooth nor uncontested. But their consequences were increasingly palpable. By 2012 the kinds of cross-border movement and habitual interethnic interaction that the Pazik bus and dilapidated interrepublican road network had afforded eight years earlier were much less common. The creation of a smooth asphalt "detour route" (*ob"ezd jol*) linking ethnically Kyrgyz villages, traversed by private minibuses accepting only Kyrgyz currency and passing exclusively through Kyrgyzstan's territory, meant that passengers from the Tajik villages of Vorukh, Khojai-A"lo and Chorkuh were far more likely to take Tajik-run minibuses traveling along Tajik roads to Tajik towns and markets than they were to come to Batken to trade.

The 2000s have, then, been characterized by the increasing *étatization* of space in this border region. However, such new manifestations of border do not simply erase older ways of apprehending and doing space—that is space produced through habits of trade, ritual visiting, seasonal migration to summer pastures or honoring the dead. To think through these dynamics, I draw on recent attempts to explore the "liveliness" of space, or as Doreen Massey (2005, 9) puts it, an account of space "as the sphere in which distinct trajectories coexist; as the sphere, therefore, of coexisting heterogeneity." Such an approach has implications for the way that we might think about borders and the work of bordering, and specifically in the Ferghana Valley, for critically questioning the tendency to treat geography as destiny.

Genealogies of Border Work

Four decades ago, in a remarkable ethnography committed to exploring how village life in the Italian Tyrol is shaped by "the play of forces larger and more powerful than themselves," John Cole and Eric Wolf described the durability of cultural differences in the context of shifting geographical boundaries (1974, 1). The authors' focus was on ethnicity and ecology in an Alpine region subject to multiple political reconfigurations during the twentieth century. Cole and Wolf showed that state boundaries are neither static nor all-determining; at the local level, they revealed that borderland villages "different in ethnic identity and often at loggerheads in politics, live side by side and share very similar modes of adaptation to a common mountainous environment" (1974, 3).

Much of the subsequent anthropological research on borders has followed the empirical concerns—if not the rich historical contextualization—of Cole and Wolf's study, attending to the social dynamics that exist across geographical boundaries and the dynamic borderland culture that particular regional and political configurations can produce. Often this has been coupled with a concern to demonstrate the challenge that such regions pose to bounded notions of culture and identity—and to expose the ideological work in identifying and marking difference. In an influential article from 1995, which served as both survey and program for the growing field of borderland studies, Robert Alvarez argued that "rather than maintain a focus on the geographically bounded community and culture, the concepts inherent in the borders genre are alert to the shifting behavior and identity and the reconfiguration of social patterns at the dynamic interstices of cultural practices" (1995, 462). Border and borderland here serve as both site and metaphor: a place of transgressive potential from which to disrupt fixed identities of gender, race, or class and thereby critique essentialized accounts of identity. "To survive the Borderlands / You must live *sin fronteras* / Be a crossroads" reads Gloria Anzaldúa's poem that captured the spirit of this critique (1987, 195). This is border as site of mixture, as place of pain and contradiction, but also of productive transgression and of possibility.

Anzaldúa, like Alvarez, was writing of the US-Mexico border, a region that has been singularly important in the development of border studies and in articulating a critical response to dominant accounts of American identity premised on notions of culture as discrete (see also Wilson and Donnan

2012, 7–8). The theoretical concepts that have been forged in this terrain—hybridity, transgression, borderland culture, deterritorialization—continue to be influential in sites well beyond the specific region in which they were forged. And yet, as Sarah Green argues in a theoretical exploration of "border" in anthropological theory, "many of the approaches within this genre in fact appeared to take for granted what constitutes 'border'" as the location of the meeting of difference (Green 2009, 3; see also Ballinger, 2002). As a result, the borderlands literature, as it developed in the 1980s and 1990s, has had considerably more to say about border as "an interstitial zone of displacement and deterritorialization" (Gupta and Ferguson 1992, 18) than it has in identifying the institutional and material processes through which state agents and ordinary people seek to make state boundaries stick: *re*territorializing space and marking difference. Such a focus reflects, in part, the distinctive disciplinary conversations through which this literature advanced: between anthropology and cultural studies, between American and Latino studies, gender and queer studies in particular. In part it reflects the generative potential of border-as-metaphor such that "borderlands" came to stand for any site of cultural contact, unmoored from reference to state territoriality.

The importance of this literature notwithstanding, one consequence of the discursive expansion of "borderlands" is that such studies were largely silent when it came to making sense of borders that were not easily open to playful possibilities for crossing. As Mathijs Pelkmans notes in a historical biography of the contemporary Georgian-Turkish border, we still know relatively little about the boundaries of states that lay along (or behind) the iron curtain. Quite apart from the difficulty of studying Soviet-era boundaries, the real-world rigidity of iron curtains "was of little use in academic agendas that proclaimed the 'fluid' nature of borders" (Pelkmans 2006, 12). The legacies of these agendas continue to be felt today, for while issues of access have eased for some of the former Soviet borders to make possible cross-border research, Cold War legacies continue to shape how such borders are conceived. Just as boundaries between socialist and capitalist economies were assumed to be self-evidently "closed," so they are assumed now to be unproblematically open: "as if their past rigidity and subsequent porosity are self-evident (and have self-evident consequences)" (ibid.).

One vigorous response to the expansion of border studies as it developed in the 1980s and 1990s has been to stress the insistent materiality and implicit, and sometimes explicit, violence of international borders—contrasting metaphorical with literal, symbolic with real. In many global settings, to ask where or what the state or the border is might seem redundant; frivolous even, as though to deny real and very unequal relations of power or institutions of violence. The border is *there*—in the line of barbed wire, in the separation wall, in the security fence, in the checkpoint, in the no-man's land that people anxiously wait to cross. The state is *there*—visible and material, in the border guards, the customs officers, the legislation making some crossings legal and others illegal, in the technological apparatus of control or punishment.

Recent scholarship has done much to illuminate the performative displays of force that characterize many global borders in an age in which cross-border movement is at once pervasive and politicized (see, for example, Aggarwal 2004; Andreas 2009; Bornstein 2002; Mountz 2010; and Nordstrom 2007). In such settings, the pressing questions are often less about what or where the state is than what it does and how it is contested: how identities, for instance, are transformed by the reality of a highly securitized international border; or how livelihoods are affected by dramatic inequalities on either side. Such studies have often positioned themselves in dialogue with, and sometimes explicitly in opposition to, the argument that globalization is gradually eroding the importance of state borders, and by extension, state sovereignty (Appadurai 1990, 1996; Kearney 1995). They serve as an important reminder that for all the heralding of our "global ethnoscape," in large parts of the contemporary world borders have become more, not less significant, and such processes may be intrinsic to the very "globalizing forces" that have led to their disappearance elsewhere (see Alvarez 2001; Brown 2010; Bruns and Miggelbrink 2011; Chalfin 2001, 2003, 2010; Navaro-Yashin 2003; Newman 2006; Nicol and Townsend-Gault, 2005; Wilson and Donnan 2012).

In their introduction to a volume on border identities, Thomas Wilson and Hastings Donnan make this argument explicitly, urging scholars to take seriously the real relations of power that are invested in such sites—and specifically, the power of the state.

> The state is an object whose reality will be denied if we focus exclusively on deconstructed representations of it, and nowhere is this more apparent than at borders, where the powers of the state are monumentally inscribed. Nations and their individual members may be in a perpetual condition of becoming, but this is only partially true of the state. The state exists. Its institutions and representations make and enforce the laws which regiment most daily activities of its citizens and residents, in direct relations of cause and effect. (1998, 8)

The authors make an important point here about the risks of treating border as mere metaphor, and thereby ignoring the very real relations of power that animate and sustain contemporary international boundaries. This is a position these authors have subsequently restated in an analysis of the development of border studies in the past two decades. The end of the Cold War, along with new literature on globalization "seemed to distract . . . many more scholars away from the political economy of territory" (Wilson and Donnan 2012, 6) As anyone who has stood nervously at a border checkpoint knows, the state at its edges is indeed often experienced in "direct relations of cause and effect" in the most explicit and intrusive ways: in orders, demands and prohibitions; in techniques of surveillance and control; in the objectification of intimate data; in the disregard for other people's time; and in the ever-present possibility that entry might be denied. The corrective offered by an approach focused on political economy to celebratory narratives of a "borderless world" is important. In the post-Soviet context such an approach acts as a sobering reminder that the opening of the iron curtain and collapse of the command economy have for many resulted in a de facto decline in opportunities for legal mobility, just as they have opened up new trajectories of movement between formerly sealed borders elsewhere (Jansen 2009; Megoran 2002; Pelkmans 2006; Reeves 2007a; Remtilla 2012).

However, the stress on the direct relations of cause and effect between state and its subject population can give the impression of a state whose spatiality and sovereignty exist a priori. In Wilson and Donnan's account quoted above (1988), identities are continuously in formation but states are political givens. As such the active work of separation through which a state boundary is produced: the visible work of checking, classifying, confiscating, as well as the more subtle forms of subjectivization through which a border comes to acquire material force are relatively unremarked in this literature. The work of spatializing the state in a region of undemarcated rural borderland, where the state is institutionally "weak" suggests some complications to this story. It is these complications that my ethnography pushes me to explore, turning Wilson and Donnan's assertion—"the state exists"—into a cluster of questions about borders and the nature of the contemporary state. What does it do for our understanding of "border" if it is not clear where and when and in which institutions the state exists? If the authority to impersonate the state— to speak on its behalf, to uphold its laws, to represent it in some way—is contested? If the very location of the border, and the entailments of "territorial integrity" are debated, both locally and in halls of political power?

The Border Multiple

To answer these questions I draw upon two distinct but related theoretical fields: the social study of science and critical studies of space. Social studies of science are productive for thinking about border work by posing as empirical questions how and when bodies and objects of various kinds come to be produced as "singular"—and when such enactments fail. If we begin with a study of situated practices, then objects that we habitually treat as unitary—medical conditions, technologies, persons, bodies, infrastructures—come to be seen in this way as the outcome of coordinated enactments, rather than as bearing singularity a priori. Annemarie Mol, in her 2002 study of ontology in medical practice demonstrates how the condition known as atherosclerosis—a condition that is something quite different in a doctor's surgery and a pathology lab—is made to cohere through a range of situated practices and tactics. It is not inherently singular; nor does "it" exist prior to the technologies that inscribe it. As Mol puts it, this approach not only grants objects "a contested and accidental history (that they acquired a while ago, with the notion of, and the stories about their construction)," but it gives them a complex present, too: "a present in which their identities are fragile and may differ between sites" (2002, 43).

This approach has two significant correlates. First, it directs attention to the kinds of "silencing" that occur in fixing the objects of knowledge. Studies of science have shown, for instance, how the vast background field of assumptions and inscription devices that allow a given scientific fact to be known (the "hinterland") get written out of scientific texts, so that the datum comes to appear autonomous and self-standing (Law 2004, 18–44; see also Latour and Woolgar 1979). Second, it draws attention to the fact that just as objects can cohere, they can also fail to cohere.[12] Focusing in this way on the practical "production of singularity" provides a useful methodological and conceptual point of entry for exploring the state at its territorial limits. Rather than starting with the border-that's-there and asking how it is subverted or contested (Bruns and Miggelbrink 2012), this approach directs attention to the multiple sites in which a border comes to materialize: in the person of the border guard, in maps, in water pipes, in cross-border volleyball matches, in informal prohibitions on movement and in the building of new "strategic" villages, as well as in the more obvious acts of document checking or the mounting of barbed wire. Such an approach does not suppose this "border" to be a singular object in a singular location; nor does it assume that these various

---

[12]John Law illustrates this in the case of the failed British fighter jet project, TSR-2, which ultimately demonstrated the "intrinsic impossib[ility]" of coordinating all the systems together to produce a functioning aircraft system. The aircraft that was enacted into some semblance of coherence over the course of two decades was ultimately unmade through equally stunning performances of disaggregation from that which had aggregated it in the first place. It failed to become a singularity (Law 2002).

practices necessarily cohere, or add up to the same thing. Indeed chapter 6 shows how the failure of this "border multiple" to coalesce was dramatically exposed following a moment of intense intercommunal conflict. The border that was being enacted by border guards, customs officers, conflict analysts, village elders, state security officials, and regional governors was not the same object. This lack of singularity had not previously been a "problem"—it was this very ambiguity that enabled water to be distributed, cattle to be taken to graze and villages on both sides of the border to profit from a shared market—but its non-coherence became a problem in a moment of conflict. As John Law has shown elsewhere, the very productive ambiguities that can enable systems to function are often the target of condemnation when a system is seen to fail (2004, 94–100).

The second methodological insight that I draw upon comes from critical studies of space, particularly as these have developed within recent cultural geography. Such approaches have diverse philosophical foundations, but share a critique of an approach to space that would treat it as an inert backdrop on which identity struggles are played out. In a subtle ethnography of spatial politics in the Zimbabwean highlands, anthropologist Donald Moore has articulated the methodological insight as follows: "Instead of viewing geographically specific sites as the stage—already fully-formed constructions that serve as settings for action—for the performance of identities that are malleable (if also constrained and shaped by multiple fields of power), this vision insists on joining the cultural politics of place to those of identity" (1998, 347; see also Moore 2005). What is entailed in such an approach is not just a call for attentiveness to the social (and political) "production" of space; nor is it only a call to recognize that space is always changing and being changed. It is, more radically, a call to think of space as inherently "lively"—that is, as the always-provisional outcome of heterogeneous trajectories of people, things, and ideas.

Such a thought is challenging because space seems so much more "material," and hence so much more static, than time (see Massey 2005). We can easily picture ourselves moving, or being hurtled "through" space in which we are active and space, as an imagined backdrop, is passive. To push us to think in a "relational" way about space, Massey encourages us to imagine ourselves accompanying her on her regular commute by train from London to Milton Keynes, a medium-size city in the south English midlands. In making this journey,

> you are not just travelling through space or across it. Since space is the
> product of social relations you are also helping, although in this case in

a fairly minor way, to alter space, to participate in its continuing production. You are part of the constant process of the making and breaking
of links which is an element in the constitution of you yourself, of London (which will not have the pleasure of your company for the day), of
Milton Keynes (which will), and thus of space itself. (Massey 2005, 118)

In this reading, space and place are not fixed coordinates, but rather
"emerge . . . through active material practices" (ibid., 118). At the end of the
journey, the city that is encountered is not some stable endpoint, but "itself
consists of a bundle of trajectories. And the same goes for the places in between. You are, on that train, travelling not across space-as-a-surface (this
would be the landscape—and anyway what to humans may be surface is not
so to the rain and may not be so either to a million micro-bugs which weave
their way through it—this 'surface' is a specific relational production), you
are travelling across *trajectories*" (ibid., 119).

This approach—attuned to space as a "specific relational production"—is
methodologically suggestive in two distinct senses. It directs our attention,
first, to the diversity of "senses of place" at the border, as elsewhere in social life: to the multiplicity of "historically sedimented practices that weave
contested meanings into the fabric of locality" (Moore 1998, 347). Further,
it alerts us to the way in which past modes of apprehending space can continue to inhabit the present, in often unexpected and unpredictable ways.
The ecological contact zone that characterizes the region around Batken has
been shaped by multiple histories of migration, population growth, religious
conflict, natural disasters, and the search for new sources of irrigation.[13] Since
the 1960s, the region has been profoundly marked by movements of other
kinds: the sendentarization and resettlement of pastoralist herders from the
high Alay Mountains into planned (*planovye*) collective farms, their grid-like
patterns contrasting starkly with the contours of older, unplanned villages;
the allocation of land to Kyrgyz returnees (*kairylmandar*) from Tajikistan's
civil war; the expansion of collective farms as new waterways were opened
up, and the state-led creation of ethnically homogenous "border villages" as
a means of materializing in quite stark fashion the new state edge.[14] What any
particular place means for these diverse groups is likely to be quite different:
one person's new "planned village" is often another's lost pasture; what to a

---

[13]On the role of population movements prior to the Russian conquest of Central Asia in
shaping the ethnic composition of southern Ferghana, see especially Kisliakov (1953), Bushkov
(1995), Gubaeva (2012), Abashin (2007b, 2007c), and Bushkov (1995).

[14]See Bichsel (2009, 115–119) for a discussion of these dynamics in Batken oblast, and Walicki
(2006) and Ferrando (2011a) on geographies of resettlement in Tajikistan.

sedentary farmer seems uncultivated hillside (*adyr*) might appear valuable grazing lands to a sheep herder (see also Bichsel 2009, 111; Bushkov 1990, 8; Humphrey 2001; van Houtum 2012, 412). Such a perspective allows us to explore the ways in which past histories of movement continue to animate the present, often in unexpected ways.

Ethnicity, Space, and the "Ethno-Spatial Fix"

There is a further reason why the relational approach outlined here can be generative. It allows us to question the reflex tendency (and sometimes quite explicit political practice) to assume an originary natural "fit" among people, culture, and territory, or to conceive of threat as emerging from the failure of these three to coincide. It foregrounds instead the political dynamics through which certain sets of trajectories come to be "stabilized" and others come to be deemed transgressive: how and why certain groups of people come to be seen as "naturally" rooted in particular places; how and when certain kinds of border-crossing movement—of people, things, and ideas—come to be seen as "risky"; in need of prevention or prohibition. If we proceed from a recognition of the "thrown togetherness" of place, to use Massey's felicitous phrase, this foregrounds the question of how policies might be articulated that "confront the challenge of the negotiation of multiplicity" (2005, 141–142).

This approach is instructive for the ways that we seek to make sense of the sources and dynamics of intercommunal conflict in the Ferghana Valley; and specifically, the destabilizing consequences of borderland militarization. As several scholars have noted (Abashin and Bushkov, 2004; Bichsel, 2009; Megoran 2007; Starr 2011), the Ferghana Valley is often characterized as overdetermined by its ethnic complexity: a "tinder-box region"; a Eurasian Balkans, vulnerable to continued fragmentation along ethnic and "tribal" lines.[15] Such concerns might appear tragically well-founded in the light of the region's recent history. In the summer of 2010, southern Kyrgyzstan was—not

---

[15]Such claims feature periodically in Kyrgyzstan's largest circulating newspaper, *Vechernii Bishkek*. On depictions in this newspaper of Central Asia as a "Eurasian Balkans," see Satybekov (2002); on characterizations of the Ferghana Valley as a "powder keg," see Satybekov (2006), Maslova (2008), and Baigaziev (2010). On the role of outside forces in destabilizing once-harmonious relations in the valley, see Ikromov (2006a). Such characterizations also feature in Western journalism about the region. Shishkin begins his *Restless Valley* by asking his readers to imagine a region "so rife with tensions and intrigue that in less than a decade it managed to produce two revolutions in the same country, murders straight out of a thriller, a massacre of unarmed civilians, a civil war, a drug-smuggling superhighway, and corruption schemes so brazen and lucrative that they would be hard to invent" (2013, ix).

for the first time—thrust into international headlines as the setting for a conflict on an alarming scale; a conflict, moreover, in which ethnicity was the decisive marker of belonging and difference. The southern towns of Osh, Jalalabat, and Bazar-Korgon were consumed by several days' violence, which pitted their respective Kyrgyz- and Uzbek-identifying populations against one another, leaving hundreds murdered, thousands of homes burned to the ground and tens of thousands of people—the majority ethnic Uzbeks—displaced from their place of birth.[16]

In such moments of collective and ethnically marked mobilization it is tempting to identify ethnic diversity or geographical complexity as politically causal: a conflict determined by the meeting of difference inside dangerously mixed-up nation-states. International news reports on the 2010 violence in Osh and Jalalabat provide a paradigmatic illustration of this kind of analysis: this was an "old-fashioned Central Asian pogrom," according to a *Guardian* editorial. For Newsweek, southern Kyrgyzstan was an "ethnic quagmire" that foreign powers would best avoid; for the *Economist*, the violence was "Stalin's harvest": the legacy of cynical gerrymandering that meant that ethnic and national borders failed to coincide in Central Asia's Ferghana Valley, with dangerous consequences.[17]

---

[16]The causes and dynamics of the conflict in Osh and Jalalabat in June 2010 remain deeply contested, the subject of sometimes heated accusations over culpability and causes. The conflict occurred against a background of significantly deteriorating interethnic relations going back to 2005 and beyond, and a crisis of state authority following the overthrow of former president Kurmanbek Bakiyev in April 2010 (Balci 2011, 470–481). In January 2011, the Kyrgyz National Commission that had been charged by the newly installed President Roza Otunbayeva with investigating the violence published a report on the June events. It blamed the conflict on the ousted President Bakiyev and the leaders of the country's Uzbek community, oriented "towards the splitting [raskol] of Kyrgyzstan and disrupting the unity of its people" (National Commission 2011). In stark contrast to this analysis, international analyses point to the undermining of interethnic trust; the increasing exclusion of Uzbek minority from positions of state power; the normalization of extra-legal force throughout the Bakiyev era and the sapping of traditional authority structures, complicating a narrative of "inter-ethnic conflict" (Human Rights Watch 2010; International Crisis Group 2010; Kyrgyzstan Inquiry Commission 2011; Matveeva, Savin and Faizullaev 2012). I have argued elsewhere that the violence of Osh is better viewed as part of a wider societal conflict that became dramatically ethnicized during the spring of 2010, rather than a conflict rooted in deep-seated differences of ethnicity (Reeves 2010b; see also Melvin 2011, 26). Ferrando (2011b, 320–330) affords a detailed analysis of the context of minority politics in Kyrgyzstan that enabled ethnicity to be mobilized so rapidly and for such dramatic effect in a moment of political crisis.

[17]See "Kyrgyzstan: Mob Rule in Osh," *Guardian*, June 15, 2010, www.guardian.co.uk/commentisfree/2010/jun/15/kyrgyzstan-mob-rule-osh-editorial; "How Kyrgyzstan Tamed Moscow," *Newsweek*, June 15, 2010, www.thedailybeast.com/newsweek/2010/06/15/how-kyrgyzstan-tamed-moscow.html; "Violence in Kyrgyzstan: Stalin's Harvest," *Economist*, June 14, 2010, www.economist.com/node/16364484.

Policy and academic studies of the region typically use more moderate language. Yet here too we often find an implicit ontology of ethnicity that treats it as stable, causal, and naturally territorialized, such that the potential for conflict springs from the fact of noncorrespondence between state and ethnic boundaries. Writing of the "host of crises" facing the Ferghana Valley in the early twenty-first century, for instance, conflict analyst Randa Slim (2002) highlights the "gap [that] exists between the ethnic divisions and the political boundaries in the Ferghana valley," the legacy of "artificially drawn" Soviet-era boundaries. In her discussion of risks and potentials for coopera-tion along Tajikistan's borders, political scientist Guzel′ Maitdinova similarly argues that "it is not coincidental that the majority of interethnic conflicts of the 1990s occurred precisely along those fault lines [v mestakh razlomov]—places of mismatch between ethnic and territorial-state borders, and specifi-cally in the border regions of Uzbekistan and Tajikistan [and] Kyrgyzstan and Tajikistan" (2010, 2). The implication in both cases is that more "natu-ral" divisions would have mapped territorial borders precisely onto ethnic boundaries; that such ethnic groups tend to form compact, coherent national units; and that it is the presence of ethnic groups on the wrong side of the ter-ritory that is an inherent threat to the region's stability.

Making sense of the violence that gripped Osh, Jalalabat, and Bazar-Korgon, as well as less extreme instances of intercommunal conflict along the Sokh and Isfara rivers requires that we take ethnicity seriously as a category of everyday practice and of potential political mobilization. Ethnicity can, at times, act as a politically charged and socially powerful category of "vision and division" (Bourdieu, [1991] 1999, 61). In the Kyrgyz- and Tajik-identifying villages that border each other along the river valleys to the west and east of Batken—such as Üch-Döbö and Khojai-A″lo, Ak-Sai and Vorukh—conflicts over water use can rapidly flare into tense stand offs between groups of young men mobilized through ties of kinship and friendship along ethnic lines. During fieldwork I regularly encountered reciprocal allegations framed in terms of ethnicity concerning the monopolizing of water; the encroachment on contested land; the improper behavior of "their" men (and especially, of "their" border guards) toward "our" women.

But it would be wrong to conclude that ethnicity—or ethnic diversity per se—is the driver of such conflict. Ethnic groups are not homogenous, stable en-tities, either analytically or in lived experience. Throughout Central Asia, where nationhood is a relatively recent mode of institutional and personal identification, there is considerable variation in localized modes of imagining and articulating what it means to be "Kyrgyz," "Uzbek," or "Tajik" (Abashin and Bushkov 2004; Finke 2006; Liu 2012; Mostowlansky 2013; Shozimov 2003). In the Ferghana

Valley this diversity is complicated by the fact of forced population movements between mountainous and lower-lying areas, which mean that ethnicity is often less salient as a dimension of popular differentiation than lineage or place of origin (Ferrando 2011b, 63–97). A Kyrgyz friend from Batken described how it was only traveling to northern Kyrgyzstan and experiencing there what was to her a very different organization of gender roles and a profoundly different ritual landscape—including that most salient of rituals, the funeral—that she came to realize that she had "more in common" with other people from Ferghana than with "*those* [northern] Kyrgyz" whose means of expressing respect for the dead was so different from her own.[18] On another occasion, after hearing a fragment of an interview with one of my elderly informants from Batken, a researcher from northern Kyrgyzstan with whom I was analyzing the taped recording of the interview insisted that my interlocutor was not speaking Kyrgyz (heavily inflected, as it was, with Tajik idioms and with a strong *Batkenchi* pronunciation) but that she was rather speaking Uzbek.[19] For this northern Kyrgyz researcher, my informant was speaking not just another dialect, but another language.

Although the Ferghana Valley is indeed an ethnically diverse region, and one where the legacy of the Soviet-era national-territorial delimitation has

---

[18]In Batken, funeral rites and subsequent gendered displays of mourning through clothing, demeanor, and spatial isolation typically bear a closer resemblance to those in neighboring regions of Uzbekistan and Tajikistan than they do funeral rituals in more northerly regions of Kyrgyzstan (although here too orthopraxy is being debated by imams who have trained abroad [Montgomery 2007, 246]). This is reflected, for instance, in the injunction to bury the deceased immediately rather than holding a three-day wake; in absolute prohibitions on drinking alcohol during the memorial feast for the deceased; and on the expectation that female relatives of the deceased wear green mourning clothes for a year following the funeral. In a study of Kyrgyz mortuary practices, Svetlana Jacquesson has described funeral rites as a "sore zone" of Kyrgyz identity because "[they] break up not only the claimed homogeneity of the nation but even the unity of an ethnic category such as the Kyrgyz" (2008, 297). For a detailed ethnographic study of contestation over the proper conduct of a funeral in Jalalabat region of southern Kyrgyzstan, see Kuchumkulova (2007, 190–291).

[19]As noted earlier, literary Kyrgyz and literary Tajik are mutually incomprehensible. However, the dialect of Kyrgyz that is spoken in Batken villages that are geographically close to Tajik majority villages in the Sokh and Isfara valleys contains a significant proportion (I would estimate as much as 20%) Tajik vocabulary. In Batken dialect, for instance, Kyrgyz numerators are modified as they would be in Tajik by adding -*ta* or -*to* (thus *bitta, ekkita, üchtö* compared with standard Kyrgyz *biröö, eköö, üchöö*), and much vocabulary relating to agriculture, trade, money, food, and construction draws on modified Tajik terms. Likewise, whereas in northern Kyrgyzstan most Kyrgyz speakers would either use the Russian names for days of the week or refer simply to "first day, second day, third day" (*birinchi künü, ekinchi künü, üchünchü künü*) Batken people typically use a modified form of the Persianate system to name the days of the week (thus *düshömbü, seishanbe, chorshanbe, panshanbe, juma, shambe,* and *bazar künü*). Greetings, exclamations, exhortations, admonitions, and nonverbal gestures of respect also tend toward convergence here between Kyrgyz and Tajik speakers. See also Gubaeva (2012, 181), Joosh kyzy (1997, 6).

created significant minority populations in each of the three states, the simple fact of ethnic diversity does not explain the presence or absence of conflict. Ethnicity can be recognized, elaborated, marked—or simply irrelevant to the nature of the encounter, as when the *aksakals* on the Batken—Ak-Sai bus greet each other as fellow elders, their ethnicity unmarked in the encounter (see Brubaker et al. 2006). Ethnic distinctions in the Ferghana Valley, like ethnic boundaries everywhere, are coproduced through the repeated, habitual navigation of linguistic, cultural, spatial, and genealogical difference (Barth 1969). They are institutionalized through multiple bureaucratic encounters; they are symbolically elaborated in television programs and school curricula. They have histories and politics. As Sergei Abashin (2004) and others have revealed through meticulous archival research, they are categories of identification that are inseparable from Central Asia's incorporation into imperial, and later Soviet administrative formations, which fostered proto-nation-states without the accompanying rights of sovereign statehood.[20] In the present, they are categories that have been politicized by the selective allocation of resources, by routine corruption, by the pronouncements of nationalist politician-patrons, and by the stresses placed on material survival by the institutionalization of new border regimes. The analytical challenge, as Matei Candea has argued in another context of politicized registers of identification, is to "take seriously the ways in which the solidity of (id)entities emerges not through the magic of social fiat, nor from the collective imagination of people, but from real, historical, traceable assemblages of people, things, places, and ideas held together by links and relations of different kinds" (2010, 4).

This argument has two consequences for the analysis that I develop in this book. To understand the contemporary salience of ethnicity as an everyday "practical category" we need to ask about the distinctive history of border drawing and redrawing in this region, of locating and relocating populations, of "shoring up" a disputed border through the creation of new villages and roads. In short, to attend to practices that have transformed land into ethnically marked territory throughout the twentieth and into the twenty-first century. These practices of social and spatial transformation have important ramifications for the way in which land and livelihood is conceived locally, as well as for the contemporary political economy of water, housing, and pastures. These Soviet and post-Soviet dynamics have created a situation where ethnicity and territory are symbolically overdetermined: that is, they have come to be so firmly linked in popular and official understandings of this

---

[20]See also Slezkine (1994), Roy (1997), Suny and Martin (2001), Sengupta (2002, 57–92), Hirsch (2005), Kassymbekova (2011), and Gorshenina (2012, 187–300).

region that the border is "read" according to the ethnic distribution of villages and homes. Attending to this history of "ethnic-spatial fixing" (Moore 2005) is crucial for understanding the way in which conflict has come to be naturalized as a function of geography—and thus for understanding the potential future dynamics of coexistence and conviviality in the region.

Further, my research foregrounds the degree to which the increasing étatization of this region, through border and customs controls, prohibitions on cross-border movement or trade, and the "shoring up" of the border through state-led resettlement and infrastructure projects are undermining indigenous socialities, informal practices of resource regulation, and local structures of dispute resolution (see also Bichsel 2009; Kuehnast and Dudwick 2008; Reeves 2009a). Some of the most consistent grievances that I recorded during fieldwork in and around Batken concerned the increasing securitization of daily life. Although disputes between local officials and border dwellers are not typically "ethnic" in nature, slurs and accusations—when these occur, say, between a Tajik conscript soldier and an ethnic Kyrgyz elder—can easily morph into a more generalized sense of grievance against the ethnic group with which one or other is identified.

Moreover, at times of heightened interstate tension, diplomatic disputes in capital cities far removed from daily life at the border can easily translate into localized tension. In such moments, official border crossings can be unilaterally closed, necessitating dangerous and illegal efforts to make it across the border for work, trade, or to visit relatives. A full year after the 2010 violence in southern Kyrgyzstan, for instance, much of Uzbekistan's border with Kyrgyzstan remained officially closed, decimating local trade and, according to local news reports, creating a boon for border guards who facilitate illegal passage (Khamidov 2011; Usmanov 2011).[21] What is at stake here, and what is important for understanding the consequences of such a dynamic, is not just

---

[21]Gavrilis (2012, 30) notes that at Kara-Suu, one of the major crossing points between Kyrgyzstan and Uzbekistan where there is a major wholesale market on the Kyrgyz side, bribes for access to the other side of the border increased threefold after the Osh events and subsequent border closures, while trade volumes declined by 60–70 percent. Political instability can also fuel intense speculation locally about whether seemingly unrelated intercommunal tension has in fact been deliberately stirred by malevolent outside forces. In the spring of 2011, heightened tension along the Kyrgyz–Tajik border in the Isfara Valley was widely rumored to have been provoked by ex-president Bakiyev, who had been ousted from power the year before, as a means of inciting instability to spur his own return to power. The status of such claims is impossible to verify, but the perception that the ousted president had been deliberately handing out weapons to ethnic Kyrgyz residents of Batken's border regions played into existing anxieties and was itself productive in inflaming cross-border relations (Komilova 2011). On the efficacy of rumor in contexts of intercommunal violence, see Spencer (1990), Tambiah (1996).

the fact that ordinary people are having to contend with the (often opaque) legal requirements of two, and sometimes three, independent nation-states to get about their daily lives. It is also that the very authority to speak on behalf of the state here is contested, creating legal uncertainty, leading to substantial abuse of power, and allowing for violence to be used to resolve uncertainty where traditional modes of authority are unrecognized. The right to impersonate the state is claimed by multiple, and often competing, formal and informal authorities; and it is a claim that is often invoked precisely to override the law.

This is undoubtedly a pervasive aspect of life in Central Asia, for city dwellers and rural farmers alike. However, it is intensified at these new international borders because the authorities here are so numerous, because the ruptures that new borders present to traditional lifeway are so sharp, because the costs of transgression can be so high, and because the spatial and institutional limits of the state are often contested.[22] After all, the soldiers who patrol Central Asia's new borders are armed; and while instances of humans being shot or livestock being seized for illegally crossing the border were sporadic rather than widespread during my period of research, the sense of fear and anger generated by such stories, and the rumors of much more extensive abuse of power, were sufficient to constitute a continuous low-level sense of insecurity.[23]

Kathleen Kuehnast and Nora Dudwick (2008) characterize this predicament of pervasive uncertainty at Central Asia's borders as a problem of knowing "whose rules rule." In a situation of weak governance, in which relationships are personalized, informal payments are widespread, and economic survival often depends on an evasion or bending of law, conflict can easily arise from the sudden intrusion of "law" into daily life. Examples of this are the decision to mount a new border post on a previously unmanned bridge, as occasionally has occurred on the route of the Batken–Ak-Sai bus; the prohibition against

---

[22]In July 2013, for instance the death of an Uzbek border guard on the Kyrgyzstan-Uzbekistan border following his shooting by a Kyrgyz border guard led to mutual accusations from the border services of Kyrgyzstan and Uzbekistan not just about who was responsible for the tragedy, but on which country's territory the incident occurred (Aijigitov 2013, Sultonov 2013).

[23]A 2011 study of peace and conflict potentials in the Ferghana Valley compiled by the Jamoat Resource Center in Vorukh (Tajikistan) with the support from the United Nations Development Programme noted that Kyrgyz border guards had "been continuously obstructing the mandated work of Tajik *mirabs* [designated local residents responsible for water allocation] in Tajik *mahallas* [village quarters]." Whereas land disputes had formerly been resolved by local authorities and community leaders, today "the major role in these disputes is played by border guards and law enforcement personnel . . . Analysis of recent events shows that virtually all incidents, even relatively minor disputes, have been accompanied by armed elements from the security sector of the two sides" (Jamoat Resource Center of Vorukh 2011, 9).

using traditional pasturelands that are now the property of a neighboring state; or the dismantling of a formerly functioning cross-border market. The other index of this predicament is the perception that some well-connected people are able to stand above the law and ignore its demands. In Batken, as a customs officer once told me, lamenting the fact that he was powerless to stop the steady trickle of narcotics through the region, "money eats the law" (*pul zakondu jep koiot*). This personalization of the state can be profoundly destabilizing, just as it can be essential, at an everyday level for getting by.[24]

There is a further twist to this story. For in a context in which local disputes over rightful use of water or access to land are increasingly identified as a regional or national problem (rather than an issue that can be negotiated by the elders of neighboring villages), the solution can easily come to be seen as requiring more fixing, more fences, or more force: a technical and military solution to problems that are fundamentally political, grounded in unequal access to resources and powers of lobby. The last few years have seen a steady increase in the presence of armed state personnel at Batken's borders, and the response in national capitals to localized tension has often been one of insisting on more state presence. At the same time, threats unilaterally to close one or other border have increasingly come to figure as blunt but efficacious tools of interstate relations. In 2006, for instance, following a local dispute along the Kyrgyz-Tajik border near the village of Surh, the populist governor of Batken region, Sultan Aijigitov, made a characteristically stark warning to the authorities in Tajikistan:

> When Uzbekistan closed its road with you [i.e., prevented cross-border movement] Batken opened its road to Tajiks. All your trade goes through Batken, even to go to Russia you go through Batken. If we close our roads too you'll just have Afghanistan left. There, you should think about that! (*Azattyk unalgysy* 2006)

These dynamics—toward increasing politicization of the border and an increasing tendency to search for technical solutions to social issues—are not unrelated. And as I elaborate further in the chapters that follow, they risk escalating local tensions over rights to place and movement if progressive attempts at materially "fixing" the border are not accompanied by complex, cross-border approaches to securing land and livelihood.

---

[24]Gavrilis (2012, 15) notes that throughout Central Asia the customs services are the most corrupt branches of the state "even in those states that had made seemingly earnest privatization and liberalization reforms." See also Martin-Mazé 2013, 533–534.

2. DELIMITATIONS

Ethno-Spatial Fixing in the Twentieth Century

In February 2011, Kyrgyzstan's third president, Roza Otunbayeva, visited Batken to meet with local officials and community activists. The focus of her speech, in the hall of the regional administration building, was the security of Batken's borders. "The protection of the territorial integrity of our state, the inviolability of the borders of our country deeply concerns every Kyrgyzstani," Otunbayeva announced, explaining that an extra 500 troops would be sent to help man the borders of southern Kyrgyzstan during the course of 2011. She urged the formation of voluntary people's militias (*narodnye druzhiny*) and mounted guards on sparsely populated or hard-to-reach parts of the border, linking the country's vulnerability to a global terrorist threat. She described the efforts the government was making on road building to enable Batken residents to move from one part of the oblast to another without having to cross into the territory of the neighboring state. She also stressed the importance of conclusively demarcating the region's borders as a way of minimizing the risk of conflict between villages located on either side:

> In 2010 alone, fifty-one [violent] incidents occurred in border regions. Of these twenty-six occurred on the Kyrgyz-Uzbek border, twenty-four on the Kyrgyz-Tajik border, and only one on the Kyrgyz-Kazakh border. As we say: "no commentary"—such numbers speak for themselves. . . . The most dangerous thing is that each of these conflicts could potentially turn into an interethnic and international conflict. Therefore, I have urged the government commission on delimitation and demarcation of the state border to continue its work to solve the tasks before it. (Otunbaeva 2011)

Eighty-seven years earlier at a meeting of Communist Party activists in Tashkent, a young Lithuanian Bolshevik, Juozas Vareikis, delivered a speech that touched on rather similar themes: conflict, external threat, and the need for clearly defined borders. The subject of Vareikis's 1924 speech was the national-state delimitation of Central Asia (*natsional'no-gosudarstvennoe razmezhevanie*), often also called the national territorial delimitation:[1] an initiative that had been conceived some years earlier in Moscow but delayed due to ongoing opposition to Bolshevik rule in Central Asia by itinerant fighters, known pejoratively as *basmachi* (bandits).[2] This radical proposal, which Vareikis had been sent to Tashkent to lead, would see the formerly czarist lands of Turkestan (by the early 1920s renamed the Turkestan Autonomous Soviet Socialist Republic) and the khanates of Khiva and Bukhara transformed into explicitly national (*natsional'nye*) republics, defined according to the majority ethnic group living in each one. This policy, Vareikis explained, would be modernizing, democratic, and revolutionary, clearing up the "national confusion" (*natsional'naia zaputannost'*) that characterized the current socio-spatial arrangement of Central Asia's diverse populations and in so doing enable the emergence of authentic historical struggle, between classes:

> In Middle Asia we have a most motley interweaving of borders, and a great deal of overlapping of national groups. The history of Middle Asia is rich in large migrations of lineages, tribes and nations from one oasis to another; and certain similarities in [these groups'] economies have led to a situation where today we have an excessively complex [*chrezvychaino zaputannyi*] interweaving of territories. (Vareikis 1924b, 49)

Overcoming this complexity, Vareikis explained, would constitute the "second revolution" in Central Asia to follow the first, Bolshevik revolution. And it would demand revolutionary fervor for its accomplishment:

> Tomorrow across the valleys and mountains of Middle Asia new state borders of independent Soviet republics will appear! The working masses

---

[1]National territorial delimitation appears to have become the more commonly used term by the 1930s (see, e.g., *O natsional'nom razmezhevanii* 1934). I suggest that this shift corresponds to a broader political move from the early 1920s to the time of the first five-year plan, away from "independence" and "sovereignty" for national republics toward a stress on their (interconnected) Sovietness. By the 1930s, with the shift toward ideological unity and anxieties about the scourge of "bourgeois nationalism" in non-Russian republics, the discursive emphasis had moved from a celebration of proto "states" toward the creation of territorially bound "republics" within a larger Soviet state.

[2]For a discussion of the political dynamics leading up to the delimitation see Gorshenina (2012, 189–214), Haugen (2003, 165–210), and Sabol (1995).

of Middle Asia, many millions of peasants will be able to realize their national yearnings under the leadership of our party. Masses of workers belonging to one and the same nationality who are currently separated, fragmented and scattered [*otdel'nye, razroznennye, rassypannye*] across the whole of Middle Asia will now be brought together by us into their own single, soviet, national state! We will gather, or rather, we will help to gather the scattered mass of workers—Uzbeks, Kirgiz, Kara-Kirgiz, Turkmens, Tajiks and other nations[3]—into unitary national republics. With revolutionary methods we will correct all of those perversions in the national history of Middle Asia that were committed by the policies of the khans, the *beks*, the emirs, and the policies of Russian imperialism. (Vareikis 1924b, 42)

For much of the twentieth century the Ferghana Valley has been subject to attempts to overcome a perceived excess of socio-spatial complexity through the delimitation of borders and the relocation of populations. This chapter examines these dynamics and the broader ideational framework within which such actions take shape and become intelligible. In exploring this history, my aim is less to provide a chronological narrative of border drawing and redrawing in the Batken zone than to draw attention to the shifting understandings of borders that are at stake in such initiatives. As Sarah Green has argued, there is a "potential multiplicity of worlds, knowledge practices and ontologies that . . . might all be differently involved in making or defining senses of border" (2012a, 581). I trace a shift from pre-Soviet conceptions of the Ferghana Valley's diversity and its "itinerant territoriality" (Mbembe 2000) to the vision of territorialized ethnicity that came to hold after the revolution, focusing on the emergence of a discourse concerning the region as peculiarly *konfliktogennyi,* or conflict-generating because of an apparent excess of heterogeneity.[4]

Historicizing contemporary discussion about the valley and its territorial, linguistic, and ethnic complexity provides a point of entry for exploring the discursive parameters of contemporary border work: the understandings of what border is and what borders should separate that animate contemporary attempts to govern this space. The historical period I chart here, from the late czarist era to the present, is marked by the emergence of a particular

---

[3]In writings from this time "Kirgiz" is used to designate those who would be today described as "Kazakh," while "Kara-Kirgiz" was used to denote today's Kyrgyz.

[4]Grant and Yalçin-Heckman (2007) make a related argument about the paradigms through which the Caucasus region has come to be known in popular and literary portrayals: as excessively, even dangerously diverse; as secretive, violent, and liable to fragmentation.

Westphalian conception of territory in which Central Asian borders came to be conceived and acted upon as properly contiguous, linear, and coextensive with the authority of the state. It is also a period, I argue, when a particular understanding of the normative relationship between ethnicity and territory came to be institutionalized—one that continues to resonate in presidential speeches such as Otunbayeva's appeal to the Batken *aktivisty*, as well as scholarship about the dangerous consequences of "mismatch" between state and ethnic boundaries. The emergence of productive contemporary discourse concerning the Ferghana Valley's vulnerability to interethnic and cross-border conflict and the concomitant need for preventive intervention (Lubin and Rubin 1999) should be understood in this broader historical context, not as a direct continuation of earlier conceptions, but as acquiring meaning within the same discursive formation (Foucault [1972] 2002).[5]

Crucial in articulating this relationship was the national-territorial delimitation (NTD) that took place between 1924 and 1936, a singularly important moment in Central Asia's recent history that also marked the triumph of a particular normative conception of territorialized nationhood, which still lives on in Central Asia today. Though not the first instance of territorial boundary-making in the Soviet Union or the first to be conducted on "national" lines, the NTD was the first in which a process of national delimitation was articulated as an explicitly modernizing move, one that would overcome backwardness and the "perversions" of previous czarist policy by propelling *nations* (*natsii*) into being. As one commentator observed during celebrations to mark the tenth anniversary of the start of the delimitation in 1934, the NTD had allowed the populations of Central Asia to "become closer [*priobshchit'sia*] to the family of soviet nations who are building socialism" by enabling "tribe, an ethnographic category, to be transformed into nation, a historical category" (Shteinberg 1934, 53).

"What Contrasts, Virtually Immeasurable!" The Ferghana Valley in Imperial Ethnography

For much of the Russian empire's history, imperial administrators had not been particularly anxious to know their subjects scientifically. However, the

---

[5]In the *Archaeology of Knowledge,* Foucault gives an account of discursive formation as referring to the realm of structured regularities within which statements, concepts, theories, claims, and hypotheses about a given object acquire meaning. The discursive formation "does not play the role of a figure that arrests time and freezes it for decades or centuries" but "determines a regularity proper to temporal process" ([1972] 2002, 83).

incorporation of Turkestan into the Russian empire following the conquest of the region by czarist forces in the 1860s and 1870s coincided with the growth of the ethnological sciences in Russia such that ethnicity would became "a servant of colonial rule" in Turkestan on a far greater scale than had occurred elsewhere in the empire (Brower 1997, 123).[6] Though Central Asia remained "in many respects a *terra incognita*" to imperial administrators (Abashin 2004, 38), the Ferghana valley, incorporated within Turkestan after the collapse of the Khanate of Kokand in 1876, was one of the few parts of formerly Russian imperial space where ethnographic mapping went hand-in-hand with physical incorporation into empire.

Under the governor-generalship of Konstantin von Kaufman, who ruled Turkestan between 1867 and 1881, there was a proliferation of scholarly work on Turkestan, featuring detailed accounts of the "natives" (*tuzemtsy*) and their way of life (*byt*) alongside discussions on climate, flora, fauna, and geomorphology.[7] In the Ferghana oblast of the Turkestan governor-generalship, a statistical service was established as part of the colonial administration, whose aim was to collect information about the local population (Abashin 2004, 46). "Progressive" techniques were introduced for making the newly acquired lands and their peoples known to the metropolis. Von Kaufman commissioned the artist Vasilii Vereshchagin to produce a series of images depicting Turkestan and its peoples, displayed in 1874 in Moscow and St. Petersburg to great acclaim. When the Third International Congress of Orientalists convened in St. Petersburg in 1876, von Kaufman personally selected "three natives" to be sent, in response to the call from the conveners for "live representatives" (Brower 1997, 125).

Despite considerable interest in studying the complex linguistic and cultural gradations that characterized the indigenous population of Ferghana, publications from this time suggest that the differences that mattered to explorers, ethnographers, and statisticians were not so much "nationality" (a category that was not directly solicited in the 1897

---

[6]On the relationship between colonial conquest and ethnographic knowledge in the Russian empire, see Brower and Lazzerini (1997); Knight (1994); Slezkine (1994). For the appropriation of ethnographic knowledge by Soviet administrators, see Hirsch (2005). As Sahadeo (pers. com.) points out, the conquest of Turkestan also coincided with the growth of race science in Russia, and imperial knowledge practices in Central Asia should be read within the context of broader European debates on race (see also Sahadeo 2007, conclusion).

[7]Middendorf (1882) includes "ethnographic information" (*etnograficheskie svedeniia*) about the valley at the end of a vast work that builds from discussion of soil and climate to forms of agriculture, pastoralism, and domestic animal breeds. Accordingly, the "ethnographic" distinction that concerns him is between pastoral and nomadic ways of life.

Imperial census) as "way of life" (*byt*).[8] In 2004, Abashin conducted a detailed study of shifting practices of ethnic accounting in Ferghana during the last half-century of colonial rule. He demonstrates how, through all the fluctuations in nomenclature and contestations over ethnogenesis, there recurred, on the one hand, a binary distinction between categories rooted in settled/nomadic way of life "to which were accorded absolutely contradictory characteristics" and, on the other, a proliferation of micro-categories based on the complex intersections of language, psychology, appearance, and *byt* (2004, 72). Hence the analytic importance at this time of the category "Sart": a term that has long gone out of official use as a statistical category, though retaining social salience to this day as a pejorative term for "Uzbek." The term was not primarily an ethnic designator, but rather described mode of life: settled, urban, and trade-based (Fragner 1994, 15).[9] This term, rather than the categories of "Uzbek" or "Tajik," provided the principle point of distinction in accounts of the Ferghana Valley with the Kyrgyz population, who were in turn defined by having a nomadic or semi-nomadic mode of life (see also Abashin 2007d).

The contrast that was stressed in Russian imperial scholarship between settled and nomadic lifestyle reflects in part the considerable difficulty facing any outsider in trying to draw clear lines of ethnographic distinction between those who described themselves as Uzbeks, Tajiks, or Sarts. In 1897, Serafim Patkanov (1860–1923), studying the results of the first imperial census to have been conducted in Ferghana, commented that, despite linguistic and other variation, "to draw a boundary between these three peoples [*narod-nosti*] would be an extremely difficult process, if indeed it would be possible at all" (Patkanov 1905, xiv).[10] Daniel Brower sees the concern with settled versus nomadic lifestyle as a direct corollary of imperial preoccupations with governance. The settled population was viewed as more of a threat to pacific incorporation within the Russian empire than the weakly Islamized and

---

[8]The 1897 census inquired, among other demographic data, about the respondent's faith, mother tongue, place of residence, literacy, profession, and rank (*soslovie*). Data on "nationality" was subsequently compiled in the published census findings according to responses for mother language, but there was no question as such about a respondent's nationality.

[9]For a detailed discussion of the role of Sart as an imperial classificatory category, and its eventual abandonment, see Abashin (2007d, 95–176) and Schoeberlein-Engel (1994, 168–172).

[10]Such classificatory difficulties continued to be echoed after the revolution. In his 1925 list of the peoples of Turkestan *krai*, Ivan Zarubin described as impossible the task of distinguishing "half-settled Uzbeks" from "Turkified Iranians" because the two shared a "common life." In such a setting, "it is unsurprising that materials from national [*natsional'noi*] statistics cannot provide satisfactory evidence" (1925, 15).

nomadic Kyrgyz, with the former containing in their midst "bigoted, hypo-critical and corrupt Muslim holy men, mullas, judges, pilgrims, saints and dervishes" (quoted in Brower 1997, 130).

The preoccupation with *byt* as the basis of ethnic classification in the Ferghana Valley also seems to derive from the challenge that the diversity of modes of life in this region posed to dominant evolutionist models, in which the rich urban culture of the oasis settlements and the "wild," nomadic life-style of the yurt-dwelling Kyrgyz were seen as lying at two poles of a devel-opmental continuum. For the imperial geographer, Alexander Middendorf (1815–1894) it was precisely this coexistence that was the source of curiosity. Writing of the diversity of lifeways he encountered in Ferghana, he noted: "In this wonderful [*zamechatel'noi*] country one encounters the most primitive nomadic life right alongside what is an unquestionably high agrarian culture and over-crowded towns overflowing with life. One finds mixed together in motley fashion [*pestro smeshivaiutsia mezhdu soboi*] diametrically opposed elements" (1882, 329). For the explorer Viktor Nalivkin and his ethnographer wife, Mariia Nalivkina, who conducted much of the base research for her hus-band's publications during their forty years in Central Asia, this distinction correlated with striking differences in the organization of gender relations between settled and nomadic populations (Nalivkin and Nalivkina 1886). What is noteworthy, Nalivkin argues, are the differences in *byt* between populations among whom he found "ethnographic" (in this context meaning "national") differences to be insignificant. This appears vividly in his contrast between Sart and Kyrgyz men in his 1913 survey of "Natives Earlier and Now" (*Tuzemtsy ran'she i teper'*):

The Sart would plough the land, sow, thresh and grind, plant trees, build houses, forge, sharpen, paint and weave, manufacture leather and trade, leaving to the responsibility of his wife only a small circle of purely do-mestic work. By contrast, the Kirgiz would make sure that his wife and children shoulder the whole burden of their cattle farming, down to the saddling and unsaddling of his horse. [He meanwhile would] eat, drink, warm himself in the sun, sing and listen to songs—especially songs about national heroes—go guesting, and from time to time take part in the business of his tribe, participating in discussions or conducting revenge attacks, making raids on the Sarts and stealing cattle [*baranta*]. [Such raids] should be considered less a case of professional robbery than a way of demonstrating one's prowess; and [a means] of getting rid of the energy that accumulates in body and soul from so much inaction. (Nalivkin [1913] 2004, 27)

As such accounts suggest, relations between Sart and Kirgiz were by no means cast as uniformly harmonious by late imperial observers.[11] However, what emerges from these accounts is an emphasis on economic and ecological complementarity, with the farmers in the fertile valley, and the cattle-herding pastoralists who lived in the mountains that ring the valley connected in complex webs of mutual dependence. Indeed, for Middendorf, it is precisely the *persistence* of these divergent but symbiotic modes of life that is the source of intellectual curiosity: "What contrasts, virtually immeasurable! Imagine a wild [*dikoe*] Kirgiz homestead, nestling between the fields of an English farmer!" he exclaimed of the way in which nomadic Kyrgyz and settled Sart populations coexisted (1882, 341). Yet, unbelievable and chaotic as it was, there was an essential interdependence between these two lifeways that deserved study:

> Cows are herded in chaotic disorder, although they are divided into herds; here a Sart one, here a Kirgiz one. Look at how decayed the Sart cows are: if you ask anyone—Sarts and Kirgiz alike, you will get one and the same answer: everything is peaceful and there are never any quarrels [*sporov vovse ne byvaet*]. And what about those times when the Sarts herd their cattle into the mountains? I enquired. Immediately I was answered with the following remark, that even Luli [gypsies] are not prevented from herding their cattle there. In the same way, everyone can keep as many head of cattle as they like: even the paltry grass can be grazed and dug *ad libitum*. This would be difficult to understand even in European conditions, but such traditions are even more incomprehensible among peoples [*narodnosti*] with ungovernable eastern blood . . . The nomads are found where barren soil gives way to the Ferghana valley. These tent-dwellers entirely reject the fertile districts; and yet for all this muddle, for all this mixing and chaos of ownership [*pri vsem etom smesheniia i khaos vladeniia*], for all the conflict of interest, the tribal contrast and imprecision, there nonetheless reigns harmony [*soglasie*] thoroughly inconceivable for the European! (Middendorf 1882, 341–342)

There are clear hierarchies of development in this account, between East and West, and between civilized agrarian populations in the Ferghana Valley and

---

[11]Nalivkin describes a situation where the "Sart," in response to the perceived arrogance of the "nomad," would deliberately charge the latter twice what he would charge a city dweller. In turn, the nomad, "who had grown up among wars and lootings," would steal the Sart's freshly ground flour from the storehouse at the end of the summer ([1886] 2003, 276). On bazaar relations at the end of the nineteenth century, see also Kudratova (2002); on the "ethnic division of labor" in cattle herding at the turn of the twentieth century, see Abdullaev (1991, 12).

their "wild" tent-dwelling neighbors. However, it is the very *indifference* to concepts of property in land that surprises and fascinates Middendorf, reflected in the tent-dwellers' disinterest in appropriating the fertile valley basin. The "natives" emerge from such accounts as a category apart—with strange lifeways and curious, unfathomable notions about property, family relations, and cleanliness. Their inclusion within the imperial polity demanded that the center know its new subjects, as well as their economy and *byt*. This, after all, would be the foundation for developing the native economy along colonial lines. But incorporation was not, at this stage, seen as presupposing dramatic cultural transformation.

The Emergence of a Cartographic Perspective: Mapping after the Revolution

This political imperative changed after the 1917 revolution, bringing about a shift in the uses to which ethnographic knowledge was put and the interpretative paradigms that were invoked. The change was less in the techniques of knowledge-gathering themselves, or even in the idioms used in ethnographic language to describe the populations mapped, as in the broader interpretative frameworks through which such studies were read and put to use. In his analysis of changing depictions of Central Asian women in the decades preceding and following the October revolution, Douglas Northrop argues that what is noteworthy at the level of techniques and tropes of investigation is precisely the continuity with earlier scholarly preoccupations. Many ostensibly Bolshevik inquiries "sounded as much Orientalist as Marxist" (2004, 39).

In the study of Ferghana's cultural and ethnic diversity there was also considerable continuity of techniques for "knowing the native." Like scholars before the revolution, statisticians and ethnographers employed by the young Soviet state debated what to do with the category Sart and whether the Sarts could properly be considered a national group (Magidovich 1924; Zarubin 1925). For this purpose, they often deployed techniques of measurement and classification that had been brought to Turkestan in the 1870s by the first imperial ethnographers (see Abashin 2004, 2007d). Despite these continuities in approach, however, knowledge of Central Asian people and places was being put to new use. Just as highly intrusive inquiries into domestic organization were deployed in order to incorporate (and ultimately "liberate") the Uzbek woman, so studies of ethnic relations were identified as essential to propel Central Asia out of backwardness.

Perhaps most important, ethno-spatial mapping was occurring in a context in which national theory and the resolution of a "national question" were central to the identity of the party-state itself. This was a teleological state: for the Bolsheviks of the 1920s the world could be remade and nations could be brought into being. In such a context, a territorial delimitation was not just an administrative act but a revolutionary one, "radically changing the national interrelations of the laboring masses" (Vareikis 1924b, 39).[12]

Lenin and the Social Democrats had been engaged in polemics about the nationality question as early as 1905. At Lenin's request in 1912, Stalin wrote on "the Nationality Question and Social Democracy." His formulation of characteristics that identified a group as a nation was to become central to national discourse in the Soviet Union and resonates to this day in scholarly and popular accounts concerning the nature of nationhood throughout Central Asia.[13] According to Stalin's definition, nations were understood to be both historically specific categories and bearers of collective rights, such that the nationality question could be solved by granting populations "real rights in the localities they inhabit" (Stalin [1913] 1973, 42–44). Stalin saw nations as real historical phenomena that no amount of proletarian internationalism could wish away. The corollary of this for the Bolsheviks was that "backward" regions could be assisted by accelerating the process of nation-formation. Ultimately such national sentiments would give way to proletarian internationalism "in true dialectical fashion" (Edgar 2004, 44).

A further consequence followed from Stalin's authoritative definition. If nations were to be defined in terms of language, territory, economy, and psychology, and if a nation was to have territorial autonomy in the area where it lived, it followed that the task of ethnological expertise was not merely to identify cultural difference *in vacuo*, but to define the precise *spatial* correlates of any particular national group. Administrative practices territorialized ethnicity. As Brower notes, Soviet officials were far more zealous than

---

[12]Vareikis was explicit about this distinction: "It would be fundamentally wrong if we were to consider the international delimitation [*mezhnatsional'noe razmezhevanie*] of Middle Asia simply as a narrowly pragmatic reform of local, internal significance . . . Such a view would be completely to misunderstand, first, the international significance that the delimitation in Middle Asia takes in the light of the general national policy of the Soviet Union, and secondly, the national confusion [*natsional'noi zaputannosti*] and deadlock of the policy of imperialism" (1924b, 41). On the need to take the delimitation seriously as an instance of "state-sponsored evolutionism," see Hirsch (2000, 203).

[13]A nation, according to this formulation, is a "historically constituted, stable community of people, formed on the basis of a common language, territory, economic life and psychological make-up manifested in a common culture" (Stalin [1913] 1973, 60). For discussion of the place of this formulation in Bolshevik nationalities policy, see Jeremy Smith (1999, 7–28); for an account that stresses the importance of the broader European context for the shaping of Soviet nationalities policy, see Hirsch (2005, 24–30).

their colonial predecessors, not only in "claiming to 'know' ethnic groups," but also in "drawing ethno-territorial boundaries" (1997, 133). This zeal had its correlate in ethnographic writing. It fostered a new concern with locating ethnic groups in space, and it signaled a shift from the elaboration of ethnographic archetypes based on mode of life ("the nomad," "the sart"), to the establishment of finite and exhaustive national categories with specific territorial locations. In July 1920, when Lenin first came to advocate the administrative reorganization of Central Asia, his first demand was for an "ethnographic" map that would show "divisions into Uzbekiia, Kirgiziia and Turkmeniia" and thereby "establish the conditions of merging [*sliianiia*] and division [*razdeleniia*] of these three parts" (Lenin [1920] 1974, 436). Populations were not just to be known, but to be located: the ethnographic map became a foundation for policy.[14]

Abashin characterizes this as a shift from a "colonial" to a "state-forming" (*gosudarstvoobrazuiushchaia*) model of ethnographic accounting. Within the former, what was important was establishing broad, indicative types (*tipazhi*), representative of one or other cultural category. Much like Vereshchagin's *Turkestan Series* of line drawings, the emphasis is on archetypes, reflected in the titles attached to the images—"an Uzbek elder," "a Sart woman." The question of the particular type that any particular individual should be ascribed to was secondary within this context. In the 1920s, a new power/knowledge nexus emerged. Scientific categories had to be converted into social-administrative ones, and "the question of how to 'fasten' one or other category to any individual person became fundamental" (Abashin 2004, 79). This resulted in more rigid classificatory schemas, a firmer hierarchy of dominant and subsidiary groups, with many once discrete categories being now subsumed into mere tribal subdivisions of other nationalities, and far greater centralization occurring in the collection and processing of knowledge. It is not insignificant, for instance, that the most detailed records of tribes and subnational groups that were gathered during the 1920s were assembled by the commission on regional delimitation (*raionirovanie*)—an institution charged with drawing up ethno-territorial boundaries.[15] In short, the

---

[14]Thus, when in 1926 Ivan Zarubin compiled an analysis of the population of Samarkand oblast as part of the Academy of Sciences' Commission for Studying the Tribal Composition of the Population of the USSR and Neighboring Countries, the work included a discussion of the "population, ethnographic composition and territorial distribution" and incorporated an accompanying ethnographic map. Although Zarubin stressed that the map was for "useful illustrative" purpose, he also noted the care that had been taken in its composition its value in reflecting the actual distribution of populations (Zarubin 1926).

[15]Schoeberlein-Engel notes that "in retrospect it seems this commission's function was to acknowledge the depth of Central Asia's diversity before it was thoroughly denied" (1994, 156).

conceptual and instrumental technologies employed for mapping the population of Central Asia had important continuities with the past, but from the 1920s on, they were put to new use.

Razmezhevanie: Revolutionary Separation

The most significant political use to which these technologies were put was the drawing of finite administrative borders along lines of putative nationality (*natsional'nost'*) and the creating of explicitly national republics. This project was celebrated by contemporaries within and beyond the Soviet Union as "one of the most progressive nationality policies in the western world" (Brown 2004, 8).[16] Half a century prior to the delimitation, when the governor-general of Turkestan had sought to draw a boundary between Bukhara and Turkestan, it was deemed sufficient that this border should lie nine *versts* (approximately 10 kilometers) south of the route through which the Russian armies were marching at the time (Vaidyanath 1967, 155). The priority then was to secure water wells to supply the Russian troops. By the 1920s the priority was to remake the world— and to do so in a manner that would be (at least temporarily) "national in form" (Khalid 2006, 238). As several scholars have argued, Soviet nationalities policy was conducted by individuals who took for granted the ontological status of nation and recognized as a political imperative the granting of national recognition. It was, in this sense, a nationalities policy "devised and carried out by nationalists" (Slezkine 1994, 412; see also Martin 2001; Suny 1993).

The national-territorial delimitation of 1924, which resulted in the transformation of the Turkestan, Bukharan, and Khivan republics into aspirationally mono-ethnic (*odnorodnye*) Soviet republics, was a product of this vision. Nationhood was a historical stage that could be traversed and overcome but not avoided.[17] In the Russian Soviet Federated Socialist Republic (RSFSR) Central Committee decree on the "National-Territorial Delimitation of Middle Asia" of October 14 of that year it is precisely this teleological vision that enabled an expressly internationalist government to celebrate the articulation of national boundaries. According to the triumphalist Central Committee decree of the time

---

[16]It is also a project that was conceived as importantly different from Western colonial models of nation-formation. In his promotion of the NTD in 1924, Vareikis went out of his way to distinguish the Soviet project from the League of Nations, decrying Woodrow Wilson as a "peddler of philistine, petty-bourgeois utopias" (1924a, 12).

[17]Initially, only Uzbekistan and Turkmenistan were given full Union status, with today's Kazakhstan an autonomous republic within the Russian Federation and today's Kyrgyzstan initially incorporated as the Kara-Kyrgyz Autonomous Oblast within the Russian Federation. Tajikistan was initially incorporated as an autonomous republic within the Uzbek SSR, gaining status as a full Soviet Republic only in 1929.

(and repeated in subsequent Soviet historiography), the Bolsheviks were simply accelerating an inevitable historical process.[18] Attaining the stage of nation-statehood was an achievement of historical import:

> The peoples of Turkestan, who formerly under czarist rule existed as powerless colonial slaves [*bespravnykh kolonial'nykh rabov*], and who today are free and equal, are building their states through the strengths of their workers. Having achieved national liberation and strengthened the foundations of workers' and peasants' power, unswervingly developing and broadening their cultural and economic construction, the peoples of Turkestan have reached a condition that will allow them to transform the Autonomous Turkestan Soviet Socialist Republic into mono-ethnic-national states [*v gosudarstva natsional'no-odnorodnye*]. (VtsIK RSFSR in Dzhumanaliev 2003, 185)

Placing the delimitation within the broader context of Soviet nationalities policy enables us to question the interpretation of much Western Sovietology (and now official Uzbekistani historiography) that the delimitation was conducted as a cynical act of divide and rule to control the periphery by dividing it against itself.[19] In a postwar classic of this genre, diplomat-scholar Olaf Caroe described the Ferghana Valley as split "by a jigsaw puzzle of convoluted lines into Uzbek,

---

[18]See, for example, Gordienko (1959, 154); Radzhabov (1968); Tuzmukhamedov (1973, 91).

[19]For variations of this argument, see Pipes (1978), Carrère d'Encausse (1987) and Shiskin (2013, 73, 238). In Uzbekistan the official history of Turkestan at the start of the twentieth century parallels the Western Sovietological account: the delimitation "interrupted the thousand-year development of Central Asian statehood" with the decision to introduce "differentiation" between ethnic groups leading inevitably to future "conflict potential" (*konfliktnost'*) (Abdullaev et al. 2000, 668–669; see also Juraev et al. 2000, 300–302). Official Uzbekistani scholarship tends to condemn the delimitation as an act of Soviet "imperialism" for having prevented the formation of an emergent and expansive Turkestani identity. However, scholarship published under the auspices of the Tajik Academy of Sciences has rather denounced the delimitation as "ax-like" (*topornoe*), with the process dominated by "pan-Turkists" who deprived the Tajiks of their historical centers in Samarkand and Bukhara (Masov 1991, 2003, 2005). Meanwhile, government-sponsored Kyrgyzstani historiography depicts the 1924 delimitation as the "foundational act of Kyrgyz statehood," which "for the first time united [the Kyrgyz people] in the framework of a single state formation on historically Kyrgyz territory [*iskonno kyrgyzskoi territorii*]" (Dzhumanaliev 2003, 317). This was a celebratory stance repeated in published histories of the twentieth century, including in President Askar Akayev's (2002, 245–250) own historical survey of Kyrgyz statehood; see also Asankanov and Osmonov (2002, 334); Chotonov (1998, 39); Dzhunushalieva (2006, 70). A full account of these literatures is beyond the scope of this book. Suffice it to say that the delimitation remains one of the most vigorously contested elements of contemporary Central Asian historiography, and the period of recent history where officially sanctioned accounts diverge most vociferously between contemporary Central Asian states. See Abashin (2007a, 177–206); Suyarkulova (2011) for an analysis of the political work of historiography in marking national difference between contemporary Uzbekistan and Tajikistan.

Tajik, and Kirghiz sections," with "large numbers of Uzbek currants in Tajik and Kirghiz cakes, and many Tajik plums in the pie of Uzbekistan." Delimitation, on this reading, was an arbitrary process intended ultimately to foster dependence upon Moscow: "It seemed as if the absurdity of the interrepublic borders was designed in order to compel a certain degree of central direction, making nonsense of a real local autonomy" (Caroe [1953] 1967, xiv–xv).[20]

Recent archival research drawing on the files of the Central Asian Bureau in Moscow suggests that, for all the hubris of their ambition, Soviet administrators saw their undertaking as anything but arbitrary. Indeed, explanatory publications from the 1920s and 1930s celebrated the delimitation as a rational, modern corrective to the "artificial [iskusstvennye] administrative boundaries" of the czarist era, which "did not correspond either to the national nor the economic demands of the peoples" (Khodzhaev 1934, 3).[21] Moreover, rather than an excess of ideological unity, Soviet leaders saw in the Central Asia of 1924 "a highly fragmented society" (Haugen 2003, 90). As Vareikis put it to the Tashkent party activists in 1924, "The revolution has inherited a whole lump of tangled national contradictions, which it remains before her to untie, for only then can the elimination of national hatred and mutual national mistrust of the workers be turned into genuine revolutionary construction" (1924a, xx). This fragmentation was understood in part to be a product of administrative incoherence: there were insufficient connections between the peoples' republics and Turkestan, with the result that republics were isolated from one another and remained untouched by the revolutionary transformations sweeping the rest of the Soviet Union (Haugen 2003, 78). In part fragmentation was seen as the product of ongoing conflicts "between various khans for a new distribution of territory and for the domination of one tribe over another" (Khodzhaev 1934, 2).

---

[20]This is a view that has received sustained critique in recent years from scholars who have made use of recently opened archival materials (Edgar 2004; Haugen 2003; Hirsch 2000; Khalid 1998 and 2007; Koichiev 2001). This view not only obscures the detailed, minutely calibrated, and positional languages of identification that characterized premodern Central Asia. It also ignores the extent to which the articulation of both the nation (halq) and the homeland (watan) were the subject of intense debate amongst the local reformist elite (Khalid 1998, 184–215). The delimitation was a project, moreover, in which local communist elites would play a crucial role (Carlisle 1994; Edgar 2004, 51–59). Martin (2001, 69) quotes a 1926 Central Asian Bureau report in which officials lamented that "local party and Soviet officials not only do not want to solve one or other national question objectively from the point of view of the overall government interest, but usually they themselves take active part, often even the leading role in inflaming national antagonism."

[21]As Gonon and Lasserre (2003) note, the assertion of "arbitrariness" in relation to borders is a political statement, suggesting that some international borders are "natural." Here what is striking is how subsequent initiatives to delimit borders are presented precisely as responses to the perceived arbitrariness of the past.

Above all, the need for a radical reconstitution of Central Asia along national lines was seen as the result of ethnic fragmentation. The civil war elsewhere in the former empire had demonstrated to the Bolsheviks just how powerful a force nationalism could be, and the question of "national antagonism" between indigenous populations dominated discussion within the Central Asian Bureau (Haugen 2003, 95–96). The hope of Bolshevik leaders, rooted in a Marxist materialism, was that such national antagonism would evaporate to reveal its true class roots if each population were given autonomy within a specified geographical area. In March 1924, at a meeting of the Central Committee of the Communist Party of Turkestan, Party leader Abdullo Rakhimbaev explicitly developed this argument in order to illustrate the "worsening of interethnic relations" in the region, alluding to a series of "scandalous" Party congresses in which the Kazakh delegates had spoken out against the Uzbeks (Abdullaev et al. 2000, 644–645). It was an argument repeated by Vareikis later that year in his appeal to the Party faithful in Tashkent. His account of the relationship between the production of national boundaries, the "untangling" of national contradictions and the possibility of temporal leap is worth quoting at length:

> While the poorest farmer cannot achieve a certain degree of economic gain, while he has not destroyed all of the feudal-slave relations in the village, until then it will be impossible to consider the revolutionary victory durable. The Soviet power will still not have a firm foundation under it. For this reason it is important to mobilize in all ways possible the class conflict in the village and the *aul* [nomadic encampment]. We must foster in all ways possible the appearance of revolutionary, class consciousness among the *batraks* [peasants] and the poorest farmers. For that reason we must unravel as quickly as possible all those interethnic contradictions [*rasputat' vse mezhnatsional'nye protivorechiia*], which are obscuring class relations, preventing class conflict. The national delimitation, illuminating the clarity of national relations among the Uzbeks, Kirgiz, Turkmens, Kara-Kirgiz and Tajiks, will untangle the network of international contradictions and in that way will clear the stage for the social, class war. . . . The national delimitation will be proven the best precondition for unleashing the authentic class line of the communist party in the republics of Middle Asia. (1924b, 61)

For Vareikis, then, the rationale is clear. The delimitation is not just a manifestation of the Bolsheviks' "chronic ethnophilia" (Slezkine 1994, 415), but a means to prevent fragmentation along ethnic lines and thus clear the stage for the real, class war.

This initial process of delimitation, conducted in 1924 and 1925, had profound and far-reaching consequences for ordinary people in Central Asia, in at least three respects. Most significant, it introduced and pervasively mobilized a language of nationality. Exclusive categories of ethnic identification—as Uzbek, Tajik, Kyrgyz, Kazakh, or Turkmen—became the vehicle for articulating claims and demanding rights. Studies of local petitioning for the readjustment of borders following the delimitation reveal how nationality rapidly came to be mobilized even by "rural and nomadic populations that previously had not exhibited 'national consciousness'" (Hirsch 2005, 145).[22] Moreover, the new national republics provided the normative and administrative framework for a host of endeavors that gave real content to this new language of nationality: practices of administrative indigenization (*korenizatsiia*) that favored the titular population; practices of cataloguing and regional studies (*kraevedenie*) that generated knowledge about the nation; and practices of narrative appropriation that rewrote complex pasts in national terms.[23] Far from "untangling" national contradictions, the delimitation served to hypostatize registers of identification that had previously been far more fluid and situational.[24] This is better understood not as the cynical manipulation often attributed to Bolshevik leaders to "divide and rule" but the consequence of the progressive institutionalization of practices that turned nationality into a salient and politically consequential category of practice.

Second, the delimitation served conclusively to territorialize ethnicity. That the Soviet state institutionalized ethnicity is an argument well made in recent Western historiography (Brubaker 1996a; Slezkine 1994). Discussed less often is the early Soviet state's particular fascination with ethnicity's *spatialization*. Populations were not just to be known, but were to be located; nationality was not just a historical category, but a geographical one. In the Soviet Union of the New Economic Policy, mapping went hand-in-hand with planning; land had to be graphed for its resources and populations to be known. When literary critic Walter Benjamin visited Moscow in 1926, he found that the newly issued maps of the Soviet state and its constituent republics were "almost as close to becoming the center of the new Russian

---

[22]For examples of such petitioning in national terms following the delimitation, see Haugen (2003, 180–210) and Koichiev (2001, 48–80).

[23]On *korenizatsiia*, see Martin (2001, 125–181); on *kraevedenie*, see Baldouf (1992); on the production of national literary heritages, see Allworth (1964).

[24]As Khalid (1998, 187) notes of premodern identities in Central Asia, "the symbiosis of Turkic and Iranian in Central Asia was not the coagulation of two pre-existing wholes; rather, it was the very encounter that shaped the two components of the symbiosis."

iconic cult as Lenin's portrait" ([1928] 1978, 118). For the leaders of the newly established USSR, the great expanse that had been acquired from the Russian empire had to be known by being incorporated (*osvoen*). As Widdis (2003, 20), puts it: cartography and planning alike were crucial to "the transformation of space into territory."

These two features of early Soviet discourse lead to a third: the inscription of a discourse of *konfliktnost'*—which can be glossed as "proclivity to conflict"—in those sites where ethnic and territorial borders failed to match. For the territorialization of ethnicity presupposes that such ethno-spatial boundaries are geographically coherent. It also implies that they are coherently mappable: that the resulting ethnic map will be one of smooth finite spaces rather than of dots, blurs, or mixed-up shades of color. Yet, from the start, the possibility of creating republics that were genuinely and not just declaratively *natsional'no-odnorodnye* was bound to fail, not least because of the Central Asians' tendency to identify themselves in ways that refused singular, exclusive national categories. In September 1920, an article published in a Moscow's magazine, *Zhizn' natsional'nostei* (Life of the Nationalities), noted that even young people who had "mastered the principles of Soviet power . . . [could] not even solve such an elementary question as what to call their people [*narod*]—Turk, Uzbek or Muslim" (quoted in Fierman 1991, 69). A few years later the celebrated orientalist, Vasilii Bartol'd, warned that "the national principle, as it was brought to life during the delimitation of Middle Asia in 1924, is a product of West European history of the 19th century and is completely alien [*sovershenno chuzhd*] to local historical traditions" (Bartol'd, [1925] 1991).

Quite apart from the difficulties of establishing where ethnic boundaries lay, conceptually and spatially, the national imperative conflicted from the start with the economic one: the need to ensure that republics were economically coherent, that mountain populations were not cut off from the markets they used, and that the integrity of irrigation systems was preserved (Haugen 2003, 188–191). The delimitation, rather than a technical process of categorization or unambiguous act of "divide and rule," was rather a fraught business of compromise—between Moscow, Tashkent, and host of competing regional elites; as well as between "national" and "economic" imperatives. These competing priorities led to a proliferation of claims and counterclaims by those living in border districts—including in parts of what are today Osh and Batken oblasts—that continued well into the 1930s (Bergne 2007; Koichiev 2001, 48–79). Indeed, by 1927 there were so many disagreements concerning the proper adjudication of lands lying in the Sokh and Isfara valleys that on May 4, after a brief spate of land exchanges in southern Ferghana, the Central Executive Committee of the USSR issued a decree prohibiting any further changes to the existing borders for three years (Koichiev 2001, 79).[25] As Martin (2001, 69) notes, the formation of national republics "not only increased ethnic conflict, but also turned local disputes, often with a clan or regional aspect, into national ones."

Allocating Land, Relocating Borders

If the initial conduct of the NTD was criticized by local elites for misrepresenting the actual distribution of ethnic communities in the Ferghana Valley, subsequent Soviet policies served to undermine the reality of putatively sovereign ethno-territorial republics in practice. In the high-modern drive for industrial agriculture, the national principle that had prevailed in the 1920s came increasingly to conflict with the economic imperatives of the 1930s and subsequent Soviet modernization.[26] Of decisive importance here was the collectivization campaign launched by Stalin at the end of the 1920s. The drive to increase agricultural outputs meant that farms dramatically expanded their lands under cultivation. A 1935 decree gave collective farms the right to "eternal use" (*vechnoe pol'zovanie*) of new lands that were brought into productive agricultural use (Alamanov 2010, 39). In the Ferghana Valley, where the contours of the 1924–1927 delimitation had often not been demarcated (i.e., inscribed in physical form on the landscape), this meant that collective farms belonging to one Union republic often came unknowingly to incorporate and cultivate swathes of grazing land that technically were part of the neighboring republic.

Already by the 1940s this was causing some concern. When in 1949 a parity commission was established to determine the rightful boundaries between

---

[25]According to Alamanov's (2005, 78–81) historical analysis of Kyrgyzstan's border negotiations, this moratorium on further delimitation had the effect of antagonizing those Kyrgyz delegates who had participated in the previous months' parity commission, who had understood that some of their territorial demands (including to the Sokh Valley) had been agreed. Three days after the moratorium was announced, the chair of the Council of People's Commissars of the Kyrgyz Autonomous SSR, Yusup Abdrakhmanov, wrote a strongly worded letter to Stalin complaining that the decision of the Central Executive Committee had ridden roughshod over the careful investigation of the parity committee. Alamanov notes that the moratorium meant that the border between the Uzbek SSR and the then Kyrgyz ASSR was, from its very inception, never based on mutually recognized and agreed borders, nor was it ever ratified as law. As a result the "border between the Kyrgyz SSR and the Uzbek SSR continued to develop naturally [*estestvennym putem*], on the basis of the de facto distribution of national groups and the formation of collective agricultural work units organized on national lines" (2005, 80).

[26]For an exploration of these dynamics in the field of irrigation, see Thurbon (1999) and Jozan (2012, 59–97). See Thorez (2005, 306–313) in the realm of transport.

Kyrgyz and Tajik SSRs, it noted that maps from a decade earlier bore little correspondence to the de facto distribution of land. The commission's report warned:

> In order to prevent future potential land conflicts and misunderstandings in the use of unallocated (*neraspredelennykh*) lands,"
> [we] . . . consider it imperative in the near future to clarify the interrepublic boundaries between the Tajik SSR and the Kirgiz SSR, considering that the borders shown on the maps . . . published in 1938–40 do not reflect the actual location of both republics [*fakiticheskogo raspolozheniia obeikh respublik*], as a result of which fourteen collective farms belonging to Batken district of the Kirgiz SSR have found themselves [having lands] within the borders of the Tajik SSR, including settlements belonging to eight of these collectives. (quoted in Alamanov 2010, 39–40)

As Christine Bichsel (2009, 111) has noted, such commissions typically recommended adjusting the republican current borders to fit current de facto land use (*fakticheskoe zemlepol'zovanie*) at the time of their work, rather than treating the original 1924–1927 delimitation as authoritative. This was the case with the 1949 commission, which decided that current kolkhoz boundaries should be taken as marking the limits of the respective Union republics. Such an approach appears to have privileged more sedentary modes of life, because it is easier to tell that land is being "used" productively when it is being cultivated rather than grazed. It also served to reinforce a working assumption that land that is being used by ethnic Kyrgyz members of a Kyrgyz collective farm de facto belongs to the Kyrgyz SSR; and vice versa for ethnic Tajiks. The commission's working assumption was that the Tajik SSR is properly the republic "of and for" ethnic Tajiks, and the Kyrgyz SSR the republic of and for the Kyrgyz.

The parity commissions' readiness to adjust the border according to current kolkhoz use meant that such border reassessments, far from resolving contention over "unallocated" lands, tended rather to replicate uncertainty. In the case of the 1949 commission, for instance, its recommendations were not ratified at an all-Union level and disagreement over where in the Isfara Valley the actual boundaries lay persisted into the 1950s, when a second parity commission was established. These new boundaries were agreed at *raion* and oblast level in both republics, but only in the Kyrgyz SSR was the agreement ratified by the respective Supreme Soviet. In the Tajik SSR the commission's recommendations were not ratified for reasons that remain unclear (Zakirov and Babadzhanov 1989). Along the Isfara River, further commissions sought to determine the interrepublic border in 1958, 1975, 1986–1987, and 1989, the last three of these initiatives in response to violent escalations of conflict between the members of what were then two neighboring collective farms located at these borders (Alamanov 2010, 39–42; *Regional'nyi dialog i razvitie* 2004; TadzkikTA 1989). This uncertainty has outlasted the end of the Soviet Union: to this day, the major obstacle slowing the delimitation of the Kyrgyz-Tajik border is disagreement over which maps and normative acts (some ratified in one Union republic but not the other) should be taken as the authoritative basis for discussion.

From the 1950s on population growth and programs to "consolidate" high-mountain settlements led to further donations and exchanges of land. Several collective farms around Batken leased lands with neighboring republics to facilitate herding arrangements and avoid taxes on uncultivated land (Popov 1989). "Uzbek" tractor stations were built on "Kyrgyz" land and there were even plans (ultimately unrealized) for a reservoir near Sokh that would be administratively part of the Uzbek republic but situated geographically on Kyrgyz SSR territory (Röhner 2007, 46). Infrastructure was constructed with little regard for republican borders or the notional sovereignty of Soviet republics, as was the case with the Machoi/Ak-Tatyr canal that winds its way between Tajikistan and Kyrgyzstan, with the explicit aim of "knitting" constituent republics together into an integrated Soviet economy.

Perhaps most important, new "planned" villages were built in this period in ways that placed increasing strain on shared sources of irrigation. In the Isfara Valley, for instance, land was being leased as late as 1985 between the Kyrgyz and Tajik republics to enable the expansion of certain settlements, such as Vorukh and Chrokuh, which were already experiencing acute pressures on irrigated land. This is how Ömürbek-Ata, the Ak-Sai elder, recalled the creation of the new village of Tojikon (which he refers to by its colloquial Kyrgyz name, Poselka), in 1985:

ÖMÜRBEK-ATA: With Poselka it all happened like this. At that time our state farm [*Sovkhoz*] was headed in Samarkandek, during the 1970s. We didn't get a separate sovkhoz here in Ak-Sai until 1980. So at that time, during the 1970s Tajiks came to all these places where we are living now and started to cultivate the land. Before that it had just been stony land [*tashtyk jer*] and the Tajiks knew how to build irrigation to make it possible for cultivation. As you know we have a *mazar* [sacred site] here, at the entrance to Ak-Sai. So when they reached the *mazar* they said we had to move the cemetery and stop burying people there because they needed the land for cultivation. But that had always been the *mazar* for the people in Kapchygai! That really offended the Kyrgyz, they got really angry [*jiini kelip turup*] and so they started fighting with the Tajiks.

MADELEINE: Because they were asking to move the cemetery?

ÖMÜRBEK-ATA: Yes, because they wanted to cultivate there. That was in 1975. If you add together all the land they were cultivating starting from that point up to the sluice at Bedek that's 1,000 hectares of land. The Kyrgyz people swapped 1,000 hectares of land for 450 liters of water! There was an instruction from Moscow. Our First Secretary and the First Secretary of Tajikistan negotiated this issue. We didn't have a pump station before [for Ak-Sai] and they gave us [access to] 450 liters of water [per second from the Isfara river] in exchange for those 1000 hectares of land. They swapped it [*almashtyrgan*], a barter of land for flowing water from the canal . . . 282 hectares [of that land] were allocated for Friendship Park, which became Poselka. When I came here in 1984 I was working for the [state farm] office and I remember all this. In 1975 the border was divided [*granitsa bölüngön*]. It was straight. The 282 hectares for Friendship Park were allocated then for ten years. And then in 1985, an agreement was made for another ten years, until 1995. But after that agreement people started building houses! Then a school appeared. And then after people started building houses, well that just led to people seizing land for themselves [*samozakhvat bolup kaldy*]. There was a law in 1985 that said that the land would be leased to Tajikistan until 1995. But the law said that people had to stick to their land. And then starting in 1991 you had the collapse [of the Soviet Union] [*razval bolot*]. And we never got that water that was promised, even though we gave the land. We were deceived, blackmailed [*aldap ketti, shantazh kyldy*].

Ömürbek's grievances here focus on policies in the recent past: with loans that became "gifts" when the Soviet Union collapsed; with temporary arrangements that became de facto permanent through the building of homes and schools; and with the mistakes of leaders who gave away land too readily.[27] In order to understand contemporary grievances over the distribution of land and water we need to attend to the late Soviet socio-spatial transformation of the landscape and its underlying rationales—including, crucially, the

---

[27]For an account presenting a divergent recollection of these events, see Shozimov, Beshimov, and Yunusova (2011, 193).

wholesale shift from small-scale farming and pastoral herding to large-scale collectivized agriculture. In short, rather than a singular event, the national-territorial delimitation of 1924–1927 should be seen as the first iteration of an ongoing story of twentieth-century border-moving, which continued beyond the Soviet Union's collapse.

"Chorkuh Has Been Left without Mountains": Understanding Post-Soviet Legacies

The legacies of these transformations can be seen in the multiple (and often non-corresponding) maps of the region. These reveal the presence of several juridical exclaves, including Sokh, a whole district of Uzbekistan's Ferghana oblast enclosed within the territory of Kyrgyzstan, as well as multiple semi-enclaves that are de facto inaccessible without passing through the neighboring state. These late Soviet processes of giving and leasing land have also created what are effectively bifurcated villages in which different streets or individual homes are subordinate to two different states. In the Isfara Valley, for instance, the village(s) of Kök-Tash/Somoniën today, although geographically a single contiguous geographical community, contains streets and individual homes that are subject to village administrations in Kyrgyzstan and Tajikistan respectively. The village(s)' two schools, two hundred meters apart, operate on different time zones, use different curricula, teach in different languages, and celebrate different independence days.[28] A mile or so away, near the home of Pirmat-Ata, the border is still harder to determine since an area of previously waterless *adyr* between Kyrgyz-administered Üch-Döbö and Tajik-administered Khojai-A″lo was settled by families from both republics after the Machoi/Ak-Tatyr canal rendered new lands irrigable from the early 1970s.

Beyond these complex geographical legacies, the history of twentieth-century boundary drawing and redrawing has consequences for the way in which this region has come to be lived, imagined, and entered public discourse.

---

[28]During my period of research it was in Kök-Tash/Somoniën that interethnic relations seemed to be most strained. Friends in Ak-Sai described the Kök-Tash folk as "too ready to fight," while those in Kök-Tash reciprocally described the people of Ak-Sai—where virtually the whole village was related by kinship or marriage—as "too harmonious" (*ötö yntymaktuu*). Strained relations in Kök-Tash/Somoniën seem to be in part due to the fact that on both sides of the border even local decisions are made elsewhere and resources tend to concentrate in other, more obviously "strategic" villages, including Ak-Sai. Kök-Tash is subordinate to the Ak-Sai village administration, while Somoniën is subordinate to the much larger village of Chorkuh. See also Trilling (2009); Yefimova-Trilling and Trilling (2012).

Perhaps most notable is the hope that with sufficient technical expertise and careful mapping, the failures of past attempts to delimit borders can be overcome: that one can, in a sense, "fix" the problem of harmonious coexistence in a context of acute resource shortage by conclusively fixing the border (Reeves 2009a). It is this aspiration that animates Roza Otunbayeva's call in 2011 for the state committee on demarcation and delimitation to proceed quickly with its work to mitigate violent cross-border "incidents," or the European Union's promise in 2012 to provide 1.3 million euro of technical equipment to allow precise GPS mapping of the Ferghana Valley borders as part of a broader project of conflict mitigation.[29]

Crucially, as can be seen from Ömürbek's discursive blurring between policy and conspiracy, compromise and blackmail, these memories of land exchange have also fostered an abiding sense that borders are not where they should be: that exchanges of land were conducted carelessly or hastily and sometimes for questionable reasons, leaving farmers needlessly deprived of agricultural or grazing land. The sense of mutual grievance here can be gauged by comparing two narratives recorded on either side of the Kyrgyz-Tajik border in the Isfara Valley. The first comes from Abdukhalil Sharipov, a retired school-teacher and amateur archaeologist from Khojai-A"lo, interviewed in 2011 by a Dushanbe newspaper; the second from a Kyrgyz elder and his daughter-in-law, now living on disputed land at the edge of Kök-Tash village, whom I interviewed in early 2010. For Sharipov, it is the Tajiks who have lost out through excessively "generous" local leadership:

The biggest problem we face [today] is the lack of irrigated land and the absence of pastures. The last time that land was swapped between Tajikistan and Kyrgyzstan was in 1989. Then the leaders of the commission from amongst the raion and oblast-level officers, those who were supposed to be representing our republic, didn't act fairly. They put together a map according to which all the lands that are beyond the reach of the last house would be considered Kyrgyz. As a result of that all four mountains surrounding our village have gone to our neighbors. Chorkuh has been left without mountains. Even the house in which I live at one time used to be considered right in the center of the Khojai-A"lo neighborhood. And now it's right on the edge of it! Twenty meters farther and you are already inside the territory of Kyrgyzstan. Now for the sake of historical justice we want to know, who was the protégé of Abdullo Rakhimbaev who so generously gave away our mountains

[29]See Delegation of the European Union to the Kyrgyz Republic (2012).

and pastures to the neighboring republic?[30] For land shares that were given away included those where an outsider's foot had never fallen [*gde nikogda ne stupala noga inozemtsev*], which were considered ours for millennia.... At the end of the 1980s there was a policy that insisted "all [should relocate] from the mountains to the valley." In the wake of that policy 400 hectares were given away at one kolkhoz meeting "as a sign of friendship" to our brother-nation [*bratskomu narodu*]. But today our neighbors don't even limit themselves to this; they continue to harass [*pritesniat'*] the local population. (Rasul-zade 2011)

Here the Tajiks are deemed to be the originary residents of the valley, with the Kyrgyz an ambiguous "brotherly nation" who benefitted disproportionately from the redistribution of land and who now continue to squeeze out the autochthonous population. For Arslan-Ata, by contrast, the Kyrgyz elder from Kök-Tash, it is the Kyrgyz as the original pastoral residents of this area who were excessively generous in giving away the mining town of Shurab to the Tajik SSR, a few miles farther down the valley from Chorkuh. This is how he recalled his own move to the town at a time when its mining output was on the rise:

ARSLAN-ATA: When we first moved there, in 1939, there was no Shurab to speak of. It was called Shor-*suu*. . . .

ELMIRA-EJE: . . . it had a Kyrgyz name

ARSLAN-ATA: It belonged to the Kyrgyz SSR. The Kyrgyz had always been there, looking after their animals. They used to call it Burovoi kishlak . . . But then when the Soviet power came they started to call it Shorsuu. And then it went over to the Tajiks.

ELMIRA-EJE: The Kyrgyz gave it as a loan, for nineteen years.

ARSLAN-ATA: And they changed the name to Shur*ob*, to make it Tajik, you see?[31] It went over to the Tajiks, but all the people living there were

---

[30]Abdullo Rakhimbaev (1896–1938) was a member of the Khujand (northern Tajik) elite and actively involved in the discussions over the national-territorial delimitation in the 1920s. An ethnic Uzbek and ardent supporter of the idea of Greater Turkestan in the 1920s, Rakhimbaev has come to be cast in contemporary Tajik historiography (and popular discourse) as an antihero who opposed the prospects of Tajik independence, along with fellow members of the Khujand elite. On Rakhimbaev's role in the NTD, see Koichiev (2001, 30) and Masov (1991, 82).

[31]Kyrgyz *suu* (water) is equivalent to Tajik *ob*. *Shor* means salty in Tajik, so Shorsuu, which for Arslan-Ata is a "Kyrgyz word," is a Persian-Turkic linguistic hybrid very typical of this region.

Kyrgyz. We were there in 1939, we saw all this. There were very few Russians then, lots of Kyrgyz, lots of Tatars from Krasnoyarsk region. No Tajiks to speak of! They were scared of working underground. But the Kyrgyz were forced to work there, conditions, the war. . . . Until 1939 it was Shor-suu.

MADELEINE: So you mean it used to be . . .

ARSLAN-ATA: Kyrgyz land! No Tajiks lived there. This is how it was. The Tajiks didn't have their own mine. Not an underground mine. The Kyrgyz had lots of mines at the time—Sülükta, Jangy-Aryk, Kyzyl-Kiya. So it was given to the Tajiks, first of all as a loan [*aren-daga berilgen*], and then in Khrushchev's time it was given to them permanently, in 1957—no, in nineteen-sixty something or other—it was to mark the fortieth anniversary of the formation of the Tajik SSR. [*As though reading a decree, in Russian:*] "To give the source of coal of the Shurab workings to the Tajik SSR." It was all official. It was an order from the Supreme Soviet. I remember reading about it in Pravda newspaper then. You could still find that article somewhere, this was in Khrushchev's time.

These two narratives have a mirroring effect. In both cases we see one ethnic group cast as having primacy in its claim on space, with lands being given to the neighboring republic by unspecified outside actors as a gesture of friendship, celebration, or solidarity. In both cases the "gift" is perceived to be unreturned and unreciprocated: a gesture that demanded return but which remained unmet by the time the Soviet Union collapsed.

Something else emerges from such narratives, which is also important for understanding the long-term implications of the NTD. Although inter-republic borders actually shifted throughout the life of the Soviet Union, the underlying rationale that state and ethnic boundaries ought properly to coincide did not. The production of never-quite-national "national" republics discursively reinscribed the very "international contradictions" that were supposed to have disappeared with the 1924 delimitation. It is here, I think, that we can locate the origins of concern with mismatches (*nesov-padeniia*) between ethnic and territorial boundaries, and the identification of such sites as *konfliktogennyi*—that is, as inherently conflict-generating. For if the rationale for delimitation is the establishment of homogenous national units that would enable the authentic class-basis of conflict to be

unleashed, then any deviation from that principle is, ideationally, a dangerous source of contradiction.[32]

In stressing the ongoing history of socio-spatial transformation throughout the twentieth century, my approach questions the conclusions of those
analyses of contemporary border dispute in the Ferghana Valley that would
trace these exclusively to insufficient "precision" in the conduct of the initial delimitation in 1924. This is an assumption well illustrated by Olaf
Caroe's condemnation of the "Tajik plums" left inside the "pie of Uzbekistan." But the assumption that today's problems spring from insufficient
accuracy in the conduct of the delimitation informs more sober scholarship too. Kyrgyz historian Arslan Koichiev, for instance, argues that insufficient preliminary work in the process of delimitation meant that around
100,000 Kyrgyz "were deprived of national unity with Kyrgyzstan" while
approximately the same number of Uzbeks were "destined [*suzhdeno*] to
become residents of Soviet Kyrgyzstan" (2001, 80), creating the conditions
for conflict between the two groups. The implication here is that with more
accuracy (*truly* national republics delimited with more precision) such conflict could have been avoided.

In Uzbekistan, a similar assumption, though with more alarming conclusions, informs Abdullaev et al.'s vast state-sponsored survey of Soviet Turkestan, which concludes with a sharp denunciation of the inaccuracies of the
NTD (2000, 668):

> The delimitation [of 1924] and the formation of new "national state-
> hood" brought new nuances to the further development of the peoples
> of Central Asia . . . The conflict-potential [*konfliktnost'*] of the situa-
> tion was deepened by the problem of "divided ethnoses," since the new
> national-territorial formations, concentrating the basic part of the
> "titular" nationality, nonetheless continued to remain polyethnic.

Only a cautious political course, the authors conclude, can avert the danger
incubated by such a situation: "In essence, a delayed-action landmine has

---

[32]My concern here is with the normative relationship that this situation established between
natsional'nost' and *territorial'nost'*. The Soviet state institutionalized some of the most extensive provisions for minority populations of any twentieth-century polity. It also reproduced a
notion of the titular population as "first among equals" due to presumed primacy of attachment to national territory. It is a situation reflected in the binaries of academic languages (of
titular vs. non-titular, indigenous [*korennoi*; lit. rooted] vs. settler), as well as in the structures
of political debate and in contemporary specifications of threat.

been laid under future ethno-national processes and interrelations among the peoples of Central Asia; one that is capable in extreme situations of erupting into all-possible conflicts and tensions" (Abdullaev et al. 2000, 669).

Locating *Konfliktogennost'*: The Ferghana Valley as Epicenter

The implication of such accounts is that ethnic heterogeneity is *inherently* destabilizing and that the normative order is the (mono-)national state. Tensions between different ethnic groups are interpreted not as the result of unequal distribution of resources or grievances at the conduct of twentieth-century land exchanges, but rather from lack of accuracy in the conduct of the 1924 delimitation, which left various populations stranded in the "wrong" republic. Within this discursive formation, the Ferghana Valley, by dint of its ethnic complexity, population density, and the presence of minority populations, is often deemed to be a particularly conflict-generating part of Central Asia (a "restless valley" in Shishkin's 2013 formulation). Similar to the Balkans, it is perceived to have the potential to draw in, and subject to inevitable conflict, a much wider area (Green 2005, 128–158). Indeed, it is not uncommon for the Ferghana Valley to be cast as a "Eurasian Balkans" which, because of its "ethnic abundance" (*etnicheskoe napolnenie*) and economic vulnerability, has "turned into a powder keg," rendering local conflicts "inevitable" (Glumskov 2000, 5).[33]

One instrumental effect of this language of *konfliktogennost'* is its tendency to naturalize and depoliticize risk. Within this discourse, undemarcated borders, geographical exclaves, or the presence of minority populations outside their titular homeland are deemed inherently destabilizing. Kyrgyzstan's most widely circulating newspaper, *Vechernii Bishkek*, described the Sokh enclave in 2000 as "an ugly appendicitis" that "cuts into Batken oblast," dangerous because "it is impossible to circumvent" (Kim and Gruzdov 2000). An article in the *Central Asia-Caucasus Analyst* similarly identified the Vorukh

---

[33]A 2005 United Nations Development Programme (2005) report on regional cooperation in Central Asia illustrates this capacity with a striking graphic, in which the relationship between Central Asia and the world is cast in terms of a series of concentric circles, with rings indicating "Central Asia," "neighbors," and "the rest of the world" working outward around a central core that is the Ferghana Valley. A box transecting the rings, marked as the "rectangle of concern," creates the visual impression that Central Asia's problems all stem from this one excessively problematic core. Tabyshalieva (1999, 24) similarly notes that "the many sources of conflict affecting Central Asia in various combinations, which can be divided into several overlapping categories, including socio-economic, demographic, ecological, political, ideological, cultural, psychological and geopolitical, have all converged in the Ferghana Valley."

exclave of Tajikistan as a hotbed of extremism, drug smuggling, and conflict (Pylenko 2005). Questions of political economy (not least the fact that as an enclave district, there is extraordinary pressure on any available arable land) are collapsed into a *geographical* explanation: there is conflict here because an anomalous piece of Tajik territory cuts a hole inside the Kyrgyz nation-state.

A further effect of this discourse is its linking effect: its capacity to weave spatially and temporally disparate incidents into a single discursive sequence. Once one has an analytical frame that sees a particular region as *konflikto-gennyi,* the most diverse and causally unrelated incidents can be invoked as evidence, tabulated as instances of the same phenomenon. Thus, for instance, local cross-border conflicts over water distribution and pasture use, the invasion of Kyrgyzstan's southern border in 1999 and 2000 by insurgents seeking to overthrow President Islam Karimov, large-scale interethnic clashes in the city of Osh in 1990, the Andijan events of 2005, and conflict in Osh in the summer of 2010, are woven into a seamless sequence of conflict. A 2005 article made this kind of linkage explicit. Under the headline, "The Conflict-Generating Potential of the Ferghana Valley Has Historical Continuities," it drew on a popular uprising in 1898 and clashes in 1990 between neighboring collective farms over canal use to assert that "the tendency towards conflict of the Ferghana valley region exists historically and objectively irrespective of the correct or incorrect politics of the powers, events in neighboring Kyrgyzstan or geopolitical influences further afield" (Razumov 2005).

Such narrative and tabular linkages have two consequences. On the one hand, they create the impression of a recurrent internal motor that condemns the region to inevitable confrontation (see, for instance the conflict timelines in Slim 2002, 143–145; and Lubin and Rubin 1999, 44–55). Diverse incidents with divergent causal sequences are flattened into manifestations of the same basic dynamic. On the other hand, the tendency to begin such accounts with events that occurred in 1990 reinforces a portrayal of conflict as subsequent to, and necessarily antithetical to, the (assumed) harmony that characterized the Soviet era, a harmony that was deemed to exist because of the strong, interventionist presence of the Soviet center. Such an approach ignores the degree to which current tensions in much of the Batken zone refer back to grievances over unequal exchanges of land in the 1970s and 1980s—events that are still recalled vividly today.

Perhaps the most significant instrumental effect is what I call the preventive imperative. The discourse of *konfliktogennost'* incites practices of anticipation; it invites intervention before conflict appears. Consider, for instance, Abdullaev et al.'s (2000) characterization of the "delayed-action landmine" that delimitation placed in Central Asia, or Slim's call on the international community to help "push the Ferghana valley away from the precipice to which it is now heading" (2002, 141). This is a language that interpolates: it urges us to intervene. In the Ferghana Valley, this concern with anticipating and preempting conflict is reflected in a proliferation of internationally sponsored programs of "preventive development"—that is, targeted development initiatives in those communities deemed at high risk of conflict. By 2004, multiple government-led aid programs, donor-funded projects, and nongovernmental organizations (NGOs) were operating in the Isfara and Sokh valleys. Some had an explicit focus on conflict mitigation, including the Foundation for Tolerance International, one of Kyrgyzstan's largest NGOs with a regional office in Batken; the Program on Regional Dialogue and Development funded by the Swiss Agency for Development and Cooperation; the Peaceful Communities Initiative funded by USAID and implemented by Mercy Corps, and the Preventive Development Component of the UNDP. Other donor organizations, such as the German Organization for Technical Cooperation, focused their activities primarily on poverty alleviation with a significant conflict mitigation component. A variety of smaller NGOs acted as implementing partners for these programs.

By 2004, conflict prevention had become an expanding field for NGOs in Batken, as the "preventive" element allowed for rapid expansion of projects into new sites. As one proponent of preventive development describes the rationale, drawing on a fire-fighting analogy: rather than wait for potentially dangerous conflagration to occur, " 'preventive development' tries to stop fires before they become emergencies by identifying and removing combustible materials, installing smoke detectors that firefighters can hear and placing extinguishers where fires are likely to start" (Clark 2004, 1).

Yet herein lies a problem, one tied to the temporality of prevention and the slipperiness of conflict (see also Austin 2004). How does one establish the relative likelihood of conflict occurring in different parts of a country or, at a more localized level, within different villages? How does one calibrate or, to use Clark's metaphor, how does one know where to put the fire extinguisher? Precisely because of the difficulty of quantifying the potential for conflict into standardized models, there is a concomitant tendency to particularize and locate failure conclusively in particular people, objects, and places. If conflict potential cannot be abstracted and a common explanatory grid established, then it must be relentlessly localized and specified. The proxy becomes the thing itself: borders and the "places of mismatch" described by Maitdinova (2010) come to be seen not just as associated with conflict, but causal of it.

From this, I suggest, follow the powerful effects of mapping—establishing, spatially and conceptually, the location of danger, fixing the root cause of an outbreak of violence. Whole projects have been dedicated precisely to the cartography of conflict (*kartirovanie konfliktov*). In Batken, for instance, the Foundation for Tolerance International has created a tabular template in order to solicit information for the construction of a map of conflicts in the south of Kyrgyzstan. This caused some frustration to those tasked with translating it in the field, as the proxies for conflict potential bore little correspondence to local perceptions of risk. In the Isfara Valley, a similar technique has been used by a Vorukh-based NGO to construct a display-size "map of problems" (*karta problem*) showing, within each village or group of villages, the various potential loci of tension. The German Organization for Technical Cooperation, in a sponsored study of *Peace and Conflict Potentials in Batken Oblast* (Passon and Temirkulov 2004), has developed a "conflict profile" of each of the sites studied. Each case is accompanied by a visual representation in which jagged danger signs (representing sites of potential conflict), hexagons (areas of past violent conflict), and circles (development interventions) are overlaid on a detailed topographic map of the affected villages and their surroundings. Danger, in this visual representation, is at once precisely knowable, geographically localized, and rendered safe by development: there is no place for contingency or for the identification of causal factors beyond the twenty or so square kilometers that are visually represented.[34]

Putting Out Fires: From Conflict Maps to Preventive Intervention

This act of graphic fixing is consequential. Conflict maps inform project documents, which in turn shape empirical interventions in border villages. Consider, for instance, the following program documents that act as the framework for the Mercy Corps Peaceful Communities Initiative (PCI) in the Ferghana Valley. Echoing Abdullaev et al.'s concerns with "divided ethnoses," the 2003 field study for the Initiative begins by identifying the Ferghana valley as a "divided" region, "with ethnic divisions refusing to fit neatly inside each country's borders" (Young 2003, 5). Target villages for PCI projects are thus selected according to their perceived geographical or ethnic complexity:

Throughout the community selection process, potential for conflict was the primary consideration for the teams . . . For PCI, community

---

[34]I have explored Central Asian conflict maps as an "inscription device" in more detail in Harvey, Reeves, and Ruppert (2013).

selection was based on the identification of communities that were located on one of the borders or that were an ethnic island within another
majority population. (Young 2003, 14)

What is notable here is that selection has little to do with whether communities identify their village as liable to cross-border conflict, or whether there
have been instances of interethnic or cross-border antagonism in the past.
Indeed, in the logic of the program report, past experience of conflict and
perception of threat are relatively insignificant as indicators because this is a
preventive, and therefore future-oriented, project. The report acknowledges
that "the potential for conflict as identified through the analysis of numerous
external organizations is not perceived in the same light by the communities
and governments themselves" but this is explained in terms of an act of local
misrecognition: not seeing all the "real" manifestations of conflict. "Conflict
as a local term implies an outbreak of fighting between countries and no one
verbalizes this as an imminent threat within the valley. Similarly, concerns
regarding religious extremism, expressed by outside observers, are not openly
articulated" (Young 2003, 18).

Rather than this being a cause for caution when it comes to preventive intervention, it is invoked to justify implementation *now*, before such fears need
become articulated openly. "Recent history elsewhere, such as the Yugoslav
conflicts . . . demonstrates that peaceful co-existence should not be taken for
granted, particularly where quality of life is poor and there are perceptions
of inequalities between the populations" (Young 2003, 6). The need for intervention is thus transformed into the analyst's ability to see what is invisible to
locals themselves—it is her awareness of other conflict situations (the report
mentions Lebanon, Georgia, and Serbia) together with an understanding of
the mechanisms of conflict escalation that enable her to see through layers
of indifference or denial. "This is not to deny that these potential triggers
for conflicts do not exist, but rather that they are not in the consciousness of
the people in the communities—arguably the best time to be implementing
conflict prevention programs (long before violence is imminent and appears
inevitable)" (ibid., 18).

This is a self-justifying argument—preventive intervention is needed before
people see a need for it. But it is also a generative one, a fact not lost on many
villagers and locally employed conflict analysts (*konfliktologi*). Demonstrating
the successful prevention of conflict can potentially lead to the exaggeration
of risk, or the local recoding of legitimate anger over lack of political voice
into *ethnic* animosity. As Parviz, the Sokh-based conflict analyst, commented
with the acerbic wit of one who has reflected much on the ambivalences of his

role in preventing and putting out conflicts: "of course we firemen also have to know how to fill our five year plans!"

The conditionality of the material aid associated with preventive development is perhaps the most striking consequence of this language of risk. Just as it was in the 1920s, the threat of conflict is recognized locally to be a productive petitionary mode and frequently spoken of as such in border villages. The program director of a Batken-based international donor organization noted with some exasperation the degree to which languages of conflict now came to inflect proposals for his organization's funding that in other settings would have been justified primarily in terms of economic need. He gave the example of a proposal recently brought to him:

> It's a run-of-the-mill build-a-school, build-a-club, do-this-and-that proposal, and [the village leaders who brought it to me] say, "you know, there's conflict potential here." But how can you blame the communities for having learnt that lesson when in fact you know it's the donors who are doing that? . . . It's different if you are working outside this area [conflict mitigation], but if you are only working in conflict and only working on issues tied to conflict and if you have a pressure by year-end or whatever to spend money and you haven't spent that money yet, you've got to do something . . . If at the end of the day you've got to spend another $200,000 you've got to *find projects*, OK? And then you tend to find projects that, you know, disperse money fast, but you don't do a "no harm" analysis, or you do but only so as to keep the donor back in Tashkent or elsewhere happy about it. But it's not serious.[35]

This particular program manager was troubled by what he saw as the pernicious effects of framing every local development initiative in terms of a "preventive" intervention, as it undermined existing indigenous mechanisms of conflict mitigation, and risked diverting funds from where they might be most needed. But there are also more subtle implications of this discourse of *konfliktogennost'*, to which conversations with Parviz drew my attention. First, it means that aspects of social life in ethnically mixed valleys that were not previously indexical of poor social relations (e.g., patterns of endogamy among Kyrgyz and Tajik communities; language differences, subtly different patterns of dress, courtship, and religious practice) now come to be marked and monitored as failures of "integration." Culturally elaborated differences between pastoral and agricultural modes of life that Middendorf had

---

[35]Author interview, Batken, July 2005.

commented on with wonderment in the 1870s and Nalivkin had described with wry affection in the 1910s come to be read now as markers of instability and lack of cohesion, which outside organizations can help overcome. Commenting on the success of PCI in the border villages of Southern Sokh, for instance, one project document notes:

> Before PCI helped organize the girls' basketball league in the Sokh enclave, there were no opportunities for girls to compete in sports outside of the schoolyard . . . This area, once belonging to the Tajik Khan of Kanibadam, has long since been overlooked by the Government of Uzbekistan, which struggles to meet the needs of its citizens in the Ferghana Valley. This neglect made Sokh sympathetic when the Islamic Movement of Uzbekistan launched multiple incursions into Uzbekistan from the surrounding mountains in the late 1990s. When one athlete, Madina, was asked her general impression about the tournament, she responded, "We need more chances to play together. Before we played volleyball (with Sogment in Batken Oblast), I had no chance to ever meet anyone from there. Now I have girlfriends there, and I hope to learn more about their community, and the life of young people there." When the league started the girls all wore traditional dress and slippers, and now they are sporting track suits and basketball shoes donated by Nike. (Mercy Corps and USAID 2003, 10)

Echoing early Soviet calls to counter "backwardness" through the transformation of female dress and *byt* (Northrop 2004, 242–283), this passage weaves together political neglect, ethnic insularity, and religious conservatism as social ills to be cast aside with the help of Mercy Corps and Nike. Practices of ethnic boundary maintenance, local gender norms that dictate appropriate boundaries of female movement, and attachment to place and community are recast in this move as marks of failure, as potential sources of instability. Culturally embedded practices of house building near to the parental courtyard, which is the basis of *mahalla* sociality, get recoded as dangerously insular, with the "mahalla concept" appearing in some analyses as a source of conflict alongside land shortages and undemarcated borders.[36]

---

[36]See, e.g., Passon and Temirkulov (2004, 50). On the importance of the *mahalla* to Tajik identity in the Isfara Valley, see Shozimov, Sulaimanov, and Abdullaev (2011, 288): "If Kyrgyz (and some Uzbeks) organize traditional events around kin and tribal structures, the Tajiks and most Uzbeks integrate neighbors into their social and cultural space through territorial *mahallas*. The Tajik proverb, 'a neighbor can be closer than a relative' could also be Uzbek not Kyrgyz." This is a generalization, to be sure, but it reflects a widely held local distinction, which can carry different normative inflection depending on the context.

Likewise, the informal land swaps of a previous generation, exacerbated by acute land pressure in the enclave districts and colossal differentials in land prices on two sides of the border, are now recoded as "creeping migration"— a term that suggests dangerously subversive transfers of sovereign property (Reeves 2009a).

This brings me to the second effect of such interventions. In failing to inquire about the actually existing dynamics of cross-border sociality (in life-cycle ceremonies, trade, cooperative herding agreements, canal-usage and clearance, tea-house chess-playing or religious instruction), and by codifying those that exist as insufficiently outward looking or engaged ("until PCI came along, children never played together!"), such approaches actually tend to produce an awareness locally of ethnic difference as something at least potentially risky. In other words, *konfliktogennost'* has become productive not just in the obvious sense that it facilitates instrumental claims vis-à-vis a grant-giving international community, but more fundamentally because it comes to shape the very imagination of what it is to be a member of a Tajik or Kyrgyz community living *here* in *this* valley, close to *this* new international border.

There is a further effect of such developments that is relevant to the book's broader exploration of border work. Such projects of preventive intervention also transform cartographic lines in southern Ferghana into material

Cross-border volleyball game in Hushiar village, Sokh district, Uzbekistan, sponsored by the Swiss-funded program of Regional Dialogue and Development, March 2005.

boundaries in important ways. There is an easy slippage between the border as a place where conflicts tend to be *concentrated* and the idea that this strand of territory is itself generating conflicts from within. When border as cartographic reality becomes the primary index of risk, interventions come to concentrate around it. A physical "bunching" on the ground comes to accompany the markers on the map. Because the pipes, pumps and other items of infrastructure through which prevention is materialized are usually legally the property and responsibility of one or other village (and thus of one or other state), and because projects tend to be organized and funded by national offices, such physical materializations often play an important role in differentiating access based on location, thus *territorializing* the state.

In an interview in June 2004, Akhmat-Agai, the director of the Ak-Sai school, commented that it was a godsend that Ak-Sai had "turned out" to be a border village and hence deemed as being in greater need:

> We had the honor, you know, to find ourselves—maybe God granted it—that these international organizations would help us as a border village, you see? A border village, the others, in other villages they don't have those kinds of opportunity. As border dwellers they help us.

This had enabled the people of Ak-Sai to have their school heating system and roof repaired by the World Bank, while other schools that had previously been part of the same collective farm but farther from the border had not. Indeed, as Akhmat-Agai pointed out to me, in the preceding year the donor funding they had received was equivalent to more than 1,000,000 Kyrgyz som ($40,000)—a figure that made the financial transfers they received form the central state budget to look like a "penny" in comparison.

Noteworthy here is Akhmat-Agai's "turned out." As a respected long-term resident of Ak-Sai who had remembered waves of new migrations to the village and instances of past contention over access to water and land, he was not unaware that his village lay close to the border. But it was recent interventions that had made this "borderness" a salient category of administrative practice. As the interview progressed, however, it became clear that this designation was also fostering new lines of division. Other schools subordinate to the same village administration had not received such funding, and there were rumors that the head of the administration was deliberately favoring his native village by selectively submitting proposals for external funding. Indeed, Ak-Sai village had become the target of so many, sometimes incompatible, projects that donors decided to set up a coordination committee to counter what one report described as the "donor shopping mentality" of village authorities (Passon and Temirkulov 2004, 51; see also Maasen et al. 2005, 22). Two organizations, unbeknown to each other, were trying to implement projects, one to repair a pump, the other to build a canal, which were "mutually exclusive." Indeed, as the regional program manager of one international grant-giving agency put it to me in interview in July 2005, the village had become "crowded out with donors."

This is a classic example of the kind of bureaucratic entrenchments described by Ferguson (1990) in his critique of the development apparatus in Lesotho. But it is a spatial entrenchment, too. The distinctive geography of preventive intervention materializes the state border even as many projects seek to counter the effects of their progressive politicization. In the following chapter, I embark on a different kind of explanation of the space than discussed here. By turning from maps to movements, and looking at the shifting trajectories of various border-crossing things and people, I ask how we might attend to the dramatic contractions and distensions of post-Soviet space in a way that does not treat the map as socially primary.

3. TRAJECTORIES

Mobility and the Afterlives of Internationalism

Khurshed, in his early thirties, turned to the group of former classmates whom he was hosting at his home in Dehkonobod *mahalla,* in Uzbekistan's Sokh district, on a chilly January evening in 2005. He picked out an apricot from one of the plates of dried fruit and nuts laid out on the tablecloth (*dastorkhon*) in front of us and held it up for us to admire. "What did the cosmonauts find when they landed on Mars?" he asked, his voice quizzical, his eyes laughing. He looked around in case any of us might venture an answer, before responding: "That the Sokh lads had got there first and were already selling apricots to the Martians!"

Khurshed bit into the apricot that he was holding and invited his guests to try the fruit for themselves. His comment at once indexed the abundance of the Sokh apricot crop and the centrality of trade to Sokh identity, something my host in Dehkonobod, Parviz, had reminded me of on numerous earlier occasions. "Turn up at any bazaar in Russia, and look at who is selling you apricots," he had told me. "Any bazaar, anywhere—you'll find Sokh lads there!" Khurshed, Parviz's former classmate, had been trading apricots from the valley since 1992 in cities across southern Siberia. He was proud to consider himself a pioneer among his friends, several of whom had subsequently joined him in the dried fruit trade. He was the first of his cohort to be able to afford a leather jacket, one of the first to buy a car, and was considered a source of authority in his *mahalla* on the state of trade and opportunities for work in Siberian Russia. Khurshed was about to leave for Russia again the following day, and this gathering at his house, with a meal of *plov* and toasts to his safe return, was the opportunity to mark the occasion among friends.

The group of eight former classmates had been meeting during the previous weeks to mark *chilu*: the period of winter rest, traditionally forty days in length, when long nights and a break in agricultural work allowed for an intense period of communal visiting. One of the men hosted the others each evening, and Parviz had invited me along to this otherwise all-male affair so that I might observe this small ritual of departure. Although Khurshed was used to leaving for Russia, he was departing this time for a rather different kind of work—a fact that turned our conversation that evening toward the risks and benefits of the increasing departures of young men from Sokh for undocumented work "in town." Import and export duties for those trying to take apricots from Uzbekistan to Russia, together with what Khurshed described as the rising "fanaticism" of antiimmigrant groups in the Russian metropolis, had made selling apricots in open-air markets too much of a headache.[1] That was why he had decided this time to leave instead for work on a construction site in the Altai region of southern Siberia. There he could work in peace and earn a steady, if less lucrative, income. I asked Khurshed whether he had to leave at all. Could he not stay in Uzbekistan and find a job there? There were times he was tempted to stay, he replied. The eight-day journey to Altai, in a car shared with the driver and three other men, was long, cold, and uncomfortable. And he had young children at home whom he would not see now for months. All the same, he told me, "I have to leave," invoking a Tajik proverb by way of explanation: "A person who has never been an outsider cannot consider himself a Muslim" (*Kas, ki musofir nashud, musulmon nashud*).[2]

Maps and Trajectories

Khurshed's gestures, his plans, and his expressions of belonging-through-mobility point us toward a rather different reading of space than the ones discussed earlier in the book. The mappings that we saw there suggest a spatial contiguity to sites that may be encountered in ruptures; they suggest a temporal continuity to sporadic events, and a basic homology to the things mapped,

---

[1] On increasing obstacles for migrant workers to trade in Russia, see Regamey and Le Huérou (2007). In November 2006, the Russian government passed legislation drastically restricting the number of noncitizens who could trade at market stalls (to 40% initially and eventually to 0%); see the decree of the Russian Federation government no. 683 "Ob ustanovlenii na 2007 god dopustimoi doli innostrannykh rabotnikov, ispol'zuemykh khoziaistvuiushchimi sub"ektami osushchestvliaiushchimi deatel'nost' v sfere roznitchnoi torgovli na territorii Rossiiskoi Federatsii," http://www.rg.ru/2006/11/16/kvota1-doc.html.

[2] Khurshed used the term "musulmon" (*Muslim*) but in a way that contextually suggests moral, upright, spiritual behavior. I am grateful to Sunatullo Jonboboev and Dilya Dorgabekova for their discussions on this theme.

which are in fact of radically different orders. By bringing together "elements of diverse origin" onto a single stage, the map, as de Certeau argues, "pushes away into its prehistory . . . as if into the wings, the operations of which it is the result or the necessary condition" (1988, 121). It is thus a productive tool of power.

Maps not only portray a deceptive coherence and presence to administrative demarcations that have to be practiced to become real; they also inscribe a fixity to geometric distance that may have little correspondence with distance that is traveled across and imagined. Maps give the impression of space-as-surface: "the sphere of a completed horizontality" (Massey 2005, 107). My aim here is to approach space in southern Ferghana in a way that remains alert to its liveliness. This is space considered not as surface, but as the sphere "of a dynamic simultaneity, constantly disconnected by new arrivals, constantly awaiting to be determined by the construction of new relations" (ibid.).

In this chapter I foreground ethnographically stories about the movements of people and things; combining this with findings from the household survey that I conducted into the shifting stakes of trans-border mobility.[3] This approach is motivated by an ethnographic reality of which I was constantly reminded during fieldwork. My interlocutors, young and old, were preoccupied with flows and limits to them: with ensuring that canal water reached gardens, apricots reached markets, sons reached Russia to work, and that money could be sent back unhindered from labor abroad. By the mid-2000s, livelihoods in southern Ferghana had come to depend on money remitted from seasonal work abroad to a degree that few could have predicted five years earlier; and this dependence had intensified in part because of obstacles to local cross-border mobility and trade.[4] New trajectories of mobility had appeared, but this was not an easy, frictionless flow (Tsing 2005); borders often seemed to emerge in conversation precisely at

---

[3]An English-language translation of the questionnaire that I developed for this purpose, together with a discussion of the methodology for selecting households for inclusion and tabulated findings from this survey can be found in Reeves (2008, 250–278).

[4]This was particularly true of trade with Uzbekistan, where export and import tariffs had rendered much of the cross-border shuttle trade that had occurred in the 1990s prohibitively expensive. Megoran, Raballand, and Bouyjou (2005) note a precipitous decline in Kyrgyzstan-Uzbekistan trade in the early 2000s and estimate that a Kyrgyz truck entering Uzbekistan in the mid-2000s would have to pay approximately US$700, around 8 percent of the container value simply to cross the border, excluding a host of informal payments. On the shift toward remittances as a primary source of livelihood in the Ferghana Valley since the early 2000s, see Röhner (2007); Thieme (2008a, 2008b); Reeves (2009b, 2012); and Rahmonova-Schwarz (2012).

the point that they represented a limit point—as a rupture to previous ways of relating, working, or doing kinship.

Inquiring into the ways borders constrain, limit, or channel movement can provide an ethnographic point of entry for exploring how and when new borders come to acquire social salience. Cunningham and Heyman note that movement has tended to be undertheorized in border studies, yet attention to material transformations in mobility and enclosure "helps us grasp concepts of dramatic social change (such as globalization) that are otherwise in danger of becoming unmoored" (2004, 296). Such an approach also gives us some conceptual understanding of the dramatic shifts in lived distance that have occurred for people in the Ferghana Valley, in which sites and categories of person that were imaginatively close are being recalibrated as distant. James Ferguson (1999) reminds us in his account of "de-modernization" on the Zambian Copperbelt how social and economic decline is often experienced precisely through a shift in spacial mobility: becoming "disconnected" is quite different from the fact or feeling of never having been connected.

As my interlocutors told me about the multiple and highly differentiated forms of connection that linked villages in southern Ferghana with sites across the Soviet space: with factories in Siberia, universities in Tashkent, markets in the Russian heartland and military barracks in the Baltics, my own mental map of the former Soviet space was progressively transformed. Grasping the experience and effects of contemporary border work in southern Ferghana demands taking seriously the multiple and highly differentiated meanings of Soviet incorporation for those living in the Soviet Union's cartographic margins.[5] This in turn requires attending to the diverse practices—of provisioning and the cutting-off of provisioning, of incorporating and deporting, of legalizing and illegalizing—through which limits were and are produced and erased.

---

[5] The emergent anthropological and historical literatures on "late socialism" are yet to fully engage with this diversity of experiences. The "last Soviet generation" of Alexei Yurchak's (2005) brilliant portrait is emphatically urban, Russophone, and secular. For Yurchak, mediating factors (class, language, ethnicity, etc.) did not fundamentally alter the "*shared* particular understandings, meanings, and processes" of the generation that came of age during the 1970s and 1980s (2005, 31). My conversations with people who were generationally part of this cohort outside Central Asian capitals (and with Kyrgyz, Tajik, or Uzbek as their first language) suggest that the meanings of late socialism were significantly more diverse, and more thoroughly mediated by the linguistic diversity of late socialist realities than Yurchak suggests (see also Ualieva and Edgar [2011]; Sahadeo [2012]). For many Tajik-speaking, Bollywood-watching young people in 1970s Sokh, for instance, the "imaginary elsewhere" of late socialism was less Paris than Bombay (ibid., 158–206).

Chasing Water: Gaz Village, Upper Sokh Valley, Kyrgyzstan

Kanysh-ai plunged her metal basin below the surface of the spring pool and immediately out again, swirling off the water so that there remained just a small layer covering the apricot stones. She flicked the basin upward, tossing the stones over each other then plunged it in again to catch more water. Swirling, swishing, tossing, and catching: a noisy percussion to accompany our conversation as we squatted, toes in water, by the side of the spring. A few more lunges of the basin, then a new rhythm as Kanysh-ai rubbed the stones against each other, handfuls at a time, to clean the traces of sugary fruit from the brown kernel underneath. The water turned a rich yellow as the stones became gradually cleaner and the remains of the fruit fell away, before another lunge into clear water, another swirl, and the process repeated again.

As we soaked and scrubbed the stones, Kanysh-ai traced for me the various trajectories of the apricots that constitute the main cash crop in the Sokh Valley. In the turbulent years of economic collapse "before Russia" (*Rossiiaga cheiiin*), apricots had been the primary source of domestic income. Now families relied primarily on remittances from Russia—a transformation, the scale and suddenness of which was indexed by her use of Russia as a temporal marker. The stones that we were washing would be sold to Uzbeks who would travel up from the valley basin to the border bazaar in Hushiar, a couple of kilometers downstream from Kanysh-ai's home. They would buy them by the kilogram, she told me, to fry and salt the tasty inner kernel for sale as *shordonak* (salty seeds). The apricot fruit, meanwhile, would be left to dry in the blazing mountain sun on boards and tiles and on every exposed part of the corrugated roof of her home. After several days of drying, a small amount of the "clean" dried apricots (*taza örük*) would be left unbleached for their own consumption, resulting in a dark, chewy fruit that clung to the teeth.

Most of the fruit would be immersed in a yellowish sulfur chemical (*dary*) producing the bright orange color and flexible texture that gave the fruit a "commercial appearance" (*tovarnyi vid*). These had a different trajectory from the Ferghana-bound stones. Most of Kanysh-ai's apricots would be purchased, in Batken or one of the border markets farther west, by Tajiks from the district center of Isfara. Kanysh-ai lamented the fact that over the past few years, she and her mother had rarely obtained a good price for their crop. In an abundant year, such as this, everyone would be trying to sell to the same few buyers and this would push the price down. Fresh apricots were being sold to wholesale buyers for as little as three soms (8 US cents) per kilogram in recent years. Better-off villagers would store their crop until the spring, when competition was less intense and prices concomitantly higher. But most people from Gaz were short on cash, and would sell at whatever price and as soon as they could. It had not always been like this, Kanysh-ai explained. Until Uzbekistan had "started to close the border," an individual

Kanysh-Ai and her mother drying apricots at their home. Gaz village, upper Sokh Valley, Kyrgyzstan, June 2005.

farmer from Gaz could take a lorry-load of apricots to Russia and still make a sizeable profit, even after paying the necessary customs dues.

By the mid-2000s, by contrast, it was only viable to take apricots to Russia if you could do so trainloads at a time: "if you have a lorry-full of apricots and you tell them on the border that it's ten tons, they can weigh your vehicle and find out that it's really seventeen," Kanysh-ai explained. "They'll give you a fine (*saga shtraf salat*). But if you have a trainload of apricots and you tell them that it's 60 tons, they are never going to know if you really have 100! You fill out your paper, you avoid the fine. But for that you need a lot of capital." That was why it was Tajiks from Isfara who dominated the commercial apricot market, she explained. A branch line built to service the coal mine on the Kyrgyz-Tajik border had left Isfara, the leafy district center just to its north, with a train station now bustling from the rise of private trade. "So of course the Isfara lads will use the trains to trade," Kanysh-ai continued. "A whole group of them will join together to buy a train-load together. The station is there, and at the station, he's got a brother, a cousin, you know." She trailed her sentence, and thrust up her hand again for another flick of the stones, the act completing the explanation. Keeping the stones in motion was the key to getting them clean.

After rinsing off the stones, and sweeping hands over her face with an *oomin*-a gesture acknowledging that this spring is also sacred (*yiyk*) space, we traced our way slowly along the path bordering the stream as it wound down from the spring pool, buckets of cleaned brown stones in each hand. As we did so, Kanysh-ai's conversation moved from the apricot flows to the water that sprung out here from below the earth and swirled off down the mountain. "All the water they drink right down as far as Hushiar begins here. They have the richer soil down there, but our ancestors knew that the best place to be is up here where the water springs from." Kanysh-ai followed with an upward flick of her head the future course of the stream that wound initially through gravel and small rocks before falling into the Tash canal that flowed through lower Sogment and Hushiar, the villages immediately downstream. Here the water was transparent and "sweet" (*shirin*), Kanysh-ai told me. By the time it reached the smaller network of channels (*aryktar*) that ran along the streets in Hushiar, it was slow and muddy, hardly reaching the lower part of the village.

Kanysh-ai's comments, like so many conversations in villages at the border, drew my attention to the importance of the canal system and its variable flows as determinants of social relations. In downstream villages around Batken during the irrigation-heavy summer months of planting and watering, there would be informal rotas in place to "chase the water" (*suu aidash üchün*) along the main canal artery to ensure that irrigation water reached the most downstream parts of the village (see also Bichsel, 2009, 49–54). Men would pace the length of the main canal to check that smaller diversionary channels had not been dug or pipes inserted to siphon off the water. Different streets would be allocated particular days on which the channels in front of their homes would be opened to enable water to run through, and by slightly adjusting the stone or tile sluice that connected a main artery to its subsidiaries, upstream villagers could ensure that there was a constant trickle to their own plots. Because this could potentially deprive those downstream of an adequate supply to water their gardens, the communal regulation of canal water was of paramount importance. Liu (2012, 132) has noted in an urban context that the collective control of *aryk* irrigation provides a paradigmatic picture of "collective coping" in a context of strained resources: an informal mechanism for ensuring water distribution, premised on an ethic of social control.

Kanysh-ai's account of the *aryk* network in Hushiar echoed this urban picture, with its emphasis on social regulation and informal sanction. Yet her depiction of the cross-border canal winding its way to Sogment and Hushiar also points to the fact that an *aryk*—with its variable flows, like natural springs and Russia-bound apricots—reveals alternative topographies of borderland space. To conventional cartography, and certainly in the normative language of preventive development, Kanysh-ai's home in Gaz is multiply disconnected: at the end of a gravel road that is barely passable in winter, cut off from the regional center by the presence of border controls, and in a mountainous location that was emphatically peripheral within the Soviet hierarchy of incorporation. Kanysh-ai had no illusions that Gaz was a "remote" (*yraaktagy*) village. She would joke about how young brides who married into to the village from warmer, lower-lying communities always got thin (*aryktap ketet*) during their first years of marriage from the harsh winters and the constant grind of carrying water uphill. But this remoteness did not mean a lack of connection; nor did it equate with categorical distance. Indeed, the very harshness of life made the connections all the more important. "When you drink from the same well," Kanysh-ai explained to me, talking about the periodic tensions that erupted between Gaz and Hushiar, the larger, downstream village across the border, "you make sure you don't spit in it [*suu ichken kuduguna tükürböi*]!" She took pride in the fact that her parents' brick home had been built according to a state standard that was replicated "across the Union" in areas subject to climactic extremes. A Stalin portrait in a dusty frame in her neighbor's home beside some World War II certificates was a reminder that remoteness did not equate affective disincorporation.

Practicing connection. A Kök-Tash elder tends a family shrine celebrating his father's service in the Soviet army. Kök-Tash, Isfara Valley, June 2005.

Kanysh-ai was acutely aware of the multiple dependencies that connected livelihoods here to those in Hushiar, Batken, Ferghana, and Moscow. Distance, her conversations suggested, could be produced and erased: it was the product of effortful activity. It was not the static relation the map suggests.

Kanysh-ai's account was punctuated by the recognition of the importance and the contingency of remaining connected. Water had to be "chased" and apricots had to be "sent": both of these activities that demanded careful coordination. Even the sending of remittances from Russia often depended on an act of coordinated "throwing" (*perekidka*), a trust-based system of informal money transfers that is largely invisible to the official banking system.[6] As other narratives pointed out, however, connections can break down, resulting in disorientation and a profound sense of loss. In southern Ferghana, this sense of becoming disconnected was most acute in those sites that had been dramatically transformed by the Soviet state: the "planned villages" that had been built to aggregate Kyrgyz herding families from the Alay Mountains in the 1970s and the international mining towns perched in otherwise barren landscapes to extract coal, mercury, and magnesium. It is to one of these villages, Ak-Tatyr, in the Isfara Valley, that I now turn.

After "Moscow Provisioning"

Wooden benches have been hastily assembled in the cavernous hall of Ak-Tatyr's school. There is a clamor of children shouting, running, and playing leapfrog over benches, while mothers chat in raised voices above the commotion. The throb of conversation is interspersed with the screech of metal across concrete as wobbly metal-legged tables are pushed to the side of the room. Patches of brown linoleum in the less trodden corners of the hall attest to better days, when villages like Ak-Tatyr could aspire to a three-story, brick school with linoleum-covered floors and a steady supply of coal for heating in winter. Now, the cost of repairs has to be met from parental contributions, and much of Burul-Ejeke's tireless work as school director is spent in lobbying, petitioning, grant-writing, and cajoling to cover the gaping holes—in roofs, linoleum, and teachers' salaries—left by the retreat of central funding.[7]

---

[6]In those instances where the sums earned by migrant workers were too large to be safely carried on the person by train through Kazakhstan, money would often be "thrown" (*perekidano*) in an informal, nonbank transfer, with building materials (pine wood and corrugated roofing sheets) the only visible border-crossing commodities. This system, widespread in northern Tajikistan, and used equally by Kyrgyzstani migrants and their families in the early and mid-2000s, relies on a minutely coordinated routine embedded in trusted kin relations, in which money is transferred from a migrant worker to his or her kin without physically crossing a border. Typically, the migrant in Russia pays a Tajik "banker" based in Russia, whose brother or cousin lives in northern Tajikistan. The "banker" phones his relative to instruct that an equivalent sum be paid to the family of the migrant. Meanwhile the sum accumulated by the banker in Russia from the deposited wages is converted into building materials that are sent for resale (at considerable profit) in Central Asia. No money ever physically crosses a border or enters a bank ledger, and the transfer costs are considerably lower than sending money through commercial banks or agencies such as Western Union. The logic of *perekidka* is similar to that of the *hawala* system well explored in the contexts of South Asian labor migration (see Ballard 2003; Mughal 2007, 75–77).

[7]Elsewhere (Reeves 2006) I have discussed in more detail the complex challenges to keep Ak-Tatyr school heated, provisioned, and supplied with teachers in a context of acute outmigration.

This evening we are here for a concert and, it turns out, a commemoration. As the largest public building of any of the villages in the area, the hall in Ak-Tatyr doubles as a club, and this evening it is packed. A young amateur band from Osh has been touring the villages around Batken, performing in schools and clubhouses for a fee that "keeps us on the road." The band members are hoping to make it big in the Kyrgyz pop scene, but tonight the atmosphere is informal and low key. The band gathers on the makeshift stage that has been formed at the far end of the room. There is a cheer as the accordionist announces that he has a cousin who lives in Govsuvar, the next village over, bordering Tajikistan and linked to Ak-Tatyr through multiple bonds of kinship and intermarriage. The accordionist uses the Tajik name for a village that in the preceding ten years has been officially changed to the more Kyrgyz-sounding Orto-Boz. Only this new name stands at the entrance to the village today, though both are used interchangeably—a small reminder, in this progressively étatized space, of the way singular histories are inscribed onto multiply lived landscapes.

Burul-Ejeke joins the band on stage and the noise gradually subsides. She welcomes the band and then explains why this concert is also to be a commemoration. The teachers' *kollektiv*, she tells us, has decided that we should hold a collection at the end of the concert for the children of School Number 1 in Beslan, the North Ossetian village that had been the site of a violent siege and botched rescue operation the preceding week.[8] After all, Burul-Ejeke told the audience, "Russia is providing for us" (*Rossiia bizge nan taap beret*; lit. "Russia finds and gives us bread") and half our men are over there, including many of our own teachers. We should give whatever help we are able.

After the concert, I accompanied Altynai, one of the teachers who had been involved in organizing the event, to the home of Tursun-Aka, the village director, where a celebratory meal was served for the band. Altynai had been among those who had proposed holding a collection for the Beslan children, and I asked her about her motivation. After all, other than the fact that Ak-Tatyr and Beslan had both been part of the USSR, there was no particular connection between these linguistically and culturally distant parts of the former Soviet south. After a pause, Altynai responded by invoking her childhood in Shurab, the small mining town straddling the Kyrgyz-Tajik border, whose renaming was lamented by Arslan-Ata (see chapter 2):

---

[8]On September 1, 2004, the first day of the new school year, School Number 1 in Beslan was sieged by militants demanding an end to Russia's presence in Chechnya. Over 1,100 people were taken hostage, including 370 children. On the third day of the standoff, Russian Special Forces stormed the school, killing 334 of the hostages. Many aspects of the crisis are still disputed, though it is widely seen as having consolidated the shift toward authoritarianism in Putin's Russia (Judah 2013, 82–84; Phillips 2008).

I don't know, how can I say? I grew up in Shurab, you know, ours was an international town. There were Russians, Tatars, Tajiks, Kyrgyz—three schools; eight mines working. A mining town, you know, it had its own Moscow Provisioning [*özünün moskovskoe obespechenie boldu*]. They sent things direct from Moscow, things you couldn't even get in Isfara! So, well, you know, Russia—there was a connection [*bailanysh bolchu ele*].

For Altynai, holding a collection for Beslan was an assertion of her own, quite conscious "feeling" (*sezim*) of internationalism, the result of having grown up in the multiethnic mining town of Shurab, with its multiple lines of connection to Moscow. Altynai was born in 1975, and at the time of our conversation was single-handedly raising three young children. Her husband worked as a casual laborer on a construction site south of Moscow, "cleaning the ground" (*jerdi tazalat*) as the euphemism for dacha-demolition went, to make way for three-story brick villas for Moscow's new rich. The connection invoked here by Altynai was subtly different from that described by Kanysh-ai: an affective link born of provisioning, and of small-town internationalism. But there was also an ambivalent cadence here: the feeling of connection persisted to the present, even as the provisioning itself was firmly confined to the past. Altynai went on to describe the town as it existed in the present:

Today the water doesn't reach [*suu jetpeit*] and they have to get water from down the mine. Only elderly [Russian] women [*starushki*] are left now and alcoholics. And Tajiks from Surh who can't get land, but they only live there in winter, since you can't grow anything.[9] It's a desert now that the mines have stopped and the water no longer reaches. It's like Afghanistan now! And we used to get things from Moscow, clean, clean [things]. People would come from Batken just to look at the shops!

Shurab was now defined for Altynai by its absences—of people, water, items for sale. What persisted were the legacies of a certain kind of "upbringing" (*vospitanie*), which gave the Shurabtsy an advantage in Russia's radically

---

[9]Several government-led initiatives, the latest of them launched in 2010, have sought to resettle land-poor families from Chorkuh and Surh, in the Tajik part of the Isfara Valley, to Shurab. See, for instance, the decree of the government of Tajikistan no. 530 on October 1: "O vnutrennei migratsii trudosposobnogo naseleniia iz malozemel′nykh i gustonaselennykh gornykh raionov v doliny respubliki, imeiushchie zalezhnye zemli na 2010–2012 gody." By encouraging immigration into Shurab and providing new workplaces with the UNDP support, the hope is that Shurab will repopulate and regain its urban identity, while the periodic tensions arising from land shortage in Chorkuh and Surh, twelve kilometers away, will be eased. The "resettlers" have been celebrated in a UNDP press release (2011) as "pioneers" who are "bravely making slow but certain steps towards a fresh and a brighter future for them and their future generations."

Disused train engine, Shurab mine, March 2008.

unpredictable informal economy. Slipping imperceptibly from the movement of water and goods to that of family members in Russia, she continued her reflection:

> Well, thank-goodness there were all those Russian teachers, that we grew up with Russian children. It meant we knew Russian too. Yesterday, they brought back my brother's youngest son, he'd been in Moscow for two and a half years. If you go [to work in Russia] and you look like you literally don't know anything well, they're going to hassle you, aren't they!? But the Shurabtsy are OK [in Russia]. Confident. An international town, after all. So maybe, maybe just because [of this] I still have, you know . . . feel . . . that connection [with Beslan].[10]

With its abandoned coal mines perched among the iron-red rock just a few miles north of Ak-Tatyr, Shurab epitomizes in stark and tragic form the legacy

---

[10]A former resident of Shurab, born there in 1985 and now studying in the United States, expressed a similar sentiment in a 2010 interview about the town where he had grown up. "Russians are amazed, [asking] why you are different, why are you so unlike the other migrants from Tajikistan, and you speak Russian without an accent? In reply [people from Shurab] don't even know how to answer. Because, it's in their roots, you see, having a wide worldview and so forth. That's why they are different. If you speak with a native Shurabets you'll be convinced of this yourself" (Rasul-zade 2010b).

of Soviet ideology of differential incorporation: an ideology of "Moscow provisioning." It is a vision in which distance can be dramatically overcome, with goods and people migrating from the center to particular, selected, provisioned parts of the periphery. It did not matter that towns such as Shurab were conceived on sites that had no obvious water supply or, like the mercury mine in nearby Aidarken, were constructed at 2,000 meters above sealevel on poorly irrigated, earthquake-prone mountainside. Such towns would be provided for—natural barriers of location would be overcome through technology, space would be transformed, distance rendered irrelevant. Such is the logic of *obespechenie*, a term of provision, but also of incorporation. It suggests not just supply (of food, goods, or security), but enclosure: linguistically *ob* implies a circular movement, the containment of an object that is enclosed, incorporated, and transformed.[11]

To have *Moskovskoe obespechenie* is not simply an indication of being materially well resourced; nor does it refer only to the kind of generalized benefits, salary additions (*nadbavki*), and compensatory payments that were enjoyed by Soviet employees in a variety of exceptionally cold, high, or remote sites. Rather, it conveyed a certain kind of cultural and aesthetic connection—of the "center in the periphery," of Moscow multiplying outward and creating a direct and specific link to chosen settlements that existed as urban "pools" largely independent of the surrounding landscape. This dedicated provisioning as a mountainous coal town meant that Shurab's water was pumped uphill over several dozen kilometers and that it was supplied with a dedicated artery of the main train line that ran through the valley to extract the coal. But it was also reflected in architectural styles, in the provision of books and school uniforms from Moscow, and even—as Altynai recalled—in the quality of underwear on sale in the town's state-run stores.

Perhaps the most striking marker of this variegated space, however, was the fact that the town's mine-driven growth from the 1950s on spread across the border of the Kyrgyz and Tajik SSRs in a way that undermined the notional sovereignty of Soviet Union republics. This was the vision of a centripetal state (Widdis 2003, 193). The mine may be technically in the Tajik SSR, but it is "of and for" the Union as a whole, and if the coal seam stretched down into Kyrgyz territory, so would the mine workings. In the words of one Russian commentator, indeed, these connections meant that Shurab was quite literally a "little Russian island" (*eto byl russkii "ostrovok"*) (Rotar' 2003): a term

---

[11]See also Widdis's (2000, 404–405) discussion of another characteristically Soviet form of incorporation—as simultaneous annexation and mastery—*osvoenie*.

that condenses at once a place (Russia), a people (Russians), and an aesthetic that set the town apart from the world around it.

There are multiple ironies today to the proud internationalism of Shurabtsy such as Altynai. First, there are the dramatic limits on Altynai's own movement. For all her sense of "connection," Altynai is one of many women who married into Ak-Tatyr from Shurab in the 1990s and who, a decade later, remained ineligible for a Kyrgyz passport and thus effectively unable to leave the country. Although she was entitled to receive a passport after seven years of residence, most of this period of residence was undocumented and hence invisible to stately practices of spatial accounting. When she married in 1994, she did not unregister from Tajikistan, which meant that her residence registration (*propiska*) indicated her home to be in Shurab long after her Tajik passport had expired. At that time, she had not anticipated crossing borders, and since a *propiska* made little difference to the entitlements that she received as mother and teacher in Kyrgyzstan, she had not rushed to reregister in Ak-Tatyr. Only when her husband, a year after leaving home, suggested that she might join him in Moscow did Altynai try to obtain a Kyrgyz passport. It was then that she learned that she would have to wait five more years before she could document her status as citizen.

An even greater irony is the fate of once centrally provisioned towns like Shurab. Evidence for the pervasive narrative of decline that seems to accompany any mention of the town is not hard to find. Its official population of 4,800 is less than one-third of its late Soviet peak of 16,000, and recent reports suggest that one-quarter of the remaining population live in the town on paper but not in person, spending most months of the year as labor migrants in Russia (Valiev 2006). Approaching the town from Ak-Tatyr, red iron-rich rocks give way to a scene of plundered buildings, with the twisted metal innards of reinforced concrete the only clue to the buildings that once stood there. The bricks have long been taken by homebuilders from neighboring villages, or bought up in bulk by masons from nearby Isfara. The mines that at one time employed 80 percent of the working-age population and at its height at the end of the 1970s extracted a million tons of coal per year now employ just over 100 people and output has declined to less than 1 percent of its 1978 peak (Rasul-zade 2010a).

It is the lack of water that is the most frequently invoked metric of Shurab's decline. The thirty-two-kilometer-long water pipe that had been built to water the town, which starts in Vorukh and now tacks back and forth between the jurisdiction of Tajikistan and Kyrgyzstan, has been the target of multiple informal appropriations by the string of villages that lie along its length. Once the state's pipe, it is now nobody's and everybody's. Small

Abandoned urban homes, Shurab, March 2004.

diversionary pipes and drainage systems (*vodootvody*) siphon off water, with 207 liters per second intended to reach the town, but in practice barely 15 do. In the urban multilevel houses, which once had functioning indoor plumping, water was "given" (as the Shurab expression goes) for only ten minutes per day by 2004. By the end of the decade, this supply dried up entirely during the summer months, and Shurabtsy came to rely almost exclusively on rainwater or tanked drinking water purchased at considerable expense.[12]

This story of urban economic decline has analogues in "structurally adjusted" sites across the globe. Mine closure is far from being a uniquely post-Soviet story. But the ambition with which the Soviet state, in industrializing, sought to transform *space*, gives such sites a particular poignancy. Brown has noted of the abandoned villages around the Chernobyl reactor—perhaps the most ambitious instance of modernist remaking of space—that the fact that the nuclear reactor was built in one of the least industrialized regions of Europe "only brings into sharper relief the determined arc of twentieth-century progress" and the silences it leaves in its wake (2004, 227). Chernobyl, like Shurab, materialized in its architecture and infrastructure the variegated provisioning

---

[12]In 2011 families who had been resettled from Surh into "new" (that is, previously abandoned) apartments paid around $5 for 200 liters of water; this is around one-fifth of an average monthly state salary.

through which the Soviet state was spatialized. It is this very disjuncture that makes Shurab so eerily quiet today: a relic, not just to a mine that has closed, but to a vision of a world inherently malleable, to the overcoming of distance and to "leaps" in time. For the people who once lived and worked there, it is precisely the spatial distanciation of once "connected" towns that is felt so acutely.

In Altynai's recollection this separation was captured in the proliferation of spatial referents: of goods and water "not reaching"; of the shift from Moscow to "Afghanistan" as a point of comparison; of people from Surh being forced in to Shurab by shortages of land and of the "locals" (*mestnye*) unable to leave because their homes are now worthless. Precisely because *Moskovskoe obespechenie* went beyond mere material benefits to include the very architecture of the town, it is these aesthetic transformations that signal its decline more than any mere drop in coal production. For the group of middle-age Ak-Tatyr women who joined in Altynai's reminiscences, it was flower beds, stucco buildings, and "civilized" shops that symbolized the town's modernity. For a visiting Russian journalist in 2003 these same markers of former glory signaled the town's decline from a "Russian island" into a war zone:

> When you arrive in Shurab today, you get the impression that the town has been attacked by mass raids from enemy aviation: the ruins of homes, rare and rag-clad people glance anxiously at the newcomer. Only the half-erased signs—club, shop, House of Culture—remind one of a time when in this fearful place there was another life entirely . . . A three-room apartment in Shurab costs about 150 Russian rubles . . . The former town park, which at one-time the Shurabtsy were so proud of, has now turned into a pasture for cows. (Rotar′ 2003)[13]

Perhaps the greatest irony is that the very people who were seen as embodying the town's progressiveness—the predominantly Russophone, predominantly immigrant "stokers" (*kochegary*) and their families—are now invoked with regard to the town's failure. For Altynai it was the proliferation of ethnically marked sex work that symbolized this decline. Russian women "who can't get out," she told me, were "selling themselves" to Tajik men to pay their way to Russia: a visibly gendered manifestation of emergent inequalities that was having a damaging impact on ethnic relations among the town's remaining population.

---

[13]A similar set of images was invoked by a *New York Times* reporter visiting Shurab: "Near the center of town, a restaurant looks as if it had been hit by a bomb. The roof is gone and there is no glass in the windows. The floor lies deep in rubble and an ornate column sprawls across the porch. Murals of dancing women in flowing dresses remain startlingly vibrant" (Frantz 2000b).

It is in this context that we should interpret the pathos and poignancy of the collection for the children of Beslan that September evening. For Altynai, as perhaps, too, for her fellow colleagues, the concert in Ak-Tatyr was more than just a gesture of sympathy for distant others. Burul-Ejeke, in introducing the collection on the grounds that "Russia provides for us," was nonetheless acutely aware of the legal entanglements, personal tragedies, and raw exploitation that such provision often entailed. The act of assisting Beslan is best understood as the reflection of an abiding affective relation to an extensive Soviet space, and a commitment to the kind of internationalism that Altynai understood to be constitutive of her identity. Holding the collection was not simply a reactive gesture, but a generative one: it is through such practices that a particular geography of imagined connection was articulated and sustained, even as the practical obstacles of reaching Russia had multiplied considerably in the preceding years.

Such connections are asymmetrical and they are not without irony. The reality of profound structural inequality between a Russia that is still imagined as "ours" and the steady stream of undocumented and readily exploitable Central Asian labor was stark, and it did not go unnoticed by people from Ak-Tatyr. Migrant workers from the former Soviet south typically undertake work that is low-paid, physically demanding, undocumented, and liable to sudden termination (in the local idiom, of being "thrown" [*kidat etti*] from work [Reeves 2013]). Raids on workplaces to check for irregular migrants are common, and campaigns to rid Russia of "illegals" (*nelegaly*) have come to constitute the acceptable face of the Russian far right.[14] The precariousness of life in Russia, one recently deported man told me, would "show you what was written on your forehead" (*mandaiga jazylganyn körösün*). Fate could be fickle in Russia. Indeed, if the villagers of Ak-Tatyr needed any reminding of the gulf between imagined geographies and the reality of categorical inequality, it was brought home when at least ten Ak-Tatyr men arrived home with five-year deportation stamps in their passports, caught in a Moscow raid on undocumented migrants prompted by the very tragedy in north Ossetia for which the school teachers had been collecting money. Grasping the shifting terrains of practical distance for Altynai and her fellow villagers entails attending to these inequalities and the languages of "(il)legality" through which they are reproduced. It also demands taking seriously the reality of continued affective connection, and the multiple past provisionings through which it is sustained.

---

[14]In the mid-2000s many of Russia's far right groups campaigned specifically on an antiimmigrant or "antiillegals" platforms, fusing xenophobic sentiment with the concern for law and order (see Zuev 2010).

Feeding Gorky

Altynai's nostalgia for an age of *Moskovskoe obespechenie* reflects the loss of a particular kind of relation and a particular dynamic of incorporation between center and periphery. In her account, one site was quite emphatically provisioned by the other. Yet for many of her neighbors from Ak-Tatyr, particularly for the privileged group of older men who had regularly traveled to Russia during summer months to sell apricots grown on private plots, provisioning and dependence was in no sense unidirectional. Several older men talked of how "we used to provide Gorky with fruit"—a reference to the Russian city where a whole generation of Ak-Tatyr men used to travel in the summer months with truckloads of fresh and dried apricots. Even the younger generation of Ak-Tatyr teenagers, who are far more likely to be working as undocumented builders than they are trading apricots in the market, still refer to what is today Nizhnii Novgorod by its long-abandoned Soviet name, Gorky.

In the Sokh Valley, other destinations figured in the stories and recollections of *mahalla* men, but the sense that "*we* were provisioning *them*," as Khurshed's reminder about the Sokh men who beat the cosmonauts to Mars, was if anything even more pronounced. Trading links with the Siberian cities of Omsk, Tomsk, Ulyanovsk, Penza, Irkutsk, Novosibirsk, and Barnaul had developed as early as the 1960s (see table 3.1). Even under Brezhnev, the relative shortage of collective farm land and dramatic population growth in the Sokh Valley had meant that apricots grown on private plots and sold in distant markets represented a substantial contribution to domestic incomes. For a generation of middle-aged Sokh men, participation in annual trading trips to the kolkhoz markets of Siberia, like military service in the Soviet army, fostered an intense affective association with Soviet cities several days' travel away.

Khojai Shamolov, an elder of Sokh's Chorbog *mahalla*, was one of the first men in the valley to meet the substantial costs of the hajj through his successful apricot business. As we paced the orchards above his home he took me on a verbal tour of his past travels, recounting with pride how his *mahalla* (and his extended family in particular) had come to dominate the apricot trade in the city of Ulyanovsk over the course of thirty years. In the 1970s, he had persuaded the directors of the Sokh sovkhoz where he worked to allow him to plant apricot trees on a stretch of stony and abandoned mountainside. The land was given to him for free and he still does not pay taxes on it, even though the trees there can yield several tons of apricots in a good year. As we walked along the steep ridge leading from his orchards to the simple wooden

TABLE 3.1
Primary destinations in Russia for migrant workers from Sokh and Ak-Tatyr, 2005

Destination	Percentage of migrant workers
Sokh district, Uzbekistan[a]	
Irkutsk	50.9
Novosibirsk	10.3
Barnaul	5.9
Tomsk	5.5
Penza	4.0
Ufa	3.7
Kazan	2.9
Gornoaltaisk	2.6
Ulyanovsk	2.6
Ak-Tatyr village district[b]	
Moscow	67.9
Nizhnii Novgorod (Gorky)	19.8
St. Petersburg	4.6
Samara	2.3
Moscow region	1.5

Source: Author's survey data, March and June–July 2005.
[a]$n = 282$
[b]$n = 132$

hut where he spends the summer months guarding his crop, he told me about the webs of connections that have made Ulyanovsk come to feel like his "second motherland" (*vtoraia rodina*).

July we live here, up in the dacha, preparing the fruit. I fix up a generator so that we can even watch television when we're up here. Then August and, *hop*! I'm off again for another month. I go there now for a rest by the Volga! Really, Ulyanovsk has become my rest home [*dom otdykha*].

Khojai Shamolov has been traveling to Ulyanovsk since the mid-1970s. In the early days, when he would trade at one of the designated kolkhoz markets, he used to appeal to the directors of Chorbog school, where he still teaches, to allow him to travel during the semester, especially before New Year's and the March International Women's Day celebrations, when demand for his dried apricots would be particularly high. At that time he was able to generate enough personal income from two weeks' trading to provide for his family for the year. "In those days it was easy—no [customs] posts, one passport, go wherever you like [*ezhai kuda khochesh´*]." With the collapse of the Soviet Union and a brief relaxation of import barriers, he began buying and selling cars—"herding back Zhigulis" as he put it, referring to the iconic Soviet car, before the import duties made this trade prohibitively expensive.

Nowadays Khojai Shamolov makes fewer journeys, but his extended presence has given him a foot in the city's lucrative wholesale market. There he spends mornings selling apricots from the back of his cavernous Kamaz truck to an extended network of relatives and neighbors who work as suppliers (*postavshchiki*) to Russian or Tatar traders throughout the city's bazaars. Trading directly is harder now, he told me, if you don't have a local *propiska*. I asked if he faced problems from the local police. "Sometimes our younger lads are stopped," he said. "But in Ulyanovsk there are fewer problems for us than in other Russian cities. The local police know Chorbog better than they know Tashkent! And anyway, they know that they wouldn't be able to conduct their *pominki* [funeral wakes] if they didn't let us trade in peace. The [locals] like our apricots too much!"

We continued walking up the ridge above Khojai Shamolov's dacha until we could see the Sokh River and the flat basin of the Ferghana Valley stretching out in a brown ribbon into the distance. The Alay Mountains were still capped in snow, even as the more sheltered trees in Chorbog showed the first flecks of spring green. As the fruit trees gave way to open pasture, and we paused to catch our breath, Khojai Shamolov gestured back to the peaks that framed the scene, then swung his arm around to bring in the Sokh Valley below and the flat expanses beyond. "Over there we have Kyshtut, then Zardaly, and after that it is already Tajikistan," he said, pointing to the mountains behind us. "But you know, although Afghanistan and Iran are closer to us and we understand their language, still Russia draws us somehow. If it weren't for the fact that I carry my father's name [*ia imenets otsa*]," he added, referring to the Sokh tradition that gave the named son a position of particular authority and responsibility for the family's welfare, "I would have long ago moved to Russia or Belarus, where I did military service."

The connections between Chorbog *mahalla* and Ulyanovsk that Khojai Shamolov had helped forge and on which a large part of his community depends are a particularly striking example of the kinds of cross-cutting dependencies that connect apricot-growing villages with particular cities throughout Siberia and European Russia. Market trading, in particular, is a realm of specific and jealously guarded connections. For Khojai Shamolov, this very specificity was a source of pride: that the Ulyanovsk police know Chorbog, with its population of 1,500, "better than they know Tashkent"; that virtually all the dried fruits consumed in that city "come from this one corner of the Ferghana Valley"; and that he in particular had come to look on Ulyanovsk as a second home where he was able to spend his afternoons strolling the banks of the Volga. Yet this very specificity of relations could also be a source of frustration, between neighboring *mahallas* and also between generations. When I later told Parviz, my host in Sokh, about the conversation that I had had with Khojai Shamolov, his response was terse: "Yes, their elders won't let anyone other than their own within 100 meters of the bazaar; they've taken over the entire place there. Monopolized. If anyone from Dehkonobod turned up there to try to get a trading place, they'd let him work for two or three days, then they'd let it be known that he'd better move on."

More important, the kind of identification with Russia as a "second motherland" that Khojai Shamolov articulated so vigorously—rooted in linguistic and cultural fluency, decades of travel, military service, and relative economic security—by 2005 was under increasing strain. The market trade that he was able to enjoy was now the preserve of a well-connected and affluent minority. When families spoke about sons having "gone to town," the reference was typically to construction sites rather than to markets, to work that was undocumented and insecure (see tables 3.2 and 3.3). Khojai Shamolov's generation had traveled to Russia and traded there as fellow citizens. His son's generation were much more likely to find themselves, often involuntarily, falling within the category of "illegal immigrants." When I asked one recently returned migrant from Ak-Tatyr how he had survived for months without a registration document in a city that is extensively policed, his response was simply "*biz Moskvada körönböibüz*" ("in Moscow we can't be seen"). Sleeping in railway wagons, dachas, and the partially constructed buildings on which working days are spent, the "new" labor migrants had a different and altogether sharper experience of city life from the cohort of established market traders who had carved out routes to Russia a generation before.

TABLE 3.2

Principle type of position occupied during most recent period of work in Russia

	District (%)	
Role	Sokh[a]	Ak-Tatyr[b]
Director of a firm	0.4	0
Intermediary	1.4	0.8
Private business/trade	15.2	12.3
Brigadier/skilled laborer	9.6	2.3
Unskilled laborer	71.6	80.8
Other	1.4	3.8

Source: Author's survey data, March and June–July 2005.
[a]$n = 282$
[b]$n = 132$

TABLE 3.3
Principle sphere of occupation during most recent period of work in Russia

Occupation	District (%)	
	Sokh[a]	Ak-Tatyr[b]
Construction		
Private building site	47.6	33.6
Commercial building site	6.7	19.5
State-owned building site	22.9	14.8
Total	**77.1**	**68.0**
Trade		
Market (dried fruit)	12.5	13.3
Market (fresh fruit)	4.8	0
Market (other)	0.7	0.8
Shop	0	2.3
Total	**18.0**	**16.4**
Catering	0.4	5.5
Service sector	0.7	5.5
Transport	1.1	0.8
Industry	0.7	0.8
Agriculture	1.1	1.6
Other	0.7	1.6

Source: Author's survey data, March and June–July 2005.
[a]$n = 282$
[b]$n = 132$

Going to Town

This gulf between the experiences of different cohorts and categories of labor migrant meant that by 2004–2005, conversations about the possibilities and risks associated with "going to town" were frequent, emotively charged, and often intensely polarized. Mass migrations of young men are perhaps always interwoven with ambivalence about the stakes of protracted absence. Marsden has described poignantly the moral assessments of work "down country" among Rowshan's Muslim men in northern Pakistan, seen as at once "character building" and "demeaning and painful" (2005, 80). In urban Bombay, Hansen has explored the pervasive discourse of moral decay surrounding migration to the Gulf states with its associated displacements of existing status hierarchies (2001, 169–171). It is not surprising that labor migration to Russia, at once profoundly exploitative and with the potential to transform family fortunes, should be the subject of intense moral debate in the Ferghana Valley borderlands, inviting reflection not just on the shifting meanings of life "over there," but on the stagnating local economy, and the obstacles to legal cross-border trade closer to home (Isabaeva 2011; Reeves 2011c, 2012; Remtilla 2010).

In order to grasp the particular significance of this long-distance migration, and its impact on local patterns of mobility, it is worth exploring for a moment its sociological particulars. By the mid-2000s, remittances from Russia were overwhelmingly the single largest source of family incomes for the villages of the Sokh and Isfara valleys, and the difference between what could be made from working a season in Russia and what could be earned locally was vast. In the summer of 2005, a mathematics teacher from Ak-Tatyr school with twenty-five years' teaching experience and a double teaching load would still be earning six or seven times less than he would as an unskilled laborer

Announcement in a Sokh shop window advertising weekly buses from Sokh to Moscow and cities throughout Siberian Russia, February 2005.

(*kara jumushchi*) on a Moscow construction site.[15] This disparity was having serious consequences for local schools, as it was widely acknowledged to be the educated, Russian-speaking, outgoing young men who were above all eager to earn a better living in town.[16] It was also felt to be reversing the normative relationship between education level and earning potential. As we took the bus together from Batken back to his home in Ak-Sai, Jengish, then a third-year university student in Batken, joked about his predicament as one of only a handful of his former school cohort who had decided to persevere with studies instead of leaving for Moscow:

> What does the student who used to get "twos" [*dvoechnik* ("F" student)] now have? A car and an apartment. What does the student who used to get "threes" [*troechnik* ("C" student)] now have? A car, an apartment, and a dacha! And what does the student who used to get "fives" [*otlichnik* ("A" student)] now have? Debts, fines, fears, illness, and hopelessness.

Jengish recounted this in jest and with more than a hint of pride that he was, despite his precarious financial predicament, still the student who got excellent grades. A year later, however, the differential with his former classmates who had returned with money to build homes and pay for weddings had become, as he put it, a source of embarrassment (*uiat*) and Jengish, too, left for Moscow, suspending his university studies. In the summer of 2006, when I traveled from Bishkek to Moscow by train, I experienced this bittersweet of life "in town" firsthand: it was Jengish who met me at Moscow's Kazan station, on his way to a twelve-hour shift cleaning shopping carts at a supermarket. As we rode the city's metro together, trading news about friends in Batken, Jengish's comments swung between the exhilaration and despair that he felt by turns in Moscow. He was managing to save money, and was navigating his way in Russian, a language that he had previously understood but not spoken. But walking the streets near his home he always felt like a "deer in the headlights" running to stay unchecked by the Moscow militia, unsure which way to leap. "Even if you don't get physically exhausted in Moscow, you will be morally exhausted [*moral´no charchasyng*]. Guaranteed."

---

[15]An unskilled laborer from Ak-Tatyr working on a construction site in Moscow in the summer of 2005 could hope to earn around 9,000 rubles (about $300) per month. With a double teaching load, a teacher in the "highest category" could earn $56.

[16]One local principal complained that in 2005 that he had lost one-third of his teachers to migration in the preceding three years. I explore the impact of labor migration on schooling in Ak-Tatyr in Reeves (2006).

Survey data flatten out the complex calculations and personal dilemmas that lie behind any single decision to migrate. But they do enable us to situate those decisions within the context of broader political and economic dynamics and thus to attend to the concrete patterns of mobility and enclosure that risk being obscured in more generalizing discussions of globalization (Cunningham and Heyman 2004). The survey I conducted in the spring and summer of 2005 in the Sokh and Isfara valleys suggests that 58 percent of households surveyed in Ak-Tatyr and neighboring Kyrgyz-majority villages of the Isfara Valley had sent at least one family member to Russia in search of work in the previous five years (see table 3.4).

In the Sokh Valley, by contrast, 78 percent of families had sent one or more family member to Russia in search of work during the preceding five years, with a further 8 percent of households deriving their income directly from the labor trade as bus drivers, intermediaries, or providing informal banking services. The relative novelty of migration as a livelihood strategy is as striking as its scale. In the Isfara Valley more than 85 percent of the migrant households surveyed first began sending family members to Russia only since 2000 (see table 3.5). Of the remainder, the majority (9.4%) were families with "historical migrants": primarily older men who traveled to Russia's kolkhoz markets during Soviet times to sell apricots from collectively owned trees.

TABLE 3.4
Summary of comparative demographic and migration data from Sokh and Ak-Tatyr

	District	
	Sokh[a]	Ak-Tatyr[b]
Total number of households surveyed (including both migrant and nonmigrant households)	361	225
Total number of households with at least one family member traveling to Russia in search of work	282	132
Mean household size (all adults and children eating together [bir qazan])	6.60	6.20
Mean number of adults per household	3.26	3.22
Mean number of children per household	3.29	2.98
Number of adults working in Russia per 100 adults at the time of survey	16.40 (March)	14.60 (June–July)
% of household sending at least one family member to Russia in the previous five years	78.10	57.60
Proportion of adults at the time of survey (%)		
with full-time paid employment	25.80	17.90
with ad hoc paid employment	7.90	7.30
without paid employment	66.40	74.80

Source: Author's survey data, March and June–July 2005.
[a]$n = 361$
[b]$n = 225$

Table 3.5
Year of first departure to Russia in search of work at the time of survey (2005)

| | District (%) | |
Year	Sokh[a]	Ak-Tatyr[b]
Before 1991	10.7	9.4
1991–1993	5.0	1.6
1994–1996	3.1	0.8
1997–1999	13.2	2.3
2000–2002	37.1	36.7
Since 2003	30.8	49.2

Source: Author's survey data, March and June–July 2005.
[a]$n = 282$
[b]$n = 132$

Acute shortages of irrigated land in the Sokh Valley, relatively lower rates of livestock ownership, and the difficulties of deriving a profitable income from cooperatively owned land in Uzbekistan mean that migration to Russia began rather earlier here.[17] But the trend toward labor migration as a *mass* phenomenon and primary source of family income can be dated to the turn of the millennium. Throughout the Sokh and Isfara valleys, income from Russia has come to sustain domestic incomes and underwrite ritual expenses in fundamental ways. Indeed, many young men would stress that the only way that they could now afford to get married or conduct a circumcision ceremony for their sons (*tūii sunnati* in Tajik; *sünnöt toi* in Kyrgyz) was to spend two or three seasons working in Russia.

The data from the survey I conducted in 2005 demonstrates a further feature of migration that is the source of considerable moral commentary: its gendered nature. From the Kyrgyz-majority villages of the Isfara Valley, one in seven migrants (14.8%) is female and there seems to be a general trend toward more family migration, in which husband and wife both work in Russia, leaving children behind in the care of grandparents or older siblings.

[17]During my research, a transformation in the administration of formerly collectively owned lands was underway, as cooperatives (*shirkats*) that were the successor to Soviet state and collective farms were being transformed into smaller private farmer (*fermer*) enterprises. All land remained owned by the state, however, with individuals leasing land and obligated to deliver a certain volume of a given crop each year. In Sokh, individual tenant farmers often looked enviously upon their Kyrgyz neighbors, who owned their own land, often had larger land plots (especially at the southern end of the Sokh Valley) and could choose which crops to grow. As Trevisani (2007, 91) notes, "in rural Uzbekistan the creation of insecurity, be it via 'structural' system shortcomings or through outright intimidation of the producers, appears to be a calculated means of state building."

Green money: circumcision ceremony (*tūii sunnati*) for Parviz's nephew, paid for with remittances from Omsk. Dehkonobod *mahalla,* Sokh Valley, December 2004.

Conversely, the proportion of female migrants from the Sokh Valley is fewer than one in fifty (1.8%) and many respondents reiterated that Russia was no place for "our women." The resultant gender imbalance often invites comparison with the wartime departure of men to the front and women to the fields (compare Heathershaw 2009, 168–169; Ikromov 2006b). When I showed pictures of women in Sokh caking bricks for an absent brother's home to one local man, he smiled and, harking at once to the authoritative codes of the Soviet ethnographic textbook and the ubiquitous slogans in Uzbekistan, read out with studied seriousness an imaginary caption to accompany the image: "Women build the state with a great future!"[18]

This regendering of work is more complex, and more ambiguous, however, than a simple appearance of female labor in sites that were previously seen as the domain of men. Life in Russia is itself complexly gendered. The work on construction sites is archetypically male, and a "season" abroad has become

---

[18]A play on the widespread official slogan: "Uzbekistan is a state with a great future" (*O'zbekiston—kelajagi buyuk davlat*). See Yurchak (1997, 178) on the "pretense misrecognition" of the official slogan under late socialism.

"Women Build the State with a Great Future!" House building, Dehkonobod *mahalla,* Sokh Valley, August 2005.

crucial now to fund the lifecycle rituals that enable one to reach mature man-
hood (Reeves 2010a). The realities of profound economic marginalization
mean that men are also taking on jobs once regarded as exclusively female:
washing clothes, baking bread, and cooking meals. Moreover, there is an
acute—and often sharply articulated—awareness among return migrants of
the extent to which migration dehumanizes. Many spoke of spending a night
in the *obez´iannik* (lit. the monkey house)—an urban detention facility used
for pretrial detention of suspected criminals whose name captures at once
its physical form and the kinds of dehumanizing (and often explicitly racialized) humiliation with which it had come to be associated in the public imagination (see also Gladarev 2011; Rushchenko 2005). One elderly man spoke
passionately about the experience of being treated "worse than dogs" by a

rude and exploitative employer building a new pet-care facility in Moscow's upscale Rublevka district.

Comparisons with animals, of course, are not unusual in settings of profoundly exploitative labor. Like languages of slavery, they are fertile metaphors for talking about physical work and of the differential capacity to speak and be heard (see also Hartman 2011, 91–128). But animal talk also does other kinds of symbolic work. Animals speak to *categorical* differences and their production. And in the context of Central Asian labor migration to Russia, it is precisely this element of social classification that such comparisons convey: what De Genova in a US context has evocatively called "the legal production of migrant 'illegality'" (2002, 419). Consider again Jengish's reference to feeling like a "deer" caught in the headlights or the fact that "moral exhaustion" is more trying than the physical exhaustion of twelve-hour shifts in a supermarket basement. What tires is the fundamental uncertainty about a predicament "before law": of making a living in a documentary regime that fosters and normalizes migrant illegality. Jengish, like the majority of his compatriots from Ak-Tatyr, was living an undocumented (or, more accurately, a fictively hyper-documented) life: reliant on undocumented work and fake residence registrations; liable to deportation. This fact is of crucial importance for understanding the shifting meanings of Russia as an affective space for the younger generation of migrants from Sokh and Ak-Tatyr. Before elaborating this claim further, it is worth delving into both the documentary regime that existed in 2004–2005 and the political economy of migrant labor to explore how this condition of deportability arises in practice.

"Clean Fake": The Economics of Invisibility

Citizens of Kyrgyzstan and Uzbekistan do not need visas to enter Russia, and if they are in possession of a migration card and a temporary residence registration, they are entitled to live in Russia for up to ninety days. Remaining longer depends on having documented work and an accompanying work permit. Whereas entering the country is relatively straightforward, remaining legally legible is extremely difficult. The system of temporary residence registration (a carryover from the Soviet system of internal regulation of movement, or *propiska* system) requires that the new arrival in the city register his or her presence with the local authorities within seventy-two hours. But only certain sites are officially recognized as a place of residence: a hotel is recognized, and so is a private apartment, as long as there are no more than a specified number of people per square meter of space.[19] In practice, however, the cost of real estate, particularly in urban centers, and the reluctance of landlords to formally register those not already in possession of a local registration means that it is extremely difficult for the newly arrived noncitizen to obtain an official registration at their place of residence. And for the significant proportion of migrants who live on the construction sites where they work, their place of residence falls entirely unrecognized within official record keeping.

A similar disjunction occurs between formal rules of labor hiring and what occurs in practice. In theory, both migrant and employer are liable to be fined for labor that is employed without a work permit (*razreshenie na rabotu*). In practice, because work permits entail taxes and uncompetitive wages, the majority of migrant labor is hired without contract, with payment not entered into any system. This is true, not just of the so-called private (*chastnye*) construction sites where a single laborer or a work brigade negotiate a deal directly with the owner of the site, but also of those instances where work is negotiated through an intermediary (*posrednik*) or on a large, commercial (*kommercheskii*) or state-run (*gosudarstvennyi*) site. As several Ak-Tatyr men pointed out to me, even the mayor of Moscow allegedly used uncontracted labor for various construction projects around the city.

Capturing the experiential blurriness of legal and illegal residence is notoriously problematic in a standardized survey—a methodology after all, premised on the production of finite categories. But the aggregate figures from Sokh and Ak-Tatyr do enable us to gain some insight into the obstacles to legal legibility faced by various categories of migrant. My 2005 survey (see table 3.6) suggests that only 22.9 percent of those who traveled from Sokh and 10.9 percent from Ak-Tatyr were in possession of a work permit during their most recent visit to Russia, and fewer than one in seven from both groups of villages had a written contract (14.5 percent and 10.3 percent respectively).

This invisibility of labor was often coupled with a "home" that was entirely invisible to official state record keeping. From Sokh, almost two-thirds of migrants (63.5%) lived on the construction site where they worked, either in a railway wagon or the partially constructed building on which they were working at the time. From Ak-Tatyr, a relatively higher proportion lived in apartments shared with other labor migrants (46%, compared to 26.9% living on a construction site), but of all the respondents from Ak-Tatyr, fewer than half had a "clean" (*taza* [legal]) residence registration obtained through official channels, and of those in possession of a registration, only 22 percent

---

[19]The legal framework regulating labor migration to Russia is described in Moiseenko, Perevedentsev, and Voronina (1999); Mezhdunarodnaia organizatsiia po migratsii (2004).

TABLE 3.6
Migrants' legal legibility in Russia

Question beginning with, "During your last period of work in Russia,"	District (%)	
	Sokh[a]	Ak-Tatyr[b]
Were you in possession of some kind of temporary residence registration for at least part of your stay in Russia?		
Yes	55.7	60.3
Sometimes	9.8	2.4
No	33.4	27.3
If in possession of a residence registration was this		
"Clean," obtained through official channels	84.0	48.1 (Moscow = 32.6)
"Clean," obtained through unofficial channels	11.7	7.6 (Moscow = 9.3)
"Fake"	1.9	43.0 (Moscow = 58.1)
Don't know	2.5	1.3 (Moscow = 0)
Did you have a work permit (razreshenie na rabotu) in Russia?		
Yes	22.9	10.9
No	71.3	80.5
I didn't need one	5.4	8.6
What kind of agreement did you have with your employer?		
Written contract	14.5	10.3
Spoken agreement	60.5	59.5
An intermediary arranged the work for me	10.4	18.3
I had my own private business	14.6	10.3
No answer	0	1.6

[a]$n = 282$
[b]$n = 132$

lived permanently in the place where they were registered. Taken together, these figures suggest that 17 percent of those from Sokh and only 11 percent of those from Ak-Tatyr were "legible" to the state in the sense of being both formally registered and actually residing at their registration address.

The degree to which the Soviet state, and its contemporary successors, has defined personhood through papers is a point well made in critical literature on the region.[20] Less studied are the kinds of practice that such a situation provokes. In Russia, whole industries exist to provide what we might call "fictive visibility": a documented persona that enables the real person to get on with life unchecked. Such practices range from the small-scale and weakly institutionalized (such as the ad hoc selling of fake [fal'shivye] registration documents by Uzbek traders in Moscow's Kazan station) to large-scale

[20]See Matthews (1993) on the history of passportization in Russia; Baiburin (2012) on the social and symbolic importance of the passport in Soviet life; Höjdestrand (2009, 20–46) on the documentary production of the homeless (bomzh) in Russia and Humphrey (2002b) on becoming "dispossessed" through documentary failure.

operations specializing in the arrangement of *propiska*-granting "fictive marriages" [*fiktivnye braki*].[21] It is not surprising that return migrants frequently commented on the centrality of stately persona to this documentary economy. After all, in a context where certification is scarce, and security depends on it, the power of *propisanie*—a term that denotes both registration and prescription— is extensive and potentially lucrative (Reeves 2013).

This situation has two significant consequences. On the one hand, it can create sites of surprising intimacy and informality between those nominally regulating movement of people within the city (in particular the local [*uchastkovyi*] police officer responsible for a particular block) and the migrant to whom protection is being afforded. Migrants would often make small, regular payments to their local policeman to ensure that they remain "invisible." In Moscow, one common practice to avoid the risk of a passport being taken, checked, and stamped consisted of the local policeman issuing, for a fee, a document (*spravka*) attesting that the migrant's passport was *already* being held at his local police station. A fictive administrative offence, in other words, was used to enable the migrant to keep the real passport at home: policeman and migrant collaborating here in a double layer of documentary obfuscation to keep the real person illegible (and temporarily undeportable).

On the other hand, the intimate involvement of law enforcement in this economy of invisibility meant a profound blurring of the boundary between documented and undocumented presence in practice. During the numerous conversations I had with returned migrants about their experiences of getting to Russia and working there, it was this discursive blurring between the domains of the "official" and the "unofficial" that was often emphasized. In the course of one discussion about her work in Solaris, a commercial catering company, I asked Tahmina-Eje, a middle-age mother of six, about her registration in Moscow. Notable in her response was the slippage between the fake and the real thing:

> I had a *taza propiska*. When they [the police] ran it through their machine it went grrrr as though it were genuine. But really it was a clean fake [*taza farshivyi*] *propiska*. The *uchastkovyi* sold it to me for 1,500 rubles. He has a deal with a grandmother who lives in an apartment. He pays her to register us in her apartment and if the police from an-

---

[21]See, for instance the messages posted on www.delbrak.narod.ru, one of many such sites. "Delbrak" here indicates *delovoi brak*, that is "marriage for business."

other beat take me to their base and telephone her to check whether I live there, she always says "yes." That's what he pays her for. We are all ghost tenants.

What matters to Tahmina-Eje is the efficacy of her "clean fake" *propiska,* not the fact of being correctly inscribed. Moreover, it follows from the police's involvement in this economy of fictive documentation that the distinction between "fine" and "bribe" blurs in practice. When state personnel themselves have a stake in maintaining one's invisibility, the normative boundary between a legal and illegal fee dissolves to reveal the true status of the payment. It is simply the "rate" (*stavka*) and nothing more. Jyldyz, an articulate journalist who, in her Bishkek life, is professionally invested in upholding the domain of law through newspaper exposés of official corruption, struggled to define the boundary when it came to her life in Russia. She described in the following way the regular checks that occurred at the market where she sold clothes and household goods (*shmotki*) in Omsk:

JYLDYZ: The *stavka* used to be between ten and fifty rubles. As soon as [the police] catch you. You haven't got a *propiska.*

MADELEINE: And was that a fine, or a bribe?

JYLDYZ: Well . . . it was kind of both a fine and a bribe, you know? It's the same thing [*odno i to zhe*]. You haven't got a *propiska.* I had a ticket [that allowed me to live unregistered] for three days and a month had gone past. So you've got to give fifty rubles if you want to deal with it there and then [*razvesti na meste*]. If they take you to the GOM [city police department] . . . you'll have to pay the state one hundred rubles.

In his penetrating critique of migrant "illegality" and deportability in the United States, Nicholas De Genova has argued that the production of legal limbos for Mexican immigrants, analogous to those in which Tahmina-Eje, Jyldyz, and Jengish found themselves, is economically productive. The state of legal vulnerability in which the migrant finds herself, together with what is effectively a "revolving door" policy of deportation and reentry, is central (and not merely incidental) to the commoditization of Mexican labor in the United States (De Genova 2005, 213–249). De Genova's argument rests on a crucial distinction between actual deportation, and the (legal and existential) condition of deportability. The US economy, his argument runs, is fundamentally dependent on the latter, as agents of law-enforcement (and Mexican migrants themselves) are well aware.

This argument can only be extended to the post-Soviet context with caution. "Law enforcement," as we have seen, is less coordinated and integrated than De Genova's rather smooth model of state intentionality conveys.[22] What his argument powerfully does, however, is to draw attention to the fact that illegality is produced and sustained by particular economic and legal formations: it is "a juridical status that entails a social relation to the state" and as such is "a pre-eminently political identity" (2002, 422). In Russia, as in other post-Soviet states, the institution of the *propiska,* which effectively renders many labor migrants "illegal" within three days of their arrival, is crucial to this social production. It was this that made deportation (*deportatsiia*) loom as an ever-present threat; it was this that enabled intermediaries to "cheat" (*aldap ketet*) and employers to "throw" (*kidat´*) employees at the end of a job without paying them—a term that vividly mirrors the "disposable, deportable, ultimately temporary character" of Mexican labor described by De Genova (ibid., 248). Above all, it was this that made the police, as Tahmina-Eje put it, "always our first [topic of] conversation" when she was with her colleagues from Solaris.

Tahmina-Eje's reflections on her permanent state of uncertainty (she used the word *nervdengen* [on edge]) points to a second insight of De Genova's account: that deportability must be explored, not merely as a legal category but as an existential reality, one of "enforced orientation to the present" in which the future is fundamentally revocable (ibid., 427). The contingency of the future was a recurrent theme in the narratives of returned migrants. Actual deportations were, in fact, relatively rare (though, as we have seen with the Moscow raid following the Beslan tragedy, they could materialize suddenly and very powerfully at times of national emergency). But the threat of deportation and of being "thrown" from work was an ongoing source of concern.

This threat fosters and reinforces forms of categorical subordination: the fact, as one elderly Ak-Tatyr woman put it, referring to a grandson's work, that the Kyrgyz in Russia "are quieter than the lamb" (*koidon joosh*). It is, at one level, a mechanism for keeping labor cheap. But it also incites less dramatic, but no less salient, practices of everyday boundary work—ones that are becoming increasingly racialized in urban Russia. When labor migrants from the former Soviet south are known to be violating a registration regime in large numbers, it is not difficult to see how skin color comes to serve as a proxy for "illegality"; or how a relationship between the two can come to

---

[22]De Genova (2002) extends his argument to examples outside the United States, but he does not explore those situations where the parameters of state law are themselves opaque and contested. In other words, situations without a clear analogue to a smoothly integrated system of law enforcement enacting the wishes of the center.

be naturalized and normalized in public consciousness and administrative praxis (see also Malakhov 2001, 146–158; 2007).

As a technology of the state's inscription, the system of residence registration is patently failing. Only a small proportion of migrants from Sokh and Ak-Tatyr were actually living in the place where they were nominally registered, if indeed, they had a registration document at all. But as a technology of border work, the *propiska* has productive and powerful effects, not least for migrants themselves and for the homes and communities whose livelihoods they sustain. In the post-Soviet context, the administrative regimes associated with the regulation of migrant labor are critical, not just for the production of cheap, deportable labor in the way described by De Genova, but also for reconfiguring understandings of what it means to be a (non-)citizen or a deportable alien. It is in the multiple daily passport checks, the selective stopping of subway passengers, the differentiated practices of hiring and pay that categorical differences are inscribed, the citizen (as well as the "immigrant") made and unmade.

Bir Ele Passport Bolchu!—There Was Just One Passport!

The significance of the routine reconfiguration of belonging resulting from this condition of deportability for contemporary spatial imaginaries—for the practical distance between Moscow and Ak-Tatyr—was brought home vividly one summer afternoon in 2005. I was at the home of Abduvali, one of the Ak-Tatyr teachers to whom Burul-Ejeke had been referring during the previous September's concert when she commented on the members of her *kollektiv* currently working in Russia. As one of the newer, "unplanned" homes in a once-planned village, Abduvali's was one of the smaller constructions: a single adobe room that had only recently acquired a corrugated roof. I was there along with several village men and Abduvali's two children because it was also one of the few village homes in 2005 to have a satellite dish. We had gathered to watch a concert from Moscow's Red Square to celebrate the city's (ultimately unsuccessful) bid to host the 2012 Olympic Games. As we sat on mattresses gathered around the television, drinking Uzbek beer and watching a live broadcast from Moscow, there was much about the scene that could be inserted within a grand narrative of globalization: a snapshot to accompany a textbook story of "an increasingly interconnected world . . . where borders and boundaries have become increasingly porous" (Inda and Rosaldo 2002, 2).

But as with many smooth stories of globalization, there were bumps, uncomfortable ones. Abduvali had bought the satellite dish earlier in the year after being deported from Moscow. His wife was still there, making dumplings for a Moscow supermarket. He had bought the satellite dish to distract his children from their mother's absence—and perhaps also to compensate for his frustration at not being there with his wife and providing for his family. For, as he told, me ought still to be working: particularly now, during the height of the summer building season. He had been making good money there when a regular month-end "clean-up" (chistka) of cowboy construction sites had left him fingerprinted and criminalized with a five-year deportation stamp in his passport.

Our viewing of the Olympic bid broadcast from a city to which Abduvali was prohibited to return was shot through with the ambivalence of fractured and complex connections, of boundaries as limit points to movement that could suddenly and violently appear. The Moscow that we watched was, despite Abduvali's deportation, still a place of affective connection, for him as much as for any of the men in the room. We were watching the Moscow bid (rather than any of others that could have been accessed at that time through the dozens of satellite channels) because we wanted *them* to win. But as the conversation slipped at the end of the concert from music to life in town (shaarda), there was a tinge of pathos in Abduvali's voice. Lighting a cigarette after his friends had left, he said, matter of factly, "you realize, when they call

Abduvali's "connected" home: Ak-Tatyr village, Isfara Valley, July 2005.

you black (*chernyi*), illegal (*nelegal*), that the Soviet Union, it turns out, really collapsed (*chyn ele buzuluptur*)."

The disjunction between forms of imagined connection and the harsh realities of documentary practice are not unique to the former Soviet space. To invoke Ferguson's metaphor, disconnections are as much a part of the "global condition" as the connections celebrated in much recent literature on global flows. What is noticeable in the case of migrations within the former Soviet space is the particular feeling associated with becoming "illegal"—and thus in an exceptional domain beyond the protection of law, in what would have once been the cities of "our" state. It is the dramatic scale of this *actual* encounter with Russia that, more than anything, distends the *imagined* distance between Ferghana and Moscow. From Sokh and Ak-Tatyr, fewer people may actually have traveled to Russia in the past than do so today—and those Soviet-era travels may have been on more unequal terms than they are now nostalgically recalled (Sahadeo 2012)—but the *promise* of incorporation, the assertion of equality and of shared socialist modernity, however formal or persistently deferred, was very real.

It is at this point that I want to return to the broader concern of this book with border work. In order to grasp the local salience of new appearances of border I have argued that we should begin, analytically and ethnographically, from mobility rather than from statis. Shifting the focus from map to the narrative tours of those who live and work at the border, from location to trajectory and from border-as-line to the laborious practice of producing boundaries affords a more nuanced understanding of contemporary connections and separations in the Ferghana Valley.

This is so in three ways. First, taking seriously the social and infrastructural connections of the past and the spatial imaginaries they sustained enables us to make sense of the pain and pathos of gaining and losing citizenship. In the radically variegated post-Soviet world of documentary privilege, where the color of one's passport can make a profound difference to your chance of getting out and getting on, the formal, categorical equality that existed in the past is of both material and symbolic importance.[23] It is in this context that we should interpret the phrase commonly used to explain the (imagined) mobility of the past, *murdagy bir ele passport bolchu* ("in the past there was just one passport"). It is in this context, too, that we can make

---

sense of the otherwise incongruous fact that more than a decade after the Soviet Union's collapse, parliamentary deputies in Bishkek could still campaign for reelection under the slogan "My Motherland is the Soviet Union" (*moia rodina—Sovetskii Soiuz*).[24] To reduce such claims to mere nostalgia, or the politics of regret, is to ignore to the degree to which the Soviet Union was felt to incorporate, connect, and provide channels of mobility—and thus the particular pathos of becoming *nelegal* with such apparent ease in one's own former capital city.

Second, it enables us to refine the critique of *konfliktogennost´* introduced in chapter 2, which demonstrated how conflict comes to be naturalized as a function of perceived "mismatches" between state and ethnic boundaries; and how assumptions about what borders are and what they should properly separate come to shape the geography of preventive interventions in the region. Such interventions are often premised on a failure or absence of connection, which can be overcome with outside assistance. This is reflected, for instance, in the perceived "insularity" of Hushiar's girls, to be countered with the help of the Peaceful Communities Initiative and Nike running shoes. Yet talking to Kanysh-ai and her mother it becomes clear just how profoundly they understand their village to be connected and how much they see their livelihood as depending on sustaining those flows. To note this is not to argue that attachment to place is irrelevant to villagers in Gaz, or that cultural boundaries between Kyrgyz and Tajiks in the Sokh Valley are not often talked of in categories that jar with contemporary celebrations of cultural hybridity. Kanysh-ai, after all, had a distinct and clearly articulated sense of cultural difference from her Tajik-speaking neighbors across the border in Hushiar. Their traditions (*salttar*) were "separate" (*bölük*), she told me categorically. Young people from Gaz did not attend celebrations hosted by Tajiks because "their men and women sit separately." The point is that such difference was not understood by Kanysh-ai as deriving from distance, or intolerance, or the absence of "dialogue." The difficulty of getting water down, apricots out, and money back from Russia was not due to an a priori lack of connection, but rather the emergence of multiple obstacles that had materialized in recent years, causing rupture to previous borderland relations: customs and border posts, registration regimes and road police, water timetables and trading regulations that made chasing water, selling apricots and sustaining livelihoods altogether more challenging than before.

---

[24]The slogan was successfully used by Klara Azhibekova, the first secretary of the Communist Party of Kyrgyzstan in her campaign to be elected as an MP.

Third, attending to trajectories allows us to see some of those connections that are not captured on the map, and thus to think about relations between villages, homes, and ethnic groups in less essentializing ways. If we start from the recognition that there have always been flows of people and things (a postulate that diverts from much of the globalization literature, premised on the radical novelty of a "world in motion"), then the analytical challenge is not so much to work out when (once static) things "started moving" and the implications of acceleration, but rather to ask when and how certain kinds of borders between people and places have come to be produced and sustained as natural (see also Maurer 2000).

What comes into focus from this perspective is the work of categorical production: the practices of classification and exclusion, infrastructures of provisioning, and technologies facilitating or limiting flow through which bordering is practically done. Seen from this perspective, Abduvali's realization that it was in an act of interpellation ("when they call you *chernyi, nelegal*") that the Soviet Union "really collapsed" can be understood as more than a mere rhetorical flourish. It is rather a recognition that state territoriality has to be enacted to become real, and that those enactments of "verticality and encompassment" occur through a range of mundane technologies and everyday practices of classification (Ferguson 2006, 110). In chapter 4 I develop this argument further by narrowing the focus to more localized trans-boundary movement. How, I ask, does a new international border work and get worked when the social and political entailments of "territorial integrity" are contested?

4. GAPS

Working a "Chessboard" Border

The outside section of Batken's Saturday market, the Özbek bazar, was unusually crowded one Saturday in early April 2004. A group had gathered around the traders, who came each week from Kokand across the border to sell Uzbek-manufactured silks, galoshes and prayer boots (*maasy*). There was a vigorous discussion underway, accompanied by the high-pitched *ooy-eee* that suggested some surprising or shocking news was being shared. I heard only fragments: a story about Gulnora Karimova, the daughter of Uzbekistan's president Islam Karimov, and a white Mercedes. I was too far away to hear the story's dénouement, and since I had been the last to show up, it was I who was blocking the narrow passageway for those anxious to get on with their browsing and shopping. I left the group quietly, and carried on to the cool indoor market behind stacked rolls of fabric.

Only later that day, after I had put this incident out of my mind, did I hear the story in full. It was told to me by my host in Batken, fifty-year-old Arapat-Eje, who sold gold jewelry at the market on Saturdays with the eldest of her three daughters. She, too, had heard it from the traders who had traveled that morning from Uzbekistan. The story was in fact recounted as a piece of news, which gave the "true" (*chyn*) reason for a series of bomb blasts that had hit Uzbekistan's capital, Tashkent, the previous week. The blasts, Arapat-Eje told me, were *not* the work of Hizb ut-Tahrir, as the official version had repeatedly claimed, but had in fact been engineered by the Uzbek authorities themselves to detract attention from a scandal involving the president's thirty-one-year-old daughter, Gulnora Karimova.[1] According to the Uzbek traders, the

---

[1] Hizb ut-Tahrir is a transnational Islamic organization professing the establishment of Islamic Caliphate, avowedly through nonviolent means, and banned throughout Central Asia.

president's daughter had been stopped by Russian police as she was driving a white, state-owned car—a Mercedes with official license plates (*gosnomera*)—across Russia on her way to Europe. When the police ordered her to open the trunk, the car was apparently found to be full of Uzbek gold that she was smuggling from Uzbekistan to her bank vault in Europe.[2]

Like many of the extravagant conspiracy theories that circulated in Batken during my period of research, this story had an air of the fantastical about it. It was easy to interpret simply as a discursive "weapon of the weak" (Scott 1985), weaving in, and subverting official Uzbek discourse about the need to retain the country's wealth inside its borders through high export tariffs.[3] Indeed, this was how I initially interpreted its significance: stories regarding gold had a particular mythic status given Kyrgyzstan and Uzbekistan's economic dependence on this resource, and it was not unusual for the substance's symbolic worth to be contained in its very materiality, especially in contexts where money and value have become progressively uncoupled (see also Humphrey 2002a, 5). I took it as just another local commentary about the morally and economically corrupt practices of those who constituted "The Family" (*sem'ia* or *üi-bülö*)—a local discourse on high-level pillage that was all-pervasive at the time in Batken.[4]

On the broad history of the movement, see Khalid (2007, 160–164); on its development in the Ferghana Valley see Mirsaiitov (2004, 52–66); on its presence in Kyrgyzstan, see Karagiannis (2005); on meanings of its membership, see the subtle portraits of Iqbol and Baktyor in Montgomery (2007, 155–158 and 191–194).

[2]I have been unable to find any independent corroboration of this story, although the US House Committee on Foreign Affairs had, just two months previously, debated allegations that Gulnora Karimova was involved in the trafficking of women to the United Arab Emirates (Smith 2004).

[3]In a notorious speech in February 1999 that was still commented on five years later, Islam Karimov had accused Kyrgyzstan of failing to feed its population, forcing Osh citizens to travel across the border to Andijan, depleting that city of bread. Justifying Uzbekistan's policy of protectionism, he made a bold attack on Kyrgyzstan's policy of liberalization: "You are building a democratic island, aren't you?! If you want to build a democratic island, first feed your own people and then start boasting! Am I right? We are trying to feed ourselves using our own potential, our own resources and using our people's hard work. But just look around us, all of them bother us. From all four sides." On the significance of this comment for Kyrgyzstan-Uzbekistan relations, see Megoran (1999). For an estimation of the economic costs of the trade barriers between the two countries, see Bouyjou (2005, 233–301), Megoran, Raballand and Bouyjou (2005), Torjesen (2007, 177–192).

[4]Although this was a full year before the "revolution" that, in local parlance, "brought down the Family" (Suleymanov 2005) in Kyrgyzstan, references to the "family parliament" (*semeinyi parlament*) and to the extended family of Mairam Akayeva in Talas who had "eaten" (*jep koidu*) the country's resources were already vigorously circulating in local discourse. For a typical dirt-digging story about the pillaging of gold in the Kyrgyzstani opposition press, see Sydykova (2003).

The more I heard renditions of the story over the following weeks, however the more I became intrigued by details to which I had not initially given much attention, including the exact route of the journey that Karimova took between Uzbekistan and Russia, and the fact that she was driving a state-registered car, which allegedly enabled her to pass through any number of Central Asian customs and border posts without being stopped. She traveled with the confidence of one who was above the law, protected by license plates that rendered her unimpedable. Indeed, it was only in Russia—a former "brotherly republic"—that she was subject to mythic justice. The remarks that would accompany this story suggested that this particular urban myth was as much a commentary about the differential permeability of state borders and the fragility of the security they provide as it was about economic pillage per se. Indeed, the two discourses were interlinked: it was precisely because Uzbekistan's borders were letting the wrong things through at the same time that they were hampering ordinary cross-border trade that its economy was suffering.

This locally circulating story captured the uncertain entailments of state sovereignty as it was experienced by traders and others living in the newly securitized borders of the three Ferghana Valley states in 2004 and 2005. A critical commentary on the "border issue" (*chek ara maselesi*) that pervaded national discourses, it was also a symbolic inversion of the increasingly virulent official depictions of their own cross-border trade as unpatriotic or threatening, and their goods as contraband. In so doing, it touched a deeper nerve. In a context where the state is identified overwhelmingly with the person of the president (Liu 2012, 148–184), this fantastical story about the destructive sovereignty of the president's daughter tapped into broader anxieties about the coherence of territorial integrity. How to have secure borders to prevent gold and other resources from being siphoned out, as well as to prevent armed militants from coming in, as had occurred during the summers of 1999 and 2000? How to have borders that are also permeable to those of us living here who depend on being able to move and visit and trade across them? How, especially, to do this in a situation where "law," like "border," presents itself in absurd forms: as an arbitrary, immobile imposition to some, and completely permeable to others? The state border "is a double bind because national prosperity appears to demand, but is also threatened by, *both* openness and closure" (Comaroff and Comaroff 2005, 129).

In Sokh, Batken, and surrounding villages on the Kyrgyz-Uzbek and Kyrgyz-Tajik borders, the "double bind" had come to acquire particular significance since 1999. Although formal independence had been declared eight years earlier, it was only since the late 1990s that passports and license plates had come to acquire practical relevance as markers of inclusion and exclusion, with one-time Soviet administrative boundaries now increasingly policed as international borders. As we have seen in earlier chapters, roads and canals had been built during the preceding seventy years ignoring the administrative boundary lines between Union republics. From the perspective of people living nearby, this meant that the border itself was encountered not as a linear formation, but as something punctuated or even mobile, materializing as repeated intrusions into village space where road and border crisscross back and forth, or erupting suddenly in the shape of a border post or soldier. To travel, for instance, from the center of Sokh to the nearest town in the Uzbek mainland, Rishton, is to cross no less than six different border and customs posts within a distance of around twenty kilometers. The effect creates a strange suspension of time as it is often unclear which state you have entered or exited. From a cartographic perspective, there is coherence to the posts' location—this is indeed where border and road recross. From the traveler's perspective, however, there is only a succession of posts across this otherwise unmarked *adyr* zone. It is these sites, like the checkpoints described by Jeganathan in Sri Lanka, where the state in the Ferghana Valley "performs the magic of its illegibility," appearing and disappearing, working "betwixt and between the recollection and anticipation of violence" (2004, 72, 74).

I draw on three ethnographic narratives in order to capture the multiplicity of border and the social work that is entailed in making territory "integral." What emerges through these accounts is a portrait of various border topoi: the border post, the "back entrance" or *chernyi vkhod*, the detour route, the canal, and the border market. "Border" is experienced as a place of both limits and gaps: a site of barbed wire and invisible landmines, but also a place of vigorous exchange, of friendship and intimacy, a site of connections and opportunities as well as of threat. It is this multiplicity that interests me, as both an ethnographic object and a prompt to theoretical reflection on a distinctive modality of power. Das and Poole (2004, 6) ask of what they call "marginal" state spaces whether "the forms of illegibility, partial belonging, and disorder that seem to inhabit the margins of the state constitute its necessary condition as a theoretical and political object." To this we might additionally ask, in terms of prevailing analytical categories, whether erupting, nonlinear borders represent less an exceptional place of subversion than a useful site from which to explore the very unexceptionality of the "exception" as suspension of law (Hartman 2008).

I argue in this chapter that we need to take seriously the entanglements between the domains of the licit and the illicit, the formal and the informal, the border post and the *chernyi vkhod*. These factors are not simply an indication of state weakness or failure but are rather *constitutive* of a particular modality of power that thrives on the pervasive reproduction of uncertainty over the location of sovereign law. Seen in this light, the habitual transgressive acts of border dwellers who negotiate, appeal to, assert, or bribe their way through the border should be interpreted not as acts of resistance toward a coherent sovereign state, but rather as participating in a particular kind of border work, in which the territorial state is both invoked and undermined.

Writing of the men and women who engage in unregulated economic activity across the porous borders of the Chad Basin, Janet Roitman notes that road banditry should not necessarily be seen as a means to critique or counter the state. Neither outlawed nor moral activity, the practices of those who extract tribute for the safe passage of goods are "rather a means to participate in prevailing modes of accumulation and prevailing methods of governing the economy, which are typical to most states in the world" (2006, 249–250). Understanding the dynamics of such processes, Roitman argues, entails taking seriously the way in which distinctions between corruption, illegality, and illicit status are made by those engaged in such activities; asking not just how such ostensibly marginal activities and spaces generate forms of livelihood, but also "how they substantiate specific modes of self-understanding" (ibid., 251). I am particularly interested in how and when different rationalities are weighed against one another in the working of a border. How and when "the state" or "the law" comes to be invoked to categorically prohibit movement, and when other kinds of appeals—to common religion, to respect for the dead, to the imperatives of harmonious borderland conviviality (*yntymak*) come to prevail. This move entails suspending the reading of "state" that assumes that it is necessarily a priori sovereign, territorial, and integrated. In reality, the geography of state regulation is more helpfully thought of as a field of competing claims to sovereignty, or as Mbembe puts it: "a proliferation not of independent power centers but of more or less autonomous pockets in the heart of what was, until recently, a system" (2001, 80). Attending to such assessments is important for understanding the ethical navigation of new borders and their associated legal forms. But they can also shed light on a distinctive modality of power: how and when appeals to the authority and coercive power of the state are used efficaciously to override the law; and what happens when such enactments fail.

Corporealities: Border as Limit

Throughout southern Ferghana, border stories were often recounted through bodies: newborn bodies, maimed bodies, trafficked bodies, ill bodies, undressed, checked, and intruded bodies and, in rare cases, raped bodies—the violent, gendered remapping of territorial transgression.[5] But it was dead bodies that seemed to have particular salience as symbols of ruptured relations. Verdery (1999, 27–28) has argued that the very corporeality and polyvalence of the deceased makes them "important means of localizing a claim," and that is perhaps especially the case in situations where every moment of delay before burial is recognized as one of torment (*kyinalysh*) for the deceased. In the Ferghana Valley, more so than in less religiously conservative areas of Central Asia, the Hadithic injunction to bury the deceased within hours of death means that funeral rites acquire enormous significance as indices of distance and connection, as well as of filial piety and relational harmony (see also Kuchumkulova 2007, 243–263). The unburied corpse is a multiply unstable object—polluting and tormented, collapsing social relations until harmony can be restored in the act of burial. It is thus in preventing the honoring of the dead that borders are felt to curse the living (Megoran 2002, 189).

In recent Kyrgyz public culture, the disruption caused to practices of filial duty by the institution of border controls has become a powerful and productive trope for commentary on the irrational inhumanity and arbitrariness of border controls. Marat Alykulov's award-winning 2006 film *Chek ara* (The Border) portrays an encounter at a small, rural checkpoint on the Kyrgyz-Kazakh border. Four Kyrgyz labor migrants who are transporting their suddenly deceased comrade home for burial are refused exit from Kazakhstan because the corpse is not in possession of a migration card. Denied passage across the bridge where the checkpoint stands because of this minor administrative error, the men are forced to carry the deceased on foot across the freezing river separating the two countries, virtually under the eye of the border guards who refused them exit. The dramatic effect lies, of course, in the visibility of the transgression. The viewer knows that an appeal to state security is being invoked merely as an excuse for the extraction of money, just as the labor migrants do. Stately authority here is understood to be profoundly performative, and even violently parasitic upon ordinary people seeking to honor the dead.[6]

One funeral story that I heard during fieldwork articulated this sense of arbitrary closure with particular force. The narrative of a Tajik student,

---

[5]Some of the ethnography in this section reworks material that I previously published in the *Anthropology of East Europe Review* (see Reeves 2007b).

[6]A radio drama written by the Kyrgyz Ministry of Culture, *Last Will* (Raev 2007) explores a similar theme on the Kyrgyz-Uzbek border. In this case however, the corpse that cannot be transported into Uzbekistan is eventually buried in Kyrgyzstan, with the soil—"which knows no division between Kyrgyz and Uzbek"—uniting the deceased with her ancestors across the border.

Image from the film, *Chek Ara* (The Border), dir. Marat Alykulov. Image courtesy of Oy Art Productions/Kyrgyzfil'm.

Firuza, was striking, for both the emotion with which it was recounted, and the dramatic context of its narrating, in a stretch of waterless *adyr* just inside Kyrgyzstan, close to the point where the three republics meet. I was traveling between the Kyrgyz towns of Batken and Osh, at the eastern end of the Ferghana Valley, with a group of Tajik students from Khujand, at the valley's western limit. We were being driven to Osh by Kadyr-Aka, Arapat-Eje's eldest son and busy father of four. Kadyr-Aka was well-connected and moderately well-off, having made a good income importing gasoline from Uzbekistan and selling it at a mark-up of one or two som (about 3 US cents) across the border in Batken.[7] By 2004 he still profited from the different regimes of value that the border creates by "ferrying Tajiks," as he put it, across the unmarked scree and dirt route that constitute the "detour road" (*ob"ezd jol*) north of the Sokh enclave. Citizens of Tajikistan need visas to enter Uzbekistan, including

---

[7]Kadyr-Aka ceased this trade a couple of years earlier for reasons that remain unclear. His cessation of this trade may have been because the differential in price of gasoline across the border no longer made this business profitable. Gavrilis (2008, 148) notes how, in the early 2000s, those transporting 200-liter gasoline drums on motorcycles near the Bürgündü canal could make $3–4 profit per trip, with Uzbek regards receiving the equivalent of 20–50 cents to look the other way.

for the fifteen-kilometer stretch of road that passes through the Sokh enclave, administratively part of Uzbekistan. For these Tajik students from Khujand to reach Osh, therefore, Kadyr-Aka took us not along the main Batken-Osh road, which would entail crossing through Sokh, but by this rocky, off-road detour, which traces the length of the Bürgündü canal before splintering into a series of unmarked tracks that cross-cut each other in otherwise barren, uncultivated territory for another sixty kilometers.[8]

Kamaz trucks and Soviet jeeps dominate this route; their loads and their quantity a frequent reminder that the "second economy" is integral rather than marginal to local livelihoods (Rasanayagam 2002a, 108–111; Seabright 2000). For this technically nonexistent road, unmarked and unmapped, constitutes one of the main routes east for the distribution of aluminum and base metals to China, Uzbek cotton for illegal processing in Osh, and Afghan opium from Tajikistan to Osh, Bishkek, and Russia. Human movement, too, is a potentially lucrative source of profit from this route. Kadyr-Aka ferries citizens of Tajikistan along this route rather than offering a more conventional taxi service on the tarmac road that crosses Sokh because the margins are higher and there is less competition from others in Batken. Soviet-era Zhigulis and the more recently imported second-hand foreign cars (*inomarki*) would both be liable to run aground on the uneven, rocky surface of the detour route. With his Soviet jeep, Kadyr-Aka is well positioned to corner the market in "ferrying Tajiks" to Osh, and because it is at the large, wholesale markets at this eastern end of the valley that the cheapest goods in the region are to be found, demand typically outstrips supply for transport along this route. The Tajik students with whom I was traveling were convinced that this longer uncomfortable ride was preferable to the inevitable delays, bribes (*pora*), and humiliation that would be liable to greet them if they tried to cross Uzbekistani Sokh without having an Uzbek visa stamped into their passport.[9]

Kadyr-Aka's intimate, embodied knowledge of the landscape also gave him the edge over those who might try working this route for the first time. He could tell our location from tiny shifts in the landscape: a chink in the canal, a conjunction of rocks. And it was this that made him king of the road, racing through the landscape with the radio on full blast, enjoying

---

[8]Since the time of this ethnography, the "detour road" has been renovated as part of a World Bank-sponsored program to assist Kyrgyzstan in becoming "transport independent" by bypassing the enclaves of Tajikistan and Uzbekistan (World Bank 2009).

[9]At around the same time that we made this journey to Osh, a Khujand-based journalist made a similar journey, condemning the extra costs and danger associated with having to take the detour route (Yusupov 2004). Citizens of Tajikistan's Sogd oblast "find themselves as hostages in a transport blockade" just to avoid travelling through Sokh: "an obstacle inexplicable to any logic."

the chance to practice skids and off-road leaps as we in the back covered our eyes to avoid being stung by the dust. Kadyr-Aka proudly reiterated to his passengers that his livelihood depended on knowing these dusty tracks intimately, just as it did on the vagaries of international relations that prohibited citizens of Tajikistan and Uzbekistan from entering each other's countries without a visa. Every bump of this route was an indignity to them—for him it was a chance to practice freedom. Like the Shabe traders described by Flynn (1997) on the Nigeria-Benin border, his livelihood depended on the particular opportunities generated by the productive configuration of gaps and limits that the borders here presented to a well-connected, jeep-owning Batken man. Indeed, the normally reserved father of young children seemed to be at his most animated here in the dusty no-man's-land at the unmarked and largely unpoliced edge of the state.

The contrast between Kadyr's sense of freedom, and the story of entrapment that was related to me by Firuza could not have been more pronounced. Indeed, the very fact that we were making this detour to avoid entering an enclave that was, as one of our passengers put it, "Tajik land since time immemorial" seemed to invite a proliferation of border talk.[10] Unable to put pencil to paper to make jottings of Firuza's story during the journey, we retreated to a café once we reached Osh, and there, slowly readjusting to the delicious motionlessness of land, she recounted her story of the corpse and its journey.

The deceased man was the father of a childhood school teacher with whom Firuza was still in close contact. Originally from a small Tajik-majority village just inside the Uzbek SSR, the teacher's father had moved in his youth to Stalinabad (now Dushanbe)—the capital of the Tajik SSR—initially to study and afterward to work as a journalist for one of the main Tajik-language newspapers. Like many of his generation, he did not see the move into another republic as constituting a move abroad. Dushanbe was geographically closer than his own capital, Tashkent, and was the natural choice for someone wanting to undertake journalism training in literary Tajik. His daughter, Firuza's school teacher, had grown up in Dushanbe as a member of the postwar Tajik intelligentsia, studying in Kiev before returning to her native city to teach. Although she had not gone to her father's village in many years, and identified little with what she saw as a "backward district" (*otstalyi raion*), Firuza's teacher knew that her father's overwhelming wish, repeated on his deathbed, was that he be buried in his ancestral land, inside what was now independent

---

[10]The Sokh enclave is administratively part of Uzbekistan, but its population identifies as Tajik and historically, there have been strong cultural and educational ties between Sokh and the cities of northern Tajikistan—ties that have been sustained only with difficulty since independence (see Introduction).

Uzbekistan. So it was, immediately after her father's death, that she set off with a small group of relatives on the 120-mile journey to the village of her father's birth. Firuza told me about her teacher's journey:

> So they'd got as far as the [border] post; they were carrying the corpse in their hands since they knew they would have to leave the car [on that side of the post]. They had come all the way from Dushanbe in the heat. They were just a few kilometers from his *mahalla*. And then they were told they can't enter. Can you imagine? All that distance in the heat. So they explain to the border guards that he is from this district [*raion*], that his fathers were buried in that *mahalla*, that they were such-and-such a family, all the things his parents had done for the *raion*. And you know what the border guards said? They were Uzbeks, they weren't even local [*oni dazhe ne byli mestnymi*]. They said to that group of relatives who were in mourning, "What do we need your corpse for? Don't you think we've got enough corpses of our own? [*U nas svoikh trupov ne khvataiut, chto-li?*]."

I pressed Firuza on the meaning of such a response from the border guards. Perhaps it demonstrated concern for a genuine lack of room in the burial ground? Or perhaps it was motivated by fear about contamination from a corpse that had been transported all day in the heat? Firuza dismissed such explanations. It had nothing to do with the paperwork, or even with money, she told me. They knew that they would have to offer money: they were prepared for that. And they were wealthy, so the cost was not going to be a barrier. No, Firuza continued firmly, this was about something else, about "nationality" (*natsional'nost'*). The border guards were Uzbek, she repeated, they were doing this to remind us that this was the territory of Uzbekistan even though Tajiks have always lived in this particular region. She continued,

> They said to [my teacher's relatives], "if he is Tajik, bury him in Tajikistan!" But Tajiks have always lived in [this *mahalla*]! And her relatives were pleading with those border guards; they tried to get them to call through to some high-up people in the district. They said to them, "aren't you a Muslim after all? Then act like one!" Let's not have this, 'you're a Tajik, I'm Uzbek.'" But they just kept on telling them to go back and bury him in Dushanbe . . . So they ended up taking the corpse all the way back to Dushanbe and they buried him there the next day. But that is a disgrace [*pozor*]! We have to bury the person the same day, not the next. And there they were going backwards and forwards, trying

to get the border guards to listen to them. You know how painful it was that they couldn't bury him according to custom? Really painful . . . So you see, in the end [the guards] broached the bounds of Nazism when they didn't let them in. Because apart from that everything was in order. They had money with them and everything.

Firuza's account had something didactic about it, something almost theatrical. At the time, sitting in the café, recording what she said, I chided myself for not having a better memory and ending up with a second-order ethnographic artifact: a dramatized reconstruction of a story that had burst out spontaneously during our earlier journey, as we had been tossed along the bumpy detour route around Sokh. I was struck by the fact that although Firuza was recounting this in the third person, her account was dotted throughout with a narrative "we," as though she personally had been there accompanying the body back to Dushanbe. This, coupled with the dramatic overstatement and the instinctive slippage from this narrative into discussion of other Tajik losses—the loss of historic Samarkand and Bukhara, the assimilation (*as-similiatsiia*) of Tajiks into Uzbeks, the closure of Tajik-medium schools in Uzbekistan—left me wondering why it was *this* message that she was so keen that I take from the story: a narrative of discrimination on the grounds of ethnicity, a story of nationalism trumping other kinds of identification as Muslims, as fellow locals.

Part of the answer lies, no doubt, in the post-Soviet prevalence in Tajikistan of a discourse of loss and historical injustice: one in which Firuza and her generation would be well versed. Accounts of the destabilizing consequences of being left with a "rump state" excised from historical centers of Tajik culture in present-day Uzbekistan are codified in official histories and have received extensive scholarly elaboration from the Tajik Academy of Sciences.[11] Particular instances of discrimination, such as that encountered by Firuza's teacher, could thus be inserted as indicative instances into a much larger, state-sanctioned narrative of historic offence (*obida*).

However, to understand why this refusal of entry was understood to be an instance of nationalism that "broached the bounds of Nazism," the

---

[11] Two of the formulations with which Firuza would likely have been familiar include Khaidarov's university textbook on the history of the Tajik people in the twentieth century (Khaidarov 2001, 126–128), and the school textbook on the contemporary history of Tajikistan (Dzhakhonov and Tukhtaeva 2002), which describes how during the delimitation of 1924, as a result of the actions of "pan-Turkist" commissioners, "all of the large Tajik towns . . . went to the Uzbek republic" (2002, 27–28). On the role of historiography in articulating competing national narratives in contemporary Uzbekistan and Tajikistan, see Suyarkulova (2011).

pervasiveness of an appropriate "narrative slot" into which it could be inserted is only part of the answer. It is also important to bring the question of the borders' perceived (il)legitimacy into the picture. Firuza saw the border guards not as mere transmitters of official Uzbek policy toward noncitizens, nor as upholding an unjust but externally derived law. She did not see the border guards as merely the last in a chain of command stretching coherently from a capital city to its margins, their authority an instance of more encompassing sovereignty that lies with the state. Her accusation, rather, is one of personal, ethnically based malice, which overrode any coherent relational appeals (to common Islamic identity, to shared Tajik-Uzbek cultural heritage, to money, to respect for the dead). The ethnicity of the border guards mattered in this encounter—their nonlocalness—precisely because they were not viewed in the encounter as mere state functionaries dutifully enacting the law; the embodiment of the state's rational-legal authority. Indeed, it is in the border guards' very refusal to do the "cooperative" thing and accept a bribe to let the body through that they were understood as having demonstrated their true nationalist intent. What is technically an act of legal exclusion based on citizenship can thus only be made sense of in terms of meaningful categories of ethnic discrimination. "State sovereignty" here collapses into the fact that "we" are stuck here unable to pay our last respects, while a youth with a Kalashnikov dictates to us as though he were the law, effecting a triple subversion of the proper rules of valley decorum: of the living before the dead, of the young before the old, of the host toward the stranger-guest (*meikhmon*).

Working the Border: Mohammed

If Firuza's story illustrates the way in which borders can appear as violent limit points, my second ethnographic example points to borders' variable permeability. Mohammed, an ethnically Kyrgyz-identifying citizen of Uzbekistan, thrives on the possibilities opened up by being a border person, able to profit from the different regimes of value and political spaces opened up on either side of the border. Mohammed works in Batken's small daily market, and after a conversation one day outside the town's newspaper office, I would regularly visit Mohammed at his stall, where he would update me on the progress of his cross-border trade.

Mohammed identifies as a Ferghana Kyrgyz and a member of the Kypchak lineage (*uruu*), which had played an important role in the Kokand Khanate. It was this shared register of identification that enabled him to get along well with the market-owner (*bazarkom*) in Batken, a fellow Kypchak, and to get a good spot in the small daily market (the so-called *p'ian bazar* or drunkard's market) selling sugar, sweets, and macaroni. Although he had grown up in Uzbekistan and had an Uzbek passport, Mohammed did not think of himself as a foreigner here, he explained: he spent most of his week in Batken, renting a small outhouse with another trader, returning to his parents in their village near Ferghana city on Saturdays, when trade in the *p'ian bazar* was quiet and the much larger weekly market was in operation. For Mohammed, the border was a zone of possibility, a place of people and connections, which needed to be known intimately in order to be exploited. The verbal tour on which he took me narrated this space not as a contiguous limit point, but rather a dense series of spaces to be passed through, officers to be befriended, checks to be avoided. Indeed, when I first interviewed him about his trade, Mohammed traced a circle on the table where we sat as he talked about the border: this was a space of constant movement for him, not a linear divide.

Each week Mohammed would buy 300 kilograms of goods (*juk*) from the market in Ferghana city, in Uzbekistan. Like many of those coming from Uzbekistan, he traded in locally manufactured Uzbek foodstuffs that could be sold at a sizeable markup in Kyrgyzstan. He reeled them off to me, with the prices and weights: chocolates, white sugar, biscuits, local *rachki* sweets, yellow lump sugar, macaroni, oil and tea. He would take his load by bus as far as Burbalyk, a small Uzbek border village that borders the village of Kyrgyz Kyshtak, a place notorious in the official Uzbek media as a site of cunning and "uncivilized" illegal trade (Orlova 2003). There he had an acquaintance (*taanysh*) who is the relative of one of the families whose home is located right on the border, the back and front gate functioning as an informal parallel crossing point (*chernyi vkhod*) to the official border post. For twenty Kyrgyz som (about 50 US cents at the time) his acquaintance would load the goods at Burbalyk onto his car and take it through his relative's yard to Kyrgyz territory on the other side of the border. The acquaintance transports it as far as the Bürgündü canal running along a stretch of the detour road that we encountered with Firuza. Mohammed himself, meanwhile, goes through the official posts a few kilometers away, giving the customs officers a cigarette or two "in order to maintain *yntymaktuu* relations," before rejoining his acquaintance at the agreed point at the canal. There another friend who drives a truck back and forth regularly along this detour route meets the two later in the day and picks Mohammed up to take him and his goods on to Batken. There are plenty of trucks passing this way, Mohammed explained, and if his friend does not show up, he simply flags down another Kamaz and negotiates a price for the journey to Batken.

Crossing the *chernyi vkhod* on the Kyrgyz-Uzbek border, with the line of the border fence in the background. Photo by Alisher Saipov/Fergana.ru.

Mohammed narrated all this with the pleasure of one who has discovered an elegant system, balanced and functioning, whose success depends on an intimate knowledge of points of informal border crossing, and on the different regimes of value that operate on either side. For Mohammed this gap was summed up in his assertion that "in Uzbekistan *rachki* sweets cost 25 som and no one has the money to buy them; here in Kyrgyzstan they cost 40 som and everyone wants to buy them!" He was quickly able to recover the 6,000 Kyrgyz som (about $150) that he spends each week at the Ferghana city market, and in 2004 was saving up to be able to pay the considerable bride price (*kalym*) that he needed in order to marry later in the year.

Mohammed's depiction of the different political possibilities on either side of the border matched his acute awareness of different economic orders. Just as he compared the prices on a range of goods in Ferghana and Batken, so he scattered our conversation with references to what was "said" and what was possible on either side of the border, reveling in the fact that here, in the Batken roadside café where we sat, he could speak his mind and be confident of the consequences. "You know," he said to me during one early conversation, grabbing the teapot in front of him and pouring it demonstratively, "everybody says, 'in Uzbekistan the state is rich and the people are poor; in Kyrgyzstan the people are rich but the state is poor.'[12] But I don't think that's true. After all, if the state is so rich in Uzbekistan, why can't they pay people normal wages?" He put the teapot down noisily, and added, "but of course *here* I can say this! Here you can say anything. If you say that in Uzbekistan, someone will come round in the night and take you away!"

His trade thrived on this difference of economic and political models—a difference of which he was acutely aware—but it also relied on the fact that the border is not fully impermeable. This is the logic of the *chernyi vkhod*. At the border the *chernyi vkhod* is typically a homestead or section of path through a *mahalla* that functions as a parallel crossing point to the official border post. The homeowner, or in some cases, a collective of *mahalla* residents, will take a small fee for allowing traffic and commercial goods to pass through unregistered and undocumented. It was generally assumed by my interlocutors that a cut of such fees would go to the official organs of border control—the customs officers and border guards—in return for quietly continuing to ignore the trade. Some of these crossing points were so well known that they had their own names. Crossing at the "eighty-fifth entrance" (so-called for the number of the house that acts as the informal crossing point on the Kyrgyz-Uzbek border), was a common euphemism in Batken for crossing into Uzbekistan without the requisite papers.

Certainly, much of this cross-border traffic continued under the noses of those nominally controlling the border. On one occasion, in the border village of Dostuk at the eastern end of the valley near the city of Osh, I ended up taking a wrong turn through the knot of residential *mahalla* streets that leads to the official border post between Kyrgyzstan and Uzbekistan. With the post close enough to be within earshot and hoping that I might be able to find a connecting path if I were to continue to the far end, I found myself walking against the flow of a group of children and teenagers who were carrying new, boxed television sets in the opposite direction through the narrow street. As

---

[12] This comment is often used to refer to very visible state reconstruction going on in Uzbekistan. In Kyrgyzstan, state-sponsored rebuilding was striking by its absence in the mid-2000s, but individual disposable incomes tend to be markedly higher. Contrasts in different state models are often articulated through comparisons in the quality of roads, the piping (or not) of natural gas and the level of pensions. Megoran (2002, 226) notes the same rich state/rich people comparison being made to him frequently during fieldwork in 1999–2000, and Liu (2012, 70) quotes one of his informants in 1999 drawing the same distinction, adding "In Kyrgyzstan, they've done away with Lenin in practice but kept his statues. In Uzbekistan it's the other way around."

I approached where they were coming from I could see a man standing at the high open gate that marks the entrance and exit of a family courtyard (*hovla*) at the street's far end. The man had a wad of 500 sum notes in his hand and as I approached he called out to me the "price" in Uzbek sum and Kyrgyz som for crossing his courtyard border. His home, which allowed this unregistered traffic in televisions to continue, was just meters below the world of uniforms, weapons, documents, and stamps that characterized the official "friendship" (*Dostuk*) border post.

A Border Ethic: *Yntymak* and *Zakon*

Far from being concealed from one another, these two forms of access—the one official and inscribed; the other unofficial—were spatially and functionally intertwined. The *chernyi vkhod* is defined not by the fact that it provides another point of access across the border from the official post, still less by any categorical "invisibility" from that which is official. Rather, it is defined by a specific relation to the official entrance: one of mutual dependence and mutual recognition. Just as the relationship between the "market" and the "black market" has been shown to be one of profound interdependence (or as Kotkin puts it in his account of Stalinism as civilization, "one economy with a dual aspect" [1995, 274]), so the functioning of the *vkhod* and the *chernyi vkhod* depend on one another.[13] Conceptually and spatially, a "front" and "back" door only make sense in relation to one another. For Mohammed, this interdependence was reflected in his matter-of-fact observation that although he would send his goods through the unofficial entrance between Burbalyk and Kyrgyz-Kyshtak, he himself would share cigarettes and pass the time of day with the border guards at the official crossing point a few hundred meters away. As he put it, the border guards, as much as the traders, had a stake in maintaining harmony (*yntymak*), by which he meant the quiet recognition that we all need to keep trade going, even as we all must deny its visibility. The realm between "law" and "outside the law" blurred and intermingled in his narrative: it was simply not relevant to his ethical assessments (see also Rivkin-Fish 2005).

The fragility of the legal-illegal divide is also reflected in Kyrgyz slang used by traders such as Mohammed to describe their business. In colloquial

---

[13]On the interdependence of formal and informal exchange in the Soviet collective, see Humphrey (1998); on the need to abandon "dual economy" models for understanding economic exchange in Uzbekistan, see Rasanayagam (2002a, 103–124; 2002b).

Kyrgyz in its southern variant, various Russian terms are used as interjections or as terms of approval.[14] Among these, the term *zakonnyi*, which carries the literal Russian meanings of "lawful" and "licit," was particularly interesting for having acquired (rather as the British slang, "wicked") a directly inverse meaning. *Zakonnyi* as used by many young people in Batken refers to those actions or eventualities that are positive and fortune generating, but not necessarily formally legal. Indeed, the expression carries the nuance of something that is (ethically) good precisely because it does not adhere to legal prescription. A *zakonnyi biznes*, for instance, is a business that is impressively productive, income- and employment generating (and thus morally good), but which relies at least potentially on the bending of law for its success.

Mohammed described his own business as *zakonnyi* in this sense. He was not, of course, unaware that his unregistered import-export activity avoided customs dues and was thus, in a formal sense, *nezakonnyi* (illegal). It was rather that he saw the ethics of his activity as deriving from something other than law—from the fact that it both depended on, and helped to foster, *yntymak* between various categories of people: between the worlds of Ferghana and Batken, between friends in Burbulak and Kyrgyz Kyshtak; between the soldiers manning the border, or "lads in uniform" (*formadagy baldar*) as he called them; and those who regularly cross through. This form of moral reasoning resembles the argument put to Janet Roitman by one of her trafficking interlocutors who runs the border in the Chad Basin, that by continuing their cross-border trade, "[we] . . . help sustain families and contribute to the well-being of agents of the force of law" (Roitman 2005, 188). Roitman is primarily concerned with the implications of this dynamic for the way that the "state" reconstitutes its authority through the appropriation of such networks. Yet striking, too, is the intimate, domestic vocabulary that is used to refer to these stately figures by the border-riding taxi drivers. As with Mohammed's references to *yntymak*, the language of familial inter-dependence signals a profoundly different logic of connection from a language of law. It is this that means that "illegality" can be experienced, not merely as an inevitable modus vivendi in a context of widespread corruption, but as an ethic of borderland exchange (Roitman 2006, 247).

---

[14] The most common of these in 2004 and 2005 among Kyrgyz speakers in Batken were *chetkii* (Russian: "precise," "efficient"), *konkretnyi* (Russian: "concrete," "specific"), *zor* (Uzbek: "great," "awe-inspiring"), all of which had been incorporated in Kyrgyz to express positive qualities. I am grateful to Elnura Osmonalieva and Burulkan Usmanalieva for sharing their insights on these terms.

Bridges and *Ballonchiki*: Muktar-Aka

Despite Mohammed's acute awareness of difference between Kyrgyzstan and Uzbekistan, his narrative shows that this border needs to be understood as a densely integrated system, involving flows, channels, and limit points. From the perspective of those living at the border, the huge trucks rumbling along the detour roads like that driven by Mohammed's acquaintance are not simply deviations from the formal traffic that gets registered in customs forms and transported along tarmac. They are rather one variety of a series of flows that all at the border have a stake in reproducing, including those nominally enacting the state at its edges.

This interdependence, and the constant erasure of the boundary between state and society, legal and illegal on which it depends, can best be understood if we turn to those whose livelihood derives most concretely from keeping the border porous. My final ethnographic example is from Muktar-Aka, a self-styled "ferry-man" (*perepravshchik*) who works a section of the canal border between Kyrgyzstan and Uzbekistan at Kara-Suu, one of the valley's easternmost towns, a short bus ride from Osh city. Kara-Suu is a site of particular importance to the Ferghana Valley's economic and symbolic geography. Since the mid-1980s, it has been divided from the Uzbekistani village of the same name (*Qorasuv*) by a twelve-meter-wide canal, and more recently, an international boundary. The different spellings that are now used to designate these identically named, historically linked, ethnically Uzbek settlements are indicative both of attempts to institutionalize difference on either side of a state border, and the complexity of this undertaking when it affects populations who, in the words of one local commentator, "have long ago become related [*davno porodnilis'*], giving away their daughters to young men from the other bank" (Zhuk 2003).

Kara-Suu is not one of the valley's larger towns but it has historically been a major trading post on the Silk Road and it continues to be one of the largest wholesale markets in the region, selling local produce, as well as clothes and household goods from China. This is where Arapat-Eje would travel each month to buy gold jewelry for resale in Batken, transporting her purchases carefully in a sheath around her waist to avoid unnecessary customs checks. Kyrgyzstan acts as a major point of entry for cheap Chinese imports, and Kara-Suu's fortuitous location at the eastern end of the valley made it a magnet for wholesale traders from throughout the Ferghana region. In 2005 there were 18,000 stallholders at the market, of whom an estimated 5,000 were from China (Torjesen 2007, 187), primarily Uighur traders from the western Xinjiang region. Kara-Suu is a town that has come to be defined in popular imagination by its market. A correspondent from *Vechernii Bishkek,* visiting the town in 2000, captured in his depiction of border town's wheeling and dealing the ambivalence of many Kyrgyz toward the proliferation of whole-sale trade at the very edges of the state.

> Everyone is doing his thing here [*kazhdyi delaet svoe delo*] . . . Many are able to make money precisely by protecting citizens from the fiscal or-gans. They act as go-betweens. In a word, they are able to fix all kinds of deals [*ulazhivaiut vsiakie raznye delishki*]. But all the same, today the border post is a source of bread not only to those guarding the fron-tier, the customs officers, agents of the veterinary-sanitary control and other state workers. On both sides of the barrier there have arisen huge car-parks, rows of traders and services, an army of people with carts. (Khamidov 2000)

In many accounts of the border market (*chek ara bazar*) as a distinct kind of social and economic space my interlocutors emphasized the extent to which trade thrives on the slipperiness of law in such locations. For the author of this article, the contained exchange of the market, with its "rows of traders and services," is contiguous with, and indeed contingent upon, the fact that the border itself is a source of income generation. Deriving income from selling bread at the market is portrayed as functionally continuous with selling a fake customs form or attaching a price to passage through the *chernyi vkhod.* As Lam puts it in his depiction of border trade in Kara-Suu, "traders and officials act in a ritualized spectacle that supports the fiction of interdic-tion" (2009, 180). It is precisely the exposure of this slipperiness between the realms of "proper" and "improper" trade that invests border towns with such moral ambiguity. In the case of Kara-Suu, the town's fame as a major trade post has been coupled in recent years with a less flattering reputation as a den of iniquity: a site of private bathhouses that double as brothels, factories il-legally processing smuggled Uzbek cotton, and speculation on the fluctuating price of goods (Khamidov 2001 and 2003). At the same time, as Montgomery (2007) notes, the sharp convergence here of "political voice, social decay and spiritual search" mean that Kara-Suu has also become home to one of Kyr-gyzstan's largest and most active memberships of Hizb ut-Tahrir al-Islami (2007, 117), an explicitly transnational organization both in structure and in its ambition for a borderless Islamic caliphate.

It is in the context of popular discourse of Kara-Suu about a town epito-mizing both the magic and danger of capitalism—a world in which every-thing, including drugs, sex, and cross-border mobility can be openly bought and sold—that the (official) border closure of 2003 needs to be explored. In early January of that year, Uzbekistan announced that it would be closing the remaining pedestrian bridge between Kara-Suu and Qorasuv as a three-day quarantine measure to prevent the spread of disease from Kyrgyzstan into Uzbekistan. Newspaper reports from the time suggest that the disease in question was influenza; my interlocutors recalled it to have been foot-and-mouth disease (*iashur*). In a way, the lack of agreement over what the disease actually was is indicative of how irrelevant the quarantine measure in the end proved to be.[15] Before the end of the three-day period, cranes had been brought in at night to dismantle the three-meter stretch of bridge that was the property of Uzbekistan, leaving the remaining nine meters (six of which are officially neutral, and three of which belong to Kyrgyzstan) dangling precariously into the canal. The symbolic weight of this tragic, broken "bridge of friendship" that now failed to stretch across the canal on which both communities depended for their livelihood was palpable in depictions of the event in Kyrgyzstan, narrated overwhelmingly in terms of invisible, agentless, night-time action.[16]

Muktar-Aka is an ethnic Uzbek living on the Kyrgyzstan bank of the canal. He made a living transporting people and goods across the twelve-meter Shahrihan-sai canal separating Qorasuv and Kara-Suu on a large inflatable tire (*ballonchik*). He saw his job as a risky but eminently ethical one: an informal route for maintaining cross-border trade at a time when formal routes had been destroyed, transporting as many as 100 passengers per day.

Like Firuza, Muktar-Aka used an account of a disrupted cross-border funeral party to illustrate the obstacles that the border closure had caused to maintaining expected practices of kinship. His narrative began with a conventional contrast between the fate of those "who pay" and those who do not:

For instance, take my father . . . My father has a sister here, close to the big customs post. She died this year, just at the time they closed

[15]The association of disease with a dangerous, polluting outside world, has become a prevailing state discourse in Uzbekistan, with state-run television featuring an almost constant litany of pollutants (from crop-eating rats to international terrorists), and exhortations to fight them. An article in Uzbekistan's government-run newspaper just after the border closure defended the move with an article titled "Defending Consumer Rights," which stressed the need to protect Uzbek consumers from "unscrupulous" Kyrgyz traders selling "hazardous" Chinese products (Eurasianet 2003).

[16]Observers at the time also noted that the timing was less than fortuitous: the removal of the bridge occurred on the eve of the tenth anniversary of diplomatic relations between the two countries. For more details on this event, see Reeves (2003).

The dismantled "bridge of friendship" across the Shahrihan-sai Canal, Kara-Suu, May 2003.

the bridge. Her relatives are on the Uzbek side, and we called them to the funeral. And there, the soldiers, all those lads standing there—they wouldn't let them through. You see, whom do they let through? Those who give money, who pay. Up to three thousand [Kyrgyz som] they can make in a day.[17] All those . . . how to say . . . soldiers, they are just there on the crossing waiting for people. They're just making money [*prosto den'gi delaiut*], that's all. Well, for example, the other day three women came across on the tire with me. I dropped them there, and they wouldn't give any money. They [border guards] wouldn't let them through—and [the women] had to come back. But if you negotiate a fee [*a kak dogovorilis' na den'gi*], "be my guest," they say. "We won't touch you." Just like that.

Muktar-Aka's narrative seemed to suggest that it was all just a matter of money. Yet when I pressed him on this his answer was revealing. The real problem was not so much people paying their way across—after all, he joked, he too, paid his "due" (*dolia*) to make sure that his small role in the cross-border economy would not be disrupted by the border guards who monitor

---

[17] Around $60 at the time of interview, or roughly equivalent to a conscript's monthly salary.

Tire-ferry across the Kyrgyz-Uzbek border at Kara-Suu. Photo courtesy of Igor' Rotar'.

this section of the canal. The problem, rather, was the way in which appeals to a higher state authority were invoked to make the border completely invisible to certain categories of people. Muktar-Aka explained:

> You see, the kind of guy who sits wearing a tie—he needs to get somewhere?[18] There! On the car, on the roof, they attach a siren, they put a flashing light, and he can get about just where he likes. And ordinary people, what about them? Even on foot they can't get through! That's humane, is it? . . . It's like a joke [*kak anekdot poluchaetsia*].

As in Firuza's account, the border guards' refusal of passage here had nothing to do with "upholding the law" and everything to do with a desire to extort money from the locals, a mercenary attitude that over-rode even filial duty or religious obligations. By denying this passage, and thus, implicitly, the obligations incumbent upon Uzbeks to pay their respects to deceased relatives, the guards were refusing to acknowledge the very culture that in fact ought to have united them, invoking an "authority" that all knew to be a

---

[18]That is, an official (*chinovnik*). Ties and suits were often used as a shorthand for officialdom.

mere pretense for the extortion of money. Muktar-Aka's contempt is echoed in the depictions of the Kara-Suu border guards that feature in newspaper accounts. According to one Bishkek newspaper:

> The Uzbek border guards and fiscal [agents], under the pretext of strengthening the execution of their duties, practice extortion [*zanimai-utsia vymogatel'stvom*] of Kyrgyzstanis and their own citizens alike . . . Of course, it is nonsense when the populations of two friendly republics [*druzhestvennykh respublik*] are obliged to cross the border illegally on home-made raised bridges. But what really angers is something else—the Uzbek guards have taken on the role at the border, not only of gendarmerie, but also of punitive raiders [*karateli*]. (Kim and Gruzdov 2003b)

Commenting on the build-up to an open conflict that occurred at the canal in April 2003, when shots were fired and stones thrown across the water, the same reporters depicted the border guards as little children, unaware of the "authority" that they were supposed to be representing at the state's edge: "Of course, it sounds absurd, but [it started] with people in Uzbek military uniform firing on our population with ordinary school-boy catapults [*iz obyknovennykh mal'chishechykh rogatok*]" (Kim and Gruzdov 2003b). Another journalist, remarking ironically on the border guards' attempts to stop him from taking photographs of "their territory," described them as "beefy lads in uniform" (*diuzhie parni v forme*) (M. Khamidov 2000). Each of these portrayals avoids calling these "lads" soldiers—and, by extension, each suggests that their violence does not really carry the authority of the state. By depicting them as oversized school boys playing with catapults or punitive raiders, arbitrarily harassing those who would seek to cross, the authors of these articles highlight the way in which stately authority is invoked merely to serve a private source of profit.

This discursive deligitimization is suggestive. Like Muktar-Aka's critique, it indicates that the real threat lies less in the low-level bribe giving that serves to lubricate social relations in an area of ruptured movement than the way that authority is invoked to override the proper border ethic. Muktar-Aka was alert to the performative dimensions of such a claim. His imitation of the portly, tie-wearing official and his image of the removable siren (a symbol, par excellence, of the way that state authority is able to be turned on and off for personal gain) emphasized the arbitrary nature of cross-border regulation, which disappeared entirely for those successfully able to impersonate the state. As though to reinforce this absurd inequality of movement, Muktar-Aka then turned from individual law-subverting officials to the fate of the country as a whole:

MUKTAR-AKA: And what's their [Uzbekistan's] problem with us? Are they scared of Kirgiziia, or something?! There's nothing to be scared of from Kirgiziia. Now, for example, with Afghanistan, earlier, there used to be a border [ran'she u nikh byla granitsa]. But now they've rebuilt bridges, something like eighteen bridges to Afghanistan.

MADELEINE: And here?

MUKTAR-AKA: Here it's the opposite. Here they are taking them away. We're probably "better" than Afghans?! They probably think so!

Muktar-Aka's discursive linkage of the funeral party, the official who overrides the law, and Uzbekistan's opening of the "wrong" bridges, points to the greater anxiety that stories of objects-in-motion serve to index. As for Firuza, the problem is not just that borders are closed, but that they have come to materialize in the wrong place, between the wrong people, and in so doing have placed a considerable strain on harmonious cross-border sociality. Border controls here are merely performative, Muktar-Aka suggests, because if ensuring protection from flows of drugs, terrorists, and weapons were really the objective, why had "something like eighteen bridges" to Afghanistan been opened in the preceding few months? The narrative structure hints at the reason: it is the very vulnerability of the state to corruption from high-ranking officials, who appeal to state for personal gain, that fosters this paradoxical situation. For Muktar-Aka this is captured in the "joke-worthy" predicament that while relations here, between Uzbeks on two sides of a canal, have been disrupted by the vagaries of state control, Afghans (the archetypal "other" of popular Uzbek discourse, whose movement ought to be controlled) have had multiple bridges opened up to them. It is the weakness of the state that the cynical siren-wearing, state-invoking, border-crossing official comes to symbolize.

Rethinking the "Strong Weak State"

The experiences of Firuza, Mohammed, and Muktar-Aka illustrate the diversity of ways in which the particular accretion of practices and sites that constitute a border regime are locally encountered in the Ferghana Valley. We have seen that sometimes the attempt to monopolize legitimate movement is efficacious, at other times it is intensely contested, and that in some cases those nominally impersonating the state have more invested in ensuring a smooth flow of goods and people over the edge of the state than in trying to stop it. Here I draw out certain features of these ethnographic narratives to make the complications to the map explicit. This is an exercise in clarification, but it is intended also to introduce a broader theoretical problematic. What do such border stories reveal about the relationship between the state and its outside; between governmentality and (il)legibility? And how might they help us to think about practices of governance in Central Asia without recourse to the paradoxical "strong weak state"?

Let us consider the way that this multiple object, "border," emerges from the ethnographies presented. In the narrative and ethnographic encounters explored here, border emerges less as a line than as a zone of possibility where the opportunities for both connection and limit are intensified. In the no-man's-land between border posts, at the *chernye vkhody* and at the border markets, there is a heightened sense of danger—the awareness that this is a particular kind of "exceptional space" where one's very location means a potential suspension of law, and where ordinary relations of deference and respect are liable to be overturned in the name of "state security." Yet these are also sites of heightened possibility for establishing connection. For those with the practical knowledge and resources to act as go-betweens, living in a borderland provides immense opportunity to profit from the different regimes of value that exist on either side.

Second, borders emerge from these accounts as personated, and the particular persons who are doing the bordering matter. Depending on respective ages, ethnicity, rank, and kin relations, a border-crossing might take two minutes, two hours, or even two days. Moreover, this very conditionality means that the "ordinary" rules of engagement between state official and civilian can (and often are) switched around. Shortly before leaving fieldwork, I was crossing through the second of the two Uzbek border posts on the main road running west to east through the Sokh enclave. The Batken-registered minibus in which I was traveling was stopped for an unusually long time at the second of these two posts. All the passengers were made to take their belongings off for a detailed inspection. The driver and passengers were frustrated by this delay because a local minibus driver on his regular route did not usually experience such treatment. The reason, the driver told me, was that this was a new shift, with whom friendly relations had yet to be established. The passengers eventually piled back into the minibus and we continued on our way. Yet on reaching "our" Kyrgyzstani post 100 meters or so farther along the road, the driver, instead of stopping when he was flagged down by two young men in military uniform, rather hooted the horn vigorously and rolled down the window. "Hey, kids! (*Ei baldar!*)" he yelled to the Kyrgyz border guards manning the post, "if any Uzbek cars come along, check them really hard!"[19] With this he sped off, ignoring the border guards' injunction to stop and trumping it with an instruction of his own.

This act of reverse interpellation points to the third characteristic feature of such spaces: the fact that the most visible manifestations of the border, the "posts," are often experienced as arbitrary intrusions into "common" space, with their function as revenue generators felt to far outweigh any nominal security they might provide. In part this perceived arbitrariness derives from the fact that many borders only appear on certain days of the week, to regulate traffic to and from weekly markets (and as people would often point out, to extract fees for goods that were being transported across the border). In part, it derives from selectivity of checks. A Kyrgyzstan-registered car is far less likely to be stopped at a Kyrgyz post than at an Uzbek one, and vice versa—a tendency that was treated as so taken-for-granted by my informants that they often responded with indignation if they happened to be stopped by border guards from their own state.[20] Those who have official state-registered cars, or so-called cool license plates (*krutye nomera*) are unlikely to be stopped by officials of either state.

Perhaps the most important reason for the experience of arbitrariness has to do with the local geography of regulation. Most posts are experienced as appearing (and as disappearing equally suddenly) in sites that are not obviously the beginning or end of anywhere. Frequently stationed on bridges across rivers or canals (that may be some kilometers inside the state), at the end of villages, near the entrance to markets, or at the edge of areas of disputed territory to act as a de facto threat against its appropriation, the law-making edge of the state is perceived to be predatory upon those sites where "we"—those of us who live at the border—are most able to sustain friendly relations. From the perspective of those who have to pass through as a condition of economic survival, the rationale is less that such posts are needed to protect against external threat than that the state sees borderland citizens as a threat to each other.

Finally, borders are sites of moral commentary. Border stories, of which the rumors surrounding Gulnora Karimova are just one example, are vehicles for reflecting on and debating the proper limits of territorial regulation. Borders are important sites for the inscription and monumentalization of stately conceptions

---

[19]"*Özbek mashina kelse, kattuuraak teksherip koigulachy!*" His word for hard, *kattuu,* has the implication, not just of thorough, but of something unpleasant. It could be rendered as "subject them to a hard checking."

[20]The scale of this selective stopping has been documented in the monitoring of various crossing points conducted by the Dolina mira network of Ferghana Valley NGOs, though it does not receive much commentary in the network's published report (Dolina mira 2004). It is also well documented in the unpublished research conducted at the request of the OSCE Field Office in Osh by the Agency for Technical Cooperation and Development into sources of tension in villages on the Kyrgyz-Uzbek border (ACTED/OSCE 2005).

of citizenship, ethnicity, and territory as well as their normative correspondence in state ideology. They are places of often massively unequal relations of power. But they are more than that, just as "the market" as an object of commentary, of knowledge, and of feeling is quite different from any particular postsocialist bazaar (Mandel and Humphrey, 2002). Journeys across borders would often incite spontaneous—and at times extremely sophisticated—comparisons between economic and political models on two sides of the border: about protectionism and trade barriers, privatization and planning, limit and flow, and the proper extent of stately regulation (see also Roitman 2005, 200).

Moreover, these debates partake in larger discursive fields—fields complexly structured by dynamics of power that are asymmetrical with state borders. Citizens of Kyrgyzstan watched, and commented on, news broadcasts from Uzbekistan and vice versa. Those whose home had a satellite dish often did not watch locally broadcast news, instead typically watching Russian news broadcasts or, for satellite-owning families in Tajik-speaking Sokh, following Persian-language news bulletins broadcast to a global Persian-speaking diaspora from Dubai (my own hosts in Sokh, Parviz, and Sharofat had given up on watching any domestic Uzbek television as soon as they had bought their satellite dish). Debates about regulation of canal water or ownership of communal grazing lands would be mediated by languages of tolerance and property rights learned from village seminars sponsored by taxpayers in the USA, Switzerland and Sweden. Normative understandings about legitimate accumulation, the proper movement of differently gendered bodies and things, and the foundations of strong statehood were as likely to be shaped by Mexican soap operas, Persian pop channels, and bootleg Uzbek religious cassette tapes as they were by state decree. In Sokh, in May of 2005, when a massacre in the nearby Uzbek city of Andijan were making headline news on CNN and BBC, many of my Uzbek interlocutors in Sokh first heard about the events from Euronews in Russian, retransmitted from Bishkek on Kyrgyz state television. The radically polarized informational sphere on two sides of the Kyrgyz-Uzbek border that Megoran encountered in 2000 was one that I found to be far more complexly structured five years later.[21] It was at the

---

[21]Megoran describes finding a population in Sokh in the summer of 2000 permeated by fear to the extent that local residents mobilized an army detachment to apprehend him (2002, 183), attributing this to the "sustained fervor of newspaper and television reporting" to which they were exposed. He contrasts this with the relaxed, joking attitude of Kyrgyz pastoralists above Sokh, the difference highlighting the "two different regimes with very different propaganda machines" to which the respective populations were exposed (ibid., 185). The year two thousand was indeed a tense time in Sokh. Yet if the "propaganda regimes" were ever as isolated in the cultural schemas of borderland populations as Megoran suggests, by 2004 the ideational field was significantly more differentiated.

intersection of (and not simply under the exposure to) profoundly different discourses of security, risk, and territoriality that understandings of borders and their flows were debated and contested.

These are some of the threads that we can draw from the narratives presented in this chapter. But what do they imply for our larger concern with border work in Central Asia? After all, at some level these are perhaps prosaic conclusions: a story of low-level resistance to state control, perhaps: of society wielding its "weapons of the weak" (Scott 1985) against the state. From an economic logic of competition and cooperation, we might conclude that there are simply insufficient incentives to proper securitization of the Uzbek-Kyrgyz border. Such stories might be invoked to bolster the argument of state "weakness" or "failure" in Central Asia.[22] And they would seem to lend yet more evidence to a well-rehearsed narrative of pervasive state corruption. Each of the accounts that I have presented could be interpreted through such frames. Each could be used as the kind of real-life story that is boxed up and inserted to enliven hefty policy documents.

I suggest that the ethnography here might also prod our analysis in another direction—one attentive to the way in which law and uncertainty (or, in the language of border-spaces, limits and gaps) function together as a particular modality of power. In other words, I explore whether the empirical border space might not give us an insight into thinking more generally about state (re)composition in Central Asia; whether a critique of the cartographic view might not also point us to a more fundamental critique of the lines we draw between "state" and "society." To illustrate what I mean, let us consider the following scene, one which is a regular sight at many of the *chernye vkhody* near the Kara-Suu market, but which we also see in a more distended form in Mohammed's account of his cross-border trade. An illegal border-crossing place is often close to the official border post. We might see women or children crossing it, day laborers grouped on the one side or the other to sell their labor, and we might see someone in uniform charged with regulating this movement. As Stina Torjesen found in her observations of a *chernyi vkhod* near the Dostuk crossing post, the distinction is locally irrelevant. On the day she made her field observations, "the women [crossing illegally] claimed that Uzbek border guards had been there until lunchtime, demanding bribes; after lunch they

---

[22]In December 2005, the International Crisis Group characterized Kyrgyzstan as "a failed state whose fate reinforces the view of its neighbors that the path to stability lies not in democracy but dictatorship" (2005b, i). Uzbekistan, meanwhile, was deemed to be "well down the path of self-destruction followed by such countries as Burma, North Korea and Zimbabwe" (International Crisis Group 2006, 1).

had been replaced by a civilian" (2007, 190; see also Lam 2009, 181). From the perspective of those doing the crossing, whether the person collecting the fee is a civilian or a state representative is in practice irrelevant: the amount to be paid is simply a "fee" and nothing else, and it is assumed by all parties that state officials are certainly not blind to the informal arrangement that exists. Indeed, the regular (and quite open) talk of the variable "fees" (*stavki*) that attach to particular positions of authority within the border and customs services speak rather of a pyramid, wherein a certain volume of money must head "upward" and "inward," from the border to the capital, from the low-level border guard to ministries and beyond.[23] These channels of patronage and tribute, as much as decrees and directives "downward," are crucial to spatializing the state.

Is this, then, simply a story of corruption? At one level, of course, it is. There is, implicitly or explicitly, some abuse of stately office underway and there is a strong local perception that certain official positions within customs and border services carry a price tag because they are financially lucrative. But casting the scene in these terms also risks missing what to me is the anthropologically interesting problem. A language of corruption suggests a normative functioning system, from which the corruption is a deviation. What we have here, by contrast, is a situation where "the state" is constituted *as state* by its appropriation of informal exchange. The goods that pass informally through the *chernyi vkhod* are not simply a deviation or a corruption "of" the state; neither are they incidental to its constitution and its everyday functioning. The state here rather thrives upon the very proliferation of informal activity. As one contributor to a web discussion noted, following an incident in which the governor of Batken oblast and the border guards of neighboring Tajikistan had got into a fight: "of course the commander of the border-unit needs to re-establish his post in order to levy money from passing cars. Because otherwise their border guards [*pograntsy*] will remain absolutely penniless" (Kashkaraev 2007). Informal fees, requests for gasoline from passing cars, demands for lifts, and so on, are not merely incidental to the functioning of the unit; they are fundamental to its very maintenance.

Roitman describes something rather similar in the context of illicit border-crossing trade in the Chad Basin, where the emergence of unregulated economic activities and violent methods of extraction, far from displacing

---

[23]Such "rates" are extremely difficult to document. I was regularly told that in Kyrgyzstan the head of a border unit (*nachal'nik zastavy*) could expect to "earn a car" (around $4,000–6,000) within half a year, though I have no way of confirming this. Satybaldieva (2010, 76) quotes an informant who explains that to become the head of the customs department on one of Kyrgyzstan's main border crossing to China, at Erkeshtam, the "applicant" has to pay $100,000–150,000, with this initial bribe recuperated through payments from lower-ranking officials, who in turn receive bribes for allowing unregulated passage.

the state, demonstrate rather how "violent practices can also be produced as a legitimate mode of the exercise of power." Violence, in the region where Roitman conducted fieldwork, had become "part of the very legibility of power" (2004, 192–193; see also Lombard 2012, 20): the state transmogrifies, it cannibalizes methods of informal seizure, but it does not disappear. Indeed, in Cameroon it is by appropriating "extra state" techniques of violent seizure that some semblance of a Weberian bureaucracy is generated, funded, and sustained. As such it confounds assumptions that states produced through highly effective forms of capillary power are "strong," while those resorting to violence are "weak."

The everyday regime of cross-border trade in the Ferghana Valley is somewhat different from Roitman's portrait, not least because violence is not—or, at least, not regularly—part of the everyday legibility of power. Most crossings are *yntymaktuu* rather than violent. But the focus of Roitman's account on the way the "state" is constituted by appropriating nonstate or illicit forms of exchange provides a useful point of entry for critiquing the binaries that continue to dominate much writing on Central Asian statehood. Writing on Central Asian "state and society" has often been premised on particular topographies of power. This has resulted in vexed conceptual and policy debates about how to theorize (and support) institutions that fit uncomfortably within such binaries. The contemporary Uzbekistani *mahalla,* for instance, is potentially a site of both grassroots social organizing and often coercive stately control: a manifestation "of the state as an NGO" (Thompson 2007, 237), which presents considerable dilemmas to western organizations committed to supporting civil society (Noori 2006, 172–221). Likewise, the emergence of strongmen "within, not outside, the state apparatus" (Jones Luong 2004, 277) has presented analysts with a problem of definition and theorization: how to account for the state that seems to be simultaneously strong and weak, "acting against itself"?

In both cases the paradox arises from an initial assumption (one emerging from a particular political ontology which has a distinct, European genealogy (Kharkhordin 2001) that the state ought, in both an empirical and normative sense, to be clearly "separate" from society—a finished construction rather than a work in progress. The ethnography presented here suggest that a more fruitful approach might be to start from a recognition of the difficulty of abstracting the state in a context of multiple formal-informal dependencies: of making "it," the state, come to appear above society and encompassing of it. The challenge is to take seriously the elusiveness of the state/society boundary, "not as a problem of conceptual precision but as a clue to the nature of the phenomenon" (Mitchell 1999, 77): the problem being *how* it is, through which material and discursive practices, the state is carved off as a separate domain from society. From this perspective the strongman who is also a state figure; the wrestler-turned-drugs baron who becomes a law-writing state deputy is less a paradoxical figure than an emblematic one. It means that what appears as a problem of the violation of a preexisting boundary between state and society, legal and illegal can rather be understood as a problem of production: How to carve off the domain of "state" as something that is constituted by law? How to make the border-guard and the civilian who alternatively guard the *chernyi vkhod* at Kara-Suu come to be understood as belonging to different domains?

This has implications for accounts that would see state power at borders as functioning exclusively through its monumental inscriptions of power. This is true for the way some borders work, or at least, how some borders in highly governmental states work most of the time. But it presupposes that the state really does "regulat[e] most daily activities of its citizens and residents in direct relations of cause and effect" (Wilson and Donnan 1998, 8). It presupposes that the state is a finished construction and that it is obvious to all parties to an encounter who and where the state is, and from whence the authorization of any particular state functionary comes. As such it provides us with few analytical tools for thinking about how state power works in sites where the causal relations are contested, or when the very *location* of state authority is up for grabs. In taking the border to be a line a priori, rather than a field of competing authoritative claims, this approach fails to see the ways in which power is enacted as much through the reproduction of uncertainty as through the demarcation of clear boundary lines. As scholars of postcolonial polities remind us, it is often precisely through "the arbitrariness with which the state displays and imposes its interests in different bodies of subjects" (Ferme 2004, 88) that thralldom for the state is maintained.

I now return to the question of what the "gaps" reveal about how a border works. The gaps alert us to the interdependency of the formal and the informal, the licit and the illicit, the state and the extra state. Wire and waterways, limits and flows, are both important to the functioning of the border economy. But gaps also speak to a different kind of gulf: between action and authorization, and the contestation over the location of legitimate authority. In order to understand the feelings that borders tend to elicit and their overdetermination as sites of contention, we need to attend to the ways in which violence here lurks as a potentiality. It is because the location of legitimate authority is contested that Firuza resorts to a language of nationalism to explain a soldier's actions. It is the fragility of (real) law that places such stakes on the maintenance of *yntymak*. And it is the performativity of stately authority that gives meaning to Muktar-Aka's gentle mocking of the tie-wearing, siren-fixing official.

Critical ethnographies of the state in the former Soviet Union have begun to explore sites of state illegibility, in encounters with the police (Rushchenko 2005) and in the ritualized violence of military service (Bannikov 2002), recognizing that here, as in postcolonial contexts, "the frontier between the legal and extralegal runs right within the offices and institutions that embody the state" (Das and Poole 2004, 14). What I have argued is that this insight needs to be extended to those sites and encounters—of which borders are a paradigmatic example—where at a distance, from the cartographer's view, there would seem to be an incontrovertible boundary between legal and extralegal, state and society, one country's territory and the next.

5. IMPERSONATIONS

Manning the Border, Enacting the State

Muktar-Aka's account of the border-crossing *chinovnik* showed how state authority is spoken of as a kind of impersonation (see chapter 4). The portly, tie-wearing official whom Muktar-Aka mocked for attaching a siren to the roof of his car was able to cross the border unchecked because of a particular, efficacious, claim to represent the state. Muktar-Aka himself was in no doubt as to the performative dimensions of such an act. The siren, the tie, and the *sluzhebnaia mashina* (official car) were temporary and fragile appeals to state authority. Interaction at the border, he suggested, was always shot through with the possibility that this claim might be challenged or overruled.

In this chapter, I explore this mode of interaction ethnographically and analytically. Ethnographically I am interested in how, in a variety of border encounters, state authority comes to be invested in particular people and objects—and what happens when that ascription collapses. Central Asia's borders provide a fruitful site for this kind of exploration because the contested location of the state—in particular people and places—is exposed here with particular clarity. Analytically I explore how violence circulates as a potential in and around Central Asia's borders and the implications of this latent threat of force for understanding how habitual practices of negotiation and differentiation become politicized, sometimes violently so.

If we recognize the state to be the product of situated practices, which achieves its effects "through a certain mundanity and banality" (Navaro-Yashin 2002, 135), then we can approach empirically the question of what are the practices and processes through which certain people, actions, places, and objects come to be invested with state-like authority. How do some mundane practices remain mundane, and others come to be imbued with stately significance?

More concretely: how and when do the conscripts who are now found throughout borderland villages, living in barracks, converted teahouses or lodging with
local families, come to be seen as state representatives enacting an externally
authorized law? Borders are productive settings for exploring these issues because they allow us to approach empirically the question of how the sovereignty
of the state is continuously reenacted through the creation of legal and political
"outsides."

In this respect, my analysis echoes Das and Poole's call to think ethnographically about the performative refounding of law in everyday life. "The
problem of the origin of law is not a ghostly specter from the past," they argue,
"but rather the result of the concrete practices in which life and labor are engaged" (2004, 15). Here I foreground one particular "concrete practice": that of
border guarding. In earlier chapters we have seen scattered references to those
who man the borders in the Ferghana Valley: the customs officers, road police,
and conscript soldiers charged with regulating the movement of people and
goods. For the most part they have remained faceless: the "rootless young men"
of Batken slang; the bribe-taking guardians with whom Mohammed would
exchange cigarettes; or the heartless "nationalists" who refused passage to the
corpse that Firuza's teacher was hoping to bury in Uzbekistan. In so doing,
I have followed a pattern that is common to much anthropological writing on
international borders, in which those who do the border guarding remain, at
best, the faceless transmitters of official state ideology. "At best" because more
striking still is the near total eclipse of border guards from the ethnographic literature on borderland culture—despite the constitutive role of these and other
state agents in forging a distinct borderland sociality. Even as faceless transmitters of official ideology their appearance in border ethnographies is rare.[1]

Attending to the work of manning a border is nonetheless significant for
understanding the dynamics through which place becomes territorialized,
habitual altercations ethicized, and illicit practices normalized in the Ferghana Valley. Border guards are rarely read or interacted with as "faceless

---

[1] See Mountz (2010) for a penetrating insight into civil servants responsible for policing
illegal immigration into Canada, and Blaive and Lindenberger (2012) for a discussion of border
guarding as social practice. Although the political significance of border enforcement has received some attention, there has been little ethnographic attention paid to the day-to-day work
of manning a border. An edited volume on *Culture and Power at the Edges of the State*, Wilson
and Donnan (2005a; 2005b, 2) emphasizes programmatically that the state is not to be treated "as
some essentialized, unitary structure, an actor just off stage whose face is never seen" and that it is
precisely this that makes borders theoretically generative. However the ethnographies contained
in the volume actually problematize the state and its personnel rather little. Of the two concepts
in the volume's title, "culture" is extensively treated, but the "state," despite the programmatic
opening essay, remains empirically little explored.

bureaucrats." They may be greeted warmly or harshly, but their age, ethnicity, provenance, rank, and length of service will be interpreted in that interaction. In Ak-Sai, for instance, where a small military barracks has been home to border troops since the early 2000s, the head of the border unit is a key authority in village life. Referred to locally by his first name, he would often be sought out by Ak-Sai men as an informal (but, crucially, armed) local authority if an altercation between Tajik and Kyrgyz young men was felt to be getting out of hand. The barracks, too, are integrated into village life. Several Ak-Sai men derive a living as drivers delivering supplies for the barracks. And in winter, those who can might call upon connections to familiar officers to make use of the barracks' bathhouse (*mönchö*)—one of the few places in the village with running water.

For border guards, the economic realities of their practice and the fact that they are, for the most part, young unmarried men embedded within a strongly age-based hierarchy, means that they necessarily develop complex social relations with those in whose communities they live: to get smoking tobacco, lifts from the village to border post, gasoline, news, or gossip. Border guarding is an activity fraught with uncertainty and negotiation; border guards' authority fragile and often undermined through appeal to higher state authority or economic power. For the most part, border guards' presence is quietly tolerated; the small-scale "gifts" that exchanged hands at border posts quietly misrecognized as "tea money" (*chai pul*) or "tobacco money" (*nas pul*)—terms that stress their benign character and the role of these exchanges in sustaining relations of friendly mutuality (cf. Patico 2002). At other times, border guards' perceived corruption invites intense moral commentary. On one occasion, at the large border market that was in operation at the southern end of the Sokh enclave, Parviz pointed out to me a group of Kyrgyz soldiers who were purchasing a satellite dish using Uzbek currency. "They didn't get that from their paycheck," he noted pointedly: their use of Uzbek sum a clear demonstration, to Parviz, that this currency must have come into their hands by illicit means.

Misunderstanding was sometimes born of difficulties of miscommunication in this trilingual environment. Most of the men policing borders in the Ferghana Valley at the time of my research were conscript soldiers (*srochniki*), posted from other parts of their respective states to conduct their military service. Often they did not share a common language with people from the neighboring state whose documents and vehicles they were charged with checking. Although Uzbek serves as a common language of everyday interaction between Kyrgyz and Uzbek speakers in and around Sokh, Kyrgyz border guards posted there from northern Kyrgyzstan often had difficulties understanding Uzbek. Likewise, language often acted as a barrier at encounters on the Kyrgyz-Tajik border in the Isfara Valley if the soldiers were not from the immediate vicinity. Few of the Kyrgyz border guards with whom I spoke around Batken knew more than a smattering of Tajik, and none of the Tajik border guards whom I encountered in the Isfara Valley knew Kyrgyz. Russian, which had served as a regional lingua franca for Kyrgyz and Tajik speakers of an older generation, now rarely functioned as a social glue between younger speakers. On more than one occasion I heard middle-age Kyrgyz men, who often pride themselves on their fluency in Russian, hurl abuse at younger Tajik border guards for their inability to speak in a "civilized manner"—meaning, in this specific situation of a borderland encounter, in Russian.

There were further social obstacles for the young men responsible for regulating the cross-border passage of cars and people around Batken. At a typical rural crossing point, manning the border would entail committing to memory a wide range of names, faces, vehicle registration numbers, and social ranks; and it required learning who should be allowed through unchecked. For a guard to stop and check the documents of the neighboring state's provincial governor, or high-ranking employees of the local police, for instance, is technically both legal and obligatory. To do so, however, would be to risk a reprimand (or worse) by the higher-ranking official. On one occasion in 2007 when the governor of Batken oblast was stopped in his white Toyota jeep by four Tajik border guards at a temporary border post near the village of Surh, this perceived insult to unspoken interstate decorum was met with a rapid escalation of force, with warning shots fired into the air and the governor allegedly seizing and breaking the offending border guard's two-way radio (*ratsiia*).[2]

Insulted at the suggestion that his official vehicle looked "suspicious," and angry that he should be stopped by Tajik guards on what he considered to be undemarcated (thus neutral) territory, the governor ignored the border guards' requests to check the contents of his jeep, instead sending his driver to bring the chief of the corresponding Kyrgyz border unit to the scene to meet force with force. The border guards from the two neighboring states

---

[2] Reports in the Tajik press emphasized that the incident occurred on Tajik territory, and that soldiers who stopped the governor's car were therefore merely performing their honest service in "guarding the sovereign national state-border of Tajikistan" (Varorud 2007). Kyrgyz-language reports were more equivocal, stating merely that the governor was stopped on the Batken-Leilek highway, thereby emphasizing the "Kyrgyz-ness" of his location and direction (e.g., Choibekov 2007). One Kyrgyz parliamentarian wrote an outspoken critique of the incident, describing it as part of a broader "predatory policy" (*khishchnicheksaia politika*) of Tajikistan to encroach on Kyrgyz lands around Batken (Omuraliev 2008). In this account the "boorish" Tajik border guards stopped the governor "on Kyrgyz territory" and their actions should therefore rightly be considered an attempt on the governor's life (*pokushenie na ubiistvo*).

were joined by the respective local chiefs of police and internal affairs, as well as a group of customs officers, and the head of the Batken TV station.[3] By the time the incident came to circulate in the national media two days later, the conflict had already reached the heads of state, with the now interstate dispute only resolved when Emomali Rahmon, the Tajik president, promised (in the Kyrgyz media's rendering, at least) to "sort his border guards out" (Foundation for Tolerance International 2007; Tazar.kg 2007).

It was not only the state officials who expected to be shown deference by soldiers manning the border. Around Batken, Arapat-Eje's son, Kadyr, would shout orders to the young conscript regulating traffic to "open up" his metal swing gate if this was a post where habit and familiarity should allow him through unchecked. On another occasion, the driver of a car that I was traveling in yelled over to a border guard who was being slow in processing the border traffic, "my brother is the procurator!" signaling in this simple (unverifiable) claim an assertion to a higher authority and a right to bypass the other cars.

Alisher, a university student from Ferghana, explained to me the unspoken codes by which the privileges of passage were granted to high-ranking officials and the way this could be extended to wealthy individuals whose purchased car license plates indexed their connections to distances centers of power:

> Take, for instance, the [license plate] number 15 FV 002. That's the plate of the *hokim* [governor] of Ferghana oblast. . . . Well, of course, no one is going to stop a car like that. . . . And then there's a whole series of other plates that, informally [*ne glasno*] no one is going to stop. I know for instance that they are never going to stop the plate AF because that's the number of the head of the internal affairs. Usually the high-ranking [*krutye*—lit. sharp or acute; here, wealthy] employees of the police drive around in cars like that. . . . Of course, you don't have to be an official to get a nice number. For instance, for private individuals 15 R 0707—you see, that's a beautiful license plate—can be bought for several hundred dollars. A plate like that says that the owner of the car is either very wealthy, such that if conflict were to arrive he could sort out the problem through the bosses [*uladit' problemu cherez nachal'nikov*]

---

[3]Although the governor and his passengers were allowed to proceed on their way, the altercation had lasting repercussions, with a conflict the following day between the heads of the respective border units, each accusing the other of illegally crossing onto the other state's territory. Meetings ensued between the oblast governors of the respective states, in which the Kyrgyz side announced that they would counter the risk that the Tajik post posed to "interethnic relations" by fortifying the provision at their own border unit at Surh (Kojotegin 2007).

or he has good contacts with people high up in the oblast. So of course you're not going to stop people like that; you don't want to delay them.

In this context of negotiated privilege, small-scale fracas between the officials of one state and those of its neighbors were a constant of local conversation. Who had been stopped by whom? How had "our" official reacted? Had he (and it was always he) shown them "who was right"? When I asked Kadyr-Aka why such formal procedures of verification so often seemed to result in tensions between the officials of neighboring states, he answered with a proverb: *karga karganyn közün chukubait* ("crows don't peck at the eyes of other crows"). A border guard, his expression suggested, ought to know better than to "peck at the eye" of another state official.

Producing State Effects

Exploring such negotiations around the right to claim state authority draws attention to the fact that the state is always encountered through multiple particular encounters with multiple particular people and things (Gupta 1995; Navaro-Yashin 2002). It is an empirical question whether and when a given official comes to be seen as "official," as the bearer of legitimate authority. A focus on the work of manning the border points to multiplicity and distribution and the problem of producing an effect of singularity and verticality: the problem for the border guard of demonstrating that he is enacting a law that is external to him; that he has meaningful claim to act on behalf of the state.

This has implications for how such sites might extend anthropological reflection on state spatialization. The tendency to treat merely as extensions of the state, or to ignore altogether, the men who do the manning—and the gendered nature of this verb is not inconsequential—means that the analytic language itself tends to participate in the production of territoriality as pregiven frame for action; to assume a depersonalized, sovereign state that is then negotiated, transgressed, or subverted. In his study of the high modern state, James Scott makes explicit a conceptual move that is often implicit in studies of international borders. "Officials of the modern state," he tells us, "are, of necessity, at least one step—and often several steps—removed from the society they are charged with governing." As a consequence they rely on typifications "that are always some distance from the full reality these abstractions are meant to capture" (Scott 1998, 76). Scott's "of necessity" occludes the very problem that we need to unpack; namely, if the state officials are understood to be "one step" removed from society, then how is that moment of abstraction achieved? What happens when it collapses? And is it, in any case, empirically the case that they are one step removed from society, or that they are seen to be such? The tendency to speak of an a priori separation between "officials" and "society" also means that the intensity of gendered sociality at borders tends to get missed, in which manning and working the border depend to a considerable degree on engaging the (male) face of the state at the border. As was discussed in chapter 4, these are sites where different cultural codes collide and are negotiated: gender, generation, wealth, localness, ethnicity, and state connections are fundamental to the encounter, and negotiating them from the "official's" perspective is rarely as simple as imposing a classificatory schema or enforcing a rule.

Perhaps most significant, by sidelining attention to the work of regulating movement across a border, we tend to screen out the ways that violence and law here circulate as each other's shadows: the way in which individuals come to be constituted as soldiers—as agents of the state's "legitimate violence"—in part through subjection to violence; and the way in which the efficacy of border as limit ultimately depends on the possibility that violation can be met with the use of force. Attending to the kinds of violence that are "internal" to the border troops can help us to think about the particular microdynamics of power at the border. It enables us to see the modality of power at the border—the kinds of arbitrary invocations of law, the contestations over who here is "the state," the potential for physical or symbolic violence—as continuous with modes of violence that circulate across the realms of what is usually parceled up as "civil society" and "the state."

My analysis proceeds from a series of extended interviews with one demobilized border guard, Kuba (short for Kubanich), whom I came to know particularly well as he was a regular visitor to the Sadyrbaev home in Batken. Kuba's case is atypical: he is now a citizen of Kyrgyzstan who served in the Russian army on the Tajik-Afghan border. For a host of historical and geopolitical reasons, this is an "exceptional" border: a Soviet-era boundary that was symbolically overdetermined as needing to be kept "under lock and key" (Shaw 2011), and one that is today both exceptionally challenging to guard and where "rule of law" is peculiarly threatened by the lucrative trade in narcotics and gemstones across it (Heathershaw 2009). For my interlocutors in the Ferghana Valley, Afghanistan was often the contrastive other against which civilization and development were charted; and the Afghan-Tajik and Afghan-Uzbek borders often served as referents for the kind of borders that should properly be closed to dangerous seepages of people and ideas.

By exploring Kuba's experiences in manning this border, I am not suggesting that his experiences of coming to guard this border (nor the everyday violence by which his life there was characterized) can easily be transposed to the very different borders of the Ferghana Valley, which did not exist as international boundaries in Soviet times. The kind of contingency over law's location that is revealed in his narrative is extreme in the sense that it illuminates with particular clarity the incompleteness of state territoriality and the fragility of recognition in ways that are more routinized elsewhere. *All* borders, Das and Poole (2004, 19) remind us, are "spaces in which sovereignty, as the right over life and death, is experienced in the mode of potentiality—thus creating affects of panic and a sense of danger even if 'nothing happens.'" As such, Kuba's reflections on border guarding provide a means of probing into a series of more general issues: concerning impersonation, military violence, stately incorporation, and the contingency of knowing whom to let through the border. I intersperse his narrative with reflections on border work from other former border guards who served on Kyrgyzstan's borders whom I came to know during fieldwork, and from written accounts of soldiering. Together they point toward the need for a processual account of the state, recognizing sovereignty to be a more-or-less contested, more-or-less violent process of assertion—not an a priori fact.

Incorporation: Military Service and the Body Politic

For twenty-six-year-old Kuba, military service on the border between Tajikistan and Afghanistan in the late 1990s represented the kind of turning point that structured recollections in terms of a binary "before" and "after." Kuba was a regular visitor to the home of Arapat and Abdumital Sadyrbaev, and a close friend of their youngest son, Üsön. A few years earlier, Kuba had lived with the Sadyrbaevs for several months, enjoying free room and board in return for his help on the family's fields. It was a time Kuba recalled with fondness, when he had "put on weight" and felt included as a family member, sharing friendship and social space with Üsön. His increasing evening drinking bouts, however, had eventually led Abdumital-Aka, an observant Muslim who never drank, to ask him to leave. Kuba now lived in much more precarious and impoverished circumstances working as a casual laborer for a family on the other side of the Sokh enclave, in Aidarken. When he came to visit friends in Batken, Kuba now made a point of drinking in private, out of sight of the Sadyrbaev family, using his flimsy one-page "temporary passport" as a deposit at the local vodka stand. As his "most precious possession" this was the best guarantee he had that he would eventually pay up.

Kuba was born in Batken, but had grown up, as "Russian" (*russkii*) Kolia, across the border in Tajikistan, the son of an ethnically Russian father and Tajik mother, but raised primarily by a Tatar-identifying paternal grandmother. His shifting between forms of identification, as (Kyrgyz) Kuba and (Russian) Kolia, mirrored a broader concern with "fitting in" to prescriptive binary nationality categories and their documentary validation. He spoke Russian, Tajik, and Kyrgyz but considered none of these languages to be fully his own. In Batken he was taken to be ethnically Tajik; in Tajikistan he was taken to be Russian. Kuba described his mixed background as a "curse" (*prokliatie*), one that was magnified by the fact that he had only recently come to acquire Kyrgyz citizenship and that he had little more than a temporary passport to document his identity for six months at a time. "I want a passport and money, in that order" Kuba used to say: both of them necessary preconditions for finding his mother who had long ago moved to Kazakhstan.

The importance of documented identity came out in the following conversation, in which, following his own question to me about my nationality, I asked Kuba about his. After a moment's hesitation, Kuba switched into declamatory tone:

KUBA: When I was a child, I always said that I was Tatar, when I was with my grandmother. But I'm Russian; I know Russian, all my documents [say I'm] Russian, but well I was brought up with Tatar traditions, and all that.

MADELEINE: Did you grow up with the Tatar language, too?

KUBA: Well, I didn't know Tatar; I could understand it but didn't speak it. It's close to Kyrgyz so maybe that's why I learnt Kyrgyz so quickly. And now I'm firmly convinced that I'm Russian [*ia tverdo uveren, chto ia russkii*]. I tell everyone, they are always asking, "Who are you by nationality?" "Russian." "Don't lie, you're not Russian" "Russian. You want, take a look at my document." He reads my document, then goes, "yeah, but all the same you're a mixture [*smes'*]. No one believes me that I'm pure Russian [*chistyi russkii*]. "You're a mixture." "Well, so what? A mixture. My mother's Tajik." "Ah, everything's clear, that's why you're so black." And proving it is hard. That's why you've got to be so insistent. Obstinacy [*uporstvo*], obstinacy. If you aren't going to insist, they'll bury you. They'll bury you with questions. They'll say, "you're not Russian, you're not Russian." I'll get a proper passport and prove it.

Kuba's concern with being documented mirrored and magnified his more
general anxiety about failing to fit within prescribed national categories.
Being "pure Russian" according to his passport did not prevent him from being questioned by document-checking officials.[4] "When I go through Sokh,
the border guards find fault with my passport [*pridiraiutsia*]," he commented
on one of his visits to Batken, which necessitated crossing the Sokh enclave.
Then, imitating the nonchalant swagger and accusatory tone of the border
guard who looked him up and down, he called out in Uzbek, "*Orusmusun?!
o'xshamaysan!*" (You think you are a Russian?! You don't look like it!), capturing in those words the gulf between the documented and physical self and
the primacy of the former. "They say that I look like a mujahid [guerrilla
fighter]. That I stuck my picture onto a fake passport. They pick at the edges
[of the picture] to make it try to come off."

Within this context of ambivalent identifications, in which everyday social categories and the pictures stuck on paper passports both failed properly to stick, military service had provided Kuba with something like a stable
point of reference: a provisional stability that acted as a turning point in his
life's narrative. If his earlier and later experiences were described in terms
of absences and failures (his failure to be given a permanent passport; his
failure to be ascribed unambiguously to one or other nationality category;
and, increasingly, his inability to afford to marry), military service stuck out
in his account as one area where the category had been able to accommodate
him. When he was given his Kalashnikov, it was the first time he had properly
been able to label himself anything: a soldier (*voennyi*). He repeated the word
slowly before continuing: "they give you the weapon and you know you can
kill someone with that. You realize then why you are there. Well, there you
are: soldier."

Kuba's official passport nationality had given him an advantage in joining
the Russian military, which, until 2004, still largely guarded Tajikistan's southern border with Afghanistan. A 1993 "friendship agreement" between the
Russian Federation and Tajikistan had meant that for most of Tajikistan's first
decade of independence, all but 70 kilometers of its 1,344-kilometer border
with Afghanistan was guarded by troops subordinate to the Russian Federation. The distinction between the forces was an ambiguous one as the majority
of soldiers in both the "Russian" and "Tajik" border forces were citizens of

---

[4]This is a reference to the "nationality" [*natsional'nost'*] line that was included in Soviet passports and is still included in contemporary Kyrgyz passports. Being "pure Russian" according
to the passport is a reference to the fact that from a documentary point of view, Kuba's national
identification was unambiguous.

Tajikistan.⁵ To ordinary conscript soldiers such as Kuba, the "Russian" military was distinguished by the origin of the commanding officers (contract soldiers from the Russian Federation), the country to which the military oath (*prisiaga*) was read out, and the quality of food, provisioning, and pay rather than by any significant difference in composition or type of operation. Kuba had wanted to join the Russian army for these very reasons, and while his passport nationality had given him an advantage in securing a place in the Russian troops, he had still had to bribe his way in. He described his entry into the Russian forces in the following terms:

KUBA: Well, really, I was from another military unit [*voenkomat*], so I was supposed to go from the raion-level [base] but I went from the oblast-level one. There were 10 of us, we took 10 bottles of whisky, each person had a bottle, we went to the colonel [of the Russian troops] and we just laid them out like that in front of him and he signed us up. But that in itself is no guarantee. All those who go to the Russian troops from there, from Khorog are bought by a purchaser [*pokupatel'*], an officer: a captain, a major, and he chooses. He won't take the skinny ones, because they'll fall ill; he won't take the fat ones either. You need to have a good body shape [*teleslozhenie*], they look at your weight, height, they check your eyes. No one who is flat-footed. They check all that, and if it all fits, then OK, they'll write down, "you go here," "you go there." In other words, they choose themselves and if he doesn't want you, he's never going to take you.

MADELEINE: In what sense do you mean they "buy"?

KUBA: In the direct sense. They buy. From the Tajik forces.

MADELEINE: For how much?

KUBA: I don't know that. They have their own tariff. They pay out [*vyplachivaiut*]. And then you see they also pay the soldiers, and they teach us. And in the Tajik army they don't teach you anything.

⁵In 2004, in an important symbolic gesture, responsibility for guarding the frontier went to the Tajik military, a change to be phased in over two years (Amirshoeva 2005). As Heathershaw has argued, this gesture had little to do with improving security. The 1993 agreement had envisaged a gradual transfer of powers to Tajik forces, but in reality this had not happened and the Tajik troops were ill-resourced to take over control. The handover, rather, was central to the post–civil war "simulation of sovereignty" in Tajikistan. "The transfer implicated political discourses which inscribed the sovereignty of the Tajik government, its authority over its territory and people, its place in the region, and its status in the international community" (2007, 232).

The techniques of objectification through which Kuba was selected—the careful checking of his passport and body; the peering into his eyes and ears, the questions and accusations, and above all the act of "purchase"—figured in his narrative less as marks of humiliation than a source of pride at being ascribed a role and an identity. Kuba's rather fractured childhood meant that military membership probably had more than usual significance as a vehicle of social incorporation. Coming to own a gun was a particularly poignant moment of self-realization. Yet the sense that the army, for all its violence and humiliation, was a site of inclusion into a particular, gendered body politic was a recurrent trope among Batken's border guards. "The army is its own little world, with its own laws," was how one conscript soldier described it to me as we sat waiting for cars in the upper Sokh Valley. "It becomes its own motherland [*rodina*], no one from outside is going to understand." In his memoir of military service in the Kyrgyz special service forces [*spetsnaz*], Il'dar Bikkenin similarly describes the army as a "big family" asking, with a nod to the institutionalized hazing of younger conscripts by their older peers, "in which family, where there are forty sons, are the father and mother going to work? Or the older brothers?" (2006, 19).

Such comments can begin to give us an insight into the complex relationship between legitimate authority, violence, and state impersonation on which post-Soviet military life is grounded. What emerges from such accounts is that external motivation for military service, in terms of such values or ideals as "patriotism," "security," or "service," are rapidly consumed by other imperatives: to survive, to dominate others as one is dominated, and to do so preserving a relatively integrated sense of self. Kuba described how service in the Russian army rapidly undermined his premilitary belief that in swearing an oath to Russia he would be serving a "superpower" (*derzhava*). "You forget about patriotism," he said, "as soon as you see of whom the officer corps consists. You soon realize that not a single normal guy, no one who is cultured and normal is going to go into the army by contract [*kontrakt-nikom*]." They were all, he said, people who were running away from something (*begushchie liudi*). Moreover, whereas the Tajik soldiers who join the Russian army swear their military oath to the Russian Federation, much of the internal disciplining of younger conscripts by the contracted officer corps is premised on reinforcing where Russia's real boundaries lie:

Up there [i.e., in the mountains], they'll remind you to your face that this isn't their motherland, even though you gave your oath to the Russian Federation. They say, "if you let someone through [the border], it's not my mother who is going to be blown up in bed. This is your own bloody motherland."

For Kuba there were multiple ironies to his serving in the Russian forces on the Tajik-Afghan border. Not only was he, like all of the Tajik conscripts who serve in the Russian army, proclaiming an oath to a country of which he was not a citizen; he was also serving on the frontiers of a state with which he only ambivalently identified. Tajikistan was where he had been raised as a child, but it was Kyrgyzstan that had belatedly granted him citizenship and where he saw his future lying. Yet for Kuba, these ironies seemed to matter less than the fact that the army incorporated, ascribing him status and giving him, at least temporarily, a stable income and a community of servicemen with whom he could identify. Being a soldier compensated for not being fully a citizen.

Within this narrative of state incorporation, material objects played a crucial transformative role. Food and uniforms were recurrent themes in recollections of military service and were overlaid with enormous symbolic agency as vehicles and indices of inclusion. Soldiers would describe in detail the provenance of different military uniforms and the qualities they contained. Hierarchies between and within units were calibrated according to who had access to which uniforms. As Kanat, a Batken border guard explained: the best were secondhand American officer uniforms, "due to last for five years," followed by commercially produced (*firmennye*) Turkish and Chinese ones. The pre-1996 Russian uniforms were poorer in quality and locally manufactured Kyrgyz ones were the worst of all, which you could "tear with your fingers."

Food, too, was much more than an index of military provisioning. It represented the difference between being able to "stay human" at the border and turning to drugs that were available there "like sunflower seeds" (*kak semechki*). For Kuba, the crucial distinction between the Russian troops in which he served, and the poorly provisioned Tajik army, was captured in the dramatic contrast between the "well-fed" Russian troops and their Tajik counterparts:

KUBA: Mine was the sixth R. detachment.[6] A good one. The soldiers were provided for, we had a building, provision; the money we received was enough for anything you could want. And the Tajiks [i.e., the soldiers in the Tajik military] went around hungry the whole time.

MADELEINE: Did they envy you for that?

KUBA: They hated us. And the locals couldn't stand us, because we had everything and they couldn't buy us off [*podkupit'*], but well they could

---

[6]I have removed the name of the detachment to protect its anonymity.

always buy the Tajiks off. They used to say how [the soldiers] would go and sweep up [for the locals], even to do their washing for them, in order somehow or other to fill their bellies, to be fed by them.

MADELEINE: You mean in the Tajik military?

KUBA: Yes. They throw them off and don't even look [at what happens to them]. There they are two years, three years they've served and then you've got your military certificate [*voennyi billet*] and they send you home like that [held up a finger to show the skinny soldier]. Even the local [soldiers] die of hunger. . . . You've got to understand that difference. A guy comes out of the Russian troops. He's full [*sytyi*], he's put on weight, done sport, he's seen people, he's gone through [lessons in] courage [*muzhestvo prokhodit*], its own kind of school. He's been conditioned, his character changes. And in the Tajik [army], they throw them out like, you know now on television "The last hero" [*poslednii geroi*], you know that Russian show where they throw them on an island with nothing to eat, well the Tajik army is bloody like that. They throw them there and say, "guard that frontier," without even asking.

For Adilet, a Kyrgyz soldier who had joined the small Russian border unit based in Kyrgyzstan's southern Alay region, it was the hope of gaining a "clean Russian passport" that provided his primary motivation. Like Kuba, he contrasted the provisioning of the Russian army in which he had served with the meager rations and secondhand uniforms that characterized the Kyrgyz troops. His own draft had been achieved with the help of his father, who had served for many years in the Russian forces serving on the Kyrgyz-Tajik border. And it was this difference in provisioning that stopped him "going crazy" on the bleak mountain climbs of the Alay:

ADILET: It's really difficult to get into the Russian troops. Because the conditions are really good there. The food, the clothing is excellent . . . My father worked there, and he had good relations. He made sure that they called me up personally. And they wrote out, "we call up Jailoobaev Adilet" so that I went to serve specifically in that unit. Because just like that they won't take you.

MADELEINE: So, for instance, from your village, the rest went to the Kyrgyz army?

ADILET: Right. Even with relations you might get in or you might not. Everyone wants to get in to the Russian army. We had a change of uniform every one and a half years, they give you new boots. Exactly [as it should be] according to the regulations. And in the Kyrgyz army, they'll only give you one uniform. Although in the Kyrgyz army they are also supposed to change, but they don't bother following the law. And they brought our uniforms from Russia, and the food was decent. . . . If you serve for three years as a contract soldier or an officer, you have the right to get Russian citizenship. They'll give you a genuine [*chistyi*; lit. clean] Russian passport. Like my father. That's why he has a photo of Putin at home.

Striking in Adilet's account is the link that emerges between the material provisioning of the army (the uniform, the boots, the food); the social entitlements attached to having a "clean [i.e., genuine] Russian passport" and the ideational linkage with Russia ("having a Putin photo"). Army service, in other words, entails both an incorporation (taking in the state) and an ascription (being recognized by the state). Rather like Kuba's recalled moment of recognition at the point that he was given his Kalashnikov, Adilet's discursive linking of uniforms and passports signals a recognition of social status accorded through military service. In this process of state incorporation, the state is, in a literal sense, wrapped around the conscript and taken in. The same is true of food. It was striking in several of the conversations I had with demobilized soldiers how "civilian food" and "army food" were spoken of as two profoundly different categories (cf. Bikkenin 2006, 17). At once a commentary on the different qualities these two kinds of food represent to the soldier, this distinction also illustrates the way in which the state incorporates by being incorporated. Army food quite literally remakes the soldier from the inside.

Decoration and Violence: The *Dembel´skaia Lenta*

If army food puts the army inside the soldier, so, in more brutal form, does violence. The institutionalized and highly ritualized hazing (*dedovshchina*) of army recruits that is still found in many post-Soviet militaries is fundamental to producing the soldier as a political subject.[7] The particular way

---

[7]The English term "hazing" only weakly conveys the phenomenon of *dedovshchina* in Soviet and post-Soviet institutional settings, including penal colonies, prisons, and other "closed" institutions. The term translates as "rule of the grandfathers" and refers to a system of institutionalized subordination based on cohorts. For a semiotic analysis of *dedovshchina,* see Bannikov

in which the conscript soldier comes to impersonate the state is profoundly conditioned by this fact. Weapons, clothing, and food are not simply neutral objects of official provisioning; they are also massively overdetermined symbols of differentiation. In the symbolic economy of the Kyrgyz army, for instance, military hierarchy is marked not just by the kind of uniform worn (whether American or Kyrgyz), but by the way it is worn and the insignia by which it is decorated. Adilet thrust back his shoulders, switched into Russian, and gave an exaggerated swagger around the room as he demonstrated the difference between the newly arrived conscripts (so-called ghosts or *dukhi*) and the "grandfathers" (*dedy*), due soon for demobilization. "You can tell a *ded* just by looking at the way he walks. You've got to have your chest back, like that. Cool, in short [*delovoi-to, koroche*]."

Konstantin Bannikov has argued in his account of army hazing in the Russian conscript forces that military clothing serves not only to mark out different generations, but also as an instrument of ritualized violence, and as the material for inscribing, quite literally, one's progress from a "ghost" to a "grandfather." The army belt is the "ultimate in this system of symbols" (2002, 116). For it is at once an instrument of punishment, a "materialization of the collective memory of the given unit" that is passed down from one generation to the next, and a material means of marking the passage of time (ibid.). Soldiers would often point to the inscriptions on their belts as they talked about their progress through their months of service and the "memory" that their belts contain: a *ded* would be entitled to add his signature to those already written in pen on the back, whereas beginning conscripts would compete to acquire the belts of the most "renowned" grandfathers.

In the contemporary Kyrgyz army, such complex symbolic work is exaggerated by the fact that the insignia with which it is decorated are those, as Adilet put it, of a "dead state": the USSR. Many soldiers serving in the Kyrgyz border troops around Batken have Soviet-issued belts and hats, embossed with a red, five-pointed star. The very ambiguity of this insignia—the sign, at once, of past greatness and contemporary weakness ("we can't even afford our own new belts!") gives it particular symbolic force as an instrument of humiliation. It is an ambiguity elaborated through violence. In a variant of a

---

(2002); for a descriptive overview, see Daucé and Sieca-Kozlowski (2006); for an analysis of the changing place of *dedovshchina* in the post-Soviet Russian military and the intimate connections that such violence instills between "pain, patriarchy, patrimonialism and patriotism," see van Bladel (2004, 153–186). It is a striking index of the degree to which Soviet military jargon is reproduced in post-Soviet contexts that in Kyrgyzstan, where the military is predominantly Kyrgyz and Kyrgyz-speaking, the informal vocabulary used to talk about *dedovshchina* is exclusively Russian.

ritual of progress through the military hierarchy that appears common across the post-Soviet space (Bannikov 2002, 116; Bikkenin 2006, 24; Sesiashvili 2006, 189–190), the soldier who is due to progress from being a "ghost" to being a "ladle" or "bucket" (*cherpak*—the second stage in the informal hierarchy of conscript cohorts) and ultimately a "grandfather," must demonstrate his preparedness by holding out his outstretched palm to receive a number of beatings corresponding to the number of remaining months' service. In a telling twist on this ritualized violence, the soldier's passage is only "approved" if, at the end of the beatings, the imprint of the five-pointed Soviet star is distinguishable in relief on his brutalized, outstretched hand.

There is a disturbingly performative element to this act of state subjectification. The civilian is transformed into an agent of the state's "legitimate violence" only by coming, quite literally, to embody that violence by bearing its signs. The state incorporates by being taken into the soldier's body through every available surface and then dramatically displayed. Hence the significance of beatings, of feeding, and of sexual humiliation to the production of the soldier as political subject—acts that constitute the "somatics and erotics of historical alterity" (Feldman 1991, 234). Hence, too, the fetishizing of surfaces, and the importance of bodily decorations through which this incorporation is symbolically elaborated. In the ritualized subjection with metal belts, it is the beating that may force submission of younger recruits to their elders, but it is the trace of the five-pointed star—the marking of the body with the state's insignia—that produces the soldier as a political subject, an agent of legitimate state violence.

This complex interdependence between violence, decoration, and state impersonation is well illustrated with the memories of *dedovshchina* recalled by former border troops. Emphasized in such accounts is the tension between secrecy and display. While the specific *agent* of violence must be kept concealed—a rule endorsed through strict prohibitions against "splitting" and the ostracism of anyone who reports on violence—the *fact* of profound intertroop hierarchies sustained through violence is, by contrast, vigorously and repeatedly elaborated. Adilet explained how it was possible for an experienced soldier to tell with one glance who is a "ghost" and who is a "grandfather." The minutely calibrated differences in the way uniforms are worn, the role of barracks graffiti and the regimented use of ostensibly "collective" space attest to the importance of displaying boundaries within and between cohorts, of establishing hierarchies, and of determining who is outside the social realm.

For soldiers nearing their demobilization (*dembely*), who had passed through all stages of the cohort-based hierarchy of the troop, the lengths that are gone to in order to display one's status are often extreme. Kuba described, for instance, how for the Russian troops guarding the border with Afghanistan, one's position as demobilizee was signaled by the wearing of a yellow ribbon (*dembel'skaia lenta* ["demob ribbon"]), which had to be extracted, at considerable risk, from one of the landmines with which border fields were dotted. The soldier awaiting demobilization is already transformed into an agent of state violence, and the moment of ritual separation back to "normal" life can only occur through an absurd and dangerous demonstration of total incorporation:

> You've got minefields, and there you'll find the demob ribbon, an ai-guillette [*aksel'banty*], you know, to decorate your uniform. Well the soldier is about to go home; he's got to get that little yellow ribbon, like a fringe, off the mine. He pulls it like that off gently towards himself, and it will look sweet on his epaulettes, his uniform when he's at his demobilization [ceremony]. Like, he's going home in a week. We had two [in my unit] who were about to go home and they went off to the mine field to get that ribbon. They had been smoking; their heads were full of fog [*tuman*]. They went off the two of them and both of them blew themselves up. One died from loss of blood from the sole of his foot, the other had a splinter fall in his eye, and they had to put a crystal in there.

The yellow ribbon that is extracted from the landmine in a state of drug-induced fog is more than just a sign of bravado that indexes a relationship to other young men. In its subsequent display it is transformed into a sign of state membership: not just a ribbon but an aiguillette to be worn on the parade uniform. It must be incorporated within a constellation of state practices and signs (the uniform, the parade, the official demobilization) in order for it to do its symbolic work. The soldier must demonstrate his mutual incorporation: of self into army, of army into self.

Bakyt, who had worked as a border guard in the Kyrgyz army and now ran an Internet café in Osh, described an analogous ritual in which social violence is dramatized through the incorporation of "state" referents in absurd form. The younger recruit, having been violently humiliated by his older peers through beatings, name callings, and an assortment of arbitrary tasks, is ultimately instructed to undress before them and then, in this state of manifest subjection (standing on one leg, saluting, wearing nothing but a military cap), he is forced to read out the official statute (*ustav*) governing military relations. The *ustav*, which soldiers are instructed to learn and memorize, is formally the foundation of all army relations, and explicitly instructs on the importance of "mutual respect" among those who constitute one's military comrades (*voiskovoe tovarishchestvo*) (*Ustav* 2002). Yet the ritual itself is a demonstration of the weakness of the *ustav* in the face of the "natural law" of *dedovshchina*. The recruit is to read it out slowly, loudly, and with exaggerated formality. The effect: an absurd undermining of the military law through the conjunction of declamation and abjection.

How are we to make sense of such gratuitous violence and the centrality of state regalia to these rituals of humiliation? First, military hazing and its symbolic excesses must be firmly located within a broader analysis of political violence. We should not start with an a priori distinction between state-sanctioned and nonstate-sanctioned violence ("legitimate" and "illegitimate" violence) but rather pay attention to the way that a boundary between these two is constituted. Second, rather than an "exception" or "deviation," the institutionalized violence of military service, as much as the guns and uniforms, is central to understanding the particular way that border guards are incorporated into the body politic. Finally, reflecting on the tense boundary between the legal and the illegal at the heart of state impersonation is critical for understanding the dynamic of power at post-Soviet borders, and the kinds of embodied response they elicit. This is so not through any simple reactive transmission (a brutalized soldier seeks in turn to brutalize the border-crossing civilian), but rather because military service produces as normal a mode of power that operates through the reproduction of uncertainty about the location of law; or rather, in which the "state" is invoked to exceed state law. To illustrate this point, I turn to a rather different setting where the boundary between legal and illegal violence was blurred: the "dirty protest" undertaken by Northern Irish political prisoners in the late 1970s.[8]

Making Sense of Military Violence?

In a series of illuminating theoretical works, Allen Feldman (1991, 1994, 1997) has sought to critique deterministic—or what he calls "processual"— accounts of political violence in which "the issue of descriptive adequacy is rarely brought to bear on the acts of violence themselves, but only on the putative origin of the irruption" (1991, 19) Violence, in such accounts, is "denuded

---

[8]The "dirty protest" was an act of sustained protest by members of the Irish Republican Army and Irish National Liberation Army held in the Maze prison, which began in 1978 and lasted for three years.

of any intrinsic semantic or causal character," treated as a mere artifact or symptom rather than having agency of its own. In contrast to such linear accounts in which causal agency is located outside of the violence itself (and thus rationalized and normalized), Feldman is attentive to the "symbolic and performative autonomy" of violence (ibid., 21) and to the ways in which contemporary forms of mass communication "anaesthetize" us to some forms of suffering more than others (ibid., 404).

His studies have accordingly focused in minute detail on the symbolic, performative, and mnemonic functions of violence, and in particular, on the politicization of the body through violence. In a departure from Foucauldian accounts of the "subjected" body that is disciplined and rendered docile, Feldman explores how the body itself can be instrumentalized against technologies of domination. Much of his ethnographic material comes from Northern Ireland of the 1970s and early 1980s. Feldman shows how, during the "dirty protest" undertaken in the late 1970s by imprisoned paramilitaries of the Irish Republican Army, the soldiers' bodies became what he calls a "weapon artifact," countering state violence with the defiling power of their own excrement. In Feldman's reading, the paramilitary's body was not passively disciplined by external technologies but was rather a "shared topos" that enabled "the reception and recirculation of violence through its semic reorganization by both the guards and the prisoners" (1991, 179). Neither guards nor prisoners are passive in this process. Rather, "the actual violence of the prison regime and the redistribution and political inversion of that violence by prisoners created a composite body whose liminality became the precondition of its symbolic fecundity" (ibid.).

There are two theoretical innovations that are worth highlighting here. The first is Feldman's emphasis on the agency of violence: the need to understand it, not as the mechanistic outcome of some elemental forces (ethnic antagonism, ideological training) but as constitutive of the political subject. The act of violence "invests the body with agency . . . Political violence is a mode of transcription: it circulates codes from one prescribed historiographic surface or agent to another" (1991, 7). Moreover, Feldman directs our attention to the communicative function of violence, or what Aretxaga has called its "symbolic overdetermination." In her own study of the gendered dimensions of the dirty protest, Aretxaga demonstrates how the excreta and menstrual blood of the women's protest "expose an excess of meaning that reveals the very character of violence as an intersubjective relation that must necessarily be interpreted" (2005a, 58). In short, we foreclose any serious analysis of violence if we dismiss it as simply "meaningless" (see also Schepper-Hughes and Bourgeois 2004, 3).

The second innovation of Feldman's research is to emphasize the symbiotic relation between prisoner and guard in generating prison violence, taking "state violence" and "nonstate violence" to be part of a single, mutually reinforcing whole. During the dirty protest, Feldman argues, the guards were caught in the violence with "the guards experienc[ing] their own violence as an organic elaboration of the defiling body of the Blanketmen [protesting prisoners]" (1991, 195). Thus, the guards' insistence that the prisoners' predicament was self-inflicted "was not only a mystification of the actual dynamics of the prison situation but the guards' inadvertent admission that their own agency had become a function of their ideological construction of the prisoners" (ibid.).

This emphasis on symbiosis represents an important step in trying to think outside the categories of "legitimate" and "illegitimate" (nonstate-sanctioned and state-sanctioned) violence. And yet in Feldman's account, the constitutive role of violence in producing the guard as a guard (and not just the inmate as an inmate) is curiously eclipsed. The "screws" (guards) remain simply "screws": faceless, nameless, and largely lacking in history. Indeed, if there are any figures in this brilliant ethnography whose actions are mechanized as merely the "playing out" of dynamics emanating from elsewhere, it is the prison guards who, during the dirty protest, "had not only been reduced to functions of the disciplinary machinery of the prison regime, but . . . had also become functions of the machinery of pollution that emanated from the body of the prisoner" (1991, 195). In the context of an ethnography that precisely seeks to critique the unexamined mechanism that pervades much anthropological writing on violence, the determinism and functionalism of this comment is striking. Implicitly, the guards' violence derives (mechanistically) from the fact that they are agents of state, but quite how or why that animates their actions in particular ways is left unexplored. There is a residual "statism" (the state as "it," as "unmoved mover") to Feldman's account.

Focusing on the constitutive role of circulating violence of the kind epitomized by *dedovshchina* enables us to examine the violence inflicted by those enacting stately authority rather differently. To push Feldman's critique to its logical conclusion, we have to ask not only about the agentive role of violence in constituting the political subject, but about the ascriptive processes through which certain kinds of violence (that of the guard, that of the soldier) come to be seen as "legitimate" and others not, not least by the guards themselves. Once we have made the analytic move to view "reified law and order as a contingent social claim, not an essence" (Heyman and Smart 1999, 13), then the empirical question of how certain individuals and their actions come to be imbued with state legitimacy comes to the fore.

In the case of border guards, a particular "formation of violence" is central to that process.

In the ritualized violence depicted by Kuba, Adilet, and Bakyt we see a symbolic elaboration of the divergence between (ineffective, nominal) "formal" law and the "real" rule of the *dedy*. When a soldier is made to read out the "military law" at the same time as he is being brutally subjected to the jibes of the *dedy*, or when, as Bikkenin (2006, 26) recalls, the commanding officer tells his younger recruits that "here the only order and the only law is me" (*zdes' poriadok i zakon—ia*), what is occurring is a reminder of the real strength of *dedovshchina* ("the rule of the grandfathers" over *ustavshchina*, "the rule of the statute"). *Dedovshchina* is not just the "meaningless" violence of the physically stronger on the physically weaker. On the contrary, *dedovshchina* is parasitic on military law and the minutely calibrated hierarchies the latter enshrines.

Thus, certain forms of violence are reproduced because the instigator holds a formal legitimizing position within the official military hierarchy (dictated by the *ustav*). Consider, for instance, the claim by the commanding officer that "law and order here is me!" It is hyperbole intended to instill fear. But it is also a fearful condensation of a statement that is experientially true for the recruit. It is the fact that the officer holds a formal position within a formal hierarchy of signs and attributions that gives his word the status of law. These attributes and the material objects by which they are signaled render his claim "legitimate" within the symbolic bounds of the military institution. The commanding officer can claim (efficaciously) to be "the law" because, within a particular, highly prescribed social formation, his claim to impersonate the state trumps all others.

Both armies and prisons are in one sense "total" social institutions. Recourse to outside arbitration is minimal, making the visibility of violence and the possibility of law's overturning particularly acute. Law in such settings can acquire an intensely performative character in a way that, in the world outside, occurs only in moments of profound social breakdown or war. But such violence should not be considered sui generis. For instance, to understand the blurring of (il)legitimate violence of military prison officers at the Abu Ghraib prison in Iraq, this violence has to be situated, as Caton (2006) has sought to do, within a constellation of hegemonic relations, circulating images, and legal contortions that embed US forces within wider processes, rather than simply dismissing the soldiers' behavior as "exceptional." Or rather, we must recognize its "exceptionality" but ask what that teaches us about the "normal" ways in which the state is invoked to exceed state law. Attending to the kinds of violence that are internal to the border troops,

I suggest, can help us to think about the particular micro-dynamics of power at the border. It enables the modality of power at the border—the kinds of arbitrary invocations of law, the contestations over who here is "the state"; the potential for physical or symbolic violence—to be recognized as continuous with modes of violence that circulate across the realms of what is usually parceled up as "civil society" and "the state." The ritualized violence of *dedovshchina* is an extreme version, certainly, but it is exceptional only to the extent that it condenses and dramatizes a particular relational dynamic that is present more generally, at least as a potentiality.

From Barracks to Border: Exploring a Modality of Power

It is this slippage between social relations within and beyond the barracks to which I now turn. My claim is not that border encounters necessarily mirror the violence of military service in scale or force, or represent merely its "replication" or "transmission" to the outside world. Nor should it be read as an argument that violence at the Ferghana Valley borders is pervasive or irrational. It is rather that the violence of military service dramatizes in elaborate and excessive form a particular modality of interaction, one in which what is important is the recognition—fragile and contested—of a claim to impersonate the state by upholding "its" laws and representing its authority. It is this same basic modality that exists in the border encounter. When the border guards around Sokh mock Kuba that he "doesn't look like his picture" or an altercation occurs at a checkpoint between a border guard and the governor of the neighboring state because both claim there to "be the law," this is not the same as the barracks violence through which military hierarchy is established, nor is it caused by the former in any instrumental sense. But it is the same basic modality of power in action grounded in the same fundamental fragility of formal law. Establishing who is "right" here consists of a sometimes subtle, sometimes overt contest over whose claim to impersonate the state is greater.

Consider the following recollection of service on the Tajik-Afghan border and the way in which an arbitrary shooting came to be transformed, not just into a "legitimate," but even a "heroic" act. This is an account of violence that is external to the barracks, yet the continuities with the ways power is articulated within the military unit are considerable. Kuba is responding here to a question about the motivations of the Russian commanding officers to serve on the Tajik-Afghan border. After describing the illegitimate activities in which commanding officers participated, spiriting drugs away in military equipment, he continued with a distinction between the contract officer and the "normal guy":

> A normal guy is going to have a wife with him, will want to buy an apartment, to go to work, to come home every evening to his wife, to his children. And here [the commanding officer] doesn't need anything, just drugs, money and that taste of freedom! He comes home and there he just goes nuts, starts picking fights [*podebilit, podebashchirit*]. All he wants to do is get back to the army. He can't live a normal life. Because what does he need? He needs drugs, definitely, and money. He's got money there, you understand? He feels himself to be God, with his automatic rifle in his hand. Someone says something, he can kill them straight away and then he just says "he was trying to swim across the river so I shot at him." And he'll be right [*i budet prav*]. He'll write a report, like "during an attempt to cross the border I fired 2–3 shots, one shot hit him in the head or the shoulder, as a result of which the wounded died instantly and was hospitalized." That's all. The boss [*nachal'nik*] puts a stamp on it and that's all—let off! [*vse, pechat' stavit i vse—svoboden!*] They'll even give him a medal because it was someone trying to cross. He kills a local guy and they can give him a medal for that! If he can show that he was trying to cross the border and they throw drugs in his pocket, he'll be a hero of the Soviet Union for the fact that he intercepted a crossing! A hero!

For Kuba, the apparent unboundedness of the commanding officer's power is shocking. It is the thrill of "playing God" that draws officers to serve on a remote stretch of unforgiving border. This is sovereign power at its most stark: both authorizing the law and remaining outside of it; what Taussig calls the "literalization, as if staged—of the mystique of sovereignty" (1997, 18). The killing of an innocent civilian will be "right" (and the Russian *prav* here carries the sense of legally right or true) simply by dint of authorizing the action. There is something deeply disturbing about the event: the exposing of a profound gulf in the regulation of power. Yet what stands out in Kuba's narrative is not simply the assertion of this gulf, but his recognition that what makes it morally repugnant is the ascription of legitimacy by means of certain formal attributes. It is the presence of the automatic rifle that gives the soldier the feeling of "being God"; it is his position in the hierarchy that means that he "*will* be right" (and not simply that he "thinks himself right" or "will be treated *as if* right"); it is the fact of putting a stamp by the boss that transforms the soldier's action into a medal-warranting act, and the placing of drugs in the victim's pocket that "proves" the latter's guilt. These are impersonations of the state that truly tremble on the brink of imposture (Fitzpatrick 2005): the commanding officer both embodies the law and imitates it; his action both legitimizes and is extra-legal. The existence of an abstract, arbitrating law which, in the final instance, will prove the honest right or redeem the virtuous is exposed as a fiction, one that the law-mocking rituals of *dedovshchina* symbolically elaborate through their violent excesses.

The correlate of such uncertainty, for Kuba, was a pervasive sense of tension between the competing demands to grant passage or refuse it. In a context where the location of law is constantly shifting, letting the "wrong" person through was dangerous, but so, equally, was not letting the "right" person across the border. His detachment had been responsible for guarding a particular bottleneck on the river border, which was a site of major traffic in opium but also a regular crossing point for villagers who had kinship links across the border, and for farmers who used to take cattle to graze in a small fertile island in the middle of the river. Manning the border was characterized by an acute tension between regulating the movement of often heavily armed locals, and following the dictates of superiors to shoot at anyone who was violating the border regime.

KUBA: They beat it into you, so you feel this great sense of responsibility. You feel it: if I let this person through, then he might start a war tomorrow in Tajikistan.

MADELEINE: Did you personally feel that sense of responsibility?

KUBA: Of course, you just keep telling yourself. You know, today my mother and father live peacefully, and tomorrow, they might never sleep again, and here I am pacing the border and it was I who let him through! . . . You've got this responsibility. If I let someone through, they can imprison me, they can even shoot me because of that. There the court decides, maybe they'll shoot you, maybe they'll give you two years, depending on which group you let through. Maybe you let through some fighters who'll chop your head off [*boevikov-golovorezov*] and maybe just one peaceful resident. Do you get that? A peaceful guy who just wants to go home! There are lots of incidents like that. Just a regular, peaceful guy, and you are like, "yes, sure, I'll let him through." And you let them through and your boss sees and that's it, your service is over. Because at the border there are no peaceful citizens, no enemies. You're just supposed not to let anyone through, full stop. Even swimming is forbidden in the streams, because they send things across quietly. No swimming at all, because the river is the border.

The other side of law's fragility is thus an abiding sense of responsibility and fear. Kuba had earlier described the physical setup of the military patrol: one that made virtually impossible any kind of continuous defense of the border as there were too many kilometers to be paced by too few soldiers. He described how he managed this uncertainty through informal calculation: did the person crossing appear "local"? Were they likely to be transporting drugs? Would he be liable to face retaliation if he fired warning shots? Would a crossing to which he turned a blind eye be caught by a commanding officer? Mediating these decisions was the acute awareness that soldiers were vulnerable to the local population, just as the locals on both sides of the border were to the soldiers. Villagers were often armed, and would occasionally take soldiers hostage as a way of extracting food, soap, and other basic goods from the commanding officers.[9] The social work involved in manning this border was fraught with uncertainty: this was a far cry from the smooth enactments of Scott's (1998) high modern officialdom.

The Tajik-Afghan border of the late 1990s was a site suffused with particular dangers. In this respect, the kinds of discrimination that Kuba had to make were unusually acute. The scale of drug smuggling, the extent of local militarization, and the war-ravaged economies on either side of the border mean that we should be cautious in extrapolating from his account to other experiences of border guarding in Central Asia. The Ferghana Valley boundaries in the mid-2000s were both less militarized and less tense than those to their south, and for the border guards around Batken in the mid-2000s, boredom rather than fear was often the dominant mood.

What Kuba's account alerts us to is the pervasive uncertainty that surrounded his own impersonation of the state, which produces the border as a site of distinct affect; not just in the clichéd sense of a place "in between," a liminal site of "fluid identities," but a site of deep, existential fear about where law lies. Is this person an innocent local or a deranged militant? Is this river a place for swimming or a place for shooting? Is the greater risk to grant or deny free passage? It is this sense of vulnerability in the face of a constantly shifting law, rather than the more obvious threat of insurgents and militants,

---

[9]Kuba described an incident in his own unit when two Russian officers were taken hostage by villagers and only released when they were presented with "a carload of flour and a carload of sugar" from the military supplies.

that pervades Kuba's account. Far from being a stable referent of action, "law" was something that was invoked sporadically, which could materialize suddenly, or be subsumed under the dominating power of money.

It is in this sense, I believe, that the "exceptional" border teaches us something about less remarkable sites and more mundane encounters. When the chief of a border unit near Batken reminds an obstructive driver that "I here am the law" (*bul jerde men zakonmun*), it may be said in jest or as a threat, but it derives its force and its effects from the same basic fact: that in such encounters, it is indeed the one who has more claim to impersonate the state who can maintain or suspend the law. It is this logic that gives authority to both the "state" license plates and the "cool" plates purchased by wealthy individuals that signal connections to those in power. Both act as licenses to suspend to the law.

"We Only Have a Border on Tuesdays"

At the Ferghana Valley borders in the mid-2000s the suspensions were usually brief, unremarkable, and likely to be overlaid with other deferential codes (the gentle bow of the border guard to a passing governor, for instance, is a delicate act of misrecognition; a violation of law that is recoded as a respectful act of welcome). But what is taking place is a suspension by the one who has more claim on the state: the one who is more efficaciously able to claim to embody the law. To convey something of the everyday sense of contingency produced by this situation, I present a final ethnographic example.

Tolib-Aka, in his late fifties, is the former administrative head (*rais*) of his *mahalla*, Navabod, in the Sokh district of Uzbekistan. He makes a living from his three hectares of land, which he farms together with his three unmarried sons. Navabod lies at the southern end of Uzbekistan's Sokh district, close in cartographic terms to the enclave's southern border with Kyrgyzstan. This particular boundary had, until a few years earlier, been completely unmarked, crossed daily in both directions by people taking their cows out to graze or to reach outlying fields. As Tolib-Aka remarked in the summer of 2004, "we only have a border on Tuesdays," a reference to the mobile border and customs control positioned on the bridge between the two sides of a cross-border market, which operated on that one day of the week.

I had first met Tolib-Aka in the early summer of 2004. I had been taken to meet him by Sultanali, his Kyrgyz maternal cousin (*bölöm*) from Batken. Learning that there was a foreigner recently arrived in Batken, Sultanali had sought me out to tell me that he was making an "ethno-psychological study" of the Uzbeks and Tajiks and that he was an expert in this sphere. He could help me to understand their psychology, he told me, an absolute precondition for understanding the dynamics of social relations in the Ferghana Valley. "You see, I grew up in Tajikistan; I understand their mentality [*mentalitet*]." As a child, Sultanali had attended an Uzbek-medium school in Dushanbe. He had gained a qualification to teach Russian in non-Russian schools and had taught Russian in Dushanbe for many years, moving to Batken at the height of the Tajik civil war, in 1992. Now, fluent in Kyrgyz (his mother-tongue), Uzbek, Tajik, and Russian, he was qualified to tell me the "objective" history of the Ferghana Valley, a version, he told me, that would be more authentic than that which I would be likely to get from other people in the town who had "never been anywhere outside Batken."

Sultanali's sense of pride in his cosmopolitan identity contrasted starkly with Kuba's characterization of his own mixed parentage as a "curse." Sultanali prided himself on his cultural fluency, and made a point of reminding me of the multiple historical contingencies that led him to find himself, after 1992, living close to the lands that his grandfather fled in Sokh during collectivization, but "on the wrong side of the border" from them, and with a different nationality listed in his passport. It was a conversation about his maternal grandparents that led Sultanali to suggest taking me to meet Tolib-Aka, with whom he shared a great-grandfather and who, because he had grown up his whole life in the Sokh Valley, might be able to tell me more about the distinctive way of life and irrigation techniques that were practiced in Sokh.

So it was that these cousins, living an hour apart, remet in 2004 for the first time since the collapse of the Soviet Union more than a decade earlier. Their conversation, like many a conversation between relatives in the Ferghana Valley who now find themselves citizens of different states, turned rapidly from discussion of family members and common friends to the metrics of livelihood now: the state of schooling, the cost of meat, the delivery of gas, the timeliness of pensions, the fragmentation of a once unified transport system. In such materials difference was measured; divergent state trajectories in the "time of the market" calibrated and compared. The border did not figure directly in the cousins' conversation until much later in the afternoon, when we set off to go and look at Tolib-Aka's fields. Sultanali had been keen to show me the distinctive farming implements and irrigation system that had enabled people to farm this unpromising mountainous terrain, citing this as an example of the "Ferghana mentality" that distinguished this region from others in Central Asia. We drove up part of the way in Sultanali's Zhiguli, and then continued on foot, through Tolib-Aka's densely planted fields. He adjusted some stones to create one waterway and close another, drawing my attention again to the importance here of irrigation as a map of social relations. Gullies and channels had been carefully dug to account for the relative gradient in different parts of the field; stones and tiles created an elaborate system of sluices and barriers.

Water and its management also dominated our conversation on the way back down from the fields, this leading seamlessly into Tolib-Aka's reflections on what constituted a well-ordered community and the need for strong, benign, unitary leadership (cf. Liu 2012, 148–184). He had decided to take us on a small detour in order to show the construction that he had overseen while director of the *mahalla*: a flood drainage channel (*sai*) that would absorb the spring mountain melt water, thereby minimizing damage to the steep mud road and the houses that faced it. This construction, he quipped, was the reason why he had been removed from his post as head of the *mahalla*. He had managed to raise the money and spend it on the people (*halq*), rather than using it to court favor with, or purchase posts from, those higher up the regional administration. This, he went on to say, is precisely the problem with the whole state: those leaders who actually try to work for the good of the people are liable to be moved sideways, "or they soon learn that they can't stay there if they keep their hands clean."

It was while we were having this conversation that we were suddenly stopped by two soldiers who appeared out of the apricot orchard at the side of this idyllic stretch of mountain road, whistling to flag us down. Sultanali turned to Tolib-Aka and, linking the latter's comment to the sudden appearance of the "state" out of the orchard, added "yes, here in Uzbekistan, even the trees have ears!"[10] Tolib, not in the mood for joking, muttered to himself, "but it's not Tuesday. What are they doing here today?" He got out of the car and walked over to the soldiers, Sultanali and I following a few steps behind. Having taken this small detour, we had at some point briefly entered Kyrgyz territory and unwittingly had illegally recrossed the border into Uzbekistan. Sultanali's license plates, with the Kyrgyz flag in the corner, easily marked this as a foreign car. Tolib was incensed. We were on what was for him indisputably local territory. We had not crossed any borders, and there was nothing on this dusty little mountain backroad, flanked by apricot orchards, to give any indication of which cars were and were not allowed. Moreover, he was, he told the young soldiers, the *rais* here, and we were his guests (*mexmonlar*). "Do you know who built that drainage channel?" Not waiting for an answer, he continued, "I am from Navabod!" Although we

---

[10] A play on the often used remark in Sokh that the "walls all have ears" [*devorning ham qulog'i bor*].

were less than ten minutes' drive away from Navabod, the significance of the village seemed not to register with the border guards, who responded by ignoring the comment and asking us for our passports. Tolib-Aka, as a local who knew that he only needed his passport on market days, had not brought his with him. "Do you know where Navabod is?" he asked of the guards, adding, in answer to his own question, "no, of course not. They would never put locals to man the borders here."

As Sultanali and I handed our passports over for inspection, Tolib-Aka continued chiding the border guards as a teacher might two insolent school boys with the backward nod of a superior to his subordinates. "Is this how you treat our guests?" he demanded. To Tolib-Aka, they were, after all, "our" Uzbek border guards, and they were less than half his age. In his understanding it was quite natural that he should address them in the same idioms, the same modality of subordination as the district governor would address him when he was the mahalla *rais* (Humphrey 1994, 24). The guards, meanwhile, made no response, but continued silently performing the state, averting their eyes from any contact with Tolib: one trying to get his two-way radio to work, presumably to contact the larger post down the mountain; the other, carefully leafing through my passport, scrutinizing its assortment of stamps and visas with exaggerated formality.

"That's a diplomatic passport!" Sultanali said to their page flicking, an assertion that he and I both knew to be untrue. The soldier glanced at me: like Tolib-Aka's assertion that he was the *rais* of his *mahalla*, Sultanali's indication that I was a "diplomat" suddenly made the authority of the state elusive and contested in this encounter. If either of these (immediately unverifiable) claims were true, then to cause us delay would at best be a profound violation of the informal code of respect (*hurmat*) that low-level state functionaries are expected to show toward those whose claim to impersonate the state is backed by a higher authority; at worst it might cause them a reprimand from their superiors. Conversely, if either or both of these assertions were untrue they could equally invite reprimand for having allowed someone to continue on their way without producing a passport, and for allowing this Kyrgyz car to continue on its journey unregistered along Uzbek territory.

The uncertainty continued for a moment longer, as the first soldier tried to get his radio to work: to assert a connection with the state that was *down there,* at the fixed post farther down the valley. But when it finally failed and he switched it off, the contingency of "legitimate authority" in this encounter on a beautiful May day in the mountains suddenly became intensely palpable. Who exactly, in this motley circle of five, was sovereign? Which side would the coin fall? Where was the state? The will to legibility, in Aretxaga's terms, was turning in this moment of uncertainty into the "repetition of illegibility and uncertainty about the outcome of the encounter" (2005b, 261). Sensing the impasse, the second soldier, passports in hand, started walking toward Sultanali's car, addressing him alone in the respectful rising tone used by young people toward an older man, *akajaan,* and beckoning him over. I wondered whether the soldier was going to make him drive down to the post to consult with a superior. But after a moment, the pair returned, this time with the passports in Sultanali's hand. *"Vatanimizga hush kelibsiz!"* (Welcome to our homeland!), the first soldier said, and the pair walked off again in the direction of the apricot orchard where they had been squatting earlier. As we got into the car, Tolib-Aka turned to Sultanali: "How much did you give?" he asked, the context obviating any need for explanation. "Akh, just some tobacco money" he replied, and we sped off, back down to Navabod, Tolib-Aka cursing at the absurdity of the border that had popped up to show its face on what ought to have been one of its days off.

At some level of course, this is a story about the efficacy of the bribe: the fact that "border" suddenly melted on this mountainside as soon Sultanali proffered some cash. As such, it would be easy to insert into a narrative of "resistance" and "collusion": society getting around the state in the act of corruption. Yet to see the incident in these terms is to treat the state as a finished construction that has to be avoided, rather than a particular kind of claim about where the authority to represent the state, to impersonate it, actually lies in any given encounter. The reason why Sultanali's bribe was efficacious is because in this particular encounter the location of the state was up for grabs: was it in the soldiers' Kalashnikov? In their dysfunctional two-way radio? In the long black coat (*chapan*) worn by elders in Sokh that gave authority to Tolib-Aka's assertion that he was the local *mahalla rais*? In my stamp-filled passport that might just have been a diplomat's? As Aretxaga (2005b) argues, the problems that are often attributed to a "deficit" of statehood, may in fact be due to the fact that it multiply and intimately impersonated.

This event was an unexceptional one, resolved through smiles, handshakes, and perhaps a moment of mutual recognition that it really did not matter whose claim to enact the state would be efficacious, for we could all safely leave "the state" elsewhere (cf. Ssorin-Chaikov 2003, 116). This is the dominant weave of life at the border: a mode that is *yntymaktuu* or convivial; in which suspensions can create spaces for friendship as well as of fear. It is these suspensions that allow border posts to become places for tea drinking and chess playing; places that allow Mohammed to get on with his legally opaque business, dependent as it is on the sharing of cigarettes and the deliberate misrecognition of his trade.

Anthropologists of the state have stressed the need to question the state's own narrative of itself as sovereign, law-bound, and territorial, stressing instead the historical and political contingency of this particular form of political ordering (Mbembe 2000). They have foregrounded attention to actual geographies of rule, and they have shown how particular practices of power are parasitical on law, even as action is justified in legal language (Asad 1992). Such approaches enable a distinctively ethnographic take on recurrent philosophical questions concerning the source of law by exploring the actions of those figures (big men mediators, paramilitary forces, brokers) who would seem at once to stand outside the law and for it, as the voice of law. As Das and Poole note, "such figures of local authority represent both highly personalized forms of private power and the supposedly impersonal or neutral authority of the state. It is precisely because they also act as representatives of the state that they are able to move across—and thus muddy—the seemingly clear divide separating legal and extralegal forms of punishment and enforcement" (2004, 14).

Attention to the work of border guarding can enable us to approach these issues in ethnographic terms. A border is both a paradigmatic state space (a place often of exceptional security and regulation of mobility) and a site where the repeated performative reenactment of "state" as a singularity can be seen and felt—by civilians and conscript soldiers alike. The anthropology of borders has tended to pay insufficient attention to the work of border guarding and the lives of those who have to man the border, with the effect that even critical studies of state power at borders often take the givenness of the state's own spatial categories and logics for granted.

The next chapter describes an incident in which contestation over the limits of law and the bounds of the state transformed an altercation between school boys and border guards into a sustained intercommunal conflict. This was an exceptional event, and one that allows us to critique the discourse of *konfliktogennost'* into which it was almost immediately inserted. It is also an instructive one, about the role of contingency in materializing a border, and the risks of an excess of state escalation of force when the bounds of legitimate authority are contested.

6. SEPARATIONS

Conflict and the Escalation of Force

In the summer of 2005, I returned, after an absence of several months, to the upper Sokh Valley. There I found Kanysh-ai and her family discussing an event that had occurred two months earlier, during which the bounds of the state and its legitimate violence became suddenly and sharply contested. On May 1, 2005, two school boys from the Tajik-majority village of Hushiar, at the southern limit of Uzbekistan's Sokh exclave, were severely beaten by border guards from the small Kyrgyz border unit stationed in the neighboring village of Sogment, just across the bridge that marks the informal boundary here between the two districts and two states. Over the course of the next several days this event had escalated into a sustained intercommunal conflict, leaving property damaged and several people hospitalized. I had been in Bishkek at the time of the incident, and my understanding of the events in early May was pieced together from a variety of different accounts, initially through a series of conflict analyses produced by local non-governmental organizations, and later from telephone calls, interviews, news reports, and conversation of the kind shared with Kanysh-ai and her mother.[1]

In this chapter I explore this multiply mediated incident and its repercussions for the way that a border materialized in the Sokh Valley during subsequent months. I revisit an event that news reports at the time cast in determinist and localizing terms: an interethnic conflict driven by resource shortage that was all but "waiting to occur." I explore how the radical uncertainty over the location of law and boundaries of the state caused a fracas between border guards and school boys to turn into a sustained conflict

---

[1] Parts of this chapter have been previously published in Reeves (2011a, 2014).

articulated along lines of ethnicity between communities on two sides of a border. By attending to the play of political contingency, the unequal powers of pronouncement available to asymmetrically positioned NGOs in Kyrgyzstan and Uzbekistan, the blurring of the boundaries between state and nonstate authorities, and the contestation over who, of those "competing to perform as state" (Aretxaga 2005b, 258), was sovereign at this moment of local contestation, I question a reading of events that would interpret conflict as the inevitable outcome of limited resources, ethnic difference, or geographical complexity.

In so doing I extend two of the book's core arguments. The first concerns the place of contingency in the materialization of a state boundary. I have argued in earlier chapters that the tendency to accord analytical primacy to the map—to treat borders as an a priori manifestation of their cartographic representation—has diverted attention from their eventful character: their capacity to erupt, crystallize, appear, and disappear with considerable speed. Here I explore ethnographically how a period of intercommunal violence, itself shaped by political dynamics occurring far from this region, caused a border to materialize in new ways at the edges of the Sokh enclave. To understand this process, it is necessary to look beyond ethnicity and water to the complex intersection of contingent factors that disrupted an existent border ethic and prompted intense local debate on the meanings of territorial integrity and the bounds of legitimate violence.

The second contribution concerns the social work of spatializing the state. The incident in question was one where the dynamics of "spatial organization, temporal arrangement, functional specification, supervision and surveillance" through which the state is produced as an autonomous structure went from being "mundane," as depicted in Mitchell's account of everyday "state effects" (1999), to being highly charged and the subject of open and sometimes heated discussion. Moreover, this was so because the authority to speak the state was, at this moment of tension, very different for people living in Kyrgyzstan and Uzbekistan. Quite how (or whether) low-ranking border guards, nongovernmental conflict analysts, elders' councils, local strongmen, regional governors, state security officials, or village leaders spoke and acted with state authority was contested and variable. As such, the incident illustrates how fixing a border is inseparable from the broader work of social inscription; how delimiting a boundary between the "state" and its "others" entails both producing and circumscribing relations (Candea 2010; Green 2005).

The May conflict and its aftermath in Sokh was a moment when the edges of the state came to matter and be made to matter in new ways. As such it is a moment that highlights the constructedness of state territoriality—the fact that territory is something to be "worked for" as Sarah Radcliffe (2001) puts it in her historical ethnography of the Ecuadorian state. But it also highlights the intense affective investment in the idea of having a bounded state: the way in which territorial integrity came to stand more generally for the coherence of the state at a moment of political turmoil. Looking at the work of border fixing not just through the enactments and justificatory statements of state officials, but also in the rather more chaotic and diffuse initiatives of border dwellers, reveals the entanglements—of "state" and "society," the symbolic and the material, the ideational and the very concrete—that undermine smooth narratives of the "seeing state" ordering society in its image (see Scott 1998).

I first learned of the May conflict by email. The title of the message that popped into my inbox was stark: "URGENT! We have a conflict." The message, written in Russian and addressed to a variety of local and foreign recipients, was sent by the director of a Batken-based NGO, Yntymak sayasaty (Politics of Harmony). It contained a stark assessment of the situation that had arisen in Sokh, and of the urgency of continued funding for initiatives of conflict prevention. "Dear Colleagues," the message read, "unfortunately it seems that it is too early to close the RDD [Regional Dialogue and Development] Project because conflicts and incidents of an interethnic character still have reason to occur." The message went on to describe how law-enforcement officials of the two neighboring states had to draw a "line of separation" to prevent an escalation of violence between Kyrgyz and Tajik crowds grouped on either side of the bridge that marks the informal border between Hushiar and Sogment. Employees of local NGOs were seeking to reach the conflict's "epicenter" in order to mediate between the two sides as all communication between the two villages had been "entirely blocked by the powers of RU [Republic of Uzbekistan] and KR [Kyrgyz Republic]."

Over the course of the following week I received several more conflict analyses, from Yntymak, the Kyrgyz NGO based in Batken, and from Mehr, the Sokh NGO where Parviz worked as a conflict analyst. During the first days of tension, these reports were coauthored in Russian, as NGOs stressed their role as mediators across ethnic and state boundaries. As time progressed, the reports became increasingly divergent in their interpretation, with their authors, in Kyrgyzstan and Uzbekistan, facing different constraints on what they could write and how critically they could position themselves with regard to state authorities. Writing for an audience of outsiders, including donor organizations, national governments, and media outlets, NGOs that had been established to collaborate and mediate across borders increasingly took on the role of spokesperson for "their" community. The accounts figure no women, no children, and rarely disaggregate "Tajik" and "Kyrgyz" sides (the reports referring to the ethnicity of the actors, rather than their citizenship). And this is not just a question of (uneven) representation, or selective framing. The events were fundamentally not coherent or linear. They were "messy" in John Law's (2004, 6) sense: complex, not just in being technically difficult to grasp but because they "necessarily exceed our capacity to know them" (ibid.).

Conflict on the Border

On May 1, 2005, a group of eleventh-grade students from Hushiar, the large village that lies at the southernmost end of the Sokh enclave, took their cattle to graze in the pastures that lie just beyond the small hamlet of Charbak, across the border in Kyrgyzstan.[2] This is customary practice during the spring months as Hushiar has no grazing lands of its own. The pastures that stretch upward to its immediate west and east are all administratively inside Kyrgyzstan, although for the most part there is no boundary fence corresponding to the cartographic border, nor any other permanent territorial marker indicating where one or other state extends. Hushiar is contiguous with both Charbak and Sogment, and crossing from one village to another the casual observer would be hard-pressed to tell which state she is in. Subtle differences in building style, the recent introduction of piped gas in Hushiar (but not in Charbak and Sogment), and larger land plots in Sogment are in many places the only clues on which the observer can fix to grasp where each state begins and ends.

On this day, two of the students who had taken their cows to graze were stopped by troops of the Kyrgyz border post stationed in Sogment. They were asked for identification, which they did not have with them, because—according to accounts from Hushiar—they had recently submitted their papers to the district passport office to apply for passports. A verbal, and then physical conflict ensued in which two boys were severely beaten by the border guards for illegally entering the territory of the neighboring state, and without appropriate documentation. The two boys were hospitalized, initially in the district hospital in Sokh, and later in a larger hospital in the Uzbek mainland. A group of relatives of the injured students confronted the commander of the Kyrgyz border unit, stationed just above the Bayaman Bridge, which acts as the informal boundary between the two villages. The commander apparently agreed to reprimand his subordinates, and the relatives dispersed.

Two days later, the weekly Tuesday market was held as usual in both Hushiar and Charbak. At about 3 o'clock in the afternoon, a group of 150–200

---

[2] The dates, times, and activities that I mention here draw on the accounts in Foundation for Tolerance International (2005), Foundation for Tolerance International, Mehr and Yntymak (2005); Mehr (2005a, 2005b); Yntymak saiasaty (2005a, 2005b).

villagers from Hushiar blocked the single small road that leads from the edge of the Charbak market to the larger road that runs through Hushiar. The villagers from Hushiar who would ordinarily have gone to Charbak to buy tobacco, spirits, or livestock were apparently warned to make sure that they left the area before the afternoon, while the remaining Kyrgyz traders and shoppers were held on the grounds of the outdoor market by the crowd that had gathered on the road. Several dozen men entered the market, apparently throwing stones and leaving some of the Kyrgyz traders injured. Three Kyrgyz-registered cars parked near the market entrance had windows broken, and sections of the water pipe that provided Charbak with irrigation water from the Sokh River, recently constructed as a Mercy Corps "consensus-building project" through its Peaceful Communities Initiative, were destroyed. By the evening, border troop reinforcements from both countries had been joined by officials from the provincial and district administrations, state security officials, and policemen. Kyrgyz troops accompanied the traders from Sogment, who had been trapped in the market, back to their village. The Hushiar villagers later dispersed, while armed troop reinforcements patrolled the informal bridge boundary between the villages, often just a few meters apart.

On May 4, several hundred men from Hushiar and Sogment gathered 150 meters apart on either side of the Bayaman Bridge, both groups surrounded by police and troop reinforcements. After a tense standoff between the two sides the governor of Batken oblast arrived, accompanied by more policemen, state security officials, and members of the local interior ministry. Uzbek officials from the oblast administration also arrived, together with military from the provincial capital, Ferghana, and some from Tashkent. Each of these two militarized delegations met with their respective populations. At stake were several issues: the allocation of water from the Sogment spring that provided both Charbak and parts of Hushiar with irrigation water, the presence of the Kyrgyz border post that had been stationed between the two villages since 2000 and was much resented by the Hushiar villagers, the use of grazing lands in Kyrgyzstan by farmers from Hushiar, and the status of several areas of disputed territory. The "Kyrgyz side," as it was now referred to in conflict analyses, demanded that the state boundary of the Kyrgyz Republic be "unambiguously determined" (*chetko oboznachena*) and requested that the number of soldiers at the Kyrgyz border post be increased. Meanwhile, a group of Hushiar elders petitioned the regional governor to remove the Kyrgyz border post altogether, and asked that the water allocation schedule which had existed prior to 2002 be reinstated.

In the early afternoon, the three NGOs working in the area persuaded the elders from the two communities to participate in "shuttle diplomacy" (*chelnochnaia diplomatiia*), during which the allocation of water between the two villages was discussed. But the discussions were aborted, apparently overtaken by incidents of violence among the assembled villagers, some of which involved the Mercy Corps water pipe that had been attacked the previous day. The two sides agreed to postpone their discussion until a later date. That evening, men from Sogment and Hushiar set up their own "self-defense" posts around their respective villages, blocking access to the cars from the neighboring state, and patrolling throughout the night. More troop reinforcements were sent from each side, and remained throughout the following days, making it impossible for people from Sogment and Charbak to leave their villages. Because the only road for any of the villages at the southern end of the valley was blocked, exiting any of the Kyrgyz villages at the southern mountainous end of the valley was impossible.

On May 7, in a closed session monitored by state security representatives, the governors of the neighboring oblasts met and discussed the allocation of water from the Sogment spring. No decision to change the timetable of water allocation was reached, and groups of men continued to block all the exit roads through the valley to the upstream Kyrgyz villages. This situation of tense standoff prevailed until six days later, when the most brutal instance of state violence against unarmed civilians since Uzbekistan's independence took place in the nearby city of Andijan. The "Andijan events" (*Andijon voqeasi*), in which a crowd of bystanders was fired on from armored personnel carriers following an armed prison break, overwhelmed events in Sogment and Hushiar and sent shock waves through the valley. With anxious rumors flying about whether similar violence might be used to break up this local standoff, the stones were removed, the road reopened, and traders began, slowly and cautiously, to frequent the "other" market as they had done before May.

Situating the Event

How are we to make sense of this event? How and why did an altercation between Kyrgyz border guards and students from Sokh escalate into a sustained confrontation between villages on two sides of the border, involving physical violence, the destruction of irrigation infrastructure and the blocking of the only road out of the valley for upstream villages? Many reports at the time suggested that it was all ultimately a fight about control over cross-border canal water between two deeply antagonistic communities: a conflict that was "waiting to happen." As such it can be inserted into an account of conflict that is already an established genre in writing on the Ferghana Valley: a cross-border incident driven by resource shortage for which the smallest altercation might act as trigger; an interethnic conflict that demands "preventive" intervention and the teaching of tolerance to limit future escalation.

I am not claiming that water was irrelevant to the dynamics of escalation, or that antagonisms did not become powerfully, indeed violently structured along ethnic lines. This was a moment of crisis when—at least for a certain category of male participants—ethnicity forcefully "happened" (Brubaker 1996b), structuring loyalties and demands, shaping the dynamics of participation. Moreover, the destruction of the neighboring village's irrigation channel and the demands that were articulated in meetings with regional authorities suggest that water was far from incidental to the dynamics of this conflict. The event occurred at the height of the spring planting season, when demands on a restricted flow of irrigation water are at their greatest. And the object of violence, the "USAID pipe" that transported irrigation water to Charbak, was not without considerable symbolic and material significance on both sides of the border. This conflict was thus, at some significant level, about differential access to resources. And it is this differential access that is crucial to understanding what happened; not the resource per se. To understand why people in Hushiar were aggrieved by the distribution of irrigation water, we need to examine the political relations that produced shortage and what they reveal about the complex business of producing state limits after independence. Doing so reveals that this conflict had little to do with an absence of toleration or dialogue, even though it rapidly came to be presented as such. It had to do with what Žižek calls "politics proper": the politics, not of asserting or affirming one's particular identity within the social order ("the postmodern identity politics of the particular"), but the kind of politics in which the specific demand "starts to function as the metaphoric condensation . . . of the entire social space" (1999, 208).

The Politics of Water Allocation

At the time of the conflict, irrigation water between Charbak and Hushiar was regulated by a schedule agreed on in April 2002 between the heads of Batken and Sokh districts. This agreement dictated that the water from the Sogment spring would be regulated on a seven-day cycle, with villagers in Hushiar having access to the water for five of those days, and those in Charbak, for two. This agreement replaced an older nine-day cycle, according to which Hushiar had had seven days' access, and Charbak had usage rights for the remaining two. The actual mechanism for irrigation regulation was a simple technology of selective sluices, which sent the water from Sogment in one direction or the other. It depended on a considerable degree of trust and mutual social control for its successful functioning. The reasons for the change in allocation had to do with relative shifts in population and the fact that water destined for users farther downstream, in the village I call Navabod, had long since failed to reach its destination. The inhabitants of Hushiar, with a population three times that of Sogment and Charbak combined, had effectively been using what was technically "Navabod's" water for the previous several years. As far as the people of Hushiar were concerned, changing the schedule meant a real and material decline in the amount of irrigation water to which they had access, at a time of considerable dependence on personal garden plots. The economic crisis of the 1990s had meant that the small plots (typically 4–6 *sotok* [0.04–0.06 hectare]) that might previously have represented a supplement to domestic incomes had now come to be central to sustaining livelihoods.[3] Losing out on irrigation water was not just an inconvenience, but a source of considerable anxiety and resentment.

The 2002 arrangement not only changed the substance of the agreement; it also rendered it more formal. The timetable for water allocation went from being a spoken, noncodified arrangement between the elders of neighboring villages to an object of official state regulation, which was to be signed and stamped by the respective regional governors. There is a long history of informal water regulation in the Sokh Valley (Dzhakhonov 1989, 44–47), just as there is of progressive state involvement in the regulation of irrigation over the course of the twentieth century (Thurman 1999; Jozan 2012). In Hushiar, there was occasional speculation that the reason for this codification "in favor of Charbak" said as much about the dynamics of relations between district and provincial governors in the two states as it did about real changes in the demand for water on both sides of the border. The Sokh district governor (*hokim*), newly appointed at that time, was keen to "prove himself" to his superior, one Hushiar man explained it to me, by showing that he could take unpopular decisions at home and still maintain order. Whatever the veracity of this claim, the 2002 agreement was interpreted in Hushiar to be indicative of far more than an unfair agreement: it was rather a visible symbol of unequal local powers of lobby and appeal.

---

[3]In contrast to Kyrgyzstan (where land had been progressively privatized since 1996), agricultural land in Hushiar was administered by a cooperative (*shirkat*) that differed little in its operational principles from the Soviet collective farm. Land is allocated on a contractual basis to leaseholders who receive a small salary for working it, but who have little say over which crops can be grown, and few opportunities to sell at a market rate. In this context, the water from the Sogment spring, which irrigated garden plots, was central to families' livelihoods. Domestic plots in Hushiar are very small, even by the Ferghana Valley standards, where population density makes for some of the smallest land plots in Central Asia. In Sogment, the average domestic land plot was twelve *sotok*, three times greater than in Hushiar.

Joint canal-clearing exercise, Kyrgyz-Uzbek border, upper Sokh Valley, January 2005.

By May 2005, recent events had given new salience to these unequal powers. To acquaintances living on the Uzbek side of the border in Sokh, broader political changes in Kyrgyzstan during the preceding few weeks provided a vivid and sobering reminder of the oft-repeated observation that "in Uzbekistan the state is rich and the people are poor; in Kyrgyzstan the people are rich and the state is poor." In Kyrgyzstan, Askar Akayev, the country's first postindependence president, had been ousted less than six weeks earlier in what the media (and even many previously indifferent citizens in Kyrgyzstan) were calling a "people's revolution" (*eldik revoliutsiia*). During the weeks immediately following this political crisis, questions of statehood and the state's "territorial integrity" had been thrust into the thick of public debate, as television bulletins and newspapers stories merged with densely circulating rumors about the disgraced President Akayev's secret sales of land to China.[4] In Bishkek, where a considerable proportion of television is directly rebroadcast from Russian channels, urbanites watched agog during the spring of 2005 as Russian political commentators earnestly

---

[4]On the role of Akayev's exchanges of land in mobilizing the opposition in a manner that was to prove decisive in 2005, see Lewis (2008, 127–145); Radnitz (2005).

debated the risks of having a "failed state" (*nesostoiavshcheesia gosudarst-vo*) in Central Asia.[5] One notorious roundtable discussion on Russia's First Channel three days after Akayev's overthrow even debated the proposition that the best option for the Central Asian region would be the "split" (*raskol*) of Kyrgyzstan into two, with the north given to Kazakhstan and the south to Uzbekistan (*Vremena* 2005). Acquaintances in Bishkek with whom I discussed these commentaries were aghast at the hubris of such claims (and the indignity that, after fleeing the country, Akayev had given his first public broadcast to a radio station based in Russia rather than Kyrgyzstan). They were also troubled by the ease with which the state seemed to have descended into chaos at a moment of crisis. Being an "integral," bordered state suddenly seemed very contingent and fragile indeed. As one Osh-based journalist put it:

> Behind the beautiful façade of independence and the loud, somber pronouncements of 2,200 years of Kyrgyz statehood, an ugly reality is concealed. Kyrgyzstan as a state does not even have its own borders [*Kyrgyzstan kak gosudarstvo dazhe ne imeet sobstvennykh granits*], and the borders that we do have more often have just an administrative character, so our neighbors can move them about just as they like. And yet—territorial integrity and borders—aren't these supposed to be the very foundation of any state? (Kalet 2006)

For more than three months, the country was without an elected president, creating a great deal of nervousness about the consequences of this political crisis. But this was also, albeit briefly, a time of tremendous hope. In Bishkek, former university colleagues who had been indifferent to political engagement in the months leading up to Akayev's overthrow began discussing the possibility of substantive change. Live broadcasts from parliament and hastily convened press conferences were suddenly the most compelling drama on television, and provided a constant narrative backdrop to the business of getting on with life in a city that had been dramatically looted following the president's ouster. Shops, offices, and public space became covered, in the space of

---

[5] In the fall of 2006, Moscow's State Institute for International Relations under the Ministry of International Affairs published the "Political Atlas of the World" in which 192 countries were ranked according to their threats, influence, well-being, bases of democracy, and "stateness" (*gosudarstvennost'*). On this last rating, Kyrgyzstan was ranked 191 of 192, behind Afghanistan and the Democratic Republic of Congo, and declared "incapable of independent existence" (*nesposobnym k nezavisimomu sushchestvovaniiu*). Russia, meanwhile was ranked twenty-seventh for its "stateness," ahead of Norway (see http://worldpolities.org/index.php?option=com_content&task=view&id=14&Itemid=308).

Public meeting on Ala-Too Square following Akayev's ouster in the Tulip Revolution, Bishkek, March 2005.

hours, with the revolution's leitmotif, "we're with the people!" (*biz el menen!*). In the spring of 2005 there was a sense that opportunities were wide open (often painfully, disconcertingly so), and that everything was potentially "up for grabs": power, property, fame, influence, jobs, contracts, and above all, land.[6]

---

[6]The sense of terrifying possibility is captured in the oral histories in Tulegabylova and Shishkaraeva (2005); on the sense of the state being "up for impersonation" in the weeks following the March 24 seizure of power, see Kniazev (2006a, 156–196). For the "official" (victors') version of the "people's revolution," see Kazybaev (2006); for the Akayev family narrative recounting of the overthrow of government, see Akaeva (2006). On the subsequent search for political ordering through the performative refounding of the constitution, see Beyer (2013).

It was this sudden shift in the quality of land—a public resource that demanded just allocation—that was the most visible spontaneous reaction to the shifts in the political landscape. Illegal land seizures consumed Bishkek and Osh, closing roads and shaking up these cities' normally quiescent residential microdistricts.[7] Property rights were being reconfigured; normally muted debates about "autochthonous" and "incomer" (*priezhie*) populations were suddenly thrust into the mix of discussion over claims to property, and the administration of justice was often rough and unforgiving.[8] As the headline of the usually moderate *Vechernii Bishkek* newspaper asserted in a mid-April edition, addressing the new powers in charge: "You grabbed power. Now give us land" (Soltoeva 2005). The "revolution" had made seizure legitimate; "grabbers" (*samozakhvatchiki*) were, for a brief moment, turned into national heroes.

Patrons and Politics

These events in no way can be said to have caused the conflict that occurred in southern Sokh in early May 2005. The ripples from political storms in Bishkek and Osh were weaker here, and most people were far too preoccupied with the business of sowing corn and weeding fields (and still more, leaving for another season's construction work in Russia) than with seizing land around Bishkek. However, among the villagers of Sogment and Gaz there was considerable pride that this was their revolution too, and that their role in propelling a new (southern) elite to power deserved recognition and reward.

---

[7] The number of informal residential districts (*novostroiki*) increased dramatically following the March overthrow of the government as new lands were claimed through a process of (technically illegal) appropriation (*samozakhvat*). Indeed, in the weeks immediately after the March 24 events, land claims around Bishkek and Osh were the number one news item, as families living in temporary accommodation saw in this moment of political transformation the opportunity successfully to press demands for land. See, for instance, the analysis published under the title, "Bishkek in panic: thousands of land-grabbers are on the loose" (*oruduyut tysiachi zemel'nykh maroderov*) (Maratova 2005).

[8] This was a time, in Bishkek, when ethnicity suddenly became a salient mark of social "vision and division" (Bourdieu 1999, 70) in a way that, in this normally comfortably cosmopolitan of cities, had previously been much more muted. Particular ethnic groups (notably Uighurs) had suffered disproportionately from the looting that followed the storming of the White House in Bishkek, and there were rumors (largely unsubstantiated, though socially consequential), of ethnic Russians having been targeted in domestic attacks. Certainly, for many Russian-speaking urbanites irrespective of ethnicity, the *el* ("people") of the revolution was perceived as remote from their own (urban, Russophone) social world.

Revolutionary border work on a Sogment shop: "Kyrgyzstan is the jewel of democracy in Central Asia! K. Bakiyev is the hero of the revolution!" July 2005.

Key to understanding why this was so is the figure of Bayaman Erkinbaev, with whose money the bridge that proved the epicenter of the May conflict had been rebuilt in 2002, and in whose honor it had been renamed. Erkinbaev, known in and around Batken simply by his first name, Bayaman, was a wrestler-turned-businessman-turned Olympic committee chair who was reputed to have control over a significant proportion of the drug trade through Osh as well as a controlling stake in Central Asia's largest wholesale market, in the border town of Kara-Suu (Lewis 2008, 150; Spector 2008, 169). By the time he turned thirty-nine, he had thrice successfully balloted for parliament as a way (many suspected) of ensuring parliamentary immunity for his business interests.[9] He was indisputably one of the country's wealthiest men and had played a critical role in the political upheavals in Bishkek.[10]

---

[9]Lewis (2008, 150) notes that when in earlier elections in 2000 Erkinbaev had been charged with electoral malpractice he simply "marched into the courtroom and beat up the judge." The case against him was dropped.

[10]For an insightful analysis of the role of elites such as Erkinbaev in mobilizing local opposition in the run up to the 2005 Tulip Revolution, see Radnitz (2010); International Crisis Group (2005a).

Erkinbaev had, until his assassination in September 2005, succeeded in impersonating the state to an exceptional degree.[11] At once reminiscent of the kind of mafia figure who stands apart from law and scorns it—the "honest bandit" of Yeltsin-era Russia (Humphrey 2002c; Ries 2002)—he was also an exemplary "state" figure. As several observers of Kyrgyz politics have noted, it is not unusual for businessmen, including those whose business activities may be of questionable legality, to enter parliament as a way of ensuring immunity from prosecution. Nor is it unusual for potential candidates to secure the patronage of prospective parliamentary constituents in very explicit and direct ways: through gifts of coal, money or clothes to individual families, and through the rehabilitation of critical infrastructure (Engvall 2011; Ismailbekova 2011; Radnitz 2010).

In the Kyrgyz villages of the upper Sokh Valley, Erkinbaev had not only paid for the rehabilitation of the bridge that was now named in his honor; he had also reputedly agreed to finance a new electricity transformer in Charbak and a new pipeline for drinking water (Bichsel 2009, 92). In the run-up to elections, his campaign team had brought the Kyrgyz pop singer, Bek Borbiev, to give a concert in Gaz—a village far off the main route for touring pop stars. He had distributed sacks of flour to needy families; he had presented new winter coats to elderly men, and there were promises of double glazing for several of the older, poorly insulated homes, including Kanysh-ai's. In this context of patriarchal provisioning, it is not surprising that for the people of Sogment and Gaz he held the status of a local hero. Bichsel notes that for many in the upper Sokh Valley, Erkinbaev was seen as a source of "humanitarian aid" alongside the various nongovernmental projects operating in the village. The only difference was the conditionality of this assistance: "Erkinbaev did not require changed attitudes towards tolerance or participatory and democratic procedures, but rather expected unity and solidarity in support of his political endeavors" (2009, 93).

When parliamentary elections were held in February 2005, Erkinbaev was one of only three candidates in Kyrgyzstan to run unchallenged in these elections. In Sogment and Gaz, which fell within his constituency, he received 95.5 percent of the vote, a figure that was strikingly consistent throughout

---

[11]Erkinbaev's death seems to have been related to disputes over control of the Turatali market in Kara-Suu. There had been a further attempt on his life on April 28, 2005, just three days before the conflict that emerged in southern Sokh. The spate of assassination attempts at this time, hitherto unusual for Kyrgyzstan, is indicative of the degree to which the rule of law was felt to have collapsed following the March overthrow of president Akayev. See International Crisis Group (2005a) for an account of the political developments at the time, and McGlinchey (2011, 102) on speculation over the causes of Erkinbaev's murder.

Kanysh-Ai on the Bayaman Bridge between Sogment and Hushiar, upper Sokh Valley, July 2005.

the entire district where he was running.[12] By the time of the conflict on the Bayaman Bridge, Erkinbaev was running for president.[13] His background in wrestling, his straddling of "legal" and "illegal" economic domains, his notoriously rough manner of speech with misogynist and nationalist overtones inspired fear and awe in equal measure.

---

[12]According to the International Crisis Group, he received 95 percent of the vote among his Kadamjai district constituency (2005a, 6). All of the parliamentary election results were archived on the website of the Central Election Committee (www.shailoo.gov.kg).

[13]Erkinbaev subsequently withdrew, throwing his weight behind the eventual victor, Kurmanbek Bakiyev.

During the May 2005 events, Bayaman was a significant figure in absentia for understanding the dynamics of conflict. For the people of Sogment and Charbak, he was known to be both a powerful and intimate friend of their villages, and a source of ultimate political authority: a patron whose successful impersonation of the state (a presidential candidate, no less) would enable him to overturn and over-ride any unpopular decisions taken by lesser state figures. He is reported to have remarked at the time that he would "take matters into his own hands" if "the authorities" should fail to resolve the conflict between Sogment and Hushiar (Bichsel 2009, 93): a rhetorical move that signals both the extent of his own power and its ambiguous status within the realm of law. He was both "within" the state and outside it; both an embodiment of "legitimate" authority and willing to override it should decisions not be taken in his favor. Das and Poole (2004, 14) remark that such figures "represent at once the fading of the state's jurisdiction and its continual refounding through its (not so mythic) appropriation of private justice and violence." In the dynamics of May 2005, he was crucial to ensuring that the newly-appointed governor of Batken oblast—a figure whom he had helped propel to power—responded immediately to the demands of the villagers in Sogment and Charbak, arriving soon after the conflict began, noting villagers' demands, and promising to "raise issues" with his opposite number in Uzbekistan.

Strained Collaborations

This political context rendered particularly stark the divergent realities facing cross-border partner NGOs. International "preventive development" in the Ferghana Valley is often dependent on the existence of partner organizations on either side of a border (indeed Mehr had been established to be the local implementing partner for donor-led initiatives). Many previously state-controlled functions in southern Sokh are now performed by nongovernmental organizations; and "civil society," especially in its transnational variant, has been identified as having an important role to play in conflict prevention (Maasen 2004; Young 2003; though see Koehler 2004 on the importance of improving state capacity). In the narrative accounts of donor reports and publications there is often a seductive symmetry to the activities of the grassroots organizations whose activities they fund. Yntymak and Mehr, for instance, had been sponsored to work collaboratively as partner organizations for joint cross-border events. The logic of such collaborations is simple and compelling: although they are independent organizations subject to different government legislation, banking rules, and reporting requirements, each organization is also embedded in its own community, and so can successfully mobilize populations for the undertaking of joint tasks. It is a model premised on balanced powers of mobilization and representation.[14]

By May 2005, the gulf between nominal institutional symmetry and the practical asymmetries of operation facing Yntymak and Mehr was vast. In Kyrgyzstan the nongovernmental sector, as the self-declared embodiment of the "people" against the "state" was celebrating a moment of intense, if ultimately short-lived, influence in political life. In the days preceding the conflict in southern Sokh, I attended Kyrgyzstan's "All-National Forum of Civil Society" (*Obshchenatsional'nyi forum grazhdanskogo obshchestva*) in the National Philharmonic Hall in Bishkek. The gathering was large and the atmosphere euphoric. Even the setting was significant: as the opening speaker noted, this was the first time that the organizers had been able to demand where such a forum be held, rather than appeal to the authorities for public space. It was a moment of consolidation and pride for leaders of civic organizations. We were addressed (in Kyrgyz, usually) as "respected relatives" (*urmattuu tuugandar*). The March events were spoken of as "*our* revolution," emphasized by repeated assertions about the importance of reminding the new powers that we—the country's "conscience" (*sovest'*)—existed. Speaker after speaker berated public officials in a way that would have been unimaginable just six weeks earlier, while newly appointed government officials sat on the stage, taking notes and listening attentively. As the printed resolutions from the forum made explicit, it was the task of "all the healthy social and political forces in the country" to unite to defend the principles of "people-power [*narodovlastiia*], freedom and constitutionalism" (Obshchenatsional'nyi forum 2005). The tension in this trio of demands notwithstanding, this was a time of palpable excitement for Kyrgyzstan's nongovernmental sector. One young speaker at the conference noted, "for the first time we are a free republic. For the first time we are able to develop a strong state. This is civil society's Tulip Revolution."[15]

The spatial ordering of the all-national forum made very visible what was occurring in more subtle ways elsewhere in Kyrgyzstan. Members of nongovernmental organizations were often being given significant administrative

---

[14]See, for an explicit statement, the "principles of prevention" in Lubin and Rubin (1999, 14–17).

[15]The "Tulip Revolution" was the name popularly given to the ousting of president Akayev and his government in March 2005, following flawed elections. The name given to the uprising evoked commonalities with the 2004 "Orange Revolution" in Ukraine and the "Rose Revolution" in Georgia, though the social and political dynamics of these colored revolutions were quite distinct. See Cummings (2010).

power. In Batken, members of the Foundation for Tolerance International, the largest NGO in the region, had played a very visible role in mediating between government and opposition factions for control of the city administration. One of its employees (an engineer who had done much of the groundwork for materializing the USAID pipe in Charbak) was invited to become the province's deputy governor.

The buoyancy felt by Batken's NGOs immediately after the Tulip Revolution stood in stark contrast to the anxiety felt by Parviz and his colleagues in Mehr. This was a dreadful year for any organization daring to call itself "nongovernmental" in Uzbekistan. New fiscal regulations made the receipt of grant funding harder and many organizations were curbing activities that could be construed as having a "political" component. Parviz frequently talked about the need to frame Mehr's activities in exclusively "economic" terms, and ultimately of giving up his NGO work to depart for unskilled labor in Russia (something he eventually did in 2007). In a speech in January 2005, Uzbek president Karimov reiterated his gradualist program of reform, stressing the need for a strong civil society to be preceded and facilitated by a "strong state," and reserving particular criticism for the "various so-called open society models" espoused by nongovernmental organizations (Karimov 2005). During the days of May tension, far from being sought out for advice, employees of Mehr were often subject to accusations from the regional and oblast administrations of having exacerbated the conflict between Hushiar and Sogment. Threats and accusations ("lack of patriotism," "collusion" with Kyrgyz partners) were used to enact a boundary between state and society, law and its violation, placing Mehr firmly outside the bounds of state. The relationship between two collaborative partner organizations on either side of the border could not have been more imbalanced.[16]

This difference was manifest in the kind of intervention that it was possible for each organization to make in the conflict, but also for the potential each had to articulate an analysis of what had occurred to the outside world. There was a striking divergence in the number of conflict analyses written, in the degree of broadcast they were permitted, and in the kinds of critique that differently positioned organizations were able to make.[17] These differences

---

[16]According to Mercy Corps (2006, 20), which sponsored the Peaceful Communities Initiative, Mehr was eventually forced to close in 2006, less than five years after it had been established, due to government pressure.

[17]This divergence in discursive possibility eventually led the employees of Mehr, in one of their conflict analyses in early May 2005, to urge their Kyrgyz partners to tone down their reporting of events. Peace-building NGOs, "of all people," they argued, should refrain from the "temptation to manipulate the situation and information [about it]" (Mehr 2005b).

generated other asymmetries. Because few journalists were present at the scene of these incidents, NGO-generated conflict analyses, along with interviews from Kyrgyzstani officials, tended to shape the broader narrative that circulated within the mass media. As a result, while Kyrgyz newspaper and online media published extensive and sometimes polemical accounts of the incident, in Uzbekistan—where writing on "conflict" is a heavily censored theme—there was no mention of the incident in the national press until over a year later. The narrative version of events that has entered international news reports therefore, has tended to exclude what seems to have been the immediate provocation for the conflict: the fact that Kyrgyz border guards beat two school boys from the neighboring village who had taken their cows to graze across the border. In much of the subsequent reporting, the violence from a group of Hushiar men at the Tuesday border market is narrated as having essentially "appeared from nowhere," unprovoked and irrational. This, for instance, is how the reporters for *Deutsche Welle* commenced their narrative sequence of events, describing Sokh as a "small Uzbek island on Kyrgyz territory":

Several people received wounds of varying severity. Three cars were overturned and the roof of one home was partially destroyed. Adylbek Shadymanov, the deputy governor of Batken oblast, told Deutsche Welle about these events.[18] In his words, the disturbances had been initiated by Tajiks [*byli initsiirovany tadzhikami*] from the Uzbek village of Hushiar, who raided Kirgiz territory unsanctioned [*samovol'no vtorglis' na kirgizskuiu territoriiu*]. They picked a fight with the local inhabitants and created a riot [*ustroili pogrom*]. Kirgiz police arrived and were able to settle the situation. However, the residents of the village of Hushiar, who are located inside the Uzbek enclave of Sokh, blocked the road out of the enclave with stones, which the Kirgiz had previously always relied on. As a result several Kirgiz villages have remained in isolation. (Pozdniakova and Chernogaev, 2005)

The reporters' narrative voice here meshes with that of Batken's new deputy governor, such that the disturbances "initiated by the Tajiks from the Uzbek village of Hushiar" acquires the status at once of descriptive fact and as the precipitating incident for the events that followed. This is a narrative structured in terms of oppositional ethnic groups confronting each other as undifferentiated crowds; of "unsanctioned raids" into already-spatialized

---

[18]Shadymanov had, until a few weeks earlier, been working for the Foundation for Tolerance International, and was appointed to the position of deputy governor after the March events.

states; and of (pacific) state officials who eventually settle the situation. By starting the account with the "unprovoked" violence of Tajik villagers against Kyrgyz property, the uncomfortable question of official violence is written out. There is no mention of border guards inflicting violence, or of popular resentment of their presence. Thus the story of interethnic conflict—of Tajiks against Kyrgyz antagonistically positioned across a border—is remade and rewritten, again.

Violent Border Work

When I returned to Sogment and Hushiar two months after the May conflict, there was still no barbed wire between Hushiar and its neighbors; the border guards were no greater in number; there were no visible material obstacles to movement; all traces of the barriers that had been mounted to block roads in May had been removed. The "state" as set of material institutions had not changed significantly. But there was a quite palpable shift in what it meant to be subject to "separate authority." New, gendered limits were being placed on cross-border movement through informal social sanction and public invocations of shame (*uiat*). More visibly, there were practical attempts to enact state spatiality in new ways: by appropriating the border guards and their "legitimate" violence for defense of private property, and by recasting once-shared social spaces in exclusive national terms.

The conflict in May 2005 did not bring about a sudden shift in mentality— a kind of collective reification or moment of sudden subordination to the nationalist rhetoric of local elites. It is rather that the events of May had intensified debate about the meanings and entailments of territorial integrity, just as the "revolution" six weeks previously had prompted considerable popular debate, in newspapers and urban kitchens, about what it meant to live in a state that "dazzles by its absence" (*blistaet svoim otsutstviem*) (Pushchaev 2005; see also Kniazev 2006b). What did being "separate" entail in terms of previously common pastureland, shared waterways, and roads on which all relied? At what point does land become exclusive national property? What role should the border guards stationed by the Bayaman Bridge have in defending "our" property? When does a border guard become a gendarme? This was not an uncontested field. In fact, it was the very disagreement about what "territorial integrity" might entail for those living here that made debates over markets, roads, pastures, mosques, water pipes, and border guards so intense.

This element of discursive intensification is significant. The "relatively sudden fluctuations in the 'nationness' of groups or relational settings" that Rogers Brubaker (1996b, 20) points to in his exploration of nationalizing regimes come about not simply through a kind of collective amnesia, or the imposing of one person's vision on an impassive mass of others, but rather through the incitement to talk. As Aretxaga argues in another context of political contestation, we have to inquire about the relationship between the "body of the state" and the work of narrating it and its excesses (2000, 51; see also Gupta 1995).

There were three sites where the body of the state and its physical edges came to be spoken of and enacted in new ways following the events of May 2005. These concerned a once-shared market, an abandoned half-constructed road, and the accessibility of a gynecologist's medical care. These were sites of enactment in a material sense: the "locatedness" of a market, a road, and a recently refurbished medical clinic were central to their production as spaces that marked a physical and moral between two communities. Territory and its "integrity" were central to what occurred. But each of these was also a site of discursive production: about the possibilities and limits of shared trade and shared resources; and about what having a "manned" border here should entail.

Bazar Bölüsh Kerek! Separating the Market

The "border market," or *chek ara bazar*, is a central institution of border-land villages, and a particularly visible and important one in the Ferghana Valley where regimes of production and value are so very different in each of the three states. At the southern limits of the Sokh enclave, the border had a form common to other border zones. What were notionally two distinct markets on either side of a border effectively functioned as a single unit, operating at the same hours on the same days of the week in close geographical proximity. Until the May conflict, the "Uzbek market" was located close to the school at the lower end of Hushiar; the "Kyrgyz market" a short walk away in the hamlet of Charbak, the site of the fated Mercy Corps pipe. When people talked of "going to the bazaar" they usually meant going to both of these markets, because many goods were sold at one site and not the other. For vodka or tobacco, one would go to the "Kyrgyz side" where production was deemed superior and spirits could be openly bought and sold. That was also the site to buy livestock, cheap Chinese clothes, and quality leather jackets brought form Bishkek. On the "Uzbek side," one could find fruit and vegetables transported from the fertile basin of the Ferghana Valley, Uzbek-manufactured sweets, household goods, bright *atlas* fabrics and rolls of locally manufactured cloth, headscarves, prayer boots, and—if one knew whom to ask—contraband fertilizer and fuel.

226 / Chapter 6

Other more subtle variations signaled the difference in economic regime. In the "Kyrgyz market," gambling was permitted and it was possible to exchange currency openly. A group of men counted out notes with lightning speed, their bags bulging with bundles of dollars, Russian rubles, Uzbek sum, Kyrgyz som, Tajik somoni, euros, and even the occasional Kazakh tenge. On the Uzbek side, such exchanges were made informally, but they were conducted out of sight, often quite literally under or behind a table piled high with other goods. Seven-seater Damaz minibuses would ply the short stretch between the two markets for heavily laden customers; and there would often be a mobile border and customs control posted on the bridge at the entrance to the Charbak bazaar. Even with this element of resented stately control, however, the markets were not spoken of as separate spaces. Most people carried both Uzbek and Kyrgyz currency, and most traders accepted either one. Morally and imaginatively, these were two parts of one social space; different, but interdependent.

When I returned to Sogment in early July, I found friends and acquaintances in the throes, quite literally, of separating the market. On a patch of rather unpromising, unirrigated land at the western side of Sogment, new trading stalls were being constructed by village men. Juniper trees had been felled from the grounds of the local mosque for timber, which was covered in corrugated metal sheeting that had been brought back from Russia by some of the village's many migrant workers. Some of the trading stalls had already been claimed, with first names written on, or scratched into, the top plank of wood.

There was a sense of anticipation in the air. I walked around the grounds with the new market director (*bazarkom*), whose home near the site had made him one of the most vocal advocates of the "separate" market. He told me about the need for Kyrgyz villagers from Sogment and upstream Gaz to be able to shop at the Kyrgyz market without crossing into the territory of Uzbekistan. "We're separate states, aren't we?" he asked. Then, interpolating me in his comment, he added: "Doesn't every normal state have a clear border? Doesn't England have a border?"

The bazarkom's assertions left me struggling for a response. Hushiar and Sogment, after all, had historically relied on a single road to connect them to their respective district centers, and beyond that, to the outside world, as well as a single spring for their drinking water and a single irrigation canal for their fields. Until 1999 there had been no visible markers of demarcation between the two villages. And here I was, just a few years later, being shown around a separate market and instructed on the importance of Kyrgyzstan having a bounded state, a discourse "more statist than the state" (Navaro-Yashin

2002, 119). As we walked through the partially constructed trading stalls, I wondered about the possible loss of trade for those who took up a place here. The previous joint market had enabled Kyrgyz traders from Sogment, Gaz, and Charbak to benefit from the volume of customers from Hushiar, with its much larger population, as well as from shoppers from farther down the Sokh Valley. In response, the bazarkom explained that he was making sure that Kyrgyz customers would turn up from elsewhere in the region instead. He was running advertisements on the regional Batken radio. He was sponsoring a series of competitive volleyball matches on market day to attract new customers, with a sheep as first prize. And he was reducing to the trade tax to attract people to trade there. He stressed the importance of the border guards' presence to ensure that the water timetable was properly adhered to. Linking our conversation about the market to the political turmoil that had gripped Kyrgyzstan for the previous few months, he commented, "Akayev never gave us a border. The new president had better delimit it (*chek arany taktap beresh kerek*; lit. 'he must define and give us the border')."

The building materials for the new bazaar were taken from the grounds of a sacred site located at the border between the two villages, the Khodjai Orif

Territorializing the *adyr:* volleyball game sponsored by the new market director on the site of the new Sogment market, July 2005.

mazar. This had been paradigmatically shared space: the resting place for a famous Sokh *Hajji,* whose village of birth is now administratively in Uzbekistan, and whose resting place, a site of pilgrimage for two communities, now lies just across the border, in Kyrgyzstan. Outcry among Hushiar elders at the felling of trees that had been collectively planted on the site of the *mazar* was met by practices of state classification. Administrators from the state registry in Batken and Sokh visited the site, asserting that establishing conclusive ownership was essential to "prevent an interethnic conflict" over the felling of the trees. The registry officials agreed that since the *mazar* indeed lay inside Kyrgyz territory, it was lawful for the trees to be felled for the Sogment bazaar (AKIpress 2005). This was one of the few remaining spaces of communally owned land in Sogment, and building materials were in short supply. But for the Hushiar elders this act of demarcation through state accounting and the felling of trees on sacred space was a bitter reminder of the way that stately logics trumped local practices of reckoning place and belonging.

The shift in the bazaar's location, to a site more fully inside Kyrgyzstan and reachable by upstream families without leaving Kyrgyz territory, was a relief to some people in Gaz in the aftermath of the conflict. When I visited Kanysh-ai and her family in July 2005, for instance, her brother warned her in

Newly built trading stalls at the site of the relocated Kyrgyz market, Sogment, July 2005.

Abandoned trading stalls on market day in the previously "joint" market, Charbak, July 2005.

stark terms not to walk down to the Charbak market, which would take her through one of the Hushiar *mahallas,* where she might be cast "bad glances." The new Sogment market would be closer to them and he was relieved that they would now be able to shop there without having to cross into Uzbekistan. But moving the market was not without opposition. The seventy-five families living in Charbak depended on the previous border market in their hamlet as a major source of livelihood: virtually everyone there was involved in trading, and many Charbak homeowners made a small income by renting out their houses as overnight storehouses for stallholders from lower-lying villages. When I visited the previously bustling Charbak bazaar on market day in mid-July, a few determined traders, mostly from Charbak itself, were still selling there, even though there were few buyers and the market felt eerily silent with the ghosts of abandoned trade.

The Akayev Road

Mirroring this concern with separate markets was a discussion about separate roads. As we have seen, the inhabitants of Sogment, Gaz, Charbak, and Hushiar rely on a single road to reach the outside world. It is the same road that connects Hushiar with other parts of the Sokh enclave, and which enables people in the Kyrgyz villages of southern Sokh to reach their oblast center in Batken, as well as the main Batken-Osh highway. Reaching any of these destinations entails crossing through the two fixed border and custom posts that stand at the main crossing point in the valley.

In 1996, construction began on a dirt road (*gruntovaia doroga*) that would link Batken to Sogment and through the mountains south of Sokh to Aidarkan on the eastern side of the Sokh enclave. This was an ambitious project, which ran into both financial and political difficulties. Constructing a road through the peaks south of Sokh was beyond the means of the Kyrgyz government in the cash-strapped 1990s, and authorities in Uzbekistan questioned the line of the proposed road, claiming that it would traverse Uzbek territory. The "Akayev road," as it was known, symbolized many of the failed undertakings of the 1990s: ambitious, expensive, mired in political complications, and eventually never more than partially realized.

The May events gave new vigor to the Akayev road, and by the summer, with presidential elections looming, it was the focus of considerable debate. The hope, at least among a vocal group of male villagers, was that a new government, keen to show its popularity after the failings of the Akayev regime, would respond to popular demand for road construction to begin. Others were suggesting that they lobby the German Organization for Technical Cooperation in Batken, which had previously sponsored a section of road building by offering "oil for work" to villagers in Sogment and Gaz. In many ways, the calls echoed those for the new market in Sogment: we are separate states, we should have separate roads. It is not "normal" for us to be dependent on a neighbor's road like this. But there was a further twist here, which had to do with the way water, as a resource, figured in these discussions. The argument vocally made by the *bazarkom* and his friends in Sogment was that it was only by having an alternative route bypassing Sokh that we could assert "real" ownership over "our" water. The Hushiar people drink our water, one of the men at the *bazarkom*'s home told me, and they use it for irrigation. This was Kyrgyzstan's water (*Kyrgyzstandyn suusu*); it comes out of Kyrgyzstan's ground (*suu Kyrgyzstandan chygyp jatat*). The problem with being dependent on the road through Hushiar, he told me, was that this meant that the Sogment villagers had no leverage over a national resource. Once the people of Sogment were to adjust the timetable in their favor, the Hushiar men could close the road out of Sokh and we "would become hostages" as had occurred in May [*zalozhnikter bolup kalabyz*]. An elder from Sogment invoked a similar logic when interviewed by a local reporter after the May conflict: "we've been left unsure whether we can trust our neighbors . . . Today we trust them—today they open the road, and tomorrow they close it again and life stops [*turmush bolboit*]. That's why the people of Gaz and Sogment need to make a tremendous effort to build a new road, so that we can reach Batken by crossing only through our own territory [*özübüzdün aimak arkyluu*]" (Abdymomunov 2005).[19]

The debate over the Akayev road was a debate about relative merits of *independence* or mutual dependence with Hushiar. In July 2005, those arguing for the need to be "separate" were more vocal and more prominent, though they were not uncontested. Others were arguing that sharing water had its advantages—the very fact that "we need their road, and they need our water" had helped to maintain harmony in the past. In this process of popular discussion, state spatiality was thrown into the weave of daily conversation: by transforming water into the "other" of a national road, and a resource that could be owned only if they were truly independent, it became not just *étatized*—an element of stately property, but *territorialized*—a resource whose spatial trajectory was central to its symbolic import.

The Border Guards and the Gynecologist

Perhaps the most striking discursive shift to occur during the summer of 2005 concerned the proper role of the border guards themselves, and the appropriate limits of their regulation of social life. Kyrgyz border guards had been stationed in the small teahouse just above the Bayaman Bridge since 2000, their presence a response to the "Batken events" of 1999 and 2000, when armed fighters, allegedly members of the Islamic Movement of Uzbekistan (IMU) tried to enter Sokh by crossing by foot over the Alay peaks from Tajikistan's Karategin district. The militants had reached as far as the Zardaly Gorge above Gaz, where many families from Gaz and Sogment pastured their animals during the summer. The border unit on the Sogment-Hushiar border had been established to protect against incursion by these same militants into Sokh itself, this dirt route into the mountains having suddenly been thrust into Uzbekistan's front line against the IMU.[20]

---

[19]Construction of the road began in 2010, drawing on a mixture of local communal labor (*ashar*) and state funds. Concerted funds have since been dedicated to road building around Sokh to secure "transport independence" from Uzbekistan, though in high mountainous terrain the challenges of road construction are extreme. See Fokus.kg (2013) for a photo reportage of the construction.

[20]Geographer Nick Megoran provides a vivid account of the fear experienced in Sokh following these incursions (2002, 183–185).

By 2005, the role of border guards in defending against incursion from Islamist militants was more ambiguous. On the gravel track leading from Hushiar up to Sogment and Gaz, there was little traffic, and virtually all of it was local. During the course of the preceding year I had occasionally spent time with the Kyrgyz border guards stationed there, chatting and watching cars go by—usually no more than three or four per hour. The guards knew virtually all of the passing cars and their drivers, and they often knew the reason why someone from Hushiar was going up the road to Sogment. "He's going to the medical clinic," one would say. "They've just come back from Adil's feast in Batken;" or "he shouldn't be allowed through really, without license plates" remarked nonchalantly to the back of an unmarked and unchecked Soviet-made Moskvich. This was border guarding at its most informal and relaxed, or in the Batken idiom, at its most harmonious (*yntymaktuu*). The prevailing attitude among the guards seemed to be that there was no point in stopping drivers whom one knew to be local, while Sogment's residents took the presence of the young army recruits for granted.

When I returned to Sogment in the summer of 2005, there was a qualitative shift in what it meant to be a "guarded" border village. In part this seems to have been because in both Hushiar and Sogment the border guards were known not to have been neutral participants in the conflict that occurred in May. In Hushiar there was anger and resentment that none of the conscripts seemed to have been so much as reprimanded for the fight that ended so violently for the Hushiar school boys. In Sogment, meanwhile, there was widespread feeling that it was only the presence of these armed conscripts who had prevented the much larger confrontation on the bridge from escalating into a violent intercommunal conflict. For the *bazarkom* and several of his neighbors with whom I participated in an extensive discussion one July afternoon about the relative (de-)merits of border militarization, the border guards were needed precisely because of this deterrent function.

This view seemed to be shared by the border troops themselves. In the summer of 2005 I interviewed Valerii, the head of Sogment's border unit, who had served in the Russian army for three years ("so that I can get Russian citizenship whenever I need it") before returning as a contract soldier to the Kyrgyz forces. When I asked him about the role of his unit on the Hushiar-Sogment border, "terrorists" seemed to be a very distant threat. Instead, he described the role of his soldiers as essentially that of armed policemen. "We need to make sure that they [the people of Hushiar] only take water on days allowed by the timetable," Valerii told me; and to make sure that they do not abuse the pastureland above Gaz. "OK, let them use the Kyrgyz pastures. But the point is that they don't pay taxes for this, whereas the Kyrgyz do."

Valerii presented himself as a kind of arbiter of last resort, whose outsider-
ness as an ethnic Russian from Kyrgyzstan's northern Issyk-Kul region gave
him the authority to rise above any local frays. As we sat chatting opposite the
teahouse-turned-border post, he waved at a couple of men passing on a green
motorcycle and told me of the brawl between the men that he had successfully
managed to diffuse the previous evening. "You see? They respect me."

In the summer of 2005, defense of "territorial integrity" had morphed
into defense of local order and village property; border guards were needed
not because of the threat of militants but to ensure that neighbors adhered
properly to a negotiated water timetable. At stake was the question of what
ought to be the role of border guards in regulating relations between two
neighboring villages and the limits of legitimate violence in enforcing territorial integrity. But it also prompted broader questions about how the "law"
ought to be balanced with other demands: of respect, of coexistence, of *yntymak*. In short, it fostered reflection on the ethical stakes and entailments of
separation and boundedness (cf. Long 2011).

Gender figured centrally in these deliberations. The importance of female
honor to nationalist projects is an argument well made in recent feminist
scholarship on the state,[21] and borderland militarization—in Central Asia
as elsewhere—is an intensely gendered project. In part this is so because
patrolling borders in Central Asia is performed overwhelmingly by men, and
is thus symbolically foundational in articulating the nation's gendered "geo-
body" (Thongchai 1994). The posters of virile Uzbek border guards accost-
ing bearded Islamic militants on display in the "centers of spirituality and
enlightenment" (*ma'naviyat va ma'rifat markazi*) of Sokh's secondary schools
served as habitual reminders of that fact. More generally, borders are gendered
spaces because control over female movement, particularly the movement
of the bride (*kelin*), is integral to the dynamics of gender and generational
hierarchy (Reeves 2011c; Reynolds 2012, 144–179). Social relationships and
expressions of authority are spatially inscribed: in the dynamics of who must
ask permission from whom to exit domestic space; in the arrangement of
differently aged and gendered bodies around the tablecloth (*dastorkhon*) at
mealtimes; in the embodied reflexes of spatial positioning when men and
women occupy the same room. Lullabies, laments, proverbs, and reprimands
all emphasize to the growing girl that as *kyz-konok* (lit. the daughter-guest or
daughter-stranger), the natal home is merely a temporary residence before

---

[21]See, programmatically, the contributions to Yuval-Davis and Anthias (1989) and Yanagisako
and Delaney (1995).

she "goes out to life" (*turmushka chygat*) at marriage. Women, physically and metaphorically, occupy space differently.[22]

Female cross-border movement, accordingly, is overlaid with anxieties about the appropriateness of movement and the limits of legibility (Kusakabe 2010; Littleton, Deng and Zhang 2012). This reality can be productively exploited—not least by women themselves. Arapat-Eje—who would transport gold jewelry that she had bought in the Kara-Suu market through the Sokh enclave for resale in Batken—laughed when she told me the "secrets" that her beautifully aging body afforded. She would strap the gold in a specially designed fabric sheath that she would tie around her waist, the latter in turn covered by the generous folds of her body and her long fabric dress and cardigan. She knew that as a grandmother and as *Batkendik* (from Batken), her chances of being searched at the two Sokh border posts were virtually none, for that would be shameful beyond belief. Her livelihood depended on the regimes of value on two sides of the border, but also on what Moore in another context has called the "politics of embarrassment" around women's bodies (2005, 212). Source of livelihood and source of threat, womanhood is overdetermined as a kind of "concealment."

But if the "politics of embarrassment" afforded opportunities for gendered border crossings, it could also lead to heightened constraints on female mobility. Border-crossing women often served as touchstones for anxieties about economic and moral decline, and anger toward the "rudeness" (*grubost'*) of the neighboring state's border guards was often articulated to me precisely in terms of "their" treatment of "our" women. Around Sokh, the emergence of Tajik female day laborers (*mardikor-ayollari*), a term that translates literally as "male-working women" who would work on the privatized land of Kyrgyz neighbors across the border rather than for their own *shirkat* (cooperative farm), was taken as indicative, not just of growing economic differentials between the villagers of neighboring states, but of a more pervasive moral collapse.[23]

It is in this context that we need to interpret the emergence of debate around one particularly gendered element of cross-border movement: that

---

[22]For subtle and poignant explorations of this socio-spatial gender regime, see Aitpaeva (1998), Peshkova (2009), and the ethnographic documentary by Helminen (2007).

[23]Etymologically, *mardikor* is gendered: the original Persian signifies work (*kor*) that is undertaken by a man (*mard*); in its colloquial usage it suggests work that is casual, physically demanding and unskilled. The *mardikor ayollar* (lit. "the women doing men's work") are thus, by definition, a sign of ruptured relations. In the early 2000s a hit by the Uzbek pop star, Yulduz Usmanova, played on this predicament, the lyrics offering a guarded critique of the conditions that led women to sell their labor "cheaper than hay." I discuss the ambivalence surrounding the emergence of female *mardikor* in Sokh in more detail in Reeves (2011c).

of Tajik women traveling to see the gynecologist Saltanat. Saltanat was one of several young Kyrgyz medical personnel employed in Sogment's recently renovated medical center. She had a two-year medical degree from the nearby town of Kyzyl-Kiya and was reputed to have considerable natural powers of healing. That there was a female gynecologist in the clinic on Sokh's southern border was treated as welcome and celebratory news by Sharofat, Parviz's wife, and her friends. In Sokh, a combination of low salaries, large-scale outmigration of the village intelligentsia, and historically low rates of female enrolment in higher education meant that by the mid-2000s qualified medical personnel were relatively few and female medical personnel, fewer still. Pressure to marry off daughters as soon as they left school, together with the practical, linguistic, and financial challenges associated with undertaking a degree in Uzbek or Russian, meant that few Sokh girls were sent to continue their studies in Ferghana or Andijan after leaving school. The medical profession—historically a largely female-dominated field in the Soviet Union—in Sokh had primarily a male face. A two-year technical college training in midwifery, in place of the final two years' school, is the most that the younger cohort of female medical staff had received. In many fields there were no female doctors at all.

For Sharofat and her friends, this shortage of female medical personnel was a source of considerable concern. It made checkups a fraught business: husbands would need to be present, or the checkup was conducted in secret so that few others would know. Nowhere was the anxiety over the absence of qualified medical personnel more marked than in the realm of reproductive health. In the winter of 2004–2005, Sokh had only two gynecologists, both of them men, to treat a population of 27,000 women. As guardians of scientific knowledge about female fertility, these figures seemed to be feared and revered in equal measure. They were often invited guests at neighborhood wedding parties, and as Valijon the musician-turned-mechanic pointed out with characteristic percipience, they were some of the "best capitalists" in Sokh, who had known how to cash in on the scarcity of their skill and the social value of their knowledge by setting up a lucrative private practice. In a context where there is enormous pressure on the young *kelin* to bear her first child within a year of marriage, and where female fertility becomes the index of family honor, this social standing is perhaps of little surprise.

In recent years, the scale of labor migration to Russia has given added importance to the gynecologists' knowledge. As Zulaikho-Opa, one of my colleagues at the technical college confided, venereal diseases were rampant now because so many of Sokh's young men had gone to work "in town" (i.e., in Russia). This context explains the relief felt by Sokh women that a female doctor had arrived farther up the valley. Her gender meant that she could be visited by women without the arousing gossip, her ethnicity and the fact that she was not "from here" meant that she was outside the realm of mutual *mahalla* obligations according to which a local doctor might also become a family guest. To Sharofat, Saltanat's lack of connection with social life in Sokh seemed almost to heighten the feeling of intimacy: one could trust Saltanat because, embedded in networks of kin that led elsewhere, she was socially distant.

Such lines of closeness were challenged by the May conflict. Saltanat had previously treated women from across the border on the same basis that she had seen those from Sogment and Gaz; she would treat whoever walked through her door, expecting no fee but gratefully welcoming gifts. Such connections were disrupted, physically and discursively, following the border incident. For not only did it become impossible for women from Sokh to cross through the (male) crowds on the Bayaman Bridge; even after the barricades were removed Saltanat was instructed by fellow villagers not to treat any patient from across the border. Saltanat's prized knowledge was, briefly and publicly, transformed into a tool for enacting lines of difference.

This moment of explicit boundary marking had receded by July. Indeed, when I returned to Sogment two months after the May conflict it was with a group of women from Hushiar who were on their way to visit Saltanat. They were visibly nervous at crossing the Bayaman Bridge and passing the border guards. It was with scarves pulled over mouths and eyes trained down that they passed the soldiers, half-walking, half-running, passports in hand. When we crossed to the other side, they told me that this was the first time they had gone to Sogment since the conflict six weeks earlier. Saltanat, then, was being cautiously, nervously visited by women from Sokh again. There were no physical obstacles to their reaching her, and the border guards at the Bayaman Bridge did not bother to ask any of us for our documents. But in Sogment in the summer of 2005, visits by women from across the border to the village clinic—movement that was intimate, gendered, and extremely hard to patrol—seemed to condense more than any other the question of what it meant to be a village that was both *at* the border, and home to border guards who were charged with "manning" its edge. What was at stake was not simply the accessibility of Saltanat's care, but the proper limits of stately verification in a context of highly coded gender relations: Should women be asked for their documents if to do so might cause embarrassment? How to maintain an ethic of gendered respect (*urmat*) and nonetheless uphold the law? Why and for whom are the border guards stationed here?

Alongside the practical business of moving markets and felling trees, such debate was integral to the border work occurring in Sogment in the summer of 2005. What was taking place over these weeks was not a sudden closure of space: the dramatic territorialization of the kind that had occurred in May, which makes news stories and becomes embedded in analyses of the Ferghana Valley's proclivity for conflict. What was occurring, rather, was a moment of intense discursive production concerning the territorial correlates of stately difference in a context of profound historical interdependence and considerable strain on shared resources. The events of May (and, indeed, the political turmoil of the preceding few months) had served to crystallize in new ways the question of what it meant to live on two sides of the border. Social boundaries of ethnicity and gender were central to defining and navigating these shifts. It was precisely by articulating and practically policing who ought to be allowed where that a state edge was inscribed. At this moment of deliberation, the production of state limits and social ones was profoundly intertwined.

This chapter has explored one particular, intense, and emotionally fraught moment of border work in the southern Sokh Valley. It reminds us of the eventfulness of borders—their capacity to appear, disappear, and de/materialize at particular moments, and of the need to attend, ethnographically, to this variability. But such moments also reveal the intensely political work of bounding the state that may be less visible at other times. This is so because the permeability of a border is profoundly shaped by political contingency and by events that have little to do with obvious shifts in threat at the border itself. The May conflict and the popular encatments of border by which it was followed need to be interpreted in the context of broader processes occurring far from Sokh and Batken; the role of informal (and powerful) patrons at a time of acute state weakness, and the gulf in political possibility that this afforded to partner NGOs struggling to collaborate at a time of crisis.

This moment of rupture also exposes the border as a site of politics in a more fundamental sense. The pervasive uncertainty that characterizes the Hushiar-Sogment border—where is the law located? What are the bounds of "legitimate" violence? Who here is sovereign of the many figures claiming to enact stately authority?—are products, not just of the peculiar realities of a new, post-Soviet border that happens to transect historically connected spaces, nor only of the difficulties of maintaining the border in contexts of limited state capacity. Such sites also point to a more general feature of the state that is revealed at its multiple limits: the radical contingency of law's legitimacy, or what Asad (2004, 287) has referred to as "the arbitrariness of the authority that seeks to make law certain." Borders, as a contested limit of state authority, are privileged points of access for probing ethnographically the problem of law's "outside."

The events of the spring and summer of 2005 are suggestive, not only for what they reveal about the contingency of claims to represent the state at its geographical margins. They also reveal the other side of this uncertainty: the immense popular investment in bounding the state at a time of political crisis, the role of ordinary people in border work, and the multiplicity of sites through which it can occur. If the empirical task is to attend to this multiplicity, it also points to an analytical challenge: to think about the state not just as a terrifying externality but as the locus of intense emotional investment, as a site of enactment or performance, as the source of legitimation, and as an object of hope. Spencer has argued through a subtle analysis of South Asian ethnography that much anthropological concern to identify "resistance" "fails to account for the moral investment that many people make in the idea of being owners, or at least members, of a state of their own" (2007, 102; see also Jansen 2013). We might add to this—to being members of a state that "bounds" and "connects" in more than merely a declarative sense. When a Kyrgyz journalist asks, rhetorically, "aren't territorial integrity and borders supposed to be the very foundation of any state?" in the context of a searing attack on "revolutionary" politics in Kyrgyzstan, it is exactly this hope for a meaningfully stable state that is being articulated.

It is in the realm of "moral investment" that we should seek to make sense of the intensely performative aftermath of a cross-border conflict in the spring of 2005: separating a market, and thus bounding a state, not reducible simply to an impulse of xenophobic exclusion—"we don't want Tajiks to shop here"—but as the enactment of a historically situated ideal of normative statehood in which state and nation properly coincide, in which borders are properly contiguous rather than holey, in which they are demarcated rather than contested or contestable, in which the young conscript soldiers are properly separate from the border villages and not financially indebted to them. This account can be reduced neither to the simple internalization of the state's new boundary lines, nor to a narrative of resistance: the familiar frame in studies of border regions of the "people" against the "state." What emerges is more complex and altogether more ambivalent: the appropriation of official discourses (of sovereignty, of territoriality, of independence and "normal" statehood) to articulate local concerns at a time of acute political upheaval.

Such arguments perhaps appear unduly abstract, particularly in a context of acute trans-border tension, in which the question of "what is to be done?" seems ever more urgent. These arguments point us toward two more specific conclusions about the dynamics of conflict and coexistence in southern Ferghana and the way these tend to be addressed. The first is the need to recognize the immensely political nature of conflicts that are depicted as "resource-driven," and thus the limits of purely technical solutions to them through conclusive delimitation of the border, the building of boundary fences, or the building of new water pipes. Internationally sponsored initiatives of preventive development in the Ferghana Valley have tended to be premised on an account of groups (typically ethnic groups) mobilizing antagonistically over limited resources. Program documents often recognize the state to be an important actor in a conflict. Mercy Corps, for instance, identifies "weak, corrupt governance structures" and "inequitable resource allocation between countries" as "root causes" of conflict in the Ferghana Valley (Young, 2003, 9). However, program *activities* tend to focus on technical interventions through infrastructure and the fostering of "tolerance" between communities divided along ethnic lines. Such interventions can, indeed, have important mitigating effects, but they can also participate in the work of spatializing the state and of heightening social tension. For if infrastructure is itself felt to be unequally distributed; or the powers to lobby governments through NGOs unequally voiced on two sides of a border, such interventions can themselves easily become a flashpoint for the articulation of difference. The violence of the Hushiar men toward the USAID pipe needs to be understood in this context: the grievances at stake less about water per se than unequal possibilities for petition, lobby and appeal that the pipe came to symbolize.

The second implication of the argument that I have developed here concerns the destabilizing effect of borderland militarization. Put simply, the presence of conscript soldiers in borderland villages is not good for peace. This is so in part because border guards are, perhaps more than any other figure in these parts, felt to ignore and undermine the proper rules of borderland sociality. They are spoken of as distant, as rude, and often as having little understanding of the codes of respect that structure social relations in southern Ferghana, particularly as these pertain to women.[24] But as the ethnography here suggests, the presence of conscript soldiers in border villages was also affecting social relations in a more fundamental way. The guards

---

[24]In their insightful analysis of two decades' initiatives of conflict prevention in the Ferghana Valley, Hiscock and Paasiaro similarly noted the destabilizing consequences of borderland militarization, with local residents "perceiving border guards as a nuisance at best and at worst as a threat in themselves" (2011, 20).

stationed at the bottom of the village were increasingly viewed as a resource whose potential for "legitimate" violence could be used to enforce individual claims or collective interests. Conscript soldiers who had been posted in the Sogment teahouse five years earlier to prevent incursions of militants from distant parts were increasingly being invoked and appropriated to protect "us" and "our property" from one-time neighbors across the border. In defending the border, their presence was also serving to spatialize the state in new and consequential ways.

CONCLUSION

Landscapes and livelihoods in southern Ferghana have been transformed in significant ways in the new millennium. Plate-glass custom posts and barbed wire fencing; military barracks and conscripts in uniform; monuments to national heroes; passport checks and body searches; bypass roads and conflict maps; seminars on tolerance and election campaigns have all contributed to spatializing the state in new ways. These transformations have had material consequences for people living near the region's new international borders. Everyday activities such as visiting relatives, burying the dead, transporting apricots, and irrigating domestic plots are often significantly harder to accomplish than they were in the past, and they entail new kinds of encounter with state authority.

However, producing the Central Asian state as territorially integral is more complex than the simple transposition of the map's orange boundary lines onto landscapes and into the consciousness of ordinary people. In the case of the Ferghana Valley this is in part because assertions of state territoriality often cut across lines of kinship, friendship, worship, work, and trade that derive from other forms of spatial practice and ways of relating. As we saw in Chapter One, a customs post that was briefly mounted on a small stretch of Tajik territory in the Isfara Valley was dismantled by villagers from either side of the border in 2003 because such impositions "stopped people from living." This was not an assertion of anger or of rebellion, simply a statement of necessity. Kyrgyz and Tajiks took action "without any kind of state directive," Akhmat-Agai, the Ak-Sai school director recounted, because if the state cannot solve the problem of harmonious coexistence, "we'll do it ourselves."

If the difficulties of materializing territorial integrity are in part due to challenges "from below"—those of society challenging statist projects of territorial control—they are also more equivocal than this, deriving not just from popular resistance or indifference, but also from the practical indeterminacy of fixing the state at its territorial limits. For Akhmat-Agai, for instance, the state to which he appeals (the state that ought to create conditions for people to live) is not "represented" by the customs officers who monitor cross-border traffic on the bridge. They are, for him, anything but the natural embodiment of its authority. This attitude holds true for many of the encounters discussed throughout the book. The border guards who stopped Firuza's teacher with the corpse of a deceased father, or the tie-wearing *chinovnik* whom Muktar mocked at the canal border in Kara-Suu, were seen as invoking the state, claiming its authority, but not as embodying the law that was external to them. Successfully enacting the state, in other words, depends on a moment of mutual recognition: that in the act of interpellation, I (civilian) recognize you (state official) to be the bearer of authority that is external to us both. Spatializing the state at new international borders depends on some kind of imagined and practical lines of connection between the soldier at the state's geographical limit and an authorizing center.

The story of state spatialization that I have explored in this book is in one sense very specific, and peculiarly post-Soviet. There are distinct historical reasons why the Ferghana Valley borders, never intended to mark the boundaries of sovereign polities, are sites of particular contestation today. The configuration of roads, waterways, and administrative boundaries that has turned multiple villages into de facto (and sometimes de jure) enclaves is the outcome of a specific conjunction of ultimately irreconcilable national-territorial ideals and economic imperatives. Shurab, the decimated "Russian island" straddling the Kyrgyz-Tajik border, is perhaps the most vivid reminder here of how the principle of *national'no-odnorodnye* republics was overtaken by the demands of a vigorously industrializing centripetal state. The scars of this ambition are visible across the post-Soviet landscape. But their coincidence with new international borders makes the eruptions of state territorialization unusually poignant here; the vectors of affective identification with a distant Soviet center often painfully at odds with the realities of post-Soviet (im)mobility.

If the gaps—both in the border fence, and between "law" and "life"—are particularly visible here, they should be treated as indicative instances rather than as exceptions to the rule elsewhere. Or perhaps, we should study them precisely as unexceptional exceptions: as examples of the everyday suspensions of law, the everyday instances of state personnel exceeding state limits, the everyday irruptions of sovereign power that are part of "normal life" for a large part of the world (Hartman 2008). As scholars of postcolonial polities have argued, the kinds of governance that are exhibited in "weak" states—the existence of parallel bureaucracies and systems of security, the tendency for money to "leap" rather than flow, the simultaneous suspension and fetishizing of law—are indicative of global reconfigurations of rule in contexts of neoliberalism that are absolutely in and of the present rather than a sign that a state has "not yet" caught up with the West (Comaroff and Comaroff 2006, 41–42, 2012; Ferguson 2006, 210; Kivland 2012). Border work at the edge of new polities, where such processes are thrust into the weave of everyday conversation, should be explored less as a post-Soviet curiosity or as a regrettable legacy of state weakness than as an indicative instance of a particular mode of governance that is by no means confined to post-Soviet or postcolonial states.

Three dimensions of border work in the Ferghana Valley help illumine more general mutations of contemporary modes of governance. First, the kind of exchange that we observe in microcosm at the border, in which "state law" (however or by whomever it is impersonated) acts as a kind of guarantee to enable informal (illicit) trading to circulate without interference, is a phenomenon that occurs in more distended ways in all sorts of settings. Explored ethnographically from the messiness of real life rather than the tidiness of analytic categories, we can see that what is important is a particular kind of authoritative claim ("I here represent the state") that enables certain practices to be sustained—practices that are remote from guarding the border or policing movement across it in any substantive sense. In other words, it enables us to see how a claim to impersonate the state in a given setting allows other, nonstate domains of effective sovereignty to appear and be sustained.

This logic of governance has parallels in sites far beyond the border. In his essay on "extractive neoliberalism" in contemporary Angola, James Ferguson suggests that in many settings of transnational oil extraction, the core feature of the sovereignty of the weakly governed state lies less in "effective control over national territory" than in the ability to provide "contractual legal authority" to enable the extractive work of transnational firms to continue unhindered (2006, 207; see also Ferguson 2005). The "state" here functions as an authorizing claim much as the individual border guard does in the microencounter of the border. What this depends on in each case is an instance of fragile and conditional recognition (that "Angola" is the locus of legitimate authority in the eyes of the international community; that the soldier here is guarding the border and not merely extracting tribute). In drawing this comparison, my aim is not to suggest that the Ferghana Valley states bear a direct resemblance to the oil states described by Ferguson. It is rather to highlight that exploring what the signifier "state" here actually does, what this authorization means, and what it enables to happen in a given setting is empirically rewarding. Above all, this way of thinking enables us to think of the "state" in a way that does not presuppose either functional sovereignty over a given territory, or to assume that it is coterminous with the domain of the licit.

This not a novel claim, but it does deserve restatement in the study of Central Asia, a field still heavily dominated by state-centric accounts that tend to treat the state and its sovereignty as analytical and empirical givens. By exploring ethnographically how and what the signifier—"state"—does, how and when "stateness" happens, and how claims to impersonate the state are made and contested, we can better "sense the political" (Navaro-Yashin 2003), including in those settings where "state" is itself an unstable referent: now intimate, now intimidating; coercive, yet full of gaps. Working through the indeterminate "chessboard" border of the Ferghana Valley not simply as a metaphor, but as a site for empirical inquiry can help us to make sense of the way in which forms of governance are sustained through the spaces of institutional and legal uncertainty, without resort to paradox (the "strong weak state") or an overwrought distinction between power and resistance. It enables us to think about the "gaps" not simply as deviations, but as sites where a particular mode of governance can flourish: one where transgression enables the "state" to exceed the state's own legitimate authority; one where "petty sovereigns" (Butler 2004) abound.

The second sense in which border work in the Ferghana Valley illumines broader processes concerns the way in which questions of *authorization* are present in particularly stark and urgent fashion. New international borders that have little popular legitimacy expose questions of ultimate authorization that are concealed, or appear merely hypothetical (or perhaps even frivolous, or dangerous) in other contexts. The authority that is prior to written rules, or what Asad (2004, 287) characterizes as "the force of the law [that] derives from beyond the general will of citizens" comes into focus here as a problem in a way that it does not in settings where there is a shared (however mythical) belief that "we" make the law by collectively willing it. What is exposed is the ultimate contingency of an assertion of law: something that the rituals of military hazing among border troops expose in violently elaborate form, but which is also visible, in more muted ways, in everyday claims to embody state law at the border. It was the giddying, visceral awareness of this contingency that comes across in Kuba's account of the officer who can "find drugs" on a civilian and thus become a "hero of the Soviet Union" (see chapter 5). But it is also present in a routinized form in many everyday border crossings, when law is briefly suspended to enable life, friendship, and *yntymak* to be sustained. The practical challenges, and the emotional poignancy of making a life at the state's limits derive from this uncertainty over when and whether there will be a suspension of law, and whose claim to impersonate the state will be efficacious. Coming to be seen to be "official" is an achievement, not an a priori fact.

This points to the third way in which the argument developed in this book sheds light on a more general problem. The border that we have encountered is a multiple object, materializing in maps and documents, in barbed wire, waterways, and the everyday discriminations of Batken's "lads in uniform." When we get up close, it is often unclear where border is, and what being bordered should entail. What exactly does it mean for people to be part of separate states, when livelihoods are fundamentally intertwined? What is a border guard *for* in a remote mountain village? From whom should he be protecting the villagers? The new international borders that are being animated in place of once internal Soviet boundaries expose this multiplicity particularly vividly. In a setting where even the head of Kyrgyzstan's delimitation commission refers to the state border as a "sieve" (*sito*) (Mamaraimov 2006), the fragile achievement of territorial integrity is an observable, empirical fact. But the multiplicity of "border" derives not just from the fact of juridical contestation, just as the "gappiness" of border is not removed by patching up the holes in the barbed wire. The multiplicity, like the gaps, is not something that can be overcome with a bit more accuracy, a bit more delimitation, or a bit more fencing. This is because border is *intrinsically* multiple—the border of the map, the border guard, the Tashkent official, the trader, and so on, are *different* borders, not merely different perspectives on a singular spatial entity.

This inherent multiplicity poses an empirical challenge because our imagination of borders is fundamentally constituted by the state's own categories and cartography. Bourdieu's elliptical warning about the difficulties of thinking a state "which still thinks itself through those who attempt to think it" (1999, 55) is particularly salient when it comes to unthinking state space. Yet trying to approach this spatiality in processual terms is instructive for thinking about territoriality in seemingly much more smoothly bounded states. Approaching an analysis of the Ferghana Valley states "through the sieve" or the chessboard reminds us that state borders can be encountered in the most diverse settings and institutional formations. As such, the work of producing state spatiality is not confined to the physical edges, the cartographic limits, or those wearing the border guard's uniform. Attending to this fact can enable us to gain better sense of how state spatiality is produced, without being beguiled "by the state's own version of itself" (Harvey 2005, 139).

Thinking of states through the sieve—that is, attending to the real multiplicity of borders—is productive in a deeper sense. It alerts us to the gaps and their potential productivity in fostering and sustaining states of transgression. It reminds us of the intimate relationship between the existence of spatial gaps and the gaps between law and life that they are used to sustain. Above all, they remind us of the extent to which the "state" may be constituted and reconstituted by those gaps—and by the sovereign enactment of attempts to close them. This may be more obvious and more coercive in some settings; more obviously benign or mundane in others. But the importance of gaps for the reconstitution of the state should not be seen as only a post-Soviet story. The contemporary productions of migrant illegality in the northern hemisphere and the intimate dependence of first world economies on the invisibility of undocumented migrant labor remind that these, too, are very gappy states (De Genova 2010; Follis 2012).

Rethinking Borders and Conflict in Central Asia

Such reflections may seem remote from the pressing issues facing the Ferghana Valley and its recent experiences of tragic, ethnically marked violence. But attending to this gappiness, the multiplicity and the fragility of law at borders has significant implications for the complex relations between borderland militarization, (il)legality, and the potential for conflict in the Ferghana Valley. The association of border with threat has tended to naturalize and ethnicize perceived sources of risk. The line of the border then comes to be seen as inherently *konfliktogennyi*—still more so if that border happens to divide two ethno-linguistic communities. Instances of cross-border violence are inserted into, and in turn serve to legitimize, an established narrative of resource-driven interethnic conflict, for which the solution is more intervention, more development, more clarity, and more force. I have argued in this book that in the absence of durable and sustainable sources of livelihood, ever-greater emphasis on "security" through increased military presence risks transforming the border into an ever more lucrative (and prospectively violent) space for the extraction of tribute, transforming issues of local resource allocation into matters of national politics.

A final example from my more recent fieldwork serves as a good illustration of this dynamic. In 2008 work began on construction of a new World Bank-funded bypass road that would connect the Kyrgyz villages in the Isfara Valley, circumventing the Tajik villages of Chorkuh and Surh, and allowing people to pass from Batken to Leilek without leaving Kyrgyzstan's territory.

Large metal barracks were built to house the Chinese laborers who had been contracted to the project; and the normally quiet mud road to Kök-Tash now hosted a regular traffic of construction vehicles. The route of the new road ran along hill tracks at the edge of Chorkuh, Surh, and Kök-Tash, alongside the canal from which people from all three villages took water and through tracts of undemarcated pastureland.

In official publications the road was justified as bringing both beneficial connectivity and removing ambiguity in a region of contested space. As the 2009 action plan for the new road noted, the project was motivated both by "the need to bypass Uzbek and Tajik territory, thereby freeing goods traffic and passengers from border tolls and delays," and by the need to mark out the bounds of the Kyrgyz state in an area subject to competing claims of ownership. "Although the proposed road does not run directly along the border at any point," the action plan noted, "it will serve to define the nearby border into the future and reduce the risk of encroachment" (National Roads Rehabilitation Project 2009). Materializing a road in the otherwise unmarked *adyr* between the two states is presented here as a means of reducing uncertainty by preventing encroachment, providing a visible marker on the landscape to the bounds of respective state territory, and affording a conduit for Kyrgyz border guards to patrol the craggy mountains (and the crucial source of firewood these mountains supply) that rise steeply to the south. In Bishkek the new bypass was celebrated in official discourse as bringing about "transport independence" (Kabar 2008a), turning Kyrgyzstan, in the words of Prime Minister Igor' Chudinov, "from a country of geographical dead-ends to one of transit" (*iz tupikovoi strany v tranzitnuiu*) (Kabar 2008b).

When I returned to Batken after an eighteen-month absence in early 2010, the effects of the new road were rather more ambiguous. Certainly many people from Ak-Sai were happy that they could now travel on smooth asphalt all the way to Batken, untroubled by Tajik customs officers. At the same time, the road—now referred to locally simply as the "Kyrgyz road" (*Kyrgyz jolu*)—had become the locus of multiple small-scale altercations between Kyrgyz border guards who patrolled its length, and villagers from Chorkuh and Surh, who relied on the pastures beyond the road to graze their cattle and gather firewood. Perhaps in retaliation for this shift in previously "shared" (undefined) space, young boys from Chorkuh would sit on the hills overlooking the road and throw stones at passing cars with Kyrgyz license plates. In March 2010 a Tajik news crew reported pessimistically that for all the hope that had been invested in the project, the new road had in fact "caused only difficulties." The road had cut off Chorkuh villagers from their orchards and lead to hostile, heated exchanges between Kyrgyz border guards and citizens of Tajikistan whose now "illegal" cross-border movement they wanted to prohibit (Komilova 2010).

The case of the road is instructive for thinking about those initiatives that foster or undermine cross-border peace. A road may promise modernity and connectivity, but if that road is also conceived to stake out a *de facto* border in otherwise undemarcated territory or to obviate the need for cross-border mobility, it also risks undermining the very spaces where mundane border-land conviviality is actually lived—of which cross-border public transport is as important as it is overlooked. Such conviviality provides the context for harmonious social relations to be practiced; for *yntymak* to be not merely asserted, but lived. In the Isfara Valley a cross-border bus route that was formerly shared, with minibuses accepting both Kyrgyz and Tajik currency, dipping in and out of one state and the next, has—by the states' second decade of independence—been effectively "nationalized," in the sense that citizens of neighboring states increasingly use different routes on different minibuses to get to different markets using different currency.

The argument that I have developed in this book suggests that we should be wary of approaches to cross-border conflict prevention that identify a solution as lying in more fixing, more clarity, and more "state"—at least in the person of underresourced border guards and customs officers. Judicially delimitating the boundaries between Kyrgyzstan, Tajikistan, and Uzbekistan is undoubtedly an important legal and administrative goal—one that could help to curb future competing claims on contested territory in a region where irrigated land is in acutely short supply. But it would be wrong to see delimitation as a panacea that would put an end to competing claims to belong *here*, in this particular place; to use those pastures, that irrigation water, to gather apricots from those trees that have been tended for years.

This is so in part because there is disagreement even over which historical agreements, ratified in one Soviet republic but not in another, should be considered juridically authoritative as a basis for today's interstate negotiations. As such, delimitation is likely to be a slow and controversial process, which fosters as many disagreements as it resolves. But it is also because past administrative boundaries bear little correspondence to the actual current distribution of homes, orchards, pastures, and waterways on which people depend for their livelihood. Delimitation, even at the scale of individual homes and land plots, risks generating further uncertainty at the very point that it is intended to foster clarity.

This is particularly true in and around the Ferghana Valley's several enclaves. In the absence of sustained attention to issues of access to irrigation water, agricultural land, markets, and historical grazing lands, delimitation may also foster a race to unilateral and militarized solutions, whereby border guards and barbed wire come to be hailed as the solution to the region's inherent *konfliktogennost'*. It is indicative, for instance, that following the 2007 altercation between the governor of Batken oblast and a group of Tajik border guards (see chapter 5), the proposed solution for countering the threat posed by the new Tajik post to "interethnic relations" was for the Kyrgyz authorities to establish its own post on the same site. This kind of "escalation of force" has been identified in other border settings (see, for instance, Heyman 1999 on the US-Mexico border)—the solution to spatial indeterminacy being seen to lie in more security and more state. But what we have here is also more complex than an escalation of legitimate violence. In a setting where those charged with regulating cross-border movement are intensely dependent on the population among whom they live, where the connections between the representative of the state and an authorizing center are fragile and contested, what we really confront is a proliferation of Butler's "petty sovereigns," "reigning in the midst of bureaucratic army institutions mobilized by aims and tactics of power they do not inaugurate or fully control" (2004, 56). This increases the opportunity for extraction in the name of state security (a proliferation of "gaps" from which to profit), but it also means a proliferation of state representatives who can be appropriated as militia, as gendarmes, even as vigilantes to enforce particular claims. It is precisely such escalations of force that are the valley's greatest source of threat.

These processes do not occur in a vacuum. The postconflict "separations" of the kind explored in chapter 6 are neither linear nor uncontested. They occur in a complex social field: one mediated as much by the vagaries of Russian urban politics and the dynamics of its oil-driven building boom as it is by the voluminous accounts of "independence" penned by Central Asian presidents. The story I have traced is not of a simple internalization of the state's new boundary lines; nor is it one of resistance: the familiar and seductive anthropological narrative of the "people" against the "state." The reality is much more complex, the cadence here imperfect. In the homes and teahouses as well as at the barracks and border posts of southern Ferghana, what "independence" should entail, socially and spatially, in a context where livelihoods are overwhelmingly reliant upon undocumented labor in cities that were once seen as "ours" is a topic that is as poignant as it is contentious. The real challenge for an anthropology of Central Asia is to capture that ambivalence: the pride at international recognition coupled with the frustrations of constricted movement; the urge to have determinate borders as a condition of "normal" statehood, coupled with anxieties about what a demarcated and barbed wire-bounded state might mean in practice; and the sharp new vectors of structural dependence that formal independence now entails. Above all, it is to recognize that territorial integrity—in a context where the state itself is a work in progress, law is fragile, and petty sovereigns abound— is a laborious and contested production. The politically urgent question, of course, is who is made to bear the burden of these spatial experiments.

BIBLIOGRAPHY

Abashin, Sergei Nikolaevich. 2004. "Naselenie Ferganskoi doliny (k stanovleniiu etnogra-ficheskoi nomenklatury v kontse XIX–nachale XX veka)." In *Ferganskaia dolina: etnich-nost′, etnicheskie protsessy, etnicheskie konflikty*, 38–101. Moscow: Nauka.

——. 2007a. "Istoriia zarozhdeniia i sovremennoe sostoianie sredneaziatskikh natsion-alizmov." In *Natsionalizmy v Srednei Azii: v poiskakh identichnosti*, edited by Sergei Abashin, 177–206. Saint Petersburg: Ateleiia.

——. 2007b. "Migratsii i etnicheskie protsessy: novyi vzgliad na formirovanie sovremenno-go naseleniia Fergany." In *Uzbekistan i Iaponiia na vozrozhdaiushchemsia Shelkovom puti (sbornik dokladov nauchnoi konferentsii)*, edited by Evgenii Abdullaev, 150–157. Tashkent: Yapon uyushmasi.

——. 2007c. "Mindontsy v XVIII–nachale XX v. Istoriia meniaiushchegosia samosozna-niia." In *Natsionalizmy v Srednei Azii: v poiskakh identichnosti*, edited by Sergei Abashin, 36–71. Saint Petersburg: Ateleiia.

——. 2007d. "Problema sartov v russkoi istoriografii XIX–pervoi chetverti XX vv." In *Nat-sionalizmy v Srednei Azii: v poiskakh identichnosti*, edited by Sergei Abashin, 95–176. Saint Petersburg: Ateleiia.

Abashin, Sergei Nikolaevich, and Valentin Bushkov. 2004. *Ferganskaia dolina: etnichnost′, etnicheskie protsessy, etnicheskie konflikty*. Moscow: Nauka.

Abdullaev, R.M., S.S. Agzamkhodzhaev, I.A. Alimov, et al. 2000. *Turkestan v nachale XX veka: k istorii istokov national′ noi nezavisimosti*. Tashkent: Sharq.

Abdullaev, Ulugbek. 1991. *Traditsionnye i sovremennye mezhetnicheskie sviazy v sel′skikh mestnostiakh ferganskoi doliny. Avtoreferat*. Candidate of Science diss., Institute of His-tory, Academy of Sciences of the Republic of Uzbekistan.

Abdymomunov, Sabyr. 2005. "Özbekistandyn sokh anklavyna chektesh kyrgyz aiyldarynyn kalky kooptuu jagdaiga tushuktu." *Azattyk unalgysy*, June 1. www.azattyk.org/content/article/1239380.html.

Abraham, Itty, and Willem van Schendel. 2005. "Introduction: The Making of Illicitness." In *Illicit Flows and Criminal Things*, edited by Willem van Schendel and Itty Abraham, 1–37. Bloomington: Indiana University Press.

Abramson, David. 1998. "From Soviet to Mahalla: Community and Transition in Post-Soviet Uzbekistan." PhD diss., Indiana University.

Abulkhaev, Rakib Abulkhaevich. 1983. "Pereselenie dekhanskikh khoziastv iz gornykh v dolinnye raiony Tadzhikistana v gody poslevoennoi piatiletki (1946–1950 gg.). *Izvestiia Akademii Nauk Tadzhikskoi SSR. Otdelenie obshchestvennykh nauk* 2 (112): 19–25.

ACTED/OSCE. 2005. "Borders of Discord: An Appraisal of Sources of Tension in Villages on the Kyrgyz-Uzbek Border in the Ferghana Valley." Unpublished report.

Adams, Laura. 2010. *The Spectacular State: Culture and National Identity in Uzbekistan.* Durham: Duke University Press.

Aggarwal, Ravina. 2004. *Beyond Lines of Control: Performance and Politics on the Disputed Borders of Ladakh, India.* Durham: Duke University Press.

Aimak News. 2011. "Burgandinskii massiv obespechit budushchee Batkenskoi oblasti." October 19. http://aimaknewsrus.kloop.kg/2011/10/19/burgandinskij-massiv-obespechit-budushhee-batkenskoj-oblasti/.

Aitpaeva, Gulnara. 1998. "Ispytanie polom." Unpublished manuscript.

Akaev, Askar. 2002. *Kyrgyz mamlekettüülügü zhana "Manas" eldik eposu.* Bishkek: Uchkun.

Akaeva, Bermet. 2006. *Tsvety zla. O tak nazyvaemoi "tiul'panovoi revoliutsii" v Kyrgyzstane.* Moscow: Mezhdunarodnye otnosheniia.

Akiner, Shirin. 2006. "Violence in Andijan, 13th May 2005: An Independent Assessment." Silk Road Paper. Washington: Central Asia-Caucasus Institute. www.silkroadstudies.org/new/inside/publications/0507Akiner.pdf.

AKIpress. 2005. "Spornaia mechet' v prigranichnom sele Sogment Batkenskoi oblasti priznana prinadlezhashchei Kyrgyzstanu." June 27. http://osh.akipress.org/news:16532/.

Alamanov, Salamat. 2005. *Kratkaia istoriia i opyt resheniia pogranichnykh problem Kyrgyzstana.* Bishkek: Friedrich Ebert Stiftung.

———. 2008. "Protsess priniatiia reshenii v uregulirovanii prigranichnykh konfliktov v Kyrgyzstane. Stennograma meropriiatiia." In *Bridging Mass Media and Public Policy Making in Kyrgyzstan*, 39–45. Bishkek: Institut obshchestvennoi politiki.

———. 2010. "Ob istorii, sovremennom sostoianii i perspektivakh iuridicheskogo oformleniia Kyrgyzsko-Tadzhikskoi gosudarstvennoi granitsy." In *Kyrgyzstan-Tadzhikistan: kurs na ukreplenie partnerstva v kontekste regional'nykh sviazei*, edited by Nur Kerim, 38–42. Bishkek: Friedrich Ebert Stiftung.

Allworth, Edward. 1964. *Uzbek Literary Politics.* The Hague: Mouton.

Alvarez Jr., Robert. 1995. "The Mexican-US Border: The Making of an Anthropology of Borderlands." *Annual Review of Anthropology* 24: 447–470. doi: 10.1146/annurev.an.24.100195.002311.

———. 2001. "Towards a contemporary understanding of the United States–Mexico border: a preface." *Human Organization* 60 (2): 95–103. http://sfaa.metapress.com/content/eykmapjf0cqhu43f/.

Alykulov, Marat. 2006. *Chek ara/Granitsa.* DVD. Oy-Art Productions, Bishkek.

Amirshoeva, Gulnora. 2005. "Tajiks Alarmed by Russian Troop Withdrawal." IWPR Reporting Central Asia 316, February 21. http://iwpr.net/report-news/tajiks-alarmed-russian-troop-withdrawal.

Amoore, Louise. 2006. "Biometric Borders: Governing Mobilities in the War on Terror." *Political Geography* 25: 336–351. doi: 10.1016/j.polgeo.2006.02.001.

Amoore, Louise, and Alexandra Hall. 2009. "Taking People Apart: Digitised Dissection and the Body at the Border." *Environment and Planning, D: Society and Space* 27: 444–464. doi: 10.1068/d1208.

——. 2010. "Border Theatre: On the Arts of Security and Resistance." *Cultural Geographies* 17: 299–319. doi: 10.1177/1474474010368604.

Andreas, Peter. 2009. *Border Games: Policing the U.S.-Mexico Divide.* Ithaca: Cornell University Press.

Anzaldúa, Gloria. 1987. *Borderlands/La Frontera: The New Mestiza.* Aunt Lute Books.

Appadurai, Arjun. 1990. "Global Ethnoscapes: Notes and Queries for a Transnational Anthropology." In *Recapturing Anthropology: Working in the Present,* edited by Richard Fox, 191–210. Santa Fe: School of American Research Press.

——. 1996. *Modernity at Large: Cultural Dimensions of Globalization.* Minneapolis: University of Minnesota Press.

Appei, Alfred, and Peter Skorsch. 2002. *Report of the EC Rapid Reaction Mechanism Assessment Mission. Central Asia, Border Management.* Brussels: European Commission Conflict Prevention and Crisis Management Unit.

Aretxaga, Begoña. 2000. "A Fictional Reality: Paramilitary Death Squads and the Construction of State Terror in Spain." In *Death Squad: The Anthropology of State Terror,* edited by Jeffrey Sluka, 46–69. Philadelphia: University of Pennsylvania Press.

——. 2005a. "Dirty Protest." In *States of Terror: Begoña Aretxaga's Essays,* edited by Joseba Zulaika, 57–74. Reno: Centre for Basque Studies.

——. 2005b. "Maddening States." In *States of Terror: Begoña Aretxaga's Essays,* edited by Joseba Zulaika, 255–268. Reno: Centre for Basque Studies.

——. 2005c. "The Sexual Games of the Body Politic: Fantasy and State Violence in Northern Ireland." In *States of Terror: Begoña Aretxaga's Essays,* edited by Joseba Zulaika, 103–123. Reno: Centre for Basque Studies.

Arslonzoda, Rakhmatjon, and O. Olimov. 2004. "Severnyi Sokh: komu on prinadlezhit?" *Varorud* 7 (95), February 18.

Asad, Talal. 1992. "Conscripts of Western Civilization?" In *Dialectical Anthropology: Essays in Honor of Stanley Diamond,* edited by Christine Ward Gailey, 333–351. Gainesville: University Presses of Florida.

——. 2004. "Where Are the Margins of the State?" In *Anthropology in the Margins of the State,* edited by Veena Das and Deborah Poole. 279–288. Santa Fe: School of American Research Press.

Asankanov, Abylbek, and Oskon Osmonov. 2002. *Istoriia Kyrgyzstana (s drevneishikh vremen do nashikh dnei). Uchebnik dlia VUZov.* Bishkek: Uchkun.

Asanov, Bakyt. 2012. "Bürgöndü: 'söögü' Kyrgyzdyki, 'eti' Özbektiki." Azattyk Unalgysy, January 27. www.azattyk.org/content/kyrgyzstan_uzbekistan_border_problem/24465254.html.

Atlas Soiuza Sovestskikh Sotsialisticheskikh Respublik. 1928. Moscow: TsIK SSR.

Austin, Alexander. 2004. "Early Warning and the Field: A Cargo Cult Science?" *Berghof Research Center for Constructive Conflict Management.* Berlin: Berghof Center. www.berghof-handbook.net/documents/publications/austin_handbook.pdf.

Azamatova, Matlyuba. 2004. "Uzbekistan: Furious Traders Riot." IWPR Reporting Central Asia 324, November 2.

Azattyk unalgysy. 2006. "Kyrgyz-tazhik chatagyna tazhik atuulary künöölüü ekenin öz moi-nuna alyshty." *Azattyk unalgysy* February 17. www.azattyk.org/content/article/1248812. html.

Baiburin, Albert. 2012. "Rituals of Identity: The Soviet Passport." In *Soviet and Post-Soviet Identities*, edited by Mark Bassin and Catriona Kelly, 91–110. Cambridge, UK: Cambridge University Press.

Baigaziev, Adyl. 2010. "Piat' voprosov s iuga." *Vechernii Bishkek*, June 25. http://members. vb.kg/2010/06/25/retush/1.html.

Balci, Bayram. 2011. "Identité nationale et gestion du fait minoritaire en Asie Centrale: analyse des affrontements inter-ethniques d'Och en juin 2010." In *La Définition des Identités*, edited by Carole Ferret and Arnaud Ruffier, 470–484. Paris: Editions Petra.

Baldouf, Ingeborg. 1992. "Kraevedenie and Uzbek National Consciousness." Papers on Inner Asia, No. 20. Bloomington: Indiana University Research Institute for Inner Asian Studies.

Ballard, Roger. 2003. *A Background Report on the Operation of Informal Value Transfer Systems (Hawala)*. Manchester: Centre for Applied South Asian Studies. http://casas.org.uk/papers/pdfpapers/hawala.pdf.

Ballinger, Pamela. 2002. *History in Exile: Memory and Identity at the Borders of the Balkans*. Princeton: Princeton University Press.

Bannikov, Konstantin. 2002. *Antropologiia ekstremal'nykh grupp. Dominantnye otnosheniia sredi voennosluzhashchikh srochnoi sluzhby Rossiiskoi Armii*. Moscow: Institute of Ethnology and Anthropology, Russian Academy of Sciences.

Barth, Frederik, ed. 1969. *Ethnic Groups and Boundaries: The Social Organization of Culture Differences*. London: Allen and Unwin.

Bartol'd, Vasilii. [1925] 1991. "Zapiska po voprosu ob istoricheskikh vzaimootnosheniiakh turetskikh i iranskikh narodnostei Srednei Azii." Unpublished document, reproduced with commentary in A.A. Prazuskas, "O national'nom razmezhevanii v Srednei Azii." *Vostok* 5: 163.

Batrakov, V.S. 1947. "Otgonnoe zhivotnovodstvo i pastbishchnyi vopros v Ferganskoi doline." *Trudy instituta ekonimiki Akademii Nauk Uzbekskoi SSR. Vypusk 1.* Tashkent: Izdatel'stvo akademii nauk UzSSR.

———. 1955. "Kharakternye cherty sel'skogo khoziaistva Ferganskoi doliny v period kokandskogo khanstva." In *Trudy Sredneaziatskogo gosudarstvennogo universiteta im. V.I. Lenina. Gumanitarnye nauki, kniga VIII*. Tashkent: Sredneaziatskii gosudarstvennyi universitet.

Bayart, Jean-François. 2009. *The State in Africa: The Politics of the Belly*. Cambridge, UK: Polity.

Benjamin, Walter. [1928] 1978. *Reflections: Essays, Aphorisms, Autobiographical Writings*, edited by Peter Demetz, translated by Edmund Jephcott. New York: Schocken Books.

Berdahl, Daphne. 1999. *Where the World Ended: Re-Unification and Identity in the German Borderland*. Berkeley: University of California Press.

Bergne, Paul. 2007. *The Birth of Tajikistan. National Identity and the Origins of the Republic*. London and New York: I.B. Tauris.

Beyer, Judith. 2007. "Imagining the State in Rural Kyrgyzstan: How Perceptions of the State Create Customary Law in the Kyrgyz *Aksakal* Courts." Max Planck Institute for

Social Anthropology Working Paper No. 95. www.eth.mpg.de/cms/en/publications/ working_papers/wp0095.html.

———. 2009. "According to Salt: An Ethnography of Customary Law in Talas, Kyrgyzstan." PhD diss., Martin Luther University.

———. 2013. "Constitutional Faith: Law and Hope in Revolutionary Kyrgyzstan." *Ethnos: Journal of Anthropology*, pp. 1–26. doi: 10.1080/00141844.2013.841270.

Bichsel, Christine. 2009. *Conflict Transformation in Central Asia: Irrigation Disputes in the Ferghana Valley*. Abingdon: Routledge.

———. 2011. "In the Name of Victory. Turning the Hungry Steppe into 'New Land' in Zafarabad, Tajikistan (1959–1979)." Public Lecture, University of Central Asia, Bishkek, Kyrgyzstan, May 17.

———. 2012. "The Drought Does Not Cause Fear. Irrigation History through James C. Scott's Lenses." *Revue d'études comparatives Est-Ouest* 43 (1–2): 73–108. doi: 10.4074/S0338059912001040.

Bichsel, Christine, Silvia Hostettler, and Balz Strasser. 2005. "'Should I Buy a Cow or a TV?' Reflections on the Conceptual Framework of the NCCR North-South Based on a Comparative Study of International Labour Migration in Mexico, India and Kyrgyzstan." National Centre for Competence in Research North-South Working Paper No. 14. Berne: NCCR North-South.

Bigo, Didier. 2002. "Security and Immigration: Toward a Critique of the Governmentality of Unease." *Alternatives: Global, Local, Political* 27 (1): 63–92. doi: 10.1177/03043754020270S105.

Bigo, Didier, and Elspeth Guild. 2005. *Controlling Frontiers: Free Movement into and within Europe*. Farnham: Ashgate.

Bikkenin, Il'dar. 2006. *Moia Armia. Povest'*. Bishkek: n.p.

Blaive, Muriel, and Thomas Lindenberger. 2012. "Border Guarding as Social Practice: A Case Study of Czech Communist Governance and Hidden Transcripts." In *Walls, Borders, Boundaries: Spatial and Cultural Practices in Europe*, edited by Marc Silberman, Karen Till, and Janet Ward, 97–111. Oxford and New York: Berghahn Books.

Borbieva, Noor O'Neill. 2012. "Empowering Muslim Women: Independent Religious Fellowships in the Kyrgyz Republic." *Slavic Review* 71 (2): 288–307. doi: 10.5612/slavicreview.71.2.0288.

Bornstein, Avram. 2002. *Crossing the Green Line between the West Bank and Israel*. Philadelphia: University of Pennsylvania Press.

Bourdieu, Pierre. 1999. "Rethinking the State: Genesis and Structure of the Bureaucratic Field." In *State/Culture: State Formation after the Cultural Turn*, edited by George Steinmetz, 53–75. Ithaca: Cornell University Press.

Brower, Daniel. 1997. "Islam and Ethnicity: Russian Colonial Policy in Turkestan." In *Russia's Orient: Imperial Borderlands and Peoples, 1700–1917*, edited by Daniel Brower and Edward Lazzerini, 115–135. Bloomington: Indiana University Press.

Brower, Daniel, and Edward Lazzerini. 1997. *Imperial Borderlands and Peoples, 1700–1917*. Bloomington: Indiana University Press.

Brown, Kate. 2004. *A Biography of No Place: From Ethnic Borderland to Soviet Heartland*. Cambridge, MA: Harvard University Press.

Brown, Wendy. 2010. *Walled States, Waning Sovereignty*. London: Zone Books.

Brubaker, Rogers. 1996a. "Nationhood and the National Question in the Soviet Union and its Successor States: An Institutionalist Account." In *Nationalism Reframed: Nationhood and the National Question in the New Europe*, 23–54. Cambridge and New York: Cambridge University Press.

———. 1996b. "Rethinking Nationhood: Nation as Institutionalized Form, Practical Category, Contingent Event." In *Nationalism Reframed: Nationhood and the National Question in the New Europe*, 13–22. Cambridge and New York: Cambridge University Press.

Brubaker, Roger et al. 2006. *Nationalist Politics and Everyday Ethnicity in a Transylvanian Town*. Princeton: Princeton University Press.

Bruns, Bettina, and Judith Miggelbrink. 2011. *Subverting Borders: Doing Research on Smuggling and Small-Scale Trade*. Weisbaden: Springer.

Bushkov, Valentin. 1990. "O nekotorykh aspektakh mezhnatsional'nykh otnoshenii v Tadzhikskoi SSR." *Issledovaniia po prikladnoi i neotlozhnoi etnologii Seriia A: Mezhnatsional'nye otnosheniia v SSSR No. 9*. Moscow: Institute of Ethnography of the Academy of Sciences of the USSR.

———. 1995. *Naselenie severnogo Tadzhikistana: formirovanie i rasselenie*. Moscow: Russian Academy of Sciences.

Butler, Judith. 2004. "Indefinite Detention." In *Precarious Life: Powers of Mourning and Violence*, 50–100. London: Verso.

Candea, Matei. 2010. *Corsican Fragments: Difference, Knowledge and Fieldwork*. Bloomington: Indiana University Press.

Carlisle, Donald. 1994. "Soviet Uzbekistan: State and Nation in Historical Perspective." In *Central Asia in Historical Perspective*, edited by Beatrice Manz, 103–126. Boulder, CO: Westview Press.

Caroe, Olaf. [1953] 1967. *Soviet Empire: The Turks of Central Asia and Stalinism*. London: Macmillan.

Carrère d'Encausse, Hélène. 1987. *Le Grand Défi: bolcheviks et nations, 1917–1930*. Paris: Flammarion.

Caton, Steven. 2006. "Coetzee, Agamben and the Passion of Abu Ghraib." *American Anthropologist* 108(1): 114–123. doi: 10.1525/aa.2006.108.1.114.

Centrasia.ru. 2011. "R. Otunbaeva: V peregovorakh po anklavam s Uzbekistanom mozhet idti rech' tol'ko o ravnotsennom obmene zemel'." February 8. www.centrasia.ru/newsA.php?st=1297167300.

Certeau, Michel de. 1988. *The Practice of Everyday Life*. Berkeley: University of California Press.

Chalfin, Brenda. 2001. "Border Zone Trade and the Economic Boundaries of the State in North-East Ghana." *Africa* 71(2): 202–224. doi: http://dx.doi.org/10.3366/afr.2001.71.2.202.

———. 2003. "Working the Border in Ghana. Technologies of Sovereignty and Its Others." School of Social Science Occasional Paper, Institute for Advanced Study Paper 16, Princeton University.

———. 2010. *Neoliberal Frontiers: An Ethnography of Sovereignty in West Africa*. Chicago: University of Chicago Press.

Choibekov, U. 2007. "Rukovodstvo pogransluzhby Kyrgyzstana trebuet nakazaniia vinovnikov intsidenta s gubernatorom Batkenskoi oblasti." Kabar.kg, January 11. www.for.kg/ru/news/21632/.

Chotonov, Usenaly. 1998. *Istoriia Kyrgyzstana XX vek. Uchebnik dlia VUZov.* Bishkek: Kyrgyzstan.

Clark, John. 2004. "A Strategy for Preventive Development in Kazakhstan: A Hudson Institute Report Commissioned by the United Nations Development Program, Kazakhstan." Almaty: UNDP. www.policyarchive.org/handle/10207/bitstreams/11752.pdf.

Cole, John W., and Eric R. Wolf. 1999. *The Hidden Frontier: Ecology and Ethnicity in an Alpine Valley.* Berkeley: University of California Press.

Comaroff, Jean, and John Comaroff. 2005. "Naturing the Nation: Aliens, Apocalypse, and the Postcolonial State." In *Sovereign Bodies,* edited by Thomas Blom Hansen and Finn Stepputat, 120–147. Princeton: Princeton University Press.

——. 2006. "Criminal Obsessions, after Foucault: Postcoloniality, Policing, and the Metaphysics of Disorder." In *Law and Disorder in the Postcolony,* edited by John and Jean Comaroff, 273–298. Chicago: University of Chicago Press.

——. 2012. "Theory from the South: Or, How Euro-America Is Evolving toward Africa." *Anthropological Forum: A Journal of Social Anthropology and Comparative Sociology* 22 (2): 113–131. doi: 10.1080/00664677.2012.694169.

Cummings, Sally, ed. 2010. *Domestic and International Perspectives on Kyrgyzstan's Tulip Revolution: Motives, Mobilization and Meaning.* Abingdon: Routledge.

Cunningham, Hilary, and Josiah Heyman. 2004. "Introduction: Mobilities and Enclosures at Borders." *Identities* 11 (3): 289–302. doi: 10.1080/10702890490493509.

Das, Veena, and Deborah Poole. 2004. "State and Its Margins: Comparative Ethnographies." In *Anthropology in the Margins of the State,* edited by Veena Das and Deborah Poole, 3–33. Santa Fe: School of American Research Press.

Daucé, Françoise, and Elisabeth Sieca-Kozlowski, eds. 2006. *Dedovshchina in the Post-Soviet Military: Hazing of Russian Army Conscripts in a Comparative Perspective.* Stuttgart: Ibidem-Verlag.

De Genova, Nicholas P. 2002. "Migrant 'Illegality' and Deportability in Everyday Life." *Annual Review of Anthropology* 31 (1): 419–447. doi: 10.1146/annurev.anthro.31.040402.085432.

——. 2005. *Working the Boundaries: Race, Space, and "Illegality" in Mexican Chicago.* Durham: Duke University Press.

——. 2010. "The Deportation Regime: Sovereignty, Space, and the Freedom of Movement." In *The Deportation Regime: Sovereignty, Space, and the Freedom of Movement,* edited by Nicholas De Genova and Nathalie Peutz, 33–66. Durham: Duke University Press.

Delegation of the European Union to the Kyrgyz Republic. 2012. "The EU Supports Border Delimitation in the Ferghana Valley." Press Release, March 1. http://eeas.europa.eu/delegations/kyrgyzstan/press_corner/all_news/news/2012/news01032012_en.htm.

Dolina mira. 2004. *Analiz situatsii po perekhodu granits v Ferganskoi Doline.* Osh: Dolina mira. www.dolinamira.org/issledovaniya.html.

Donnan, Hastings, and Thomas Wilson. 1999. *Borders: Frontiers of Identity, Nation and State.* Oxford and New York: Berg.

Dudoignon, Stéphane. 1998. "Communal Solidarity and Social Conflicts in Late 20th Century Central Asia: The Case of the Tajik Civil War." Tokyo: Islamic Area Studies Working Paper Series.

Dzhakhonov, Usto. 1989. *Zemledelie Tadzhikov doliny Sokha v kontse XIX–nachale XX v. (Istoriko-etnograficheskoe issledovanie).* Dushanbe: Donish.

Dzhakhonov, Usto, and Gulnora Tukhtaeva. 2002. *Tojikiston navii/Noveishii Tadzhikistan.* Dushanbe: Matbuot.

Dzhumanaliev, Akylbek. 2003. *Kyrgyzskaia gosudarstvennost' v XX veke. (Dokumenty, istoriia, kommentarii).* Bishkek: Natsional´naia akademiia nauk Kyrgyzskoi Respubliki.

Dzhunushalieva, Gulmira. 2006. "Ob otsenkakh natsional´no-gosudarstvennogo razmezhevaniia Srednei Azii v 1924 g." *Kyrgyzstan tarykhynyn maseleri/Voprosy istorii Kyrgyzstana* 1: 67–70.

Edgar, Adrienne. 2004. *Tribal Nation: The Making of Soviet Turkmenistan.* Princeton: Princeton University Press.

Elden, Stuart. 2006. "Contingent Sovereignty, Territorial Integrity and the Sanctity of Borders." *SAIS Review* 26 (1): 11–24. doi: 10.1353/sais.2006.0008.

Engvall, Johan. 2011. "The State as Investment Market: An Analytical Framework for Interpreting Politics and Bureaucracy in Kyrgyzstan." PhD diss., Uppsala University.

Eurasianet. 2003. "Uzbek Border Row Introduces New Element of Tension in Central Asia." *Eurasianet Insight,* January 27. www.eurasianet.org/print/53386.

Féaux de la Croix, Jeanne. 2010. "Moral Geographies in Kyrgyzstan: How Pastures, Dams and Holy Sites Matter in Striving for a Good Life." PhD diss., University of St. Andrews.

——. 2011. " Moving Metaphors We Live By: Water and Flow in the Social Sciences and around Hydroelectric Dams in Kyrgyzstan." *Central Asian Survey* 30 (3–4): 487–502. doi: 10.1080/02634937.2011.614097.

Feldman, Allen. 1991. *Formations of Violence: The Narrative of the Body and Political Terror in Northern Ireland.* Chicago: University of Chicago Press.

——. 1994. "On Cultural Anesthesia: From Desert Storm to Rodney King." *American Ethnologist* 21 (2): 404–418. doi: 10.1525/ae.1994.21.2.02a00100.

——. 1997. "Violence and Vision: the Prosthetics and Aesthetics of Terror." *Public Culture* 10 (1): 24–60. doi: 10.1215/08992363-10-1-24.

Ferguson, James. 1990. *The Anti-Politics Machine. "Development", Depoliticization and Bureaucratic Power in Lesotho.* Cambridge, UK: Cambridge University Press

——. 1999. *Expectations of Modernity: Myths and Meanings of Urban Life on the Zambian Copperbelt.* Berkeley: University of California Press

——. 2005. "Seeing Like an Oil Company: Space, Security and Global Capital in Neoliberal Africa." *American Anthropologist* 107 (3): 377–382. doi: 10.1525/aa.2005.107.3.377.

——. 2006. *Global Shadows: Africa in the Neoliberal World Order.* Durham: Duke University Press.

Ferguson, James, and Akhil Gupta. 2002. "Spatializing States: Towards an Ethnography of Neoliberal Governmentality." *American Ethnologist* 29 (4): 981–1002. doi: 10.1525/ae.2002.29.4.981.

Ferme, Mariane. 2004. "Deterritorialized Citizenship and the Resonances of the Sierra Leonean State." In *Anthropology in the Margins of the State,* edited by Veena Das and Deborah Poole, 81–115. Santa Fe: School of American Research Press.

Ferrando, Olivier. 2011a. "Soviet Population Transfers and Interethnic Relations in Tajikistan: Assessing the Concept of Ethnicity." *Central Asian Survey* 30 (1): 39–52. doi: 10.1080/02634937.2011.554054.

———. 2011b. "La question minoritaire en Asie centrale post-Soviétique. Recompositions identitaires dans la vallée du Ferghana (1989–2008)." PhD diss., Institut d'Études Politiques de Paris.

Fierman, William. 1991. *Language Planning and National Development: The Uzbek Experience*. Berlin: Walter de Gruyter.

Finke, Peter. 2006. "Variations on Uzbek Identity. Concepts, Constraints and Local Configurations." Habilitation diss., University of Leipzig.

Fitzpatrick, Sheila. 2005. *Tear off the Masks! Identity and Imposture in Twentieth Century Russia*. Princeton and Oxford: Princeton University Press.

Flynn, Donna. 1997. "'We are the border': Identity, Exchange, and the State along the Benin-Nigeria Border." *American Ethnologist* 24 (2): 311–330. doi: 10.1525/ae.1997.24.2.311.

Fokus.kg. 2013. "Fotoreportazh: Stroitel'stvo dorogi Bel'-Sogot-Bozhoi vokrug anklav Sokh." June 17. http://focus.kg/news/polytics/14577.html.

Follis, Karolina. 2012. *Building Fortress Europe: The Polish-Ukranian Frontier*. Philadelphia: University of Pennsylvania Press.

Foucault, Michel. [1972] 2002. *The Archaeology of Knowledge*. London and New York: Routledge.

Foundation for Tolerance International. 2005. "Kratkaia informatsiia ob intsidente mezhdu zhiteliami s. Khush″iar Sokhskogo raiona RU i Charbak, Sogment Batkenskogo Raiona KR." Unpublished document, May 3.

———. 2007. "Konflikt na pogranichnoi zastave 'Surkh' na granitse Kyrgyzstana s Tadzhikistanom." *Ezhenedel'nyi Vestnik proekta "Rannee preduprezhdenie dlia predotvrashcheniia nasiliia"* 54, January 10–16.

———. n.d.a. "Conflict Analysis in Samarkandek-Chorku-Surkh Area: Project "Kyrgyzstan-Tajikistan." Unpublished document.

———. n.d.b. "Informatsiia dlia sostavleniia karty konfliktov na iuge Kyrgyzstana." Unpublished document.

Foundation for Tolerance International, Mehr and Yntymak, 2005. "Informatsiia o tekushchem konflikte mezhdu zhiteliami s. Khush″iar Sokhskogo raiona RU i Charbak, Sogment, Gas Batkenskogo raiona KR." Unpublished document, May 8.

Fragner, Bert. 1994. "The Nationalization of the Uzbeks and Tajiks." In *Muslim Communities Reemerge: Historical Perspectives on Nationality, Politics and Opposition in the Former Soviet Union and Yugoslavia,* edited by Edward Allworth, 13–32. Durham: Duke University Press.

Frantz, Douglas. 2000a. "Sokh Journal; Good Fences, but, Some Will Say, Bad Nieghbors." *New York Times,* November 30. www.nytimes.com/2000/11/30/world/sokh-journal-good-fences-but-some-will-say-bad-neighbors.html?pagewanted=all&src=pm.

———. 2000b. "Rich Slice of Soviet Central Asia, Left to a Lonely Despair." *New York Times,* December 19. www.nytimes.com/2000/12/19/world/rich-slice-of-soviet-asia-left-to-a-lonely-despair.html.

Friedman, John T. 2011. *Imagining the Post-Apartheid State. An Ethnographic Account of Namibia*. Oxford: Berghahn Books.

Galemba, Rebecca. 2012a. "Remapping the Border: Taxation, Territory, and (Trans)national Identity at the Mexico-Guatemala Border." *Environment and Planning D: Society and Space* 30 (5): 822–841. doi: 10.1068/d7710.

——. 2012b. "Taking Contraband Seriously: Practicing 'Legitimate Work' at the Mexico-Guatemala Border." *Anthropology of Work Review* 33 (1): 3–14. doi: 10.1111/j.1548-1417.2012.01072.x.

Gavrilis, George. 2008. *The Dynamics of Interstate Boundaries.* Cambridge, UK: Cambridge University Press.

——. 2012. "Central Asia's Border Woes and the Impact of International Assistance." Central Eurasia Project Occasional Paper Series No. 6. www.soros.org/sites/default/files/occasional-paper-series-20120601.pdf.

Gladarev, Boris. 2011. "Korni rasizma v rossiiskoi militsii." In *Militsiia i etnicheskie migranty. Praktiki vzaimodeistviia,* edited by Victor Voronkov, Boris Gladarev, and Liliia Sagitova, 424–507. Saint Petersburg: Ateleiia.

Glumskov, D. 2000. "Evraziiskie balkany." *Vechernii Bishkek,* March 30.

Gonon, Emmanuel, and Frédéric Lasserre. 2003. "Une critique de la notion de frontières artificielles à travers le cas de l'Asie centrale." Cahiers de géographie du Québec, 47 (132): 433–461. doi: 10.7202/008090ar.

Gordienko, Andrei Art'emevich. 1959. *Sozdanie sovetskoi natsional'noi gosudarstvennosti v Srednei Azii.* Moscow: Gosiurizdat.

Gorshenina, Svetlana. 2012. *Asie centrale: L'Invention des frontières et l'héritage russo-soviétique.* Paris: CRNS Editions.

Grant, Bruce. 1995. *In the Soviet House of Culture: A Century of Perestroikas.* Princeton: Princeton University Press.

Grant, Bruce, and Lale Yalçin-Heckmann. 2007. "Introduction." In *Caucasus Paradigms: Anthropologies, Histories and the Making of World Area,* edited by Bruce Grant and Lale Yalçin-Heckmann, 1–19. Münster: Lit Verlag.

Green, Sarah. 2005. *Notes from the Balkans: Locating Marginality and Ambiguity on the Greek-Albanian Border.* Princeton: Princeton University Press.

——. 2009. "Lines, Traces and Tidemarks: Reflections on Forms of Borderli-ness." East-BordNet Work Group 1 2009 Working Paper No. 1. www.eastbordnet.org/working_papers/open/documents/Green_Lines_Traces_and_Tidemarks_090414.pdf.

——. 2010. "Performing Border in the Aegean." *Journal of Cultural Economy* 3 (2): 261–278. doi: 10.1080/17530350.2010.494376.

——. 2012a. "A Sense of Border." In *A Companion to Border Studies,* edited by Thomas Wilson and Hastings Donnan, 573–592. Oxford: Wiley-Blackwell.

——. 2012b. "Reciting the Future: Border Relocations and Everyday Speculations in Two Greek Border Regions." *HAU: Journal of Ethnographic Theory* 2 (1): 111–129. www.haujournal.org/index.php/hau/article/view/66/105.

Greenhouse, Carol. 2002. "Introduction: Altered States, Altered Lives." In *Ethnography in Unstable Places: Everyday Lives in Contexts of Dramatic Political Change,* edited by Carol Greenhouse, Elizabeth Mertz, and Kay Warren, 1–34. Durham: Duke University Press.

Gubaeva, Stella Sitdikovna. 1983. *Etnicheskii sostav naseleniia Fergany v kontse XIX–nachale XX v. (po dannym toponimii).* Tashkent: Izdatel'stvo Fan.

——. 2012. *Ferganskaia dolina. Etnicheskie protsessy na rubezhe XIX–XX vv.* Saabrucken: Lambert Academic Publishing.

Gullette, David. 2010. *The Genealogical Construction of the Kyrgyz Republic: Kinship, State and "Tribalism."* Folkstone: Global Oriental.

Gupta, Akhil. 1995. "Blurred Boundaries: The Discourse of Corruption, the Culture of Politics, and the Imagined State." *American Ethnologist* 22 (2): 375–402. doi: 10.1525/ae.1995.22.2.02a00090.

——. 2012. *Red Tape: Bureaucracy, Structural Violence, and Poverty in India.* Durham: Duke University Press.

Gupta, Akhil, and James Ferguson. 1992. "Beyond 'Culture': Space, Identity, and the Politics of Difference." *Cultural Anthropology* 7 (1): 6–23. doi: 10.1525/can.1992.7.1.02a00020.

Hansen, Thomas Blom. 2001. *Wages of Violence: Naming and Identity in Postcolonial Bombay.* Princeton: Princeton University Press.

Hartman, Tod. 2008. "States, Markets, and Other Unexceptional Communities: Informal Romanian Labour in a Spanish Agricultural Zone." *Journal of the Royal Anthropological Institute* 14 (3): 496–514. doi:10.1111/j.1467–9655.2008.00514.x.

——. 2011. "The Economy, Labour and the New Romanian Migration to Spain." PhD diss., University of Cambridge.

Harvey, Penny. 2005. "The Materiality of State Effects: An Ethnography of a Road in the Peruvian Andes." In *State Formation: Anthropological Perspectives*, edited by Christian Krohn-Hansen and Knut Nustad, 123–141. London and Ann Arbor, MI: Pluto Press.

Harvey, Penny, Madeleine Reeves, and Evelyn Ruppert. 2013. "Anticipating Failure: Transparency Devices and their Effects." *Journal of Cultural Economy* 6 (1): 1–19.

Haugen, Arne. 2003. *The Establishment of National Republics in Soviet Central Asia.* London: Palgrave Macmillan.

Heathershaw, John. 2007. "Peace as Complex Legitimacy: Politics, Space and Discourse in Tajikistan's Peacebuilding Process, 2000–2005." PhD diss., London School of Economics and Political Science.

——. 2009. *Post-Conflict Tajikistan. The Politics of Peacebuilding and the Emergence of Legitimate Order.* London: Routledge.

Helminen, Suvi. 2007. *Love and Broken Glass.* DVD. Nordlys Film, Denmark.

Heyman, Josiah McC. 1999. "State Escalation of Force: A Vietnam/US-Mexico Border Analogy." In *States and Illegal Practices*, edited by Josiah Heyman and Alan Smart, 285–314. Oxford and New York: Berg.

Heyman, Josiah McC., and Alan Smart. 1999. "States and Illegal Practices: An Overview." In *States and Illegal Practices*, edited by Josiah Heyman and Alan Smart, 1–24. Oxford and New York: Berg.

Hilgers, Irene. 2006. "The Regulation and Control of Religious Pluralism in Uzbekistan." In *The Post-Soviet Religious Question: Faith and Power in Central Asia and East-Central Europe*, edited by Chris Hann, 75–98. Münster: Lit Verlag.

——. 2011. *Why Do Uzbeks Have to Be Muslims? Exploring Religiosity in the Ferghana Valley.* Münster: Lit Verlag.

Hirsch, Francine. 2000. "Toward an Empire of Nations: Border-Making and the Formation of 'Soviet' National Identities." *Russian Review* 59 (2): 201–226. doi: 10.1111/0036–0341.00117.

——. 2005. *Empire of Nations: Ethnographic Knowledge and the Making of the Soviet Union.* Princeton: Princeton University Press.

Hiscock, Duncan, and Maija Paasiaro. 2011. "Looking Back to Look Forward. Learning the Lessons of Conflict Prevention in the Ferghana Valley." London: Saferworld. www.

saferworld.org.uk/downloads/pubdocs/Ferghana%20Valley%20May%202011%20re-
port.pdf.

Höjdestrand, Tova. 2009. *Needed by Nobody: Homelessness and Humanness in Post-Socialist Russia*. Ithaca: Cornell University Press.

Horstmann, Alexander, and Reed L. Wadley. 2006. *Centering the Margin: Agency and Narrative in Southeast Asian Borderlands*. Oxford: Berghahn Books.

Human Rights Watch. 2005. *Burying the Truth: Uzbekistan Rewrites the Story of the Andijan Massacre*. Human Rights Watch Report. September. www.hrw.org/sites/default/files/reports/uzbekistan0905.pdf.

——. 2010. *"Where Is the Justice?" Interethnic Violence in Southern Kyrgyzstan*. Human Rights Watch Report, August. www.hrw.org/sites/default/files/reports/kyrgyzstan0810 webwcover_1.pdf.

Humphrey, Caroline. 1994. "Remembering an 'Enemy': The Bogd Khaan in Twentieth-Century Mongolia." In *Memory, History and Opposition under State Socialism,* edited by Rubie S. Watson, 21–44. Woodbridge: James Currey.

——. 1998. *Marx Went Away—But Karl Stayed Behind*. Ann Arbor: University of Michigan Press.

——. 2001. "Contested Landscapes in Inner Mongolia: Walls and Cairns." In *Contested Landscapes: Movement, Exile and Place,* edited by Barbara Bender and Margot Winer, 55–68. Oxford: Berg.

——. 2002a. "'Icebergs', Barter and the Mafia in Provincial Russia." In *The Unmaking of Soviet Life: Everyday Economies after Socialism,* 5–20. Ithaca and London: Cornell University Press.

——. 2002b. "Mythmaking, Narratives, and the Dispossessed in Russia." In *The Unmaking of Soviet Life: Everyday Economies after Socialism*, 21–39. Ithaca and London: Cornell University Press.

——. 2002c. "Russian Protection Rackets and the Appropriation of Law and Order." In *The Unmaking of Soviet Life: Everyday Economies after Socialism*, 99–126. Ithaca and London: Cornell University Press.

Ikromov, Bobodzhon. 2006a. "Fergana—dolina angelov." *Varorud* 1 (187), January 4.

——. 2006b. "Sotsial'nye iavleniia, skazyvaiushchiesia na degradatsii obshchestva." In *I zvezdy plachut. Publistika.* Kazan': Mir bez granits.

Imanaliev, Muratbek et al. 2006a. "Tsentral'naia Aziia: granitsy na zamke?" *Sbornik statei o Tsentral'noi Azii*, 91–107. Bishkek: Institut Obshchestvennoi Politiki.

——. 2006b. "Pravovye aspekty upravleniia granitsami Kyrgyzskoi Respubliki." OSCE Academy Research Report on Legal Aspects of Border Regulation. Bishkek: OSCE Academy.

Inda, Jonathan Xavier, and Renato Rosaldo. 2002. "Introduction: A World in Motion." In *The Anthropology of Globalization: A Reader*, edited by Jonathan Inda and Renato Rosaldo, 1–34. Oxford: Blackwell.

Ingold, Tim. 2007. *Lines: A Brief History*. Abingdon: Routledge.

Integrated Regional Information Networks News. 2005. "Kyrgyzstan-Tajikistan: Landmine Threat Along Uzbek Border Removed." www.irinnews.org/Report/29426/KYRGYZ-STAN-TAJIKISTAN-Landmine-threat-along-Uzbek-border-removed.

International Crisis Group. 2002. "Central Asia: Border Disputes and Conflict Potential." *Asia Report* 33. Osh and Brussels: International Crisis Group. www.crisisgroup.org/~/media/Files/asia/central-asia/Central%20Asia%20Border%20Disputes%20and%20Conflict%20Potential.ashx.

———. 2005a. "Kyrgyzstan: After the Revolution." *Asia Report* 97. Bishkek and Brussels: International Crisis Group. www.crisisgroup.org/en/regions/asia/central-asia/kyrgyzstan/097-kyrgyzstan-after-the-revolution.aspx.

———. 2005b. "Kyrgyzstan: A Faltering State." *Asia Report* 109. Bishkek and Brussels: International Crisis Group. www.crisisgroup.org/en/regions/asia/central-asia/kyrgyzstan/109-kyrgyzstan-a-faltering-state.aspx.

———. 2005c. "Uzbekistan: The Andijon Uprising." *Asia Briefing* 38. Bishkek and Brussels: International Crisis Group. www.crisisgroup.org/en/regions/asia/central-asia/uzbekistan/B038-uzbekistan-the-andijon-uprising.aspx.

———. 2006. "Uzbekistan: In for the Long Haul." *Asia Briefing* 45. Bishkek and Brussels: International Crisis Group. www.crisisgroup.org/en/regions/asia/central-asia/uzbekistan/B045-uzbekistan-in-for-the-long-haul.aspx.

———. 2010. "The Progroms in Kyrgyzstan." *Asia Report* 193. Bishkek and Brussels: International Crisis Group. www.crisisgroup.org/en/regions/asia/central-asia/kyrgyzstan/193-the-pogroms-in-kyrgyzstan.aspx.

Isabaeva, Eliza. 2011. "Leaving to Enable Others to Remain: Remittances and New Moral Economies of Migration in Southern Kyrgyzstan." *Central Asian Survey* 30 (3–4): 541–554.

Ismailbekova, Aksana. 2011. ""The Native Son and Blood Ties': Kinship and Poetics of Patronage in Rural Kyrgyzstan." PhD diss., Martin Luther University.

Jackson, Michael. 2002. *The Politics of Storytelling: Violence, Transgression and Intersubjectivity.* Copenhagen: Museum Tusculanum Press.

Jacquesson, Svetlana. 2008. "The Sore Zones of Identity: Past and Present Debates on Funerals in Kyrgyzstan." *Inner Asia* 10 (2): 281–303. doi: 10.1163/000000008793066669.

Jahonov, Usto. 1995. *Ta"rikhi Sūkh (Tadqiqoti ta"rikhī-etnologī.* Khudjand: Gosudarstvennoe izdatel′stvo im. R. Dzhalila.

Jamoat Resource Center of Vorukh/UNDP Tajikistan. 2011. *Potential for Peace and Threats of Conflict: Development Analysis of Cross-Border Communities in Isfara District of the Republic of Tajikistan (Vorukh, Chorkhuh, Surkh, Shurab) and Batken District of the Kyrgyz Republic (Ak-Sai, Ak-Tatyr, and Samarkandek).* Dushanbe: UNDP. www.undp.tj/files/Report in English(2).pdf.

Jansen, Stef. 2009. "After the Red Passport: Towards an Anthropology of the Everyday Geopolitics of Entrapment in the EU's 'Immediate Outside.'" *Journal of the Royal Anthropological Institute* 15 (4): 815–832. doi: 10.1111/j.1467–9655.2009.01586.x.

———. 2013. "Hope For/Against the State: Gridding in a Besieged Sarajevo Suburb." *Ethnos* (January 16): 1–23. doi: 10.1080/00141844.2012.743469.

Jeganathan, Pradeep. 2004. "Checkpoint: Anthropology, Identity and the State." In *Anthropology in the Margins of the State*, edited by Veena Das and Deborah Poole, 67–80. Santa Fe: School of American Research Press.

Jones Luong, Pauline. 2004. "Conclusion: Central Asia's Contribution to Theories of the State." In *The Transformation of Central Asia: States and Societies from Soviet Rule to Independence,* edited by Pauline Jones Luong, 271–281. Ithaca: Cornell University Press.

Joosh kyzy, Mairam. 1997. *Kara Tooluk Kyrgyzdar (Manas atanyn izi menen)*. Batken: Batken raionduk basmakana.

Jozan, Raphaël. 2012. *Les débordements de la mer d'Aral: Une Sociologie de la guerre de L'eau*. Paris: Presses Universitaires de France.

Judah. Ben. 2013. *Fragile Empire: How Russia Fell in and Out of Love with Vladimir Putin*. New Haven: Yale University Press.

Juraev, M., R. Nurullin, S. Kamolov, *et al*. 2000. *O'zbekistonning yangi tarikhi ikkinchi kitob: O'zbekiston sovet mustamlakachiligi davrida*. Tashkent: Sharq.

Kabar. 2008a. "Bakiev prinial uchastie v prezentatsii tekhniki, priobretennoi Mintransom." Kabar News Agency, August 4. www.cis-news.info/read/64313/.

Kabar. 2008b. "I. Chudinov prinial uchastie v torzhestvennom sobranii ko dniu rabotnikov avtomobil'nogo transporta." Kabar News Agency, October 24. www.for.kg/ru/news/74922/.

Kalet, Almaz. 2006. "Rostki tiul'panov." *Oazis* 24 (44): 1, 3.

Kandiyoti, Deniz. 2003. "The Cry for Land: Agrarian Reform, Gender and Land Rights in Uzbekistan." *Journal of Agrarian Change* 3 (1–2): 225–256. doi: 10.1111/1471–0366.00055.

Karagiannis, Emmanuel. 2005. "Political Islam and Social Movement Theory: The Case of Hizb ut-Tahrir in Kyrgyzstan." *Religion, State and Society* 33 (2): 137–150. doi: 10.1080/09637490500118638.

Karimov, Islam. 1999. "Uzbek President on Real Economic Independence." Transcript of a television broadcast, February 27. www.uzland.info/news/02_27_99.htm.

——. 2005. "Nasha glavnaia tsel'—demokratizatsiia i obnovleniia obshchestva, reformirovanie i modernizatsiia strany. Doklad Prezidenta Respubliki Uzbekistan Islama Karimova na sovmestnom zasedanii Zakonodatel'noi palaty i Senata Olii Mazhilisa." Press Service of the President of the Republic of Uzbekistan. www.uzbekistan.pl/index.php?goto=249.

Kashkaraev, Nurlan. 2007. "Pogranichniki Tadzhikistana ugrozhali raspravoi gubernatoru Batkenskoi obl. KR." *Kyrgyz Ordo*, Web discussion. www.kg-rdo.net/system/forum/viewtopic.php?topic=3191&forum=25.

Kassymbekova, Botakoz. 2011. "Humans as Territory: Forced Resettlement and the Making of Soviet Tajikistan, 1920–1938." *Central Asian Survey*, 30 (3–4): 349–370. doi: 10.1080/02634937.2011.607916.

Kazybaev, Pamirbek. 2006. *Kyrgyzstan: eldik revoliutsiia, 24-mart 2005*. Bishkek: Uchkun.

Kearney, Michael. 1995. "The Local and the Global: The Anthropology of Globalization and Transnationalism." *Annual Review of Anthropology* 24 (1): 547–565. doi: 10.1146/annurev.an.24.100195.002555.

Kenenbaev, Aidar. 2009. "Gde brov', a gde glaz? Kak Tadzhikistan i Kyrgyzstan reshaiut territorial'nye voprosy." Centrasia.ru, April 10. www.centrasia.ru/newsA.php?st=1239374940.

Kivland, Chelsey. 2012. "Unmaking the State in 'Occupied' Haiti." *Political and Legal Anthropology Review* 35 (2): 248–270. doi: 10.1111/j.1555-2934.2012.01202.x

Khaidarov, Gafur. 2001. *Istoriia Tadzhikskogo naroda: XX vek*. Khudzhand: Khudzhandskii Gosudarstvennyi Universitet.

Khalid, Adeeb. 1998. *The Politics of Muslim Cultural Reform: Jadidism in Central Asia*. Berkeley: University of California Press.

——. 2006. "Backwardness and the Quest for Civilization: Early Soviet Central Asia in Comparative Perspective." *Slavic Review* 65 (2): 231–251. www.jstor.org/stable/10.2307/4148591.

——. 2007. *Islam after Communism.* Berkeley: University of California Press.

Khamidov, Alisher. 2011. "Closed Uzbekistan-Kyrgyzstan Border Ratcheting Up Tensions." Eurasianet.org, April 6. www.eurasianet.org/node/63237.

Khamidov, Mohammedzhan. 2000. "Bereg levyi—bereg pravyi." *Vechernii Bishkek,* June 30.

Khamidov, Oibek. 2001. "Svet i teni Kara-Suu." *Vechernii Bishkek,* August 10.

——. 2003. "Demontazh uzbekskimi vlastiami most prichinil mnozhestvo neudobstv grazhdanam dvukh gosudarstv." *Vechernii Bishkek*, February 20.

Kharkhordin, Oleg. 2001. "What Is the State? The Russian Concept of *Gosudarstvo* in the European Context." *History and Theory* 40 (2): 206–240. doi: 10.1111/0018–2656.00163.

Khodzhaev, Faizulla. 1934. "Doklad predsedatelia SNK Uzbekskoi SSR tov. Faizully Khodzhaeva." In *O natsional' nom razhmezhevanii. Doklady na plenume Sredazbiuro TsK VKP(b) 1934 5 sentiabria 1934 g,* 1–16. Moscow and Tashkent: Ob"edinenie gosudarstvennykh izdatel'stv, Sredneaziatskoe otdelenie.

Kim, Aleksandr, and Iurii Gruzdov. 2000. "Pokhishchenie po-sokhski." *Vechernii Bishkek,* June 12.

——. 2003a. "Ch´i miny i na ch´ei zemle? Kyrgyzstan i Uzbekistan razbiraiustia." Centrasia. ru, February 27. www.centrasia.ru/newsA.php?st=1046293260.

——. 2003b. "Obstrel Kara-Suu." *Moia stolitsa—novosti,* April 18.

Kisliakov, Nikolai Andreevich. 1953. "Tadzhiki doliny Sokha." In *Sbornik statei po istorii i filologii narodov srednei Azii posviashchennyi 80-letiiu so dnia rozhdeniia A.A. Semenova,* 111–119. Stalinabad: Izdatel'stvo akademii nauk Tadzhikskoi SSR.

Kniazev, Aleksandr. 2006a. *Gosudarstvennyi perevorot. 24 marta 2005g. v Kirgizii.* Bishkek: Obshchestvennyi fond Aleksandra Kniazeva.

——. 2006b. "Kyrgyzstan—strana bez gosudarstva?" *Delo Nomer* 4 (626), February 1.

Knight, Nathaniel. 1994. "Constructing the Science of Nationality: Ethnography in Mid-Nineteenth Century Russia." PhD diss., Columbia University.

Koehler, Jan. 2004. "Assessing Peace and Conflict Potentials in the Target Region of the GTZ Central Asia and Northern Afghanistan Programme to Foster Food Security, Regional Cooperation and Stability." Berlin: ARC-Berlin. www.arc-berlin.com/pdf/Integrated%20 Report_04.pdf.

Koichiev, Arslan. 2001. *Nasional' no-territorial' noe razmezhevanie v ferganskoi doline (1924– 1927 gg.).* Bishkek: Kyrgyz State National University Press.

Kojotegin, Ulan. 2007. "Surkh postu küchötülgön rezhimge ötöbü?" *Zaman.kg,* January 19.

Komilova, Khosiat. 2010. "Zhizn´ na prigranich´e." Stan.tv, March 5. www.stan.tv/news/14897/.

——. 2011. "Eksliusivnoe interv´iu: Nematboi Olimov, glava dekhkanskogo khoziaistva Chorkukh." Stan.tv, April 13. www.stan.tv/news/20565/.

Kotkin, Stephen. 1995. *Magnetic Mountain: Stalinism as a Civilization.* Berkeley: University of California Press.

Kuchumkulova, Elmira. 2007. "Kyrgyz Nomadic Customs and the Impact of Re-Islamization after Independence." PhD diss., University of Washington.

Kudratova, D.K. 2002. "O roli torgovykh vzaimootnoshenii naseleniia Ferganskoi doliny v ukreplenii mezhetnicheskikh sviazei (konets XIX–nachalo XX veka). *Obshchestvennye nauki v Uzbekistane* 1: 61–64.

Kuehnast, Kathleen and Nora Dudwick. 2008. *Whose Rules Rule? Everyday Border and Water Conflicts in Central Asia.* Washington, DC: World Bank Group, Social Development Department.

Kurbskii, Andrei. 2000. "Khronika Batkenskikh sobytii 1999ogo goda." *Tsentral´ no-aziatskii tolstyi zhurnal.* http://ctaj.elcat.kg/tolstyi/c/c010.htm.

Kyrgyzstan Inquiry Commission. 2011. "Report of the Independent International Commission of Inquiry into the Events in Southern Kyrgyzstan in June 2010." http://reliefweb.int/sites/reliefweb.int/files/resources/Full_Report_490.pdf.

Lam, Cheng-Un Stephen. 2009. "Cooperation in the Ferghana Valley Borderlands: *Habitus*, Affinity, Networks, Conditions." PhD diss., King's College London.

Latour, Bruno, and Steve Woolgar. 1979. *Laboratory Life: The Construction of Scientific Facts.* Princeton: Princeton University Press.

Law, John. 2002. *Aircraft Stories: Decentering the Object in Technoscience.* Durham: Duke University Press.

———. 2004. *After Method: Mess in Social Science Research.* London: Routledge.

Lenin, Vladimir. [1920] 1974. *Polnoe sobranie sochinenii*, Vol. 41. Moscow: Gosudarstvennoe izdatel´stvo politicheskoi literatury.

Lentz, Carola. 2003. "'This Is Ghanaian Territory!' Land Conflicts on a West African Border." *American Ethnologist* 30 (2): 273–289. doi: 10.1525/ae.2003.30.2.273.

Lewington, Richard. 2010. "The Challenge of Managing Central Asia's New Borders." *Asian Affairs* 41 (2): 221–236.

Lewis, David. 2008. *The Temptations of Tyranny in Central Asia.* London: Hurst.

Liu, Morgan Y. 2012. *Under Solomon's Throne: Uzbek Visions of Renewal in Osh.* Pittsburgh: University of Pittsburgh Press.

———. 2014. "Massacre through a Kaleidoscope: Fragmented Moral Imaginaries of the State in Central Asia." In *Ethnographies of the State in Central Asia: Performing Politics*, edited by Madeleine Reeves, Judith Beyer, and Johan Rasanayagam. Bloomington: Indiana University Press.

Lombard, Louisa. 2012. "Raiding Sovereignty in Central African Borderlands." PhD diss., Duke University.

Long, Nick. 2011. "Bordering on Immoral: Piracy, Education, and the Ethics of Cross-Border Cooperation in the Indonesia-Malaysia-Singapore Growth Triangle." *Anthropological Theory* 11 (4): 441–464. doi: 10.1177/1463499611423869.

Loy, Thomas. 2006. "From the Mountains to the Lowlands: The Soviet Policy of 'Inner-Tajik' Resettlement." *Trans: Internet Journal for Cultural Studies* 13 (2). www.inst.at/trans/16Nr/13_2/loy16.htm.

Lubin, Nancy, Barnett R. Rubin, Council on Foreign Relations, and Century Foundation. 1999. *Calming the Ferghana Valley: Development and Dialogue in the Heart of Central Asia: Report of the Ferghana Valley Working Group of the Center for Preventive Action.* New York: Century Foundation Press.

Lukashova, Irina, and Irina Makenbaeva. 2009. *Vozdeistvie mirovogo ekonomicheskogo krizisa na trudovuiu migratsiiu iz Kyrgyzstana v Rossiiu: Kachestvennyi obzor i kolichestvennoe issledovanie.* Bishkek: OSCE. www.osce.org/ru/bishkek/40542.

Maasen, Kristel, Bektemir Bagyskulov, Akyn Bakirov, Asylbek Egemberdiev, Anara Eginalieva, Abdygapar Karatov, Lubov Kolesnikova, and Abror Mirsangilov. 2005. *The Role and Capacity of Civil Society in the Prevention of Violent Conflict in Southern Kyrgyzstan.* Bishkek: Foundation for Tolerance International.

Magidovich, I.P. 1924 "Naselenie TASSR v 1920 g." In *Statisticheskii ezhegodnik 1917–1923 gg.* Tashkent: Tsentral´noe statisticheskoe upravlenie.

Maitdinova, Guzel´. 2010. "Pogranichnye problemy Tadzhikistana: reali i mezhdunarodnoe sotrudnichestvo po obespecheniiu bezopasnosti granits." Working Paper, Center for Geopolitics Research, Russian-Tajik (Slavic) University.

Malakhov, Vladimir. 2001. "Skromnoe obaianie rasizma." In *Skromnoe obaianie rasizma i drugie stat´i,* 141–158. Moscow: Dom intellektual´noi knigi.

——. 2007. "Rasizm i migranty." In *Ponaekhali tut . . . Ocherki o natsionalizme, rasizme i kul´turnom pliuralizme,* 95–103. Moscow: Novoe Literaturnoe Obozrenie.

Mamaraimov, Abdumomun. 2006. "Salamat Alamanov: granitsa mezhdu Kirgiziei i Uzbekistanom napominaet sito." Fergana.ru, November 27. www.fergananews.com/articles/4745.

Mandel, Ruth, and Caroline Humphrey, eds. 2002. *Markets and Moralities: Ethnographies of Postsocialism.* Oxford: Berg.

Maratova, Madina. 2005. "Bishkek v panike: oruduiut tysiachi zemel´nykh maroderov." *Delovaia nedelia* 15 (643), April 15.

Marcus, George. 1998. *Anthropology through Thick and Thin.* Princeton: Princeton University Press.

Marsden, Magnus. 2005. *Living Islam: Muslim Religious Experience in Pakistan's North-West Frontier.* Cambridge, UK: Cambridge University Press.

Martin, Terry. 2001. *The Affirmative Action Empire: Nations and Nationalism in the Soviet Union, 1923–1939.* Ithaca: Cornell University Press.

Martin-Mazé, Médéric. 2013. "Le gouvernement international des frontiers d'Asie centrale." PhD diss., Institut d'Études Politiques de Paris.

Maslova, Dina. 2008. "Shkatulka s dragotsennostiami na porokhovoi bochke." *Vechernii Bishkek,* August 1.

Masov, Rakhim. 1991. *Istoriia topornogo razdeleniia.* Dushanbe: Irfon.

——. 2003. *Tadzhiki: Vytesnenie i assimiliatsiia.* Dushanbe: Natsional´nyi muzei drevnostei Tadzhikistana.

——. 2005. "'Nasledie' Mangitskoi vlasti: ili pochemu akademik Masov ne soglasen s akademikom Shukurovym." In *Aktual´nye problemy istoriografii i istorii Tadzhikskogo naroda.* Dushanbe: Paivand.

Massey, Doreen. 2005. *For Space.* London: Sage.

Matthews, Mervyn. 1993. *The Passport Society: Controlling Movement in Russia and the USSR.* Boulder, CO: Westview Press.

Matveeva Anna, Igor Savin, and Bahrom Faizullaev. 2012. "Kyrgyzstan: Tragedy in the South." Ethnopolitics Papers no. 17, April. www.ethnopolitics.org/ethnopolitics-papers/EPP017.pdf.

Maurer, Bill. 2000. "A Fish Story: Rethinking Globalization on Virgin Gorda, British Virgin Islands." *American Ethnologist* 27 (3): 670–701. doi: 10.1525/ae.2000.27.3.670.

Mbembe, Achille. 2000. "At the Edge of the World: Boundaries, Territoriality and Sovereignty in Africa." *Public Culture* 12 (1): 259–284. doi: 10.1215/08992363-12-1-259.

——. 2001. "On Private Indirect Government." In *On the Postcolony*, 66–101. Berkeley: University of California Press.

McBrien, Julie. 2008. "The Fruit of Devotion? Islam and Modernity in Kyrgyzstan." PhD diss., Martin Luther University.

McGlinchey, Eric. 2011. *Chaos, Violence, Dynasty: Politics and Islam in Central Asia.* Pittsburgh: University of Pittsburgh Press.

Megoran, Nick. 1999. "The Borders of Eternal Friendship: Kyrgyz-Uzbek Relations in 1999." *Eurasianet Insight*, December 19.

——. 2002. "The Borders of Eternal Friendship? The Politics and Pain of Nationalism and Identity along the Uzbekistan-Kyrgyzstan Ferghana Valley Boundary, 1999–2000." PhD diss., University of Cambridge.

——. 2004. "The Critical Geopolitics of the Uzbekistan–Kyrgyzstan Ferghana Valley boundary dispute, 1999–2000." *Political Geography* 23 (6): 731–764. doi: 10.1016/j.polgeo. 2004.03.004

——. 2005. "The Critical Geopolitics of Danger in Uzbekistan and Kyrgyzstan." *Environment and Planning D: Society and Space* 23 (4): 555–580. doi: 10.1068/d56j.

——. 2007. "On Researching 'Ethnic Conflict': Epistemology, Politics, and a Central Asian Boundary Dispute." *Europe-Asia Studies* 59 (2): 253–277. doi: 10.1080/09668130601125585.

Megoran, Nick, Gaël Raballand, and Jerome Bouyjou. 2005. "Performance, Representation and the Economics of Border Control in Uzbekistan." *Geopolitics* 10 (4): 712–740. doi: 10.1080/14650040500318498.

Mehr. 2005a. "Kratkaia informatsiia ob intsidente mezhdu zhiteliami s. Khush"iar Sokhskogo raiona RU i Sogment, Charbak Batkenskogo raiona KR." Unpublished document, May 4.

——. 2005b. "Napriazhennost' v sele Khush"iar." Unpublished document, May 6.

Melvin, Neil. 2011. "Promoting a Stable and Multi-Ethnic Kyrgyzstan: Overcoming the Causes and Legacies of Violence." Central Eurasia Project Occasional Papers Series 3. New York: Open Society Foundations. www.opensocietyfoundations.org/sites/default/files/OPS-No-3-20110305.pdf.

Mercy Corps and USAID. 2003. *Semi-Annual Report: The Peaceful Communities Initiative. Conflict Mitigation Initiative in the Ferghana Valley.* http://pdf.usaid.gov/pdf_docs/PD-ABY751.pdf.

Mercy Corps. 2006. *USAID's Peaceful Communitities Initiative.* Almaty: USAID http://pdf.usaid.gov/pdf_docs/PDACJ077.pdf.

Mezhdunarodnaia organizatsiia po migratsii. 2004. *Pravovaia pamiatka migrantu v Rossiiu.* Moscow: Mezhdunarodnaia organizatsiia po migratsii.

Middendorf, Aleksandr Theodor von. 1882. *Ocherki Ferganskoi doliny, s prilozheniem "Khimicheskikh issledovanii pochv i vod," K. Shmidta.* Saint Petersburg: Tipografiia Imperatorskoi akademii nauk.

Mikhailov, Grigorii. 2012. "Bishkek idet na obostrenie s Tashkentom." *Nezavisimaia gazeta*, May 16. www.ng.ru/cis/2011–05–16/1_bishkek.html.

Mirsaiitov, Ikbol. 2004. *Osobennosti formirovaniia politicheskogo islama v Ferganskoi doline.* Bishkek: Mezhdunarodnyi institut strategicheskikh issledovanii pri Prezidente Kyrgyzskoi Respubliki.

Mitchell, Timothy. 1999. "Society, Economy and the State Effect." In *State/Culture: State Formation after the Cultural Turn*, edited by George Steinmetz, 76–97. Ithaca: Cornell University Press.

Moiseenko, Valentina, Viktor Perevedentsev, and Natal'ia Voronina. 1999. *Moskovskii region: migratsiia i migratsionnaia politika*. Moscow: Carnegie Moscow Center.

Mol, Annemarie. 2002. *The Body Multiple: Ontology in Medical Practice*. Durham: Duke University Press.

Mol, Annemarie, and John Law. 2002. "Complexities: An Introduction." In *Complexities: Social Studies of Knowledge Practices*, edited by Annemarie Mol and John Law, 1–22. Durham: Duke University Press.

Montgomery, David. 2007. "The Transmission of Religious and Cultural Knowledge and Potentiality in Practice: An Anthropology of Social Navigation in the Kyrgyz Republic." PhD diss., Boston University.

Moore, Donald S. 1998. "Subaltern Struggles and the Politics of Place: Remapping Resistance in Zimbabwe's Eastern Highlands." *Cultural Anthropology* 13 (3): 344–381. doi: 10.1525/can.1998.13.3.344.

——. 2005. *Suffering for Territory: Race, Place, and Power In Zimbabwe*. Durham: Duke University Press.

Mostowlansky, Till. 2013. "Azan on the Moon: Entangling Modernities Along Tajikistan's Pamir Highway." PhD diss., University of Berne.

Mountz, Alison. 2010. *Seeking Asylum: Human Smuggling and Bureaucracy at the Border*. Minneapolis: University of Minnesota Press.

——. 2011. "Where Asylum-Seekers Wait: Feminist Counter-Topographies of Sites between States." *Gender, Place & Culture* 18 (3): 381–399. doi: 10.1080/0966369X.2011.566370.

Mughal, Abdul-Ghaffar. 2007. *Migration, Remittances and Living Standards in Tajikistan*. Dushanbe: IOM Tajikistan. www.iom.tj/pubs/Impact%20of%20remittances%20in%20 Khatlon%20by%20Mughal.pdf.

Musabekova, Chynara. 2003. *Gosudarstvenno-pravovye voprosy territorii i granits Kyrgyzskoi Respubliki (po materialam dissertatsionnogo issledovaniia)*. Bishkek: Obshchestvennyi fond sodeistviia obrazovaniiu.

Nadzhibulla, Farangis. 2010. "Uzbekskii anklav Sokh v Kyrgyzstane, naselennyi Tadzhikvami." *Azattyq Radiosy*, June 14. http://rus.azattyq.org/content/Sokh/2068831.html.

Nalivkin, Vladimir Petrovich. [1886] 2003. "Kratkaia istoriia kokandskogo khanstva." In *Istoriia srednei Azii. Sbornik istoricheskikh proizvedenii*, edited by A.I. Buldakov, Sergei Shumov, and Aleksandr Andreev, 250–418. Moscow: Evrolints; Russkaia panorama.

——. [1913] 2004. "Tuzemtsy ran'she i teper'." Reproduced with commentary in *Musul'manskaia sredniaia Aziia. Traditsionalizm i XX vek*, edited by Dmitrii Arapov and Sergei Poliakov. Moscow: Russian Academy of Sciences.

Nalivkin, Vladimir Petrovich, and Mariia Nalivkina. 1886. *Ocherk byta zhenshchiny osedlogo tuzemnogo naseleniia Fergany*. Kazan: Tipografiia Imperatorskogo Universiteta.

National Commission of Inquiry. 2011. "Zakliuchenie natskommissii po rassledovaniiu iiunskikh sobytii na iuge Kyrgyzstana." http://pda.kabar.kg/politics/full/1669.

National Roads Rehabilitation Project. 2009. "National Roads Rehabilitation Project Osh-Isfana Section Updated Feasibility Study. Resettlement Action Plan." December 2009.

Navaro-Yashin, Yael. 2002. *Faces of the State: Secularism and Public Life in Turkey*. Princeton: Princeton University Press.

——. 2003. "'Life Is Dead Here': Sensing the Political in 'No Man's Land.'" *Anthropological Theory* 3 (1): 107–125. doi: 10.1177/1463499603003001174.

Nelson, Diane. 1999. *A Finger in the Wound: Body Politics in Quincentenial Guatemala*. Berkeley: University of California Press.

Newman, David. 2006. "The Lines That Continue to Separate Us: Borders in Our 'Borderless' World." *Progress in Human Geography* 30 (2): 143–161. doi: 10.1191/0309132506ph599xx.

Nicol, Heather, and Ian Towsent Gault, eds. 2005. *Holding the Line: Borders in a Global World*. Vancouver: University of British Columbia Press.

Niksdorf, Viktor. 1989. "Trudnosti dolzhny byt' preodoleny." *Sovetskaia Kirgiziia*, July 18, 1.

Noori, Neema. 2006. "Delegating Coercion: Linking Decentralization to State Formation in Uzbekistan." PhD diss., Columbia University.

Nordstrom, Carolyn. 2007. *Global Outlaws: Crime, Money and Power in the Contemporary World*. Berkeley: University of California Press.

Northrop, Douglas. 2004. *Veiled Empire: Gender and Power in Stalinist Central Asia*. Ithaca: Cornell University Press.

Obshchenatsional'nyi forum grazhdanskogo obshchestva. 2005. "Rezoliutsii foruma." Unpublished document.

Omuraliev, Kubanich. 2008. "Intsidenty na kyrgyzsko-tadzhikskoi granitse mogut vylit'sia v vooruzhennyi konflikt." Centrasia.ru, April 5. www.centrasia.ru/newsA. php?st=1207375260.

Omuraliev, Nurbek, and Ainura Elebaeva. 2000. "Batkenskie sobytiia v Kyrgyzstane: khronika sobytii." *Tsentral'naia Aziia i Kavkaz*. www.ca-c.org/journal/cac-07-2000/04.omural. shtml.

O natsional'nom razmezhevanii. Doklady na plenume Sredazbiuro TsK VKP(b) 1934 5 sentiabria 1934 g. 1934 Moscow and Tashkent: Ob"edinenie gosudarstvennykh izdatel'stv, Sredneaziatskoe otdelenie.

Orlova, Tat'iana. 2003. "Detektiv, ili Lenin pomeshal?" *Moia stolitsa—novosti*, August 18.

Otunbaeva, Roza. 2011. "Ia veriu, chto nashi pogranichniki i v dal'neishem budut nadezhno okhraniat' granitsy nashego gosudarstva." Press Service of the President of the Kyrgyz Republic, February 7. www.president.kg/ky/posts/4d6cf5527d5d2e720d00081a.

Pallitto, Robert, and Josiah C. Heyman. 2008. "Theorizing Cross-Border Mobility: Surveillance, Security and Identity." *Surveillance and Society* 5 (3): 315–333. www.surveillance-and-society.org/articles5(3)/mobility.pdf.

Pannier, Bruce. 1999a. "Kyrgyzstan: Soldiers, Refugees, Journalists Converge on Batken City." Radio Free Europe/Radio Liberty, September 9. www.rferl.org/content/article/1092179. html.

——. 1999b. "More Refugees Flee to Camps as Fighting Spreads." Radio Free Europe/Radio Liberty, September 9. www.rferl.org/content/article/1092215.html.

——. 2012. "Uzbekistan." *Freedom House Nations in Transit Report*. www.freedomhouse. org/report/nations-transit/2012/uzbekistan.

Parker, Noel, and Nick Vaughan-Williams. 2009. "Lines in the Sand? Towards an Agenda for Critical Border Studies." *Geopolitics* 14 (3): 582–587. doi: 10.1080/14650040903081297.

Passon, Daniel, and Azamat Temirkulov. 2004. *Analysis of Peace and Conflict Potential in Batken Oblast*. German Organization for Technical Cooperation. http://arc-berlin.com/wp-content/uploads/2013/01/Kyrgyzstan.pdf.

Patico, Jennifer. 2002. "Chocolate and Cognac: Gifts and the Recognition of Social Worlds in Post-Soviet Russia." *Ethnos* 67 (3): 345–368. doi: 10.1080/0014184022000031202.

Patkanov, Serafim Keropovich. 1905. *Obshchii svod po imperii resul'tatov razrabotki, dannykh pervoi vseobshchei perepisi naseleniia, proizvedennoi 28 ianvaria 1897 goda*. Sankt-Peterburg: Parovaia tipo-litografiia N.L. Nyrinkina.

Pelkmans, Mathijs. 2006. *Defending the Border: Identity, Religion, and Modernity in the Republic of Georgia*. Ithaca: Cornell University Press.

Peshkova, Svetlana. 2009. "Bringing the Mosque Home and Talking Politics: Women, Domestic Space, and the State in the Ferghana Valley (Uzbekistan)." *Contemporary Islam* 3 (3), 251–273. doi: 10.1007/s11562-009-0093-z.

Pétric, Boris-Mathieu. 2005. "Post-Soviet Kyrgyzstan or the Birth of a Globalised Protectorate." *Central Asian Survey* 24 (3): 319–332. doi: 10.1080/02634930500310402.

Phillips, Timothy. 2008. *Beslan: The Tragedy of School Number One*. London: Granta Books.

Pipes, Daniel. 1978. "The Third World People of Soviet Central Asia." In *The Third World: Premises of U.S. Policy*, edited by Willard Scott Thompson, 155–174. San Fransisco: Institute for Contemporary Studies.

Polat, AbduMannob. 2007. *Re-Assessing Andijan: The Road to Restoring U.S.–Uzbek Relations*. Washington, DC: Jamestown Foundation.

Polat, Necati. 2002. *Boundary Issues in Central Asia*. Ardsley, NY: Transnational Publishers.

Poliakov, Sergei. 1992. *Everyday Islam: Religion and Tradition in Rural Central Asia*. Armonk, NY: M.E. Sharpe.

Popov, M. 1989. "Konflikta moglo ne byt'." *Kommunist Tadzhikistana*, 28 June, 1.

Pozdniakova, Natal'ia, and U. Chernogaev. 2005. "Konflikt raionnogo mashtaba: situatsiia vokrug uzbekskogo anklava Sokh i Kirgizii ostaetsia napriazhennoi." *Nemetskaia volna*, May 10. www.centrasia.ru/newsA.php?st=1115788380.

Proekt zakona Kyrgyzskoi Respubliki. 2011. "O pridanii osobogo statusa otdel'nym prigranichnym territoriiam Kyrgyzskoi Respubliki i ikh razvitii," debated in parliament April 8. www.kenesh.kg/Articles/1142-Proekt_Zakona_KR_O_pridanii_osobogo_statusa_otdelnym_prigranichnym_territoriyam_KR_i_ix_razvitii.aspx.

Pylenko, Zoya. 2005. "Batken's Border Problems." *Central Asia—Caucasus Analyst Bi-Weekly Briefing* 6 (21): 12–13.

Raballand, Gaël. 2005. *L'Asie centrale ou la fatalité de l'enclavement?* Paris: L'Harmattan.

Radcliffe, Sarah. 2001. "Imagining the State as a Space: Territoriality and the Formation of the State in Ecuador." In *States of Imagination: Ethnographic Explorations of the Postcolonial State*, edited by Thomas Blom Hansen and Finn Stepputat, 123–145. Durham: Duke University Press.

Radnitz, Scott. 2005. "Networks, Localism and Mobilization in Aksy, Kyrgyzstan." *Central Asian Survey* 24 (4), 405–424. doi: 10.1080/02634930500453368.

———. 2010. *Weapons of the Wealthy: Predatory Regimes and Elite-Led Protests in Central Asia*. Ithaca: Cornell University Press.

Radu, Cosmin. 2010. "Beyond Border-'Dwelling': Temporalizing the Border-Space through Events." *Anthropological Theory* 10 (4): 409–433. doi: 10.1177/1463499610386664.

Radzhabov, S.A. 1968. "Razvitie sovetskoi natsional'noi gosudarstvennosti v respublikakh Srednei Azii." *Pravovedenie* 1: 25–32.

Raev, Sultan. 2007. *Last Will.* Radio play, broadcast as part of *Seven Wonders of the Divided World.* BBC Radio 3, September 9.

Rahmonova-Schwarz, Delia. 2012. *Family and Transnational Mobility in Post-Soviet Central Asia: Labor Migration from Kyrgyzstan, Tajikistan and Uzbekistan to Russia.* Baden-Baden: Nomos.

Rasanayagam, Johan. 2002a. "The Moral Construction of the State in Uzbekitan: Its Construction Within Concepts of Community and Interaction at the Local Level." PhD diss., University of Cambridge.

——. 2002b. "Spheres of Communal Participation: Placing the State within Local Modes of Interaction in Rural Uzbekistan." *Central Asian Survey* 21 (1): 55–70. doi: 10.1080/02634930220127946.

——. 2006. "'I Am Not a Wahhabi': State Power and Muslim Orthodoxy in Uzbekistan." In *The Post-Soviet Religious Question: Faith and Power in Central Asia and East-Central Europe,* edited by Chris Hann, 99–125. Münster: Lit Verlag.

——. 2010. *Islam in Post-Soviet Uzbekistan: The Morality of Experience.* Cambridge: Cambridge University Press.

Rasanayagam, Johan, Judith Beyer, and Madeleine Reeves. 2014. "Introduction: Performances, Possibilites and Practices of the Political in Central Asia." In *Ethnographies of the State in Central Asia: Performing Politics.* Bloomington: Indiana University Press.

Rasul-zade, Tilav. 2010a. "Zhuravli uleteli, zabyv o rodnykh gnezdakh i gorode Shurab, prevrativshemsia v beskhoznye ruiny." Fergana.ru, June 23. www.fergananews.com/article.php?id=6626.

——. 2010b. "Shurab—bol' kazhdogo, kto s nim sviazan." Fergana.ru, July 1. www.fergananews.com/article.php?id=6639/

——. 2011. "Chorkukh, ostavshiisia bez gor." *Asia-Plus,* May 26. http://news.tj/ru/newspaper/article/chorkukh-ostavshiisya-bez-gor.

Razumov, Yaroslav. 2005. "Konfliktogennost' Ferganskoi doliny imeet istoricheskie traditsii." *Panorama* 19, May 20. http://panoramakz.com/archiv/2005/19.htm.

Reeves, Madeleine. 2003. "Dis/locating the State: Making, Crossing and Contesting Borders in Kyrgyzstan." MPhil diss., University of Cambridge.

——. 2006. "Schooling in Ak-Tatyr: A Shifting Moral Economy." In *Surviving the Transition? Case Studies of Schools and Schooling in the Kyrgyz Republic since Independence,* edited by Alan De Young, Madeleine Reeves, and Galina Valyayeva, 159–198. Charlotte, NC: Information Age Publishing.

——. 2007a. "Travels in the Margins of the State: Everyday Geography in the Ferghana Valley Borderlands." In *Everyday Life in Central Asia Past and Present,* edited by Jeff Sahadeo and Russell Zanca, 281–300. Bloomington: Indiana University Press.

——. 2007b. "Unstable Objects: Corpses, Checkpoints, and 'Chessboard Borders' in the Ferghana Valley." *Anthropology of East Europe Review* 25 (1): 72–84.

——. 2008. "Border Work: An Ethnography of the State at Its Limits in the Ferghana Valley." PhD diss., University of Cambridge.

——. 2009a. "Materialising State Space: 'Creeping Migration' and Territorial Integrity in Southern Kyrgyzstan." *Europe-Asia Studies* 61 (7): 1277–1313. doi: 10.1080/09668130903068814.

——. 2009b. "Po tu storonu ekonomicheskogo determinizma: mikrodinamiki migratsii iż sel'skogo Kyrgyzstana." *Neprikosnovennyi zapas* 4 (66): 262–280. http://magazines.russ. ru/nz/2009/4/ri24-pr.html.

——. 2010a. "Migrations, masculinité et transformations de l'espace social dans la vallée de Sokh." In *Dynamiques migratoires et changements sociétaux en Asie Centrale,* edited by Marlene Laruelle, 131–147. Paris: Editions Petra.

——. 2010b. "A Weekend in Osh." *London Review of Books* 32 (13), 17–18.

——. 2011a. "Fixing the Border: On the Affective Life of the State in Southern Kyrgyzstan." *Environment and Planning D: Society and Space* 29 (5): 905–923. doi: 10.1068/d18610.

——. 2011b. "Introduction: Contested Trajectories and a Dynamic Approach to Place." *Central Asian Survey* 30 (3–4): 307–330. doi: 10.1080/02634937.2011.614096.

——. 2011c. "Staying put? Towards a Relational Politics of Mobility at a Time of Migration." *Central Asian Survey,* 30 (3–4): 555–576. doi: 10.1080/02634937.2011.614402.

——. 2012. "Black Work, Green Money: Remittances, Ritual, and Domestic Economies in Southern Kyrgyzstan." *Slavic Review* 71 (1): 108–134. doi: 10.5612/slavicreview.71.1.0108.

——. 2013. "Clean Fake: Authenticating Persons and Documents in Migrant Moscow." *American Ethnologist* 40 (3): 508–524. doi: 10.1111/amet.12036.

——. 2014. "The Time of the Border: Contingency, Conflict and Popular Statism at the Kyrgyzstan-Uzbekistan Boundary." In *Ethnographies of the State in Central Asia: Performing Politics,* edited by Madeleine Reeves, Judith Beyer and Johan Rasanayagam. Bloomington: Indiana University Press.

Regamey, Amandine and Anne Le Huérou. 2007. *Les migrants en Russie. Des populations fragilisées, premières victimes des crises politiques internes et externes.* Paris: FIDH/ Grazhdanskoe Sodeistvie. www.fidh.org/IMG//pdf/Migranrussie472fr2007.pdf.

Regional'nyi dialog i razvitie. 2004. "Adresnaia zona Samarkandek-Chorku: otchet o situatsii Todzhikon-Ak-Sai ot 04.04.04." Unpublished report.

Remtilla, Aliaa. 2010. "Home Alone: Keeping Home the Same in the Wake of the Migration of Others." Paper presented at the biannual meeting of the European Association of Social Anthropologists, Maynooth, August 24–27.

——. 2012. "Re-Producing Social Relations: Political and Economic Change and Islam in Post-Soviet Tajik Ishkashim." PhD diss., University of Manchester.

Reynolds, Rebecca. 2012. "Locating Persons: An Ethnography of Personhood and Place in Rural Kyrgyzstan." PhD diss., University of Glasgow.

Ries, Nancy. 2002. "'Honest Bandits' and 'Warped People': Russian Narratives about Money, Corruption, and Moral Decay." In *Ethnography in Unstable Places: Everyday Lives in Contexts of Dramatic Political Change,* edited by Carol Greenhouse, Elizabeth Mertz, and Kay Warren, 276–315. Durham: Duke University Press.

Rivkin-Fish, Michele. 2005. "Bribes, Gifts and Unofficial Payments: Rethinking Corruption in Post-Soviet Russian Healthcare." In *Corruption: Anthropological Perspectives,* edited by Dieter Haller and Chris Shore, 47–64. London: Pluto Press.

Röhner, Irene. 2007. "National and International Labour Migration. A Case Study in the Province of Batken, Kyrgyzstan." National Centre for Competence in Research North-South Working Paper No. 8. Berne: NCCR North-South.

Roitman, Janet. 2004. "Productivity in the Margins: The Reconstitution of State Power in the Chad Basin." In *Anthropology in the Margins of the State,* edited by Veena Das and Deborah Poole, 191–224. Santa Fe: School of American Research Press.

——. 2005. *Fiscal Disobedience: An Anthropology of Economic Regulation in Central Africa*. Princeton: Princeton University Press.

——. 2006. "The Ethics of Illegality in the Chad Basin." In *Law and Disorder in the Post-colony*, edited by Jean Comaroff and John Comaroff, 247–272. Chicago: University of Chicago Press.

Romero, Fernando. 2008. *Hyperborder: The Contemporary U.S.-Mexico Border and Its Future*. New York: Princeton Architectural Press.

Rotar', Igor'. 2003. "Zhivye teni goroda-prizraka." *Novye Izvestiia*, August 4. www.newizv.ru/news/2003-08-04/226/.

Roy, Olivier. 1997. *La nouvelle Asie centrale ou la fabrication des nations*. Paris: Editions du Seuil.

Rubin, Barnet. 2002. *Blood on the Doorstep: The Politics of Preventive Action*. New York: Century Foundation Press.

Rushchenko, Igor'. 2005. "Bez statusa, ili 'v iame neopredelennosti'. K probleme nezakonnogo nasiliia v organakh militsii po dannym ukrainskikh issledovanii." *Neprikosnovennyi zapas*, 4 (42). http://magazines.russ.ru/nz/2005/42/ru16.html.

Sabol, Steven. 1995. "The Creation of Soviet Central Asia: The 1924 National-Territorial Delimitation." *Central Asian Survey*, 14 (2): 225–241. doi: 10.1080/02634939508400901.

Sahadeo, Jeff. 2007. *Russian Colonial Society in Tashkent, 1865–1923*. Bloomington: Indiana University Press.

——. 2012. "Soviet 'Blacks' and Place Making in Leningrad and Moscow." *Slavic Review* 71 (2): 331–358. doi: 10.5612/slavicreview.71.2.0331.

Samadov, Saidakbar. 2008. "Komu prinadlezhit anklav Sokh?" Centrasia.ru, April 1. www.centrasia.ru/newsA.php?st=1207062000.

Satybaldieva, Elmira. 2010. "The Nature of Local Politics in Rural Kyrgyzstan: A Study of Social Inequalities, Everyday Politics and Neo-Liberalism." PhD diss., University of Kent.

Satybekov, Erlan. 2002. "Zona nasiliia." *Vechernii Bishkek*, September 18.

——. 2006. "Porokhovaia bochka." *Vechernii Bishkek*, August 11.

Schatz, Edward. 2004. *Modern Clan Politics: The Power of "Blood" in Kazakhstan and Beyond*. Seattle: University of Washington Press.

Schepper-Hughes, Nancy, and Philippe Bourgois. 2004. "Introduction: Making Sense of Violence." In *Violence in War and Peace: An Anthology*, edited by Nancy Schepper-Hughes and Philippe Bourgois, 1–31. Oxford: Blackwell.

Schoeberlein, John. 2000. "Shifting Ground: How the Soviet Regime Used Resettlement to Transform Central Asian Society and the Consequences of This Policy Today." In *Migration in Central Asia: Its History and Current Problems*, edited by Hisao Komatsu, Chika Obiya and John Schoeberlein, 41–64. Osaka: Japan Center for Area Studies.

Schoeberlein-Engel, John. 1994. "Identity in Central Asia: Construction and Contention in the Conceptions of 'Özbek', 'Tâjik', 'Muslim', 'Samarqandi' and Other Groups." PhD diss., Harvard University.

Scott, James. 1985. *Weapons of the Weak: Everyday Forms of Peasant Resistance*. New Haven: Yale University Press.

——. 1998. *Seeing Like a State. How Certain Schemes to Improve the Human Condition Have Failed*. New Haven: Yale University Press.

Seabright, Paul. 2000. *The Vanishing Rouble. Barter Networks and Non-Monetary Transactions in Post-Soviet Societies*. Cambridge: Cambridge University Press.

Sengupta, Anita. 2002. *Frontiers into Borders: The Transformation of Identities in Central Asia*. Delhi: Hope India.

Sesiashvili, Ikrali. 2006. "Hazing in the Georgian Army: The Association 'Justice and Liberty' Reports on Non-Statuary Relations." In *Dedovshchina in the Post-Soviet Military: Hazing of Russian Army Conscripts in a Comparative Perspective*, edited by Francoise Daucé and Elisabeth Sieca-Kozlowski, 187–204. Stuttgart: Ibidem-Verlag.

Shaw, Charles. 2011. "Friendship under Lock and Key: The Soviet Central Asian Border, 1918–1934." *Central Asian Survey* 30 (3–4): 331–348. doi: 10.1080/02634937.2011.607966.

Shishkin, Philip. 2013. *Restless Valley: Revolution, Murder and Intrigue in the Heart of Central Asia*. New Haven: Yale University Press.

Shozimov, Polat. 2003. *Tadzhikskaia identichnost' i gosudarstvennoe stroitel'stvo v Tadzhikistane*. Dushanbe: Irfon.

Shozimov, Pulat, Baktybek Beshimov, and Khurshida Yunusova. 2011. "The Ferghana Valley during Perestroika, 1985–1991." In *The Ferghana Valley: The Heart of Central Asia*, edited by S. Frederick Starr, 178–204. Armonk, NY: M.E. Sharpe.

Shozimov, Pulat, Joomart Sulaimanov, and Shamshad Abdullaev. 2011. "Culture in the Ferghana Valley Since 1991: The Issue of Identity." In *The Ferghana Valley: The Heart of Central Asia*, edited by S. Frederick Starr, 278–295. Armonk, NY: M.E. Sharpe.

Shteinberg, Evgenii. 1934. "Sredneaziatskoe razmezhevanie i protsess natsional'noi konsolidatsii." *Revoliutsiia i natsaional'nosti* 12: 47–54.

Slezkine, Yuri. 1994. "The USSR as a Communal Apartment, or How a Socialist State Promoted Ethnic Particularism." *Slavic Review* 53 (2): 414–52. doi: 10.2307/2501300.

Slim, Randa. 2002. "The Ferghana Valley: In the Midst of a Host of Crises." In *Searching for Peace in Central and South Asia: An Overview of Conflict Prevention and Peace-Building Activities*, edited by Monique Mekenkamp, Paul von Tongeren and Hans van de Veen, 489–515. Boulder, CO: Lynne Reiner.

Smith, Christopher. 2004. "Prepared statement to the House of Representatives Committee on International Relations." February 11. http://commdocs.house.gov/committees/intlrel/hfa91796.000/hfa91796_0.HTM.

Smith, Jeremy. 1999. *The Bolsheviks and the National Question, 1917–23*. London: Macmillan.

Soltoeva, Anara. 2005. "Vlast' vziali. Zemliu davai!" *Vechernii Bishkek*, April 8.

Spector, Regine. 2008. "Securing Property in Contemporary Kyrgyzstan." *Post-Soviet Affairs* 24 (2): 149–176. doi: 10.2747/1060–586X.24.2.149.

Spencer, Jonathan. 1990. *A Sinhalla Village in a Time of Trouble: Politics and Change in Rural Sri Lanka*. Oxford: Oxford University Press.

———. 2007. *Anthropology, Politics and the State: Democracy and Violence in South Asia*. Cambridge: Cambridge University Press.

Ssorin-Chaikov, Nikolai V. 2003. *The Social Life of the State in Subarctic Siberia*. Stanford: Stanford University Press.

Stalin, Joseph. [1913] 1973. "The Nation." In *Marxism and the National Question*. Reproduced in *The Essential Stalin: Major Theoretical Writings, 1905–1952*, edited by Bruce Franklin. London: Croom Helm.

Starr, S. Frederick. 2011. "Introducing the Ferghana Valley." In *Ferghana Valley: The Heart of Central Asia*, edited by S. Frederick Starr, ix–xx. Armonk, NY: M.E. Sharpe.

Stewart, Kathleen. 1996. *A Space on the Side of the Road: Cultural Poetics in an "Other" America*. Princeton: Princeton University Press.

Suleymanov, Muzaffar. 2005. "Bringing Down 'The Family': Implications for Central Asia." *Peace and Conflict Monitor*, April 14. www.monitor.upeace.org/pdf/Central_Asia.pdf.

Suny, Ronald. 1993. *The Revenge of the Past: Nationalism, Revolution, and the Collapse of the Soviet Union*. Stanford: Stanford University Press.

Suny, Ronald, and Terry Martin. 2001. *A State of Nations: Empire and Nation-Making in the Time of Lenin and Stalin*. New York: Oxford University Press.

Suslova, Svetlana. 2000. "Dnevnik Batkenskikh sobytii." *Tsentral' no-Aziatskoe Agentstvo Politicheskikh Issledovanii*, October 1.

Suyarkulova, Mohira. 2011. "Becoming Sovereign in Post-Soviet Central Asia: 'Discursive Encounters' between Tajikistan and Uzbekistan." PhD diss., University of St. Andrews.

Sydykova, Zamira. 2003. "Zoloto Kyrgyzstana: pravda i vymysel." In *Gody ozhidanii i poter', vremia peremen*. Bishkek: Res Publica.

Tabyshalieva, Anara. 1999. *The Challenge of Regional Cooperation in Central Asia. Preventing Ethnic Conflicts in the Ferghana Valley*. Washington, DC: United States Institute for Peace.

TadzhikTA. 1989. "Suchetom vzaimnykh interesov." *Kommunist Tadzhikistana*, 20 July, 1.

Tambiah, Stanley. 1996. *Levelling Crowds. Ethnonationalist Conflicts and Collective Violence in South Asia*. Berkeley: University of California Press.

Taussig, Michael. 1997. *The Magic of the State*. New York: Routledge.

Tazar.kg. 2007. "Sovbez Tadzhikistana nameren ubrat' blokpost 'Surkh' na granitse s Batkenskoi oblast'iu KR." January 26.

Thieme, Susan. 2008a. "Living in Transition: How Kyrgyz Women Juggle Their Different Roles in a Multi-Local Setting." *Gender Technology and Development* 12 (3): 325–345. doi: 10.1177/097185240901200303.

——. 2008b. "Sustaining Livelihoods in Multi-Local Settings: Possible Theoretical Linkages between Transnational Migration and Livelihood Studies." *Mobilities* 3 (1): 51–71.

Thompson, Chad. 2007. "Epistemologies of Independence: Technology and Empire in the Post-Soviet Borderlands." PhD diss., York University, Canada.

Thongchai, Winichakul. 1994. *Siam Mapped: A History of the Geo-Body of a Nation*. Hawai'i: University of Hawai'i Press.

Thorez, Julien. 2005. "Flux et dynamiques spatiales en Asie centrale. Géographie de la transformation post-Soviétique." PhD diss., University of Paris X-Nanterre.

Thurman, Jonathan. 1999. "Modes of Organization in Central Asian Irrigation: The Ferghana Valley, 1876 to Present." PhD diss., Indiana University.

Torjesen, Stina. 2007. "Understanding Regional Co-operation in Central Asia, 1991–2004." DPhil diss., University of Oxford.

Trevisani, Tommaso. 2007. "After the Kolkhoz: Rural Elites in Competition." *Central Asian Survey* 26 (1): 85–104. doi: 10.1080/02634930701423509.

——. 2014 "The Reshaping of Cities and Citizens in Uzbekistan: The Case of Namangan's 'New Uzbeks.'" In *Ethnographies of the State in Central Asia: Performing Politics*, edited by Madeleine Reeves, Judith Beyer, and Johan Rasanayagam. Bloomington: Indiana University Press.

Trilling, David. 2009. "Ferghana Valley: Tajik-Kyrgyz Border a Potential 'Karabakh.'" Eurasianet Insight, June 4. www.eurasianet.org/departments/insightb/articles/eav060509.shtml.

Tsing, Anna L. 2005. *Friction: An Ethnography of Global Connection*. Princeton: Princeton University Press.

Tulegabylova, Nurjan, and Elmira Shishkaraeva, eds. 2005. *The Spring of 2005 through the Eyes of People of Kyrgyzstan: Anxieties, Expectations and Hopes (Oral Histories)/Vesna 2005 goda glazami Kyrgyzstantsev: Trevogi, ozhidaniia, nadezhdy*. Bishkek: Tsentr izdatel'skogo razvitiia.

Turnbull, David. 2005. "Locating, Negotiating, and Crossing Boundaries: AWestern Desert Land Claim, the Tordesillas Line, and the West Australian Border." *Environment and Planning D: Society and Space* 23 (5): 757–770. doi: 10.1068/d357t.

Tursunov, Bakhrom, and Maria Pikulina. 1999. "Severe Lessons of Batken." *Conflict Studies Research Paper* No. K 28. Sandhurst: Royal Military Academy.

Tuzmukhamedov, Rais Abdulkhakovich. 1973. *Natsional'noe osvobozhdenie narodov Srednei Azii (otvet klevetnikam)*. Moscow: Progress.

Ualieva, Saule, and Edrien [Adrienne] Edgar. 2011. "Mezhetnicheskie braki, smeshannoe proiskhozhdenie i 'druzhba narodov' v sovetskom i postsovetskom Kazakhstane." *Neprikosnovennyi zapas*, 6 (80). http://magazines.russ.ru/nz/2011/6/u18-pr.html.

United Nations Development Programme. 2005. *Human Development Report Central Asia. Bringing Down Barriers: Regional Cooperation for Human Development and Human Security*. Bratislava.

——. 2011. "First Resettlers Have Received Their Land Certificates for House Building in Shurab." Press release, UNDP Tajikistan (Khujand office), September. www.globe-expert.eu/quixplorer/filestorage/Interfocus/3-Economie/32-International/32-SRCNL-UNDP_News/201109/First_reset_letters_have_received_their_land_certificates_for_house_building_in_Shurab.html.

Usmanov, Seyitbek. 2011. "'Closed' Kyrgyz-Uzbek Border: A Recipe for Clashes." *Eurasia Daily Monitor*, August 12. www.jamestown.org/programs/edm/single/?tx_ttnews%5Btt_news%5D=38323&tx_ttnews%5BbackPid%5D=27&cHash=f03cb3439cf1a4e5b43cc16fc54f5eee.

Vaidyanath, R. 1967. *The Formation of the Soviet Central Asian Republics: A Study in Soviet Nationalities Policy, 1917–1936*. New Delhi: People's Publishing House.

Valiev, Bakhtior. 2006. "Bol' Tadzhikskoi kochegarki." *Varorud*, August 4.

van Bladel, Joris. 2004. "The All-Volunteer Force in the Russian Mirror: Transformation without Change." PhD diss., Rijksuniversitet Gronigen.

van Houtum, Henk. 2012. Remapping Borders. In *A Companion to Border Studies*, edited by Thomas Wilson and Hastings Donnan, 405–418. Oxford: Wiley-Blackwell.

van Schendel, Willem. 2001. "Working through Partition." *International Review of Social History* 46 (3): 393–421. doi: 10.1017/S0020859001000256.

van Schendel, Willem, and Itty Abraham. 2005. *Illicit Flows and Criminal Things: States, Borders and the Other Side of Globalization*. Bloomington: Indiana University Press.

Vareikis, Iozas [Juozas]. 1924a. "Predislovie." In *Natsional' no-gosudarstvennoe razmezhe-vanie Srednei Azii*, edited by Iozas Vareikis and Isaak Zelenskii, 1–2. Tashkent: Sredne-Aziatskoe Gosudarstvennoe Izdatel'stvo.

———. 1924b. "Novyi etap natsional'nogo stroitel'stva v Srednei Azii." In *Natsional' no-gosudarstvennoe razmezhevanie Srednei Azii*, edited by Iozas Vareikis and Isaak Zelenskii, 39–68. Tashkent: Sredne-Aziatskoe Gosudarstvennoe Izdatel'stvo.

Varorud. 2007. "Podrobnosti ob intsidente na tadzhiko-kyrgyzskoi granitse s gubernato-rom Batkenskoi oblasti Kyrgyzstana." January 12.

Vaughan-Williams, Nick. 2010. "The UK Border Security Continuun: Virtual Biopolitics and the Simulation of the Sovereign Ban." *Environment and Planning D: Society and Space* 28 (6): 1071–1083. doi:10.1068/d13908.

Vechernii Bishkek. 2001. "Anklav Sokh bol'she ne sushestvuet?" April 25. http://members.vb.kg/2001/04/25/01.htm.

———. 2003. "Mina zamedlennogo deistviia, ili kogda smertonosnye 'igrushki' perestanut pugat'." *Vechernii Bishkek,* April 18.

Verdery, Katherine. 1991. *National Ideology under Socialism: Identity and Cultural Politics in Ceauşescu's Romania.* Berkeley: University of California Press.

———. 1999. *The Political Lives of Dead Bodies: Reburial and Postsocialist Change.* New York: Columbia University Press.

Vremena. 2005. "Razvitie situatsii v Kirgizii." Roundtable television discussion, Russian First Channel, March 27. Transcript available at http://vladimirpozner.ru/?p=6998.

Walicki, Nadine. 2006. "Tajikistan Unravelled: The State Resettlement of Citizens." MA thesis, Carleton University.

Whitlock, Monica. 2004. "Civil Unrest Erupts in Uzbek City." BBC news, November 1. http://news.bbc.co.uk/1/hi/world/asia-pacific/3971281.stm.

Widdis, Emma. 2000. "Borders: The Aesthetic of Conquest in the Soviet Cinema of the 1930s." *Journal of European Studies* 30 (120): 401–411. doi: 10.1177/004724410003012004.

———. 2003. *Visions of a New Land: Soviet Film from the Revolution to the Second World War.* New Haven: Yale University Press.

Wilson, Thomas M., and Hastings Donnan. 1998. "Nation, State and Identity at Interna-tional Borders." In *Border Identities: Nation and State at International Frontiers*, edited by Thomas Wilson and Hastings Donnan, 1–30. Cambridge, UK: Cambridge University Press.

———. 2005a. *Culture and Power at the Edge of the State. National Support and Subversion in European Border Regions.* Münster: Lit Verlag.

———. 2005b. "Territory, Identity and the Places In-Between: Culture and Power in Euro-pean Borderlands." In *Culture and Power at the Edge of the State: National Support and Subversion in European Border Regions,* edited by Thomas Wilson and Hastings Donnan, 1–29. Münster: Lit Verlag.

———. 2012. "Borders and Border Studies." In *A Companion to Border Studies*, edited by Thomas Wilson and Hastings Donnan, 1–26. Oxford: Blackwell.

Wimmer, Andres, and Nina Glick Schiller. 2002. "Methdological Nationalism and Be-yond: Nation-State Building, Migration and the Social Sciences." *Global Networks* 2 (4): 301–334.

World Bank. 2009. "Press Release: World Bank Supports Rehabilitation of the Osh-Batken-Isfana Road." http://web.worldbank.org/WBSITE/EXTERNAL/NEWS/0,,contentMDK:2 2377794~menuPK:34463~pagePK:34370~piPK:34424~theSitePK:4607,00.html.

Yanagisako, Sylvia, and Carol Delaney. 1995. *Naturalizing Power: Essays in Feminist Cultural Analysis*. New York and London: Routledge.

Yefimova-Trilling, Natalia, and David Trilling. 2012. "Kyrgyzstan and Tajikistan: Disputed Border Heightens Risk of Conflict." Eurasianet.org, August 2. www.eurasianet.org/node/65744

Yntymak saiasaty. 2005a. "Informatsiia o konflikte ot 1–3.05.2005 v regione Sokh KaraTokoi." Unpublished document, May 3.

——. 2005b. "Informatsiia o konflikte ot 1–3.05.2005 goda v regione Sokh KaraTokoi. Na 19:00 vechera 04.05.2005." Unpublished document, May 4.

Young, Anna. 2003. *Ferghana Valley Field Study: Reducing the Potential for Conflict through Community Mobilization*. Portland, OR: Mercy Corps.

Yurchak, Alexei. 1997. "The Cynical Reason of Late Socialism: Power, Pretense, and the Anekdot." *Public Culture* 9 (2): 161–188. doi: 10.1215/08992363-9-2-161.

——. 2005. *Everything Was Forever, Until It Was No More: The Last Soviet Generation*. Princeton: Princeton University Press.

Yusupov, Khul´kar. 2004. "Vyidet li iz transportnogo tupika Ferganskaia dolina?" Fergana. ru, May 27. www.fergananews.com/article.php?id=2904.

Yuval-Davies, Nira, and Floya Anthias, eds. 1989. *Woman-Nation-State*. Houndmills: Macmillan.

Zakirov, I. and K. H. Babadzhanov. 1989. "Isfara: press-konferentsiia K. M. Makhkamova." *Kommunist Tadzhikistana*, 21 July, 1.

Zanca, Russell. 1999. "The Repeasantization of an Uzbek Kolkhoz: An Ethnographic Account of Post-Socialism." PhD diss., University of Illinois.

Zartman, I. William. 2010. *Understanding Life in the Borderlands: Boundaries in Depth and in Motion*. Athens: University of Georgia Press.

Zarubin, I.I. 1925. *Spisok narodnostei Turkestanskogo kraia*. Vol. 9 of *Trudy komissii po izucheniiu plemennogo sostava naseleniia Rossii i sopredel´nykh stran*. Leningrad: Rossiiskaia akademiia nauk.

——. 1926. *Naselenie Samarkandskoi oblasti*. Vol. 10 of *Trudy kommissii po izucheniiu plemennogo sostava naseleniia Rossii*. Leningrad: Akademiia nauk SSSR.

Zhuk, Oleg. 2003. "Uzbekistan szhigaet mosty?" *Delo No*, January 15.

Žižek, Slavoj. 1999. *The Ticklish Subject*. London and New York: Verso.

Zokirov, Alisher. 2012. "Kyrgyzskie strasti po uzbekskomu gazu: Zhogorku Kenesh opiat´ vyshe mezhdunarodnogo prava?" *Belyi Parus,* February 16. www.paruskg.info/2012/02/16/57723.

Zuev, Dennis. 2010. "The Movement against Illegal Immigration: Analysis of the Central Node in the Russian Extreme-Right Movement." *Nations and Nationalism* 16 (2): 261–284. doi: 10.1111/j.1469–8129.2010.00430.x.

INDEX

Abashin, Sergei, 61, 70, 75
Abduvali (Ak-Tatyr resident), 136–38, *137*, 140
Abu Ghraib prison in Iraq, 194
Adilet (Kyrgyz soldier in Russian army), 186–89, 194
adyr (arid foothills), 1, *227*, 248
affective identification with Russia, 108, 112, 118–19, 122, 130, 136–38, *137*, 207, 242
Afghan-Tajik border, 179–80, 185, 195–98; friendship agreement with Russian Federation (1993) and, 182–83
Afghan-Uzbek border, 179
agency of violence, 192
agriculture, 18; interdependence of pastoral and agricultural modes of life, 8, 19–20, 40. *See also* apricot crops; collective farms
Aijigitov, Sultan, 64
Akayev, Askar (Kyrgyz president), 26–27, 213–14
Akayev road, 229–31
Akhmat-Agai (Ak-Sai resident), 47–48, 99, 241–42
Ak-Sai, 99; Akhmat-Agai (resident), 47–48, 99, 241–42; border unit head in as local authority, 175; bus from Batken to, 38–44; "donor shopping mentality" in, 99–100; Ömürbek-Ata (resident) narratives on collective farms and land exchange in, 45–47, 84–85; World Bank-funded bypass road ("Kyrgyz road") in, 247
Ak-Tatyr, 110–12, 118–19, 126; Abduvali (resident), 136–38, *137*, 140; irrigation and

irrigation canal of, 1–3, *3*, 18–19. *See also* Russia, out-migration to
Alamanov, Salamat, 25–26
Alay Mountains in Kyrgyzstan, 18
Alisher (university student from Ferghana), 177–78
Altynai (former Shurab resident), 111–19
Alvarez, Robert, 50
Alykulov, Marat, 146
Andijan events *(Andijon voqeasi)*, 36, 167, 210
Angola, extractive neoliberalism in, 243
animals, 129–30
anthropological research. *See* ethnography and ethno-spatial mapping; fieldwork and research
Anzaldúa, Gloria, 50
apricot crop (Sokh and Isfara Valleys), *5*, 101–2, 105–10, 126; as main income "before Russia" (economic collapse), 105–7, 119–22
Aretxaga, Begoña, 192, 202–3, 225
Arslan-Ata (Kyrgyz elder from Kök-Tash), 88–89
aryk irrigation, 107–10; collective control of as "collective coping," 108
Asad, Talal, 237, 244
ascription. *See* state ascription
atherosclerosis, 54

Bakyt (former border guard), 190, 194
Bannikov, Konstantin, 188

Poole, Deborah, 144, 174, 180, 204
Post-Soviet, 243, 246; state spatialization as, 242
power modalities. *See* modalities of power
preventive development, 8, 57, 211, 220, 238–39. *See also* conflict and conflict prevention; nongovernmental organizations
propiska (residence registration). *See* documentary economy; Russia, out-migration to

Qorasuv: closing of pedestrian bridge between Kara-Suu and Qorasuv for quarantine in 2003 and, 160, *161*, 162; conflict at Kara Suu/Qorasuv canal in 2003, 158, 163

Radcliffe, Sarah, 207
Radnitz, Scott, 11
Rahmon, Emomali (Tajikistan President), 177
Rakhimbaev, Abdullo, 79
razmezhevanie. See national-territorial delimitation
remittances from Russia, 33, 39, 103, 105, 109–10, 124, 128
research. *See* fieldwork and research
ritual expenses, 127, *128*, 129
roads: detour road *(ob"ezd jol)* north of Sokh enclave, 144, 147–49; road banditry, 145. *See also* Akayev road; "Kyrgyz road"
Roitman, Janet, 145, 169–70, 175
Russia: affective identification with, 108, 112, 118–19, 122, 130, 136–38, 137, *137*, 207, 242; Moscow Provisioning (*moskovskoe obespechenie*) and, 111–19. *See also* ethnography and ethno-spatial mapping; national-territorial delimitation; Soviet era ethno-territorial transformations; Soviet era socio-spatial transformations
Russia, out-migration to, 21–22, 101–2, 125–26; Abduvali (resident of Ak-Tatyr) and, 136–38, *137*; affective identification with Russia for migrants, 118–19, 130, 137; in Batken, 39; debate on, 123; dehumanization and, 129–30; earnings disparities and, 124–25; effect of on medical profession in Sokh, 235; experience of historical migrants *vs.* current (2005), 118–23, 130, 137; gendered nature of, 123, 127–30, 235; household survey of, 103; in Isfara Valley, 21; of Jengish (Batken university student), 124–26, 130, 134; of Khojai Shamolov, 119–22; of Khurshed in Sokh, 101–3; lack

of irrigated land and, 127; migrants' legal legibility in Russia, 131–32, 136; percent of migrants with "clean" temporary residency/work permits, 131–32; primary destinations in for migrant workers from Sokh and Ak-Tatyr (2005), 120; principle sphere of occupation during most recent period of work in Russia, 123; principle type of position occupied during most recent period of work in Russia, 122; remittances and, 33, 39, 103, 105, 109, 127–28; ritual expenses and, 127, *128*, 129; in Shurab, 115; summary of comparative demographic and migration data from Sokh and Ak-Tatyr, 126; weekly buses from Sokh to Moscow and other Russian cities, *124*; year of first departure to Russia in search of work at the time of survey (2005), 127. *See also* deportation and migrant legality; documentary economy
Russian military, 182–85; Adilet (Kyrgyz soldier in Russian army) and, 186–89, 194; Kuba in, 179–80, 182–86; military hazing and, 172, 187, 189, 191, 193–95, 197

sacred sites, 107; Khodjai Orif *mazar,* 227–28
Sadyrbaev, Arapat-Eje (Batken resident), 24, 141, 147, 158, 234
Sadyrbaev, Kadyr-Aka, 147–49
Sadyrbaev family, 22–24, 27–28, 32, 180
Saltanat (Kyrgyz gynecologist in Sogment), 235–36
Sart ethnic-occupational group, 70–73, 75
School Number 1 in Beslan, collection for, 111, 118
science, social study of, 53–54
Scott, James, 178, 198
Shahrihan-sai Canal, *161*
Shamolov, Khojai (Sokh resident), 119–22
Sharipov, Abdukhalil (Khojai-A"lo resident), 87–88
Sharofat (Sokh resident), 235–36
Shurab, 242; abandoned homes in, *116*; abandoned train engine in, *113*; Altynai's (Shurab resident) narrative of decline of, 111–19, 242; ethnically marked sex work in, 117; lack of water as factor in decline of, 115–16; out-migration in, 115
Siberia, 12, 101–2, 119
silencing, 54
singularity, 10, 37, 54–55, 111, 178
Slim, Randa, 59

provisioning and, 104–10, 119; Russian military and, 180, 184–90
state inscription, 166, 171, 206, 237; registration system in Russia and, 136
state spatialization, 7, 9, 16, 231, 244–45; border guards and, 239–40; marginal state spaces, 144; patronage and tributes at borders and, 169; as post-Soviet, 242; social work involved in, 206; spatial politics in the Zimbabwean highlands, 55; in undemarcated rural borders with weak state governance, 53
state territoriality, 231; enactment of to be real, 140; ethno-territoriality from Soviet national-territorial delimitation (NTD) and, 80–81; incompleteness of, 180; itinerant territorialty, 68–73; material boundaries as creating, 99; as "worked for," 206–7. See also territorial integrity
stories so far, border as location of, 8
strong weak states in Central Asia, 10, 12
"subversive clientalism," 11
Sultanali (Batken resident), 199–203
Surh (Tajik village in Isfara Valley), 64; detour road and, 48–49, 49, 246–47; lack of deference shown to governor of Batken oblast at border near, 176–77, 249

Tahmina-Eje (recent return migrant), 133–35
Tajik-Afghan border, 179–80, 185, 195–98; friendship agreement with Russian Federation (1993) and, 182–83
Tajik ethnic group and language, 16, 20, 59, 235; imperial classification and, 70; lack of deference shown to governor of Batken oblast by four Tajik border guards, 176–77, 249; language barriers, 175–76, 181; as majority language spoken in Uzbekistan's Sokh Valley, 31; mobilization of language of nationality from NTD classification, 80; place names in Tajik, 40–41; Tajik female day laborers (mardikor-ayollari), 234; Tajik proverbs, 102
Tajikistan, 10, 18; Ak-Tatyr canal and, 1; bypass road and, 246–48; chessboard (shakhmat) formation of alternating and contested jurisdiction of border, 3–6, 43–44; delimiting of borders, 248; discourse of loss and historical injustice in, 151; Emomali Rahmon (Tajikistan President), 177; female cross-border movement and, 235–36; friendship agreement with

Russian Federation (1993), 182–83; map of, 2; Sultan Aijigitov (governor of Batken region) warning to the authorities in, 64; visa for entering Uzbekistan and, 147–48; Vorukh enclave of, 18; as "strong weak" state, 10. See also Krygyz-Tajik border; national-territorial delimitation
technology of border work, 6–7, 136, 140
temporality of borders, 6–8
territorial integrity, 6–7, 65, 67–68, 206, 233, 250; coherence of multiplicity of boundaries and, 143–44; defined in anthropological terms, 37; difficulties in materializing, 241–42; fragility of, 245; of Kyrgyzstan post-revolution, 213–14, 224–25, 238; as messy, contested and social, 6–8, 208; territorialized nationhood, 67–68. See also national-territorial delimitation; state territoriality
Tolib-Aka (former administrative head (rais) of Navabod), 199–203
Torjesen, Stina, 168
trade, cross-border, 14, 22, 104–10, 119, 143; at chernyi vkhod (back entrance) on the Kyrgyz-Uzbek border, 153–57, 154; at Kara-Suu market, 158–60; obstacles to legal, 123; trade routes, 20. See also apricot crop (Sokh Valley); Russia, out migration to
trajectories, 44, 49, 53, 55–57, 100–103, 138–40, 200, 231
trans-border mobility. See deportation and migrants legality; Russia, out-migration to
tribute. See patronage
Tulip Revolution, 213–20, 215, 221–22
Turkish statehood, 13

Üch-Döbö, 9, 16, 59, 86–89; Ak-Tatyr canal border of, 1, 3, 3, 5–6; irrigation of, 18; NGOs in, 12; Pirmat-Ata (resident of Üch-Döbö), 4–6; water tension along ethnic lines, 59
uncertainty, 63–64, 143, 237–38, 244–45; delimitation of boundaries as risking increased, 248; as modality of power, 168; pervasive at borders, 63
US-Mexico border, 50
Uzbek ethnic group, 16, 20, 58–59; imperial classification and, 70; mobilization of language of nationality from NTD classification, 80; Uzbek language, 175–76. See also May events